AF704122

The Law-Governed Universe

The Law-Governed Universe

John T. Roberts

OXFORD
UNIVERSITY PRESS

OXFORD
UNIVERSITY PRESS

Great Clarendon Street, Oxford OX2 6DP

Oxford University Press is a department of the University of Oxford.
It furthers the University's objective of excellence in research, scholarship,
and education by publishing worldwide in

Oxford New York

Auckland Cape Town Dar es Salaam Hong Kong Karachi
Kuala Lumpur Madrid Melbourne Mexico City Nairobi
New Delhi Shanghai Taipei Toronto

With offices in

Argentina Austria Brazil Chile Czech Republic France Greece
Guatemala Hungary Italy Japan Poland Portugal Singapore
South Korea Switzerland Thailand Turkey Ukraine Vietnam

Oxford is a registered trade mark of Oxford University Press
in the UK and in certain other countries

Published in the United States
by Oxford University Press Inc., New York

© John T. Roberts 2008

The moral rights of the author have been asserted
Database right Oxford University Press (maker)

First published 2008

All rights reserved. No part of this publication may be reproduced,
stored in a retrieval system, or transmitted, in any form or by any means,
without the prior permission in writing of Oxford University Press,
or as expressly permitted by law, or under terms agreed with the appropriate
reprographics rights organization. Enquiries concerning reproduction
outside the scope of the above should be sent to the Rights Department,
Oxford University Press, at the address above

You must not circulate this book in any other binding or cover
and you must impose the same condition on any acquirer

British Library Cataloguing in Publication Data

Data available

Library of Congress Cataloging in Publication Data

Roberts, John T.
The law-governed universe / John T. Roberts.
p. cm.
Includes bibliographical references and index.
ISBN 978–0–19–955770–7 (alk. paper)
1. Law (Philosophy) 2. Philosophy of nature. 3. Natural law. I. Title.
B105.L3R63 2008
113—dc22

Typeset by Laserwords Private Limited, Chennai, India
Printed in Great Britain
on acid-free paper by
CPI Antony Rowe, Chippenham, Wiltshire

ISBN 978–0–19–955770–7

10 9 8 7 6 5 4 3 2 1

With love and gratitude, this book is dedicated to Tom and Doris Roberts, to Heather Gert, and to Susanna Gert-Roberts.

Preface

This book is longer than I would like it to be. I believe that it is a fairly common practice to read just the first and last chapters of long philosophy books, hoping to get the main ideas. Sometimes doing this really will give you a good picture of the main ideas in the book; sometimes it will not. In the case of this book, it will. (But please read some of the other chapters!)

Much of the research for this book was done while I was being generously supported by the American Council of Learned Societies through a Charles A. Ryskamp Fellowship, in residence at the Center for Philosophy of Science at the University of Pittsburgh, having been granted a leave of absence by my own department at the University of North Carolina at Chapel Hill. I am very grateful to all three of these institutions.

Much of the writing for this book was done while I was a visitor at the Department of Philosophy and Humanities at Texas A&M University. I am grateful to that wonderful department for many things.

The account of laws of nature offered here benefited from helpful discussions with many people. They include James Bogen, Joseph Camp, John Earman, Bernard Gert, Michael Hand, Katya Hosking, William Lycan, Tim Maudlin, Chris Menzel, Ram Neta, Michael Pendlebury, Alexander Rosenberg, Jay Rosenberg, Adina Roskies, Wesley Salmon, Roger Sansom, Sarah Sawyer, and Roy Sorensen. The main argument of Chapter 4 is a descendant of an argument that I developed in collaboration with John Earman. I also received helpful feedback on parts of this material from audiences at Dartmouth College, North Carolina State University, Texas A&M University, the University of Kansas at Lawrence, and the University of North Carolina at Chapel Hill. I must have forgotten someone, and I apologize.

My wife Heather Gert and my friends John Carroll and Marc Lange were extremely generous with time and with advice about this book. Heather is my standard of philosophical sanity. John and Marc are my philosophical role models; they are great philosophical theorists of laws of nature, and even though they disagree with many of the central claims I make, their influence is all over this book. I also received very helpful comments from two anonymous referees for Oxford University Press.

Just in case it isn't as obvious as I think it is: Serendipides, the Ionian philosopher discussed in Chapter 3, Section 3.3.10, is fictitious.

Contents

1

The law-governed world-picture

1.1 A remarkable idea about the way the universe is

Many of us believe that the scientifically informed common sense of our culture includes a particular striking idea. I am going to call this idea *the law-governed world-picture*. Here is one way to express it:

Scientific inquiry has revealed to us a universe that is governed by laws of nature. It has also found out what some of those laws are. Or at least, it has made some very good guesses: it has found principles that are, under certain circumstances, very good approximations to the laws of nature. And there is no principled limit to how much better its guesses and approximations might get; so in principle, science can discover particular laws of nature, whether it has already done so or not.

The laws of the land can be violated by those on whom they are binding, but doing so carries certain consequences, for there are enforcement mechanisms in place. Laws of nature, by contrast, have no enforcement mechanisms. None are required, for there are no violations.

That doesn't mean that the laws of nature do not govern the universe at all, or that they 'govern' only in the figurative sense that nature does its elaborate dance *as if* it were obeying laws. The laws of nature govern the universe in the sense that the universe cannot but conform to them; their requirements are not merely required but also inevitable; with them, resistance is futile.

This has important consequences for our understanding of the universe and what makes it go. The evolution of natural things is not wholly determined by some inscrutable fate; it is not an inexplicable sequence of events, 'just one damned thing after another'; it is not a puppet show in which the action is directed by capricious gods according to fickle whims. It must proceed in a certain way because that way is determined by certain principles. Those principles can be grasped by reason, formulated in a language, and discerned by empirical inquiry. Just as a well-ordered state has a 'government of laws, and not a government of men,' this well-ordered universe has a government of laws, and not a government of unprincipled gods, or fairies, or demons, or fates, or what have you.[1] Understanding of the natural universe and of the events it contains can be achieved only by understanding its laws.

If you buy all of that, you buy the law-governed world-picture. I call it a 'picture' rather than a 'theory' or an 'account,' because as it stands it is pretty impressionistic. It is hard to say what its literal content is. It insists that laws really do govern the universe, and that this is not merely a figure of speech—but as of yet, we don't know how to understand what the non-figurative meaning of 'govern' might be here. It is a vision of reality based on a metaphor—the metaphor of government by laws—and what guidance we have for understanding the meaning of this metaphor is supplied mostly by a list of things it is meant to rule out, most of which are pretty hard to pin down themselves. As it stands, we cannot yet see what would count as a reason in favor of the law-governed world-picture or a reason against it. Nevertheless, it is a powerful idea, and it seems plausible that it is an important part of what is called 'the modern scientific world-view.' This book is about what exactly it would mean for the law-governed world-picture to be right, and about whether it is right. I am going to argue that the law-governed world-picture is right—but only if its content is understood in the right way, and the right way turns out to be a surprising way.

It is easy for modern, scientifically educated Westerners to take the law-governed world-picture for granted, as if it were a truism, or part of the universal common sense of humanity. It is nothing of the kind. As J. R. Milton writes:

> The idea of nature as a system governed by laws and the idea that the main aim of a scientist (or natural philosopher) should be the discovery of these laws is . . . historically quite specific. They are not ideas, like that of time, which can be traced back in one form or another as far as our sources permit; still less are they Kantian categories which govern any possible thought about the subject.
>
> (Milton 1998, p. 680)

[1] This does not mean that the law-governed world-picture is incompatible with theism, or with supernaturalism more generally. It just means that what goes on in the natural world goes on according to laws, and not according to the wills of lawless beings. If there are supernatural beings, then either they are themselves subject to the laws of nature whenever they attempt to intervene in the natural world, or else their influence on the natural world consists in having set up the laws of nature to begin with. (In the latter case, perhaps they have the power to suspend the laws on special occasions.)

Historians who have written on the origin of the modern concept of a law of nature disagree on many things: Zilsel argues that the concept emerged only in the seventeenth century; Ruby claims to find the modern concept of a scientific law already in the thirteenth century, in Roger Bacon's optical writings; Milton agrees that the idea of law-governed nature occurs earlier than the seventeenth century, but argues that it remains too vague to play a genuine role in scientific research until Descartes begins the search for the laws of motion.[2] Zilsel and Needham both argue that the concept of a law of nature originated in the idea of God imposing laws on the created world, but Ruby argues that it did not.[3] But there is no controversy among them on the point of the passage just quoted: whether it arose in the thirteenth century or the seventeenth, the idea of a law-governed universe and a science oriented toward discovering the laws came into being in a particular historical context. It was not known to the ancient Greeks,[4] and Needham argues that it did not arise indigenously in China at all.[5] In short, the law-governed world-picture is not something that 'everybody knows.' It is a comparatively recent addition to human thinking. If it is true, then that is a surprising and fascinating thing about the universe.

The law-governed world-picture has a powerful effect on the imagination. But it has different powerful effects on different imaginations. For some, the idea that science has revealed a law-governed universe is liberating: it releases us from the dreadful belief that we are at the mercy of capricious or vengeful powers, and brings with it the promise that we can learn the laws of nature and use this knowledge to control our destiny, at least to some degree. On the other hand, for some it brings with it the terrifying thought that we are cogs in a great machine that we are powerless to control. The idea of a law-governed universe can seem alienating, since the laws of nature are imposed on us from without and we have no say in them; but it can also make us feel at home in a universe that, like us when we are at our best, acts in accordance with principles that reason can grasp. To many, a universe governed by laws of nature necessarily implies a deity to serve as the supernatural lawmaker, since otherwise the power of the laws to govern would be inexplicable.[6] But there is also the view

[2] Zilsel (1942), p. 245; Ruby (1986), pp. 342–3; Milton (1998), p. 699.
[3] Zilsel (1942); Needham (1951); Ruby (1986), p. 342, p. 347.
[4] On this point, see especially Milton (1998), p. 680.
[5] Needham (1951). [6] Foster (2004) is a recent defense of this view.

that a law-governed universe is precisely the kind of universe that does not require a supernatural creator for its existence; having its own laws, it is self-sustaining and nothing from outside of it need be called on for any explanatory purpose—thus the line attributed to Laplace, 'Sire, I have no need of that hypothesis.'[7] In short, it is clear that if we accept the law-governed world-picture, this must have a big effect on our world-view. But it is far from clear what that effect should be.

If we are interested in the most basic question of metaphysics—'What is reality like?'—and we are inclined to take modern science seriously, then we should be interested in the question of whether the law-governed world-picture is accurate, and in the question of how exactly that picture should be interpreted. I think that this is the most important reason why the philosophical problem of lawhood is worth working on. There are other reasons that are commonly given in the literature: our concept of a law seems closely connected to other concepts that philosophers are interested in, such as causation, determinism, and explanation; there are interesting philosophical theories of things like induction, counterfactuals, explanation, reduction, and content which take the concept of a law of nature for granted, so that we won't really know what those theories say until we know what a law is; and so on. Those are reasons that are internal to contemporary professional philosophy: you become sensitive to them after you have already been initiated into the game. They are good reasons to be interested in the problem of laws. But I think the main reason why the problem is interesting is not internal to contemporary professional philosophy at all: it is just that anyone with a philosophical temperament wants to know what kind of world we live in, and any such person who takes modern science seriously has encountered the law-governed world-picture, recognized that if that picture is accurate then it makes a huge difference to the question of what kind of world this is, and can appreciate that that picture is extremely puzzling. So, any such person wants to know whether the law-governed world-picture is right, and just what it would mean for it to be right.

I said that *many of us believe* that the law-governed world-picture is part of our scientific common sense. Not all of us do, though. Some say that the very idea of a law of nature is a metaphysical holdover from

[7] Barbour (1997), pp. 34–5.

a bygone age when science, theology, and metaphysics had yet to be properly distinguished from one another; the law-governed universe is not something that science has revealed to us, but an interpretative construct that we have illegitimately imposed on the output of science.[8] By contrast, some agree that there really are such things as laws of nature, and empirical science is in principle capable of discovering them, but say that it is a mistake to think of these laws as 'governing' the universe in any but a thin metaphorical sense. For these philosophers, the laws are nothing more than a special set of exceptionless regularities—patterns in the great cosmic mosaic—which are privileged by their comprehensiveness and their simplicity.[9] Others think that while the concept of a law of nature does play an important role in modern science, the laws do not govern the universe, and the universe does not even conform to them; they are principles we use in constructing models of the world, rather than a feature of the world itself.[10]

So there are many ways in which philosophers deny that science really does present us with a vision of the world as governed by laws. I hope to show that all these ways of denying it are mistaken.

1.2 Cosmos and compulsion

Two ideas are commonly associated with the idea of a law-governed universe. The first is that our universe is characterized by a cosmic order: though we are confronted with a buzzin' bloomin' confusion, it is not as chaotic as it might have been; there is the regularity of the seasons, the cycles of life, the music of the spheres. The universe conforms to regularities and uniformities that are aptly described as 'harmonious.' Perhaps this is the aspect of the law-governed world-picture that most often inspires awe; perhaps it is the one that leads people to suppose that this law-governed universe must have a divine lawgiver.

The second idea is that the development of the universe is characterized by a kind of inevitability or compulsion: if it is a law of nature that nothing

[8] Bas van Fraassen is this view's most prominent contemporary defender; see his (1989).

[9] David Lewis is this view's most prominent contemporary defender. See, e.g., his (1994).

[10] Nancy Cartwright, Ronald Giere, and Paul Teller are among this view's defenders; see Cartwright (1983) and (1999), Giere (1999), Teller (2004).

travels faster than light, then it does not *just happen* that nothing ever gets going that fast; nothing ever *could*. Perhaps this is the aspect of the law-governed world-picture that makes many people feel alienated and fear for their autonomy as agents.

The ideas of cosmos and compulsion are distinct and logically independent of one another. You can have compulsion without cosmos: there can be deterministic systems that are 'chaotic' in the technical sense, and if the entire universe were such a system then there may well have been compulsory laws but nothing like a cosmic order.[11] On the other hand, it is at least conceivable that the world is cosmically ordered, though it has no compulsion to it; it could be a lovely, orderly universe that is nothing but a four-dimensional mosaic of 'loose and separate' states of affairs. So a universe can exhibit cosmos without compulsion, or compulsion without cosmos: cosmos and compulsion are two different things.

Although the law-governed world-picture involves the idea of compulsion as well as that of a cosmic order, the very idea that there are such things as laws of nature need not. Perhaps there are such things as laws of nature which are nothing more than universal regularities that constitute the harmonious order we find in the universe; cosmos without compulsion. This way of thinking about laws has been cultivated by partisans of the *best-system* approach to laws, which was pioneered by John Stuart Mill and Frank Ramsey, and refined and defended by David Lewis.[12]

1.3 The laws as the cosmic order: the best-system approach

According to the best-system account of laws, what it is to be a law of nature is to be a generalization that belongs to the best deductively closed system of true propositions about what actually goes on in the universe. There are many such systems; the weakest contains only the logical truths, and the strongest contains all the details—an exhaustive biography of every last bird, bee, quark, and lepton. The weakest one is admirably simple,

[11] See Earman (1986), chapters 8 and 9.

[12] Mill (1904), p. 230; Ramsey (1978), p. 138; Lewis (1973a), p. 73; Lewis (1994). See also chapter 5 of Earman (1986) and Halpin (1999) for further defense and elaboration of the best-system approach. I suggested a revision to Lewis's version in my (1999).

but woefully lacking in information content; the strongest one has as much information content as anyone could ask for, but it is enormously complicated. In addition to these two, there are many others, containing some but not all of the logically contingent truths. Each of these is more informative but less simple than the system that contains only the logical truths, and each is less informative but simpler than the system that contains all the truths. The two virtues of simplicity and informativeness tend to conflict: other things being equal, if you want more information, you need more axioms—and other things being equal, adding axioms makes a system less simple. The 'best' system is the one that strikes the best balance between information content and simplicity.

To see how this works, let's momentarily adopt the convenient fiction that the only things in the universe are the sun and planets of our solar system, and that they all conform perfectly to Kepler's laws. The strongest possible true deductive system will specify the exact positions of all the planets at each moment in the history of the universe. This is a great deal of information, and any system that contains it all is going to have to be rather complicated. A much less complicated system will consist only of Kepler's laws. This system will convey a great deal of information about the history of the universe—not all of the information there is, but enough to provide a 'big picture' and to enable one to make predictions about what will happen tomorrow based on where the planets are today. So it is plausible that the best system in this simplified fictional universe will consist of Kepler's laws and all their consequences; at any rate, this system will be a serious contender in the race for 'best system.' This is a pleasing result: in a universe containing nothing but the major bodies of our solar system and obeying Kepler's laws completely, it is intuitively plausible that the laws of nature are just Kepler's laws; the nomologically contingent facts include the details about which planet happens to be where when, and these details are exactly the ones left out by the system that seems 'best.'

In this toy universe, the laws turn out to be the basic principles that describe the way in which the planets form a harmonious, cosmic system. That is no accident: the generalizations that belong to the best system are the true general propositions that provide the best summary of what goes in the world; they give you the most information content by the most economical means. The more harmonious the universe is, the more information content you can get from a comparatively simple set of true generalizations. And when the universe is harmonious, its harmoniousness will consist in the existence of such a set. The members of that set just are the laws of nature. When we switch from this toy Keplerian world to the actual universe, the set of facts that have to be systematized becomes enormously more complicated, and so it is predictable that the best system will be more complicated as well. But the key idea remains: we have laws of nature just in case there is a relatively simple system of true generalizations that delivers a tremendous amount of information content—that is, just in case we live in a cosmically ordered universe. And the laws themselves are the members of this system—that is, they are the principles that constitute the cosmic order.

But this discussion of the Keplerian toy universe leaves something to be desired; it depends on a brute appeal to intuitions about which system is best. In particular, it depends on the assumption that if we start out with the system containing only Kepler's laws, and then add to it enough additional information to make it possible to deduce the positions of all the planets at all times, then the gain in information content will be outweighed by the cost in simplicity. How can this assumption be justified? In order to justify it, it seems that we would need a principled method for comparing the value of a certain increase in information content with a certain decrease in simplicity. (Or at least, we would need some principled constraints on any acceptable method for making this comparison, which would be sufficient to determine the outcome of the comparison in at least some cases.) Where is such a method to come from?

Lewis says it comes from scientific practice: when choosing which theories to accept, scientists must balance a number of virtues against one another, and two of these are information content and simplicity. The way we should compare gains in information content with losses in simplicity (and vice versa) in order to pick out the best system is the same way in which scientists compare these things in order to decide which theory to accept.[13]

But it isn't clear that scientific practice will do the job Lewis needs it to do here. Scientists don't work with an explicit formula for deciding how to trade off various theoretical virtues against one another. There are methods scientists can use in solving 'curve-fitting' problems, but here the

[13] Lewis (1986).

competing virtues that must be balanced against one another are simplicity and closeness of fit with the data, rather than simplicity and information content.[14] (And if two theories or deductive systems differ in their degree of fit with the data, then they could not both be true, so they are not both in the running for the title of 'best true deductive system'; hence, scientists' methods for solving this kind of problem are not relevant to the problem of picking out the best from among all the true deductive systems.) So, the standards for balancing information content against simplicity that Lewis needs must come from regularities in what scientists actually do, or from conventions implicit in their behavior, rather than from methods they explicitly endorse. But in choosing which theories to accept, scientists don't ever face a choice like the choice between the two systems in the toy example. One of those systems is just Kepler's laws; the other is Kepler's laws together with the equations of motions of all the planets. The two are not incompatible with one another; in fact, the second one entails the first one. Scientists might have to face the question of whether they have sufficient evidence to justify accepting the stronger theory, or whether they should be more conservative and merely accept the weaker theory. But this is a judgment about the strength of the available evidence, and not a judgment about the competing theoretical virtues of the two systems. So it is hard to see why we should expect that scientific practice will ever need to rely on standards for balancing information content against simplicity, in the way that Lewis's best-system account of laws requires. Scientists just don't ever need to make the kinds of trade-offs that it must be possible to make if the best-system account of laws is correct. So we still face the problem of where the standards of balance presupposed by the best-system account are supposed to come from.

Lewis's best-system analysis has been criticized on the grounds that it makes the extension of lawhood depend inappropriately on the standards of informativeness, simplicity, and balance that we (members of our species and culture) happen to employ.[15] Why should our species and culture have anything to do with what lawhood is? Isn't it ad hoc and chauvinistic to build in a reference to ourselves in an analysis of the concept of lawhood? Elsewhere I've argued that Lewis can give an adequate response to that

[14] Sober and Hitchcock (2004) contains an interesting discussion of the trade-offs between simplicity and fit involved in theory selection.

[15] For example, by Carroll (1994), pp. 49–55.

worry without giving up the spirit of his analysis.[16] The problem I am raising here is more radical, and I don't think it can be dealt with in the same way: it is not just that building our own species-and-culture's standards of the balance between informativeness and simplicity illegitimately privileges our own species-and-culture; it's that our species-and-culture's standards of this kind of balance are not there to be appealed to. We *have no practice* of weighing the competing virtues of simplicity and information content for the purpose of choosing one deductive system over others, where all are presumed to be true. So we have no explicit formulated standards, and no standards that are implicit in unstated conventions either.

This is not yet a refutation of the whole best-system approach to laws. Perhaps there is yet some way in which the standards for balancing information content against simplicity can be specified, otherwise than by adverting to standards that are allegedly implicit in a non-existent practice; perhaps there is some other way of characterizing the 'best system' than as the system that achieves the 'best balance' of information content and simplicity. The question of whether there is some way of getting around this problem is interesting, because the general best-system approach to laws is powerfully attractive to anyone who adopts a certain reasonable point of view—namely, that there are such things as laws of nature, but they consist in nothing more than the elegant system of harmonious regularities that our universe exhibits. Or, in a slogan: 'Laws of nature are about cosmos, rather than compulsion.' The mere fact that extant formulations of this general view have problems at the level of their details is not sufficient to kill the best-systems approach altogether.

1.4 The three ways: No-Laws, Non-Governing-Laws, Governing-Laws

I reject the best-system approach for a different reason: it seems to me to be a misguided attempt to carve out a middle position between two extremes, between which there is no tenable middle ground. It turns out to share the most important vices of one of the two extremes it tries to steer between.

[16] Roberts (1999).

The other extreme is the one I think we must go with, if we want to do justice to a couple of interesting things that go on in scientific practice and scientific reasoning.

At one extreme, we have *No-Laws*: the view that the very idea of a law of nature has no legitimate work to do in science or the philosophy of science—it is a metaphysical-cum-theological holdover from a bygone age, a philosophers' toy for which science has no use. At the other extreme, we have *Governing-Laws*: there are laws of nature, and they really do govern the universe.

No-Laws strikes many as counterintuitive, and it deprives us philosophers of a concept that would be very useful to appeal to in accounts of causation, explanation, determinism, and many other things. But Governing-Laws seems to have certain metaphysical and epistemological liabilities. If laws are things that can govern the universe, then in what does their governing of the universe consist? It seems that any good answer is going to have to appeal somewhere to 'necessary connections between distinct existences,' and many philosophers would call those unintelligible. If laws are things that govern the universe, rather than simply pervasive regularities in the course of events, then how can we have any epistemic access to them? All we can observe, after all, is that something happened; we cannot empirically detect whether it happened because it was necessitated by a law, or whether it happened just as a brute fact. So, empiricist qualms make many philosophers uneasy with Governing-Laws.

It is tempting to try to steer down the middle, and go for *Non-Governing-Laws*: there are laws of nature, and science does discover them, so lawhood is available for philosophers to appeal to in their accounts of explanation, determinism, and so forth, and we can save our intuitions about there being such things as laws of nature. But these laws don't literally govern the universe, so we avoid all of the empiricists' nightmares that Governing-Laws threatens us with. The best-systems approach to laws is the most well received, and probably the most promising, attempt to steer such a middle course.

The reason why I reject the best-system approach is that I reject all such attempts to steer a middle course. There are certain things that go on in science, I claim, that cannot be made sense of on any view that rejects the law-governed world-picture, whether of the No-Laws variety or the Non-Governing-Laws variety. It is logically possible, of course, that those elements of science cannot in fact be made sense of. Perhaps they are based on the same confused notions that the outmoded idea of a law-governed universe is based on. Perhaps we would be justified in believing in that possibility, if we were steadfast in our empiricist scruples and certain that governing laws of nature would violate them. But that is not how things are: I will argue in this book that there is a view of lawhood that vindicates the law-governed world-picture without offending against even the most radical Humean metaphysical prejudices.[17] Since making sense of some of the interesting things that go on in science requires adopting the law-governed world-picture, and even the most severe empiricist hang-ups turn out not to forbid adopting it, we have a good reason to adopt it. Going for a middle-way compromise would lose us the ability to make sense of some stuff that it would be great to be able to make sense of, and for no good end.

In the following section, I will explain why I am dubious of the No-Laws view. In the section after that, I will explain a reason for being dissatisfied with the middle way offered by the best-systems approach—or with any view that acknowledges laws but rejects governing. Later on in this chapter, I'll say something about why we need not be disturbed by the broadly 'Humean' or empiricist worries about the law-governed world-picture that motivate many to favor the best-system approach.

1.5 Work that laws do in science

One of the crowning accomplishments of the physics of the nineteenth and twentieth centuries is statistical mechanics. This branch of physics involves studying the large-scale behavior of macroscopic systems by treating them as aggregates of smaller and simpler systems. It is the tool whereby thermodynamics is reductively explained in terms of the statistical behavior of huge collections of particles.

A statistical-mechanical treatment of a macroscopic system begins by treating the system as an aggregate of a large number of smaller systems, each of which is supposed to be subject to the laws of some general physical

[17] To some readers that will sound like a contradiction. I hope to have shown otherwise by the end of this book; the case is summarized in Chapter 10, Section 10.5.

theory, such as classical (Hamiltonian) dynamics[18] or quantum mechanics. The physically possible states of this aggregate system comprise an abstract space, the *state space* of the system. For example, if the background theory is Hamiltonian dynamics, then for a system of N particles, the state space is the *phase space* of the system, which is an 6N-dimensional space, with one dimension for each component of the position of each particle (that gives us 3N dimensions), and one for each component of the momentum of each particle (that gives us 3N more). Specifying all 6N values—in other words, specifying a point in the 6N-dimensional phase space—amounts to completely specifying the physical state of the entire aggregate system at a particular moment in time.[19]

The evolution of the system over time is represented by a trajectory through the state space which is consistent with the laws of the background theory (e.g., Hamiltonian dynamics). Given any point in the space as an initial condition, at least one trajectory through the space begins at that point; there will be a unique trajectory running through any given point if the theory is deterministic. Every one of these possible trajectories, of course, will be consistent with every consequence of the background theory; so, for example, each possible trajectory will respect the conservation of energy. But there are other interesting features a trajectory might have that are not consequences of the background theory alone. Some of these features are shared by *almost all* of the possible trajectories—i.e., by the trajectories beginning at *almost any* point in the state space—though not by all. If it can be shown that this is the case for a given feature, then we can predict with some confidence[20] that the evolution of the actual world will exhibit that feature, and we will have a rather satisfying explanation of why it does—even though it is not a deductive consequence of our theory that the evolution of the universe will have that feature.

One example is the second law of thermodynamics, that entropy never decreases. Other examples are provided by other generalizations of thermodynamics, such as that in a glass of iced water outside on a hot summer day, the ice cubes will gradually melt, and the liquid water will not convert into ice. Almost all total states of the microscopic constituents of the system that are consistent with the fact that they compose a glass of iced water

[18] Hamiltonian dynamics is a powerful and elegant generalization of Newtonian mechanics, developed in the early nineteenth century by William Rowan Hamilton.

[19] Khinchin (1949), pp. 13–15.

[20] Assuming we are confident in our background theory.

outside on a hot summer day will evolve, under the laws of Hamiltonian mechanics, into a state consistent with their being a glass of liquid water with no solid ice in it. There are some exceptions: if the water molecules in the glass happened to be lined up and moving just right when they were placed in the glass, then they might all suddenly fall into place to form a seamless chunk of ice five minutes after the glass is taken outside. But the set of possible initial states of the water molecules that would lead to that kind of evolution are vanishingly small within the space of all possible initial states of the water molecules consistent with their making up a glass of iced water on a hot summer day. So we should not expect to see that happen, and no further explanation is called for when we do not find it happening.[21]

The reasoning I've been describing uses phrases like 'almost all' and 'almost every' a lot; those are vague, but they can be made precise, and they are made precise in statistical mechanics. 'Almost all possible states' means all points in the state space *except a set of measure zero*—that is, except for a set of points that is assigned the value zero by a suitable measure function.[22] The standard measure that is employed, when the background theory is Hamiltonian dynamics, goes by volumes in phase space: the measure of a region of the phase space is directly proportional to the volume of that region. So to say that *almost all possible trajectories lead to an increase in entropy* is to say that *the points in phase space at which a dynamically possible trajectory originates which fails to exhibit an increase in entropy make up a portion of phase space with volume zero*. But what justifies this choice of measure?

The standard answer is that it is the unique possible measure that satisfies a certain important constraint, namely *invariance under the dynamics*. Let R be a region within the phase space, and let t be a real number, and let R(t) be the region within the phase space that consists of all and only the points that a dynamically possible trajectory through phase space could reach if it started out at a point in R and then evolved for a time-interval of length t. A statistical measure over the phase space is dynamically invariant just in

[21] The reasoning here is of course far more complicated and subtle than this brief sketch reveals, and there are many unsolved problems about exactly how it works. Excellent discussions of some of its difficulties are found in Price (1996) and Albert (2000).

[22] A measure function assigns a number to each subset of the points in a space, subject to certain formal constraints; e.g., the null set is assigned a measure of zero; if A is a superset of B, then the measure of A must be at least as great as that of B; if A and B are two disjoint sets, then the measure of their union must be the sum of their measures.

case the measure of R is equal to the measure of R(t), for any R and any t. What this means can be put loosely by saying that we cannot gain or lose any information about where in phase space the system is just by waiting; if we learn at time zero that the system is in a region R with measure m, and we wait t units of time and then calculate the region in which the system might be then, this region will also be one of measure m. If the second measure were greater, then we would have lost information; what we know later about where the system is in phase space narrows down the possibilities less than what we knew before did. If the second measure were smaller, then we would have gained information; what we know later about where the system is in phase space narrows down the possibilities more than what we knew before did. Surely, whatever statistical measure we propose to use, it had better satisfy this constraint. A result called Liouville's Theorem says that for classical systems, the measure defined by the volume of a region in phase space satisfies this constraint.[23]

In this reasoning, the concept of a law of nature plays a key role. The dynamically possible trajectories of the system are just the trajectories that are consistent with the laws of nature to which the component particles of the aggregate are subject. The requirement that the measure be invariant under the dynamics is, roughly, the requirement that so long as the system evolves in a way consistent with the laws of nature, we can neither gain nor lose information just by waiting. Without the distinction between laws of nature and other propositions that happen to be true, we cannot draw the distinction between dynamically possible trajectories and merely logically possible trajectories, and we cannot formulate the constraint that dynamical invariance imposes.

The distinction between laws and other truths that is required to make sense of the basic techniques of statistical mechanics cannot just be the distinction between true universal regularities and other propositions. Suppose that as a matter of fact, nowhere in the universe does an ice cube ever spontaneously form out of the molecules in a glass of water at room temperature. Then this is a true universal regularity. Statistical mechanics does not treat it as a law, though; if it did, then there would be no dynamically possible trajectories through the state space that resulted in this sort of anti-thermodynamic macroscopic behavior—yet there are

[23] Khinchin (1949), pp. 15–19.

such trajectories, it is just that they all start out in initial states that are located in a phase-space region of measure zero. In any given system, there might turn out to be various regularities (such as symmetries) in the initial microstate; these might give rise to other regularities that obtain throughout the evolution of the system. But no such special feature of one particular possible initial microstate counts as a law, for purposes of statistical mechanics: for any such regularity, there are states in the state space that violate it.

In short, statistical mechanics presupposes a distinction between dynamically possible trajectories (trajectories consistent with the underlying laws) and merely logically possible trajectories, and this distinction plays a crucial role in the definition of the statistical measure: that measure must be such that it is invariant under all of the dynamically possible trajectories, but it need not be invariant under all of the logically possible trajectories. This example alone is enough to show that at least in some regions of scientific research, the distinction between a law and a true non-law does real work. This does not yet tell us how we should understand that distinction. But it does provide us ample reason to reject the claim that the very idea of a law of nature is a mere metaphysical holdover from the seventeenth century.[24] It is a concept that does at least some real work in at least some real science, and the philosophical problem of explicating it is a legitimate problem for the philosophy of science.

This rules out one of the three ways surveyed above: the No-Laws option. (Unless, that is, we are prepared to say that statistical mechanics rests on a bogus distinction.) It leaves us with two others to consider: the view that there are such things as laws of nature but they do not 'govern the universe' except in a figurative sense; and the full-blown law-governed world-picture.

1.6 An important difference between the laws of nature and the cosmic order

If we accept the view that the laws of nature are nothing more or less than the regularities that constitute the harmonious order of the

[24] But it does not give us a reason to reject the view of Mumford (2004), that what we call 'laws of nature' are really metaphysical necessities grounded in the essences of natural properties.

universe—whether we cash this out in terms of Lewis's version of the best-system account or not—then we must pay a certain price. Many scientists recognize a difference between striking and pervasive regularities that are consequences of the laws of nature alone, and striking and pervasive regularities that depend on the initial conditions of the universe as well as the laws. On the view that laws just are the regularities constituting the harmonious system of the universe, this distinction is obliterated. For on this view, if any regularity is striking enough and pervasive enough and is free from exceptions, it automatically counts as one of the laws of nature.

We should not obliterate this distinction lightly. To show why, I want to begin by discussing one of the paradigmatic expressions of the idea of the law-governed universe: Newton's *Principia*. There Newton succeeds in showing that known regularities in the motions of the planets, moons, and comets could be explained by subsuming them under the three laws of motion and the law of universal gravitation. However, he also recognizes that these laws are not sufficient to explain why such an orderly machine as our solar system exists in the first place. As he writes in the General Scholium to Book Three:

> . . . planets and comets must revolve continually in orbits given in kind and in position, according to the laws set forth above. They will indeed persevere in their orbits by the laws of gravity, but they certainly could not originally have acquired the regular position of the orbits by these laws.
>
> (Newton 1999, p. 940)

What does Newton mean by this? He goes on to describe the dazzling degree of order that we find in our solar system:

> The six primary planets revolve about the sun in circles concentric with the sun, with the same direction of motion, and very nearly in the same plane. Ten moons revolve about the earth, Jupiter, and Saturn, in concentric circles, with the same direction of motion, very nearly in the planes of the orbits of the planets. And all these regular motions do not have their origin from mechanical causes, since comets go freely in very eccentric orbits and into all parts of the heavens.
>
> (ibid.)

How is all of this harmonious order to be explained? Why do the planets all go around the sun in the same direction? Why do their orbits lie almost in the same plane? Why do their moons all go around them in the same direction in which the planets go around the sun? For that matter, why are there any stable planetary orbits at all? Given the current positions, velocities, and masses of the bodies in the solar system, the laws of motion and of gravity guarantee that they will continue on in the harmonious way that we know they do. But not just any old set of positions, velocities, and masses are like this. If you were building a solar system from scratch, endowing the celestial bodies with masses, arranging them in their initial locations, and giving their initial velocities, by far the majority of arrangements you might contrive would not result in anything like the harmonious system of the world that we actually find. The vast majority would result in wildly unstable orbits, trajectories that eventually crash into the sun, or ones that escape the solar system altogether. What's more, if the solar system were initially situated too near to another body at least as massive as the sun, its gravitational influence would disrupt the stability of the solar system. So, the regularities that characterize the motions of the solar system—although they appear 'lawlike,' and some of them are even called 'Kepler's laws'—are not consequences of the laws alone; they depend also on the initial conditions of the solar system. And the initial conditions required for these regularities to obtain are extremely special ones. They appear to be *finely tuned* to produce the kind of world we find.

Newton wastes no time drawing an important consequence from all of this:

> This most elegant arrangement of the sun, planets and comets could not have arisen without the design and dominion of an intelligent and powerful being. And if the fixed stars are the centers of similar systems, they will all be constructed according to a similar design and subject to the dominion of *One*, especially since the light of the fixed stars is of the same nature as the light of the sun, and all the systems send light into all the others. And so that the systems of the fixed stars will not fall in upon one another as a result of their gravity, he has placed them at immense distances from one another.
>
> (ibid.)

This argument of Newton's is of course one version of the Argument From Design. But more specifically, it is an early example of what has come to be known as a *fine-tuning argument*. In this argument, Newton does not appeal to the laws of nature themselves as evidence of the existence of God; rather, he points to the existence of amazing regularities that could not have resulted from the laws of nature alone. It is cosmic order that is *not* subsumed under the laws that shows the work of an intelligent designer.[25]

Newton's response to the appearance of fine-tuning is not the only possible response. Another is to see the problem as a scientific one, calling for a scientific solution. This is what Laplace did when he formulated his Nebular Hypothesis. On the assumption that the bodies in the solar system coalesced out of a large rotating disk, Newton's laws lead us to expect that the result would be a system of bodies exhibiting the kind of large-scale regularities we find. Had the system started out as a set of discrete bodies which had to be positioned and set in motion in such a way that they would form a system exhibiting the kind of harmony we actually find, then fine-tuning would have been required; but on the hypothesis that they all condensed out of a gigantic rotating disk, no fine-tuning is required; 'generic' initial conditions for such a rotating disk can be expected to lead to an orderly solar system.[26]

Note that both Newton's argument, and the reply to it offered by the Nebular Hypothesis, implicitly respect a distinction between two different kinds of generalization, both of which belong to the harmonious system that characterizes our world: on the one hand, there are the laws of nature, which remain in the background throughout the argument—they are not said (in the Newtonian argument quoted above) to cry out for an explanation in terms of divine action, and no mechanism is called for to explain why generic initial conditions would lead to a world in which they are true. On the other hand, there are other regularities, such as the ones more-or-less summed up by Kepler's so-called 'laws': these are not consequences of the real (Newtonian) laws, and so they do require an explanation, either by appeal to a supernatural agent or to a natural mechanism—and the fact that, given the laws, they depend so sensitively on a special choice of initial conditions makes the need for explanation all the more urgent. Among the harmonious and stable regularities that constitute the cosmic order we see around us, there are the ones that are laws of nature, and then there are the ones that are not, and this distinction

[25] Another conclusion Newton draws is that the stability of the solar system also depends on active divine intervention in the world. For Newton believed, mistakenly, that in the long run the gravitational attractions of the planets on one another would cause their orbits to degenerate. (But that aspect of Newton's argument is not relevant to our story here.) See Barbour (1997), pp. 34ff.

[26] See Barbour (1997), pp. 34–5.

makes a difference for what still stands in need of being given an explanation of some kind.

Situations with the same logical structure can be found in more recent physics and astronomy. Contemporary advocates of fine-tuning arguments note that given our best guesses about what the fundamental laws of nature are, those laws involve numerical constants whose values are 'free parameters,' such that only values within a very small region of the space of possible values would lead to a universe containing large amounts of condensed matter, which is a necessary condition for the evolution of life. This leaves us with an explanatory problem: why are the values of the fundamental constants located in the life-supporting range, given that that range is such a tiny portion of the range of possible values? We have the same two options that we had in the Newtonian case: we can posit a supernatural designer to supply the needed explanation; or we can seek some kind of mechanism that would reliably produce the special conditions we happen to find. A third option has appeared in the contemporary literature: perhaps reality consists not of just one universe, but of a 'multiverse' of different universes exhibiting a very wide range of possible values for the fundamental constants; since we can only find ourselves in a universe that can support life, it is no surprise, and needs no further explanation, that we find ourselves in a universe where the values of the fundamental constants are in the life-supporting range.[27]

Closer to Newton's original fine-tuning argument are contemporary arguments that focus on the fact that given some contemporary theory about what the laws are, only very special initial conditions could give rise to a universe with certain large-scale properties that our universe seems to have. For example, thermodynamic temporal asymmetries (e.g., entropy tends to increase and never decreases in macroscopic systems) are puzzling in the light of our best fundamental theories, for the laws of those theories are temporally symmetric, respecting no difference between the 'forward' and 'backward' directions of time. Given that we have temporally symmetric fundamental laws, why do macroscopic systems exhibit temporally asymmetric behavior? One standard answer to this question appeals to the idea that the universe (or at least the present epoch) began in an initial state of very low entropy. But this does not seem

[27] For discussion of contemporary fine-tuning arguments, see the articles in Manson (2003).

satisfactory as a complete solution to the problem. For low-entropy states are (more or less by definition) extremely rare within the space of all possible states the universe could have started out in. It is thought to be very troubling that our current theories force us to posit, as a brute fact, that the initial conditions of our universe were of such a special kind, in order to explain why the second law of thermodynamics should hold. For this reason, there is a tradition of trying to do better than simply positing special initial conditions. This tradition begins with Boltzmann, who hypothesized an eternal universe that is almost always in a state of very high entropy. Given an infinite amount of time, it is overwhelmingly probable that there will eventually be statistical fluctuations away from the high-entropy norm, of any given magnitude. We just happen to find ourselves living temporally close to one of those fluctuations (and we could hardly find ourselves living at any other time, since we need a relatively low-entropy environment to survive).[28]

Recently, Craig Callender has argued that we should consider the possibility that the special low-entropy initial conditions of the universe are in fact nomologically necessary, pointing out that on Lewis's best-system analysis, it seems likely that they will be (Callender 2004). This may be a case of one philosopher's *modus ponens* being another's *modus tollens*: Callender argues that since an otherwise plausible account of laws, the best-system analysis, yields the result that the 'special initial conditions' of the universe are in fact consequences of the laws of nature, we should take seriously the possibility that they are—a possibility that incidentally provides a solution to the problem of explaining the thermodynamic temporal asymmetries. By contrast, I argue that the fact that the best-system analysis renders the special initial conditions lawlike is a reason to reject that analysis of lawhood.

If we run the argument in Callender's direction, I think we prove too much: *whenever* a pervasive and simple regularity is found to play an important role in our scientific theories, it will automatically count as a law of nature, and insofar as derivation from a law is explanatory, it will no longer stand in need of explanation.[29] The same argument would have been available in the early eighteenth century, with respect to the

[28] See Albert (2000); Price (1996).

[29] Of course, given an explanation that appeals to a law, we can always ask for a further explanation of that law itself. But when we do so, we will not be looking for a causal or mechanical explanation such as the Nebular Hypothesis.

special initial conditions required to generate the kind of harmonious solar system that we find. Laplace could have skipped the task of framing a hypothesis describing a mechanism whereby a coplanar system of stable and unidirectional orbits could have formed, and simply pointed out that given what was known, the best system seemed to include the fact that the initial conditions were such as to give rise to such a system, therefore it is a consequence of the laws of nature that such a system exists, and there is nothing left to explain.

A second example is given by the apparent flatness and homogeneity of the universe, which, given the standard Big Bang cosmological model, would result only from extremely special initial conditions. This fact was one of the early motivations for the research program of Inflationary Cosmology, which seeks to replace the standard Big Bang model with an alternative model of the early universe, in which generic initial conditions would predictably lead to a universe with the large-scale properties we actually observe.[30] This is not the only virtue of Inflationary Cosmology, but it is one of the virtues that initially made it popular. But it is an advantage that Inflationary Cosmology enjoys over the standard Big Bang model only because the latter posits cosmic regularities that are not explained by the laws alone, but only by the laws together with special initial conditions. On any view of laws that obliterates this distinction, there is no advantage for Inflationary Cosmology here.

It isn't part of my project to examine these arguments in detail, or to assess the merits of fine-tuning arguments for the existence of God, inflation, or anything else. The reason I bring all of this up is that it illustrates something important about the way many scientists, past and present, think about the laws of nature. Newton's fine-tuning argument, and its successors, take for granted that when we find a striking regularity whose existence is not guaranteed by the laws of nature alone, but depends also on special features of the initial conditions, this regularity stands in need of some explanation. Newton thought that the needed explanation would refer to God. The Nebular Hypothesis and its successors—such as Inflationary Cosmology—agree with the Newtonian assumption, but look for the needed explanation in a different direction than Newton himself looked. Those scientists and philosophers who see a deep problem in

[30] Guth (1997), pp. 176–86; Earman and Mosterin (1999).

the temporal asymmetry of thermodynamics, and do not see a complete solution in the bare posit of low-entropy initial conditions for the universe, agree that when a large-scale regularity depends sensitively on special initial conditions, there is still explanatory work to be done. What all of these players have in common is the assumption that when we find a striking large-scale feature of our world that is not a consequence of the laws of nature, but depends on very special initial conditions, a further explanation is called for. And that assumption in turn presupposes *that it makes sense to speak of large-scale regularities in the world that are not laws of nature and are not consequences of the laws of nature.* All these players also assume *that we are aware of some such regularities.* If the laws of nature were nothing more than the basic regularities constituting the harmonious regularity of the universe, this would be nonsense: the stability and harmony of the solar system, the flatness and homogeneity of the universe, the constant and universal increase in entropy, the availability of large amounts of condensed matter for the formation of galaxies, planets, and heavy elements, are all among the general features of our universe that constitute the cosmic order—so they would be among the laws of nature, rather than improbable consequences of special initial conditions. In short, unless all of the players I have been talking about are deeply confused, there is more to the notion of the laws of nature than there is to the notion of the order of the cosmos. 'Law and order' is not a redundant phrase.

What should an advocate of the best-system approach to laws say about all of this? Well, it is hard to see how striking large-scale regularities in the world such as the general increase in entropy, the flatness and homogeneity of the universe, and the existence of large quantities of condensed matter could fail to make it into the best system. Adding any of them to a given system involves a relatively small cost in simplicity, since each can be formulated fairly briefly as a simple generalization; leaving any of them out of a system incurs a great cost in information content, since so many of the salient large-scale features of our universe depend on them. So it is hard to see how to avoid the conclusion that either the best-system approach to laws is simply wrong, or else all of the arguments involving apparent fine-tuning surveyed above are fundamentally confused. Fans of the best-system approach can be expected to go for the second verdict.[31]

[31] As I mentioned above, Callender (2004) makes a case for this second verdict.

If they do, they have to face the question of why we should place more confidence in a philosophical idea barely a century old than in intuitively plausible assumptions that surface in scientific reasoning time and time again. To this question, they can give answers: the only alternative to the best-systems account seems to be to posit some kind of non-logical, necessary connections in nature; to posit such necessary connections is to engage in supra-empirical metaphysics, and it incurs terrible epistemological liabilities.

We seem to have a stand-off here. On the one side, we have the history of arguments about fine-tuning, which requires a distinction between the laws of nature and all the other pervasive regularities that go into constituting the harmonious order we find around us. These arguments have the authority of some great figures in the history of science behind them, and they are undeniably intuitively appealing in their own right. (Even if you don't think Newton's fine-tuning argument justifies the conclusion that the world-system had an intelligent designer, can you really deny that Newton pointed out a glaring need for an explanation? That if the Nebular Hypothesis had not worked out, we would have had a real problem on our hands?) On the other side, we have broadly Humean concerns about necessary connections in nature.

One of my goals in this book is to show how to achieve a peaceful resolution of this stand-off. We can give a serious philosophical account of lawhood that makes room for compulsion over and above cosmic order, and allows us to make sense of the debates over various forms of apparent fine-tuning, but which does not run afoul of the metaphysical and epistemological reservations that motivate advocates of the best-system approach. You can be a good empiricist without rejecting the basic assumptions about laws of nature that give life to the issues about fine-tuning.

1.7 The picture in four theses

Suppose the law-governed world-picture is right. What would things have to be like, then?

In order to make progress on this question, it would be useful to formulate the law-governed world-picture as a short list of theses. That would make it easier to think about it systematically. It would help us to articulate necessary conditions and sufficient conditions for its accuracy, and so help us search for arguments for it and against it, and evaluate such arguments when we find them.

There is a danger in trying to do this, though. For the law-governed world-picture isn't really a short list of theses. It's a large-scale view of the world, one that you can pick up from having learned a certain amount of science without ever finding it distinctly expressed in any particular scientific text. It was not born into the world by being explicitly formulated by anyone, but rather by emerging as a very general way of thinking about things suggested by the progress of the modern natural sciences.[32] Perhaps we find more-or-less precise and explicit formulations of it in various seventeenth-century authors like Descartes, but there it appears as a hybrid scientific-theological view, as much about God's relation to the natural world as about the natural world itself. Since then, the view has been liberated from its theological entanglements. This is not to say that one may not consistently accept the law-governed world-picture and interpret it in the light of one's theological views; it is only to say that the law-governed world-picture is something you can buy without buying a theological interpretation of it.[33] For example, consider the views of Laplace: his imaginative account of a universe in which an ideally intelligent and well-informed being could use its knowledge of the laws of nature together with the global state of the universe at a given instant is surely a paradigm articulation of one version of the law governed world-picture.[34] But Laplace's version of the picture has no need of the hypothesis of a creator—or at any rate, it doesn't appeal to one. As much as Laplace differed with Descartes and Newton about theological matters, he and they agreed in their adoption of the law-governed world-picture. So even if that picture was first articulated as a set of partly theological theses, it soon became something else. But what replaced it has no canonical formulation. So, like materialism, it may prove difficult to pin down.

[32] Especially by that of the physical sciences, where candidate laws are comparatively easy to identify. But not exclusively by that of the physical sciences: on one inviting reading of the Darwinian revolution, its most important general lesson is that law-governed processes, as opposed to inherently teleological processes, are all that it required to explain the existence and diversity of life.

[33] But for a defense of the contrary view, see Foster (2004).

[34] Laplace (1952), p. 4. Laplace's demon usually appears in the philosophical literature in discussions of determinism; I stole the idea of using it as a paradigm articulation of the very idea of a law-governed universe from Carroll (1994).

At any rate, we shouldn't be too complacent about our ability to pin it down.

Nevertheless, I shall plow ahead. It seems to me that there are four theses such that anyone who accepts all four deserves to count as a friend of the law-governed world-picture, and anyone who rejects any one of them does not. Here they are:

The Lawhood Thesis: There is a distinct class of facts, or true propositions, fittingly called *the laws of nature*; alternatively, there is a property fittingly called *lawhood* that some but not all facts or true propositions (and no false propositions) have.[35]

The Discoverability Thesis: Science is in principle capable of discovering which propositions are the laws of nature—i.e., which true propositions have the property of lawhood.

The Governing Thesis: The laws of nature govern the universe, in some robust, non-figurative sense of 'govern.' It is not just that everything behaves *as if* it were governed by laws; the evolution of the universe *really is* governed by laws.

The Science-Says-So Thesis: We can be justified in believing that the laws of nature govern the universe (in whatever sense of 'govern' makes the Governing Thesis come out true) without appealing to any extra-scientific source of epistemic justification.

Anyone who rejects the Lawhood Thesis denies that there are such things as laws of nature. Anyone who rejects the Governing Thesis may allow that there are such things as laws of nature, but denies that they govern the universe in any meaningful sense. Anyone who rejects the Discoverability Thesis may allow that there are such things as laws of nature, but locates them outside the ken of science. Anyone who denies the Science-Says-So Thesis may allow that there are laws of nature, that they are discoverable by science, and even that they really do govern the universe—but must place *the fact that* they govern the universe outside the ken of science; perhaps it is something that we must turn to pure metaphysics or theology

[35] Some philosophers might complain that laws of nature are not really propositions, but rather concrete entities of some kind, such as facts or states of affairs. (One motivation for this complaint might be the thought that mere propositions could not govern the universe; they are just not the sort of thing that could push planets around.) But I do not think that I really have any substantive quarrel with those philosophers; see Chapter 2, Section 2.2.

to discover.[36] None of these characters accepts everything in the sketch of the law-governed world-picture that I offered at the very beginning of this chapter.

Of course, these four theses are not perfectly perspicuous. In particular, the Governing Thesis and the Science-Says-So Thesis both make use of the term 'governing' without giving an account of it. So both of them stand in need of interpretation. In later chapters, and especially in Chapter 5, I will turn to the problem of interpreting them. But even before we have a good interpretation of the relevant notion of 'governing,' it is useful to have this list of four theses. For different ways of rejecting the law-governed world-picture correspond nicely to different subsets of the list. Those who locate laws in the models scientists produce rather than in the world reject all four theses. Those who allow that there are such things in the world as laws of nature and that science is the right tool to investigate them accept the Lawhood Thesis and the Discoverability Thesis. But some stop there; 'Humeans' like David Lewis are naturally interpreted as denying the Governing Thesis, and so denying the Science-Says-So Thesis. And on one reading of van Fraassen's views, they are *at least consistent* with the conjunction of the Lawhood Thesis and the Governing Thesis, but not with either the Discoverability Thesis or the Science-Says-So Thesis. For according to van Fraassen's view of laws, science has no use for them, and it certainly has no use for the notion that they 'govern' the universe;[37] but according to Constructive Empiricism, science does not have the final word in what we may believe about the world; it only covers the observable surfaces of things, and while these surfaces contain no laws, the hidden parts of the world may.[38]

1.8 The strategy of this book

Our question is: what would things have to be like, in order for the law-governed world-picture to be correct? Well, the Lawhood Thesis, the Discoverability Thesis, the Governing Thesis, and the Science-Says-So

[36] I will discuss the Science-Says-So Thesis, the need to include it in an adequate formulation of the law-governed world-picture, and the notion of an 'extra-scientific source of epistemic justification' further in Chapter 7, Sections 7.1 and 7.2.

[37] van Fraassen (1989). [38] van Fraassen (1980).

Thesis would all have to be true. Having said this, we can break down our original question into four sub-questions: what would things have to be like in order for each of these four theses to be true?

I will argue in Chapter 4 that the Lawhood Thesis, the Discoverability Thesis, and the Governing Thesis can all three be true only if some *meta-theoretic* account of laws is true. Chapter 3 will explain in detail what a meta-theoretic account of laws is; Section 1.9, below, will give a brief overview.

Starting with Chapter 5, I will consider the question: what would things have to be like, in order for the Governing Thesis and the Science-Says-So Thesis both to be true? In Chapters 5 through 9, I will argue that the answer is that a certain condition must obtain. From that condition, we can almost read off an account of laws. At any rate, the satisfaction of that condition is both necessary and sufficient for the truth of a certain account of lawhood. This account is a meta-theoretic one. I call it the *measurability account of laws*, or the 'MAL' for short.[39]

The overall argument of the book splits into two distinct pieces: the argument of Chapter 4 is completely independent of the argument of Chapters 5 through 9. If you are convinced by the first argument but not the second, then you have a good reason to think that if the law-governed world-picture is right, then the correct philosophical account of lawhood is a meta-theoretic one. This is very informative, since most of the philosophical accounts of lawhood on the market today are not meta-theoretic. (In fact, as far as I know, the MAL is the only meta-theoretic account of laws that has been stated[40]—so you also have at least some reason to look favorably on the MAL.) On the other hand, if you are convinced by the second argument but not by the first, then you have a good reason to think that if the law-governed world-picture is right, then so is the MAL. (And so, you have a good reason to accept the conclusion that the correct account of lawhood is meta-theoretic, since the MAL *is* a meta-theoretic account of lawhood.)

Each argument shows something conditionally: *if the law-governed world-picture is correct*, then the first argument shows that the correct account of

[39] In Roberts (2004), I defended a different account of laws under the same name. The account I defend in this book is a descendant of that one. I trust that my reusing the name will cause no great confusion.

[40] Apart from the earlier version of the MAL in Roberts (2004).

laws is some meta-theoretic conception, and the second argument shows that it is the MAL in particular. Of course, this gives anyone committed to the law-governed world-picture a reason to accept the MAL. But many people don't believe that the law-governed world-picture is right. What can I say to them?

The MAL turns out to have some remarkable features. It specifies truth conditions for lawhood-ascriptions, and it does so in informative terms, in a way that does not make reference to any ontological or metaphysical posits that are not obviously required by scientific methodology anyway. The only basic non-logical concept that it makes use of is that of a legitimate procedure for measuring some quantity—and we cannot practice science without at least implicitly making use of that concept. So the metaphysical/ontological price of accepting the MAL is very low. Ironically, if the arguments of this book succeed, they show that the *only* way you can do justice to the law-governed world-picture is by adopting an account of lawhood that does *not* offend against Humean metaphysical scruples.

Moreover, the MAL can be tested in a certain way. If we take any candidate scientific theory T, and rewrite it so that it just talks about what happens in the world without saying of any proposition that it is or is not a law of nature, then the MAL makes predictions about which propositions we should call laws of nature if T were our theory. (This is true of all meta-theoretic accounts of laws; in fact, it is one way of defining what it is for an account of laws to be meta-theoretic.) When we apply the MAL to a decent range of candidate theories for which there is little or no controversy about what 'the laws of that theory' are, we find that we get the right answers. For example, when we apply it to the theory consisting roughly of Books I and III of Newton's *Principia*, we find that if this theory were our theory, then we should call the three laws of motion and the law of universal gravitation 'laws of nature,' but we should withhold that appellation from the rest of what Newton says—even the other things he says that have a 'lawish'-looking form, for example that all of the planets go around the sun in the same direction.

So, suppose that we deny the law-governed world-picture: we either deny that there really is any such thing as lawhood, or else we say that the propositions we call 'laws' don't really 'govern' the world except perhaps in a figurative, 'as-if' sense. Then, we encounter the MAL, and all the arguments I was just talking about. We now see that if we wanted to, we could introduce a new predicate, 'L', by specifying truth conditions for L-ascriptions in exactly the way the MAL specifies truth conditions for lawhood-ascriptions. Doing this would not require us to accept any metaphysical or ontological posits that we don't already have to accept anyway in order to do science. If we did so, then it would turn out that we should predicate L of exactly those principles that we normally predicate lawhood of. It will also turn out that the things we attribute L to also have some of the important features that philosophers have traditionally attributed to the laws of nature—such as counterfactual robustness. And most importantly, it will turn out that there is an important non-metaphorical sense of 'govern' in which it is correct to say that the Ls govern the universe. Lo and behold, all along we have had the resources to define a kind of proposition that includes all the propositions that people are inclined to call 'laws of nature,' and that has exactly the features that the law-governed world-picture attributes to the laws of nature. Why in the world should we balk at saying that this new predicate 'L' picks out exactly the laws of nature?

There are two things we could say now: either that we have discovered good evidence that this new predicate means exactly what people have meant by 'law of nature' all along, or else that if we stipulatively redefine our term 'law of nature' so that it is equivalent with the new predicate 'L', then the newly redefined 'law of nature' will do all the work that the old term was expected to do. (I prefer to say the second thing, but if you prefer to say the first then I won't argue with you.) If we were inclined to reject the law-governed world-picture on the grounds that it is unintelligible to say that the laws of nature govern the universe, or that to say so is to adopt an extravagant metaphysical thesis, or that if the laws of nature do govern the universe then there is no way we could ever discover that they do, or what the laws of nature are, we can now see that we've lost those grounds.

1.9 The meta-theoretic conception of laws

In this section and the next, I will present a brief overview of the account of lawhood that I will defend in this book; details and serious arguments will have to wait for the chapters to follow. If you would rather get straight to the feature film without watching a trailer first, feel free to skip the remainder of this chapter.

The view of lawhood I will defend is a *meta-theoretic* account. Let me start by explaining what that means.

A given scientific theory T can be divided into two parts: its non-nomic part, which consists of everything T says or entails that can be stated without the use of the term 'law of nature' or its cognates; and its nomic part, which consists of all statements of the form 'It is a law that P' and 'It is true but not a law that P' that T says or entails. According to the MAL, the non-nomic part of T determines its nomic part. This means that there cannot be two scientific theories T1 and T2 that share the same non-nomic part but differ in their nomic parts. This is perhaps a surprising claim. Consider, for example, the theory presented in Newton's *Principia*. Its non-nomic part includes the following propositions:

f=ma: For every massive body, the total impressed force on the body equals the body's mass multiplied by its acceleration.[41]

same-direction: All the planets go around the sun in the same direction.

Its nomic part includes the following propositions:

(1): **f=ma** is (not just true but also) a law of nature.

(2): **same-direction**, though true, is not a law of nature; it is an accidental regularity.

It seems that there is an alternative to Newton's theory, which is exactly like Newton's theory except that it says that **f=ma** and **same-direction** are *both* laws of nature. There also seems to be an alternative according to which neither of these propositions are laws of nature, and both are accidental regularities. These theories might have very little to recommend them, but for all that, they do seem to be theories a scientist could propose, and they are clearly alternatives to Newton's theory since they are logically inconsistent with it. The MAL denies this. Since it implies that the non-nomic part of a theory fixes its nomic part, it implies that at most one of these three rivals is a genuine scientific theory.

This seems surprising because we are used to thinking of the laws of nature as one feature of the reality that scientific theories are supposed to

[41] I have presented this Newtonian law in its usual modern form rather than Newton's own.

tell us about—like the causes of cancer, the moons of Saturn, and the ingredients of the sun. And what a theory says about one such feature of reality can be varied independently of what it says about other such features of reality, subject to the requirement of logical consistency. I call this view *the first-order conception of laws*. The MAL rejects the first-order conception of laws in favor of what I call *the meta-theoretic conception of laws*. On the meta-theoretic conception, laws of nature are not part of the first-order subject matter about which science theorizes; the laws of a theory are not just whatever that theory says are laws of nature—since scientific theories don't *say anything* about the laws of nature. Rather, the laws of a theory are the propositions that play a certain special role within that theory. In this respect, the laws of a scientific theory are like the postulates of a mathematical theory: the postulates of Euclidean geometry, for example, are not the propositions that Euclidean geometry *says* are *the postulates*—Euclidean geometry does not say anything at all about postulates (though texts on Euclidean geometry often do); it just says things about points, lines, planes, and things like that. The first-order subject matter of Euclidean geometry consists of geometrical objects; postulates are meta-theoretical, i.e. they are the subject matter of meta-mathematics rather than mathematics. Just so, according to the meta-theoretic conception of laws, are laws meta-theoretical: Newton's theory's first-order subject matter is not the laws of nature, but rather masses, forces, and things like that; the laws of this theory are the propositions that play a certain role within it. Newton's theory doesn't *say* anything about what the laws are, any more than Euclid's theory *says* anything about what the postulates are—though texts on Newton's theory (including Newton's own) often do say things about what the laws of Newton's theory are. For this reason, according to the meta-theoretic conception of laws, any two apparent presentations of scientific theories which agree on their non-nomic parts but identify different propositions as laws would not be presentations of two different theories: they would be two different presentations of the same theory, at least one of which is confused, since it fails to identify the theory's laws correctly. This is why the two alternatives to Newton's theory I mentioned above are not genuine rivals to Newton's. The three 'theories' (Newton's own, and the two alleged alternatives) are really different formulations of the same theory, of which at most one correctly identifies the laws of that theory. The other two are like garbled presentations of Euclid's geometrical theory which misidentify a theorem as a postulate or vice versa, and do not thereby state some coherent alternative to Euclid.

Of course, the analogy between laws and postulates is far from perfect. One of the ways in which it fails is that we do sometimes say that, or conjecture that, or wonder whether, some proposition is a law of nature (and not just whether it is a law of some particular scientific theory). By contrast, we never say that, or conjecture that, or wonder whether, some proposition is a *postulate*, full-stop. Indeed, the meta-theoretic conception of laws must acknowledge this in order to be coherent: for the meta-theoretic conception is a way of thinking about what it is for some proposition to be a law of a particular scientific theory T—but what does 'a law of T' mean? Presumably, it means: a proposition that is a law of nature if T is true, or perhaps a proposition that we would be committed to calling a law of nature if we were committed to the truth of T. So, the subject matter of the meta-theoretic conception of laws is not well defined unless there is such a thing as *being a law of nature*, or at least such a thing as *being committed to calling something a law of nature*. But we cannot allow that there is such a theory-neutral natural state of affairs as P's being a law of nature without sliding back into the first-order conception of laws.

Hence, the meta-theoretic conception of laws must provide an account of what it is to say that something is a law of nature (rather than a law of some theory), without giving an account of what it is for there to be a law of nature (which is not relativized to a particular theory). The way to do this is to adopt a contextualist semantics of statements of the form 'P is a law of nature.' The basic idea is that 'P is a law of nature' is true in context k just in case P is a law of some true theory that is salient in k. This allows us to make sense of statements of the form 'P is a law of nature,' in addition to statements of the form 'P is a law of theory T,' while maintaining that lawhood is at bottom a role that a proposition plays within a theory rather than a theory-neutral feature of the world.[42]

A worry naturally arises at this point: the MAL was supposed to be a way of vindicating the law-governed world-picture, according to which the universe is really governed by laws of nature. But the MAL makes lawhood a role played within a scientific theory, rather than a theory-neutral feature

[42] This move requires an account of what makes a theory 'salient' in a given context; I'll give an account of that in Chapter 3.

of reality. And the MAL makes the truth conditions of a statement of the form 'P is a law of nature' dependent on what theories happen to be salient in the context of utterance. In the light of this, how could the laws govern the universe in any meaningful sense? Surely, if anything really governs the universe, then it is not in any way beholden to or dependent on the activity of scientific theorizing!

There is an answer to this worry, but I can only gesture at it here. The way in which laws of nature may be reasonably said to 'govern the universe' has to do with inevitability: the laws of nature are inevitably true, and always have been. Ascriptions of inevitability are closely related to assertions of counterfactuals: roughly, if I say that it has always been inevitable that P, I commit myself to saying that even if things had been different in this way or that, P would still have been true. (That's just a first approximation; we will have to refine it later.) And counterfactuals are notoriously context-dependent. So it should not be a surprise that judgments about what is inevitable—and hence, which propositions govern the universe—are themselves context-dependent. But this raises the disturbing prospect that what governs the universe is in an important sense up to us: by changing the features of our present context in the way that makes counterfactuals shift their truth values, we can make the principles that govern the universe jump around. This worry is misplaced, though. It will turn out that whenever we are engaged in empirical-scientific inquiry, the truth conditions of the counterfactuals relevant to the way in which the laws govern the universe are not 'up to us.' We do not in any sense have the power to make the principles that govern the universe change.[43]

1.10 The measurability approach to laws

1.10.1 The connection between laws and measurements

One thing that laws of nature do is make it possible to design ways of measuring things. Newton's laws of motion and gravitation make it possible to measure the masses of the sun and planets by means of astronomical observations; the law of thermal expansion makes it possible to measure temperature using a mercury thermometer; the laws governing

[43] I explain why in Chapter 8.

the propagation and reflection of light waves make it possible to use radar to measure the distance between one object and another; laws of electrodynamics make it possible to measure the strength of the electromagnetic field by observing the motions of small charged particles and the distribution of scattered iron filings; Ohm's and Kirchoff's laws make it possible to measure differences in electric potential; and so on. In general, whenever we can set up a situation in which one or more laws guarantee that some quantity we would like to measure will be correlated with some other quantity we already know how to measure, a method of measurement is available to us. Undoubtedly, one of the greatest practical benefits conferred by knowledge of the laws is that it makes it possible to design new methods of measurement in this way.

Conversely, it seems that whenever we have a method of measurement that we are inclined to trust, we believe (at least implicitly) that the reliability of this method is underwritten by the laws of nature. Consider a case in which we measure one quantity by means of contriving a situation in which we can read off the value of the quantity we would like to measure—call this *the object variable*—from the value of another quantity, which we are able to detect more or less directly—call this *the pointer variable*. One example is when we use an ammeter to measure the current in an electrical circuit: the circuit is run through a coil that induces a magnetic field, which in turn displaces a pointer that is connected to a torsion spring. When the spring is in its equilibrium position, the pointer stands still and vertical; the presence of a magnetic field induced by the current in the coil exerts a force on the pointer that causes it to rotate either to the left or the right; as the angle through which it has rotated becomes greater, the torsion force pushing it back in the direction of its equilibrium position becomes greater; the pointer will stop oscillating and come to rest at the point when this torsion force exactly balances the magnetic force pushing the pointer in the opposite direction. Thus, the further the pointer is displaced, the greater the torsion force that keeps it in place; hence the greater the magnetic force pushing it away from the equilibrium position; hence the greater the magnetic field induced by the current in the coil; hence the greater the current in the coil. In this way, things are contrived so that the angular displacement of the pointer from its equilibrium position is proportional to the amount of current in the circuit. The pointer variable (the displacement of the pointer), which we can detect just by looking at it (with the help of a numbered scale directly behind the pointer), is a function of the object variable (the current).

When we take this kind of instrument to be a good one for measuring current, we do not simply take it that the position of the pointer *just always is* a function of the current. For we suppose that this relation between them is not merely a fortuitous coincidence. One indication of this is that we take the reliability of the instrument to be counterfactually robust: had the current been twice what it actually is, then the pointer would not still have been displaced by the very amount it actually is displaced by; rather, it would still have been displaced by an amount proportional to the current. Thus, when we trust the instrument, we seem to be taking it to be *nomologically necessary* that the pointer variable is proportional to the object variable; we take it that there are laws of nature that guarantee this proportionality. In this particular example, many laws of nature are involved: Newton's second law of motion, which guarantees that the pointer will stop moving back and forth when and only when the forces acting on it balance each other; the torsion force law (the analogue of Hooke's law for torsion springs), which guarantees that the spring exerts a force on the pointer in the direction of the equilibrium position and proportional to the angular displacement from that position; the Lorentz force law, which guarantees that the force on the pointer is proportional to the strength of the induced magnetic field; and the law of magnetic induction, which guarantees that the strength of this field is proportional to the current. The important point here, though, is not which laws are involved, but that *some* laws or other guarantee that, when the instrument is properly constructed and properly employed, its pointer variable will be a function of the object variable. If we did not believe this, then it is not clear that we would regard the use of this instrument as a good way of measuring current at all.

So in general, it seems that wherever there is a good measurement procedure, there are some laws of nature. The pointer variable (the output) of the measurement is correlated with the object variable (the thing getting measured), and this correlation is nomologically necessary, i.e. it is a consequence of the laws of nature. When we know (or take ourselves to know) some laws of nature, we can exploit them to design new ways of measuring things; when we trust a method of measurement, we thereby implicitly take that method to be nomologically reliable.

All of this suggests an analysis of measurements in terms of laws of nature. But all it really shows is that there is an important connection between laws and measurements. The idea I want to try out is that things actually run in the opposite direction: we can give an analysis of laws in terms of measurements. Briefly and roughly, the idea is that *laws are those principles that guarantee the reliability of measurements*. This is intended not as an empirical identification, such as the identification of water with H_2O, but as an analysis of the significance of calling or treating something as a law of nature: *what it is for someone to regard something as a law of nature is for it to be one of the principles that guarantee the reliability of the methods they regard as good measurement methods*. In both of these italicized slogans, it is tempting to read 'reliability' as *counterfactual* reliability; but if the slogans are read in that way, then they purport to analyze lawhood in terms of counterfactuals. But counterfactuals are the focus of much the same philosophical perplexities as laws themselves; if we want to really illuminate the nature of lawhood, it seems that we had better not analyze in terms of counterfactuals.[44] So, let us understand 'reliability' in these two slogans as meaning *actual, de facto* reliability.

This proposal is the heart of the MAL.

1.10.2 *A helpful objection*

Someone might object that this idea is hopeless from the start, for the following reason:

> We are willing to treat something as a legitimate measurement method only if we believe it to be reliable; the kind of reliability that is required is not mere *de facto* reliability, but the kind of reliability that carries over to counterfactual scenarios (as you yourself have just pointed out); the only way we have of telling that some regularity is reliable in this counterfactual sense is to determine that it is a consequence of the laws of nature. Thus, we don't even know what to count as

[44] This is not to say that developing an analysis of laws in terms of counterfactuals is a trivial or pointless activity. Lange (2000) shows clearly that the task of analyzing laws in terms of counterfactuals is not nearly as straightforward as it might seem. He goes on to work out one sophisticated way of defining laws in terms of counterfactuals. This analysis sheds much light on the relation between laws and counterfactuals—but if counterfactuals are in the end just as mysterious as laws, and mysterious for very similar reasons, then such an analysis only reduces two mysteries to one, rather than removing the mystery. Lange does not claim otherwise: his stated goal is not to give an account of the metaphysical nature of laws of nature, but only to make clear the nature of the commitment one undertakes when one calls something a law of nature.

a good way of measuring something until we already have some idea of the laws of nature. The idea of a law of nature is thus prior to the idea of a measurement, and our beliefs about the laws of nature must be prior to our beliefs about what is a good way to measure something. If we are going to do any analyzing here, we ought to analyze measurement in terms of laws, rather than the other way around.

This objection is a very helpful one to consider. For there is a response to it that brings out an important virtue of the MAL. The objector is responding from a point of view that is, I believe, closer to the mainstream than mine. So the response to it will bring out some important differences between my proposal and the dominant approaches to laws on the market today, and highlight some of my proposal's peculiar advantages.

Consider first what the objector and I agree on: we both hold that it is absolutely essential to science and to empirical knowledge more generally that we are able to make measurements; further, we both agree that whenever we regard a method as a good method for making measurements and rely on it as a source of evidence in scientific reasoning, we take that method to be reliable in a way that extends to counterfactual scenarios. Neither of us, as of yet, has offered any explanation for why these two principles should be true or why we should believe them; they are both taken as primitive at this point. I propose to stop with these two primitive assumptions, and add no more. On the basis of them, I propose the hypothesis that what we take to be the laws of nature are exactly the principles that guarantee the actual reliability of the methods we take to be good measurement methods—that *what it is* to take a proposition L to be a law of nature *is* to take some set of methods to be good measurement methods, where L is one of the principles that collectively imply that these methods are actually reliable. Now, on the basis of my hypothesis, I can offer an explanation of why laws support counterfactuals: appealing to the second primitive principle that I share in common with the objector—that we regard something as a good method of measurement only when we regard its reliability as extending to counterfactual situations—I infer that the principles that collectively imply the actual reliability of the methods we regard as good measurement methods must extend to counterfactual situations as well. And those principles are exactly what we take to be the laws of nature, according to my hypothesis. This explains why taking something to be a law necessarily involves taking it to be counterfactually resilient: we cannot coherently hold both that some proposition is a law of nature, and that it would fail to remain true in a wide range of counterfactual scenarios—or at least, we cannot coherently hold both of these things while we are engaged in scientific inquiry.[45]

Now consider the position of the objector. His assumptions, like mine, include that we regard something as a method of measurement only when we take it to be reliable in counterfactual as well as actual situations. He adds the assumption that we regard a principle as extending to counterfactual situations only when that principle is a law or a consequence of the laws—a further primitive assumption that he has as of yet offered no explanation for. And it cries out for explanation: why are the laws of nature such special features of the world that they, by contrast with all the other important features of the world, must be held constant when considering hypothetical scenarios? If they were logically necessary, this would be no great mystery, but they are not logically necessary. They seem to have some special potency that enables them to remain in place even when we hypothetically rearrange other aspects of the world. The objector owes us an explanation of why this is so. (Recall that this is exactly the point that my hypothesis enabled me to explain.) Furthermore, the objector goes on to conclude that we can say that some method is a good method for making measurements only when we are already confident that there are laws of nature that guarantee its reliability. So before we can start making any measurements at all, we must already have some idea of not only what regularities are *true* in our world, but also of which ones are *laws*. It is hard enough to understand how we can find out which propositions are laws of nature when all we have direct empirical access to is what actually happens in the actual world; it is only harder when we add that we cannot even be sure that something is a good way of measuring the *actual* value of some physical quantity without *already* knowing something about the laws.

So in the final analysis of the dialectical situation *vis-à-vis* me and this objector at this stage of the discussion, our situations seem to be as follows: both of us take for granted as basic premises, without any further justification or explanation, that science requires measurements, and that anyone who regards something as a good measurement method also regards it as counterfactually reliable. I have introduced a hypothesis

[45] The line of argument gestured at here is worked out in much more detail below, in Chapter 8.

which, if true, explains why we must regard the things we take to be laws as counterfactually stable. The only problem that remains for me is that of explaining how we decide what to regard as a good method of measurement. The objector, by contrast, has as yet no explanation of the fact that laws of nature are counterfactually stable; this is a further basic assumption for him, and he owes us some explanation of why it should be so. And he faces both the problem of how we are ever able to find out what we should regard as a good measurement method, and the problem of finding out what the laws of nature are—each of which, it seems, must be solved before the other one can be if his view is right. Thus the objection stated above is not as threatening as it first appears: in the very course of stating the objection, one takes up a position with liabilities that my proposal easily avoids.

1.10.3 The proposal is meta-theoretic

Above, I expressed my proposal in two ways: first, *the laws of nature are the principles that guarantee the reliability of measurements*; second, *for someone to regard something as a law is for it to be a principle that guarantees the reliability of a method they regard as a good measurement method*. The first formulation might be seen as shorthand for the second one, but taken at face value it says something quite different: for it focuses on *what a law of nature is*, whereas the second formulation focuses on *what it is to regard something as a law*.

Consider for a moment the first formulation, taken at face value. It makes the question of what the laws of nature are depend on the question of which measurement methods are good ones. What does this imply about a world in which there is no intelligent life, and thus no measurements at all? The implication seems to be that there are no laws in such a world. This implication can be avoided by saying that in a world without laws, there are nevertheless principles that guarantee that certain methods *would* be good measurement methods, if only there were anyone there to employ them. After all, surely we want to allow that even in some worlds where there are intelligent beings making measurements—indeed, even in the actual world—there are some perfectly good measurement methods that no one will ever employ, either because no one thinks of them, or because they are too expensive to carry out, or just because no one ever gets around to it. Still, they are good measurement methods, and there will be principles that guarantee their reliability. So what makes a principle guarantee the reliability of measurements cannot be that it guarantees the reliability of some methods of measurement *that actually get performed.*

So the worry about worlds without intelligent life in them is not fatal to my proposal. But it points to another one that is more serious. Being a measurement is a matter of being *used* in a certain way for a certain epistemic purpose. There is nothing intrinsic about any natural process in virtue of which it is a measurement; presumably, just about any kind of physical process could be exploited by a suitably placed and suitably endowed creature in a measurement process, and just about any kind of physical process that is used in a measurement could occur naturally when no measurement is going on at all (though for some of the more sophisticated measurement techniques of modern science, it would presumably require an extremely improbable set of initial conditions for these processes to occur spontaneously). What makes a physical process a measurement at all is that some sapient being is employing it for the purpose of finding something out. To define laws of nature in terms of measurements renders the concept of a law of nature an epistemological concept, whereas it seems to be an ontic or metaphysical concept.

The second formulation of my basic proposal is less vulnerable to this sort of worry. For it does not define laws of nature as such in terms of measurements; it defines regarding something as a law of nature in terms of regarding something as a good measurement. Here both terms of the identification are clearly epistemological concepts, so the same worry does not arise.

But of course, what we want to know is not only what it is to regard something as a law of nature; we want to know *what we are saying about the world* when we say that something *is* a law of nature. The second formulation of the proposal appears unable to deliver what we want. We seem to be in a bind here; neither formulation of the proposal seems able to avoid some difficulty or other. But there is a way out of this bind.

Suppose that M is the set of methods that are good measurement methods, according to my point of view. What are the propositions that are laws, according to my point of view? They are the propositions that serve to guarantee the reliability of the methods in M. But M should not simply be identified with the set of measurement methods that I explicitly call 'good measurement methods.' There might be many methods of measurement that must be good ones if everything else I believe is true, though I have never thought of them; there might also be methods of measurement that I am in the habit of using and depending on in practice, though it has not risen to the level of conscious awareness that I constantly trust them. So the methods that are good ones from my point of view are the ones I consciously recognize as good ones, the ones that I practically count on, and all the methods whose status as good measurement methods is entailed by everything else I believe. And the laws, according to my point of view, are the propositions that guarantee the reliability of all of these methods. These need not coincide with the propositions that I would list if you asked me for my opinion about what the laws of nature are. They are not the laws of nature *according to my explicit conscious opinions*; they are the laws of nature *according to my point of view*, which means that they are the propositions that I am *committed* to regarding as laws.

So, I inhabit a point of view, a context, within which a lot is presupposed about the world. *If all of these presuppositions are true*, then I would speak truly if I said that a member of *M* is a legitimate measurement method, and I would speak truly in calling P a law of nature if and only if P is one of the principles that guarantees the reliability of methods in *M*.

The upshot of these reflections is that the proposal I introduced above is best understood as a meta-theoretic one. Recall that a meta-theoretic account of laws is one that identifies lawhood as a role played within a theory, and says that a lawhood-ascription 'It is a law that P' is true in a context k just in case P plays the law-role within a true theory that is salient in k. What we have to do in order to specify a particular meta-theoretic account is say what the law-role is, and say what the salient theory in a given context k is. Suppose the 'salient theory' in my own context is just everything true that I believe about the world, explicitly or implicitly—including what I believe about which measurement methods are good ones. Suppose that a proposition P plays the law-role within a theory T just in case T is one of the propositions that collectively guarantee the reliability of all of the methods of measurement that must be good methods if T is true. These two suppositions give us a meta-theoretic account of laws. If this meta-theoretic account is right, then what it is for P to be a law of nature in a given context k is for P to be one of the propositions that collectively guarantee the reliability of the methods of measurement that are good ones according to the true beliefs and presuppositions of the speakers in k. That vindicates the second formulation of the proposal, that what it is for someone to regard something as a law is for it to be one of the principles that guarantees the reliability of a method of measurement that they regard as legitimate.

What's more, the first formulation of the proposal turns out to be presupposed to be true in every context. For in a given context k, it is (trivially) presupposed that whatever background theory is presupposed in k is true, and it is (also trivially) presupposed that whatever is presupposed to be a good measurement method in k is a good measurement method, so it follows that in k, the presuppositions imply that the propositions truly called laws of nature are the ones that collectively guarantee the reliability of the good measurement procedures.

This meta-theoretic account does not fall prey to the objection that it identifies a metaphysical concept with an epistemological concept. It does not define the property of being a law of nature as a property having to do with what sapient creatures can do to find things out. For it does not identify *any* property as 'the property of being a law,' period; the truth conditions it assigns to law-statements are context-dependent ones, and they refer to the role a proposition plays within a theory when it is a law of that theory, but not to any non-relativized notion of lawhood. But on the other hand, this meta-theoretic account does not fall prey to the objection that it only tells us what it is to regard something as a law, without telling us what we are saying about the world when we say that something is a law. For it supplies objective (though context-dependent) truth conditions for any token utterance of 'P is a law of nature.' So the meta-theoretic proposal provides us with a way of spelling out the proposal without running afoul of the dangers we saw for both of its original formulations.

1.11 What comes where

Throughout the book, I'll depend on a few simple assumptions about what laws of nature must be like, if there are any. These assumptions once had the status of 'received views,' but each has come under attack recently. In Chapter 2, I'll defend these assumptions.

In Chapter 3, I'll explain the meta-theoretic conception of laws in more detail, and in Chapter 4, I'll present my argument that the Lawhood, Discoverability, and Governing Theses can all three be true only if the meta-theoretic conception of laws is correct.

In Chapters 5 through 9, I'll lay out my argument that the Governing and Science-Says-So Theses can both be true only if the MAL is the correct account of lawhood. I will provide some defense for the claim that the MAL makes the right predictions about what we should be willing to call a law of nature in Chapter 9, Section 9.5; a more detailed defense of this claim is given in the Appendix.

In Chapter 10, I'll take up the controversy between 'Humean' and 'non-Humean' views of laws of nature, and argue that the MAL is not comfortably classified on either side of this debate. The MAL implies the thesis called 'Humean Supervenience,' though it avoids other commitments typical of 'Humean' views (most importantly, the rejection of the law-governed world-picture). I'll explain how the MAL can avoid some important arguments that purport to show that any view that implies Humean Supervenience must be false, and how the MAL provides a way of understanding our universe as truly governed by laws of nature, though in a surprising way.

2

In defense of some received views

2.1 Some assumptions that will be in play

In this chapter, I will state and motivate some assumptions about laws that I will take for granted throughout the rest of the book. None of these assumptions is idiosyncratic, but none of them is completely uncontroversial. These assumptions are: that the laws are *propositions*, that they are *true*, that *all of their logically contingent logical consequences are laws themselves*, and that at least some of them are *metaphysically contingent*. The reader who already believes all of these assumptions can skip this chapter without missing anything very important to the rest of the book. But since there are many philosophers who disagree with one or more of these assumptions, I had better take a little time to explain why I make them.

2.2 The laws are propositions

Sometimes laws are defined as *statements* of a certain sort, but most philosophers insist on a distinction between law-statements and laws themselves. Statements are human products, which come into existence when humans make them; we do not want to say that there were no laws before there were law-statements, or that there would be no laws if there were no law-statements.

If we define a law-statement as a statement of the form 'It is a law that P,' then the laws themselves are what is stated by the that-clauses (the 'that P's) that occur in true law-statements. What is stated by a that-clause is generally taken to be a proposition, though some philosophers maintain that some that-clauses state facts, or represent states of affairs, which must be distinguished from propositions. If there is anything substantive at stake in the question whether laws are facts or propositions, then I don't want to take a stand on it. Henceforth, I'll speak as if I assume that a law is a kind of proposition, but I don't think anything important will be lost if 'proposition' is systematically replaced by 'fact.'

I need to address one objection. Some philosophers think that if a law of nature is the kind of thing that governs the universe, then it cannot be a mere proposition. The truth of a proposition might be a consequence of the existence of some law of nature and its governing, but a proposition itself (even a true one) is just not the right sort of thing to govern the universe. The universe consists of concrete entities such as atoms and galaxies; propositions are abstract entities—mere shadows of what goes on in the universe, or ways that things might be in the universe. A shadow of the universe, or a way that things might be in the universe, is not the sort of thing that could govern the universe. So if we want to take the law-governed world-picture seriously, we had better not understand laws of nature as propositions.

I think this objection results from taking the grammatical form of the statement that the laws of nature govern the universe too seriously. 'The laws of nature' occurs in the subject position, the verb is 'govern,' and the direct object is 'the universe.' This suggests the picture of laws as some kind of agent, that is able to do something to the universe. But we shouldn't take this grammatical appearance seriously. Consider the parallel case of the laws of the land: it is a law of the United States of America that every citizen must file a federal income tax return on or before April 15 of each year. This has the form 'it is a law (of the USA) that P,' where P is here a proposition about what citizens must do. And of course, the laws of the USA govern the citizens of the USA. But how could a mere proposition govern robust concrete entities like the citizens of the USA? The answer to this puzzle is that, well, strictly speaking, it is the *government* of the USA that governs the citizens of the USA, and the government of the USA is a concrete entity (or at least, it is as concrete as a social institution can be). But the government of the USA governs its citizens *via making the laws of the land*. Its governing activities have *contents*; the bit of governing that got done when the law in question was enacted is a bit of governing to the end *that everyone must file a tax return by April 15*. The proposition which we call the law is not the agent of the governing, but the content of the governing.

Something similar is going on in the case of laws of nature. The laws of nature are not agents that somehow manage to influence the concrete physical universe in a way that it makes sense to describe by means of the verb 'to govern.' Rather, the universe is governed, and its governance has a content, which is to say that there are certain things it is *governed to do or not to do*; the laws of nature are the propositions that give the contents of this governing. This is what we really mean (or, what we should really mean) when we say things like, 'the laws of nature govern the universe.' We mean that the universe is governed, and the laws of nature are the contents of the governing.

This way of putting it suggests that in addition to the laws of nature, there must be something that plays the role of the government—some concrete entity or agent that actually does the governing. That might be so. For example, it might be that whenever it is a law of nature that all Fs are Gs, this is so in virtue of a concrete state of affairs involving the universals F and G, as Armstrong (1983) holds. In this case, the law in question is still the proposition that all Fs are Gs—after all, we say 'it is a law of nature *that all Fs are Gs*'—even though the lawhood of this proposition consists in the existence of something other than a proposition.

But it might not be so. Consider a second analogy: the rules of English grammar, which govern the speech of English-speakers. The proposition that the subject must agree with the predicate is one of these rules; just like the laws of the land, it is not an agent of governing, but a content of governing. But in this case, unlike the case of the laws of the land, it is far from obvious whether there is any concrete entity that it makes sense to think of as the governing agent here. At any rate, it is far more clear that it makes sense to say that the rules of our grammar govern our speech, and that these rules are contents of governing rather than governing agents, than it is that there exists some concrete governing agent in this case. So it is at least coherent to suppose that there could be contents of governing without a concrete governing agent.

We are still a long way from being clear about the sense in which the universe is 'governed.' It is like the sense in which the land is governed, in that the governing has a content that takes the form of a proposition. This much we can agree on whether or not we think there must also be some concrete agent that does the governing. If there is such a concrete agent, then it of course is not a proposition; it is a governor of some sort. But then *it* is not what we call the laws of nature, any more than the legislature of our land is what we call the laws of our land. For this reason, I think I am on safe ground assuming that the things we call laws of nature should be thought of as propositions.

2.3 The laws are true

It might seem to go without saying that laws of nature are true: something that has been taken to be a law of nature might turn out to be false, but if it does, then it thereby turns out not to have been a law of nature after all.

But there are grounds on which a reasonable person might doubt that all laws must be true propositions. For a great deal of attention has been paid in recent literature to what are called *hedged laws* or *ceteris paribus laws*. These are laws that, as usually formulated, take the form of generalizations that have exceptions. Even though they have exceptions, it is alleged that such laws can still be laws. But for a generalization to have exceptions is, of course, for that generalization to be false. Hence, it seems that if there are such things as hedged laws, then there are laws that are false propositions. And a large and growing chorus of respectable voices in the philosophical community proclaims that there are indeed such things as hedged laws, and that science has discovered many of them. Perhaps we should not be so quick to assume that laws must be true.[1]

Perhaps the most oft-cited examples of putative hedged laws are rather over-simplified examples of putative laws from psychology. For example:

> **Caramels:** Any person who wants to eat a caramel, sees a dish of caramels in front of her, and does not believe that eating a caramel from the dish would lead to undesirable consequences, will eat a caramel.

Plausible enough; perhaps it's even a law. But surely Caramels has exceptions: once in a great long while, surely some neurological mechanism will fail to work properly, and the person's beliefs and desires won't lead to action. Sometimes a person in the situation described will be struck by

[1] The recent literature on hedged laws is large and growing; some of the highlights are Cartwright (1983), Fodor (1991), Schiffer (1991), Pietroski and Rey (1995), and Lange (2002).

lightning just as she was about to begin reaching for a caramel. And so on. Further examples come from biology:

Ravens: All ravens are black.

Ravens might be a law of zoology, if there are such things as laws of zoology—but surely there are exceptions, such as albino ravens. Cartwright (1983) famously argues that there are even examples in physics:

Grav: For every pair of bodies of masses m and M separated by a distance d, each member impresses a force on the other in the direction of the other with a magnitude given by GMm/d^2, where G is a constant.

Grav is false whenever the bodies in question are electrically charged, in which case the forces they exert on one another are not purely gravitational.

None of these examples is beyond question.[2] I have argued that there are no hedged laws,[3] and I stand by this claim. But for purposes of this book, I can remain neutral on this question.[4] The important point here is that even if there are such things as hedged laws, it does not follow that any false proposition is a law. If Caramels is a hedged law, then although Caramels is false, something else is true, namely *that other things being equal, a person who wants to eat a caramel . . . will eat a caramel.* This proposition, not Caramels itself, is the proposition that should be called a law here, and it is evidently true. And in general, whenever we have a hedged law, we have a true, hedged proposition. (Similar remarks apply to Ravens and Grav.[5]) One might adopt the view that in a hedged law-statement, the hedging clause ('other things being equal') really modifies the lawhood operator ('it is a law that'), rather than the proposition that is said to be a law, so that we have a false proposition that is truly said to be a hedged law. But this view seems to have no advantage over the alternative view

[2] Grav, for example, can be rescued from falsehood simply by reformulating it to make it clear that it asserts the existence of one component force exerted by each body on the other, and does not purport to specify the value of the total force exerted by one body on the other. This requires realism about component forces. But component forces are theoretical entities that seem to pull their weight quite well in Newtonian physics.

[3] Earman and Roberts (1999); Earman, Roberts, and Smith (2002).

[4] I discuss the way my view of laws can accommodate hedged laws in Chapter 9, Section 9.4.

[5] In the case of Ravens, the true proposition that is a law might be best formulated as a generic: 'Generically, ravens are black.' In the case of Grav, it might (following Cartwright (1999)) best be formulated as a proposition about powers, rather than regularities in behavior: 'Every massive body has a power to exert an attractive force on every other body given by the equation GMm/d^2.'

that the lawhood operator in a hedged law-statement is just the ordinary, unmodified lawhood operator, and the proposition it is applied to is a true, hedged proposition. The latter view is simpler, and allows us to maintain the simple generalization that all laws of nature are true.[6]

2.4 The logically contingent consequences of the laws are laws themselves

Are the laws of nature logically closed? In other words, is every proposition that is a logical consequence of a set of laws of nature itself a law of nature?[7] If so, then a lot of propositions that are very complicated and do not seem to have much generality are going to count as laws of nature: for example, if it is a law of nature that all copper objects conduct electricity, then the closure of the laws would imply that it was also a law of nature that every copper statue of a cat that was made by a left-handed sculptor with hazel eyes is electrically conductive.

There are some impressive reasons to think that the laws are logically closed. For example, it seems plausible that the laws are distinguished from other truths by, among other things, the fact that they are *necessary* in a certain sense (weaker than logical necessity), and the fact that they would all still have been true under a broad range of counterfactual scenarios. Given any sense of necessity, the logical consequences of the propositions that are necessary in that sense are necessary in that sense themselves. If a set of propositions would all still have been true in some counterfactual scenario, then it must be that all of the logical consequences of those propositions would also have been true in that counterfactual scenario. So, the logical consequences of the laws of nature must share these two distinguishing features of the laws of nature. If these are the features that distinguish the laws from other truths, then the consequences of the laws must be laws themselves.

[6] John Carroll and an anonymous referee for Oxford University Press both made very helpful comments on this section.

[7] Since the laws presumably must be stated in a language that includes that of arithmetic, it makes a difference whether 'logically closed' means 'closed under derivability' or 'closed under semantic consequence.' Surely the interesting suggestion here is that laws are closed under semantic consequence: any derivation-system is going to capture only a subset of the semantically valid consequences; different derivation-systems will capture different subsets; and what is a law and what is not should not depend on which system of derivation we choose to use.

But on the other hand, there are also some impressive reasons to think that the laws of nature are not logically closed. For example, if the laws are logically closed, then every logically necessary truth is a law of nature. This is disquieting; it just feels wrong to say that it is a law of nature that either there is a talking donkey or else there isn't. If we understand logical closure in a broad sense, so that the logical consequences of the laws of nature include their mathematical consequences, then every mathematical truth is a law of nature. And this seems outrageous: one of the most important things about the laws of nature seems to be the way in which they are different from theorems of pure mathematics.

There are other reasons to doubt the logical closure of the laws as well. Laws are supposed to play a special role in explaining their instances. Suppose we want an explanation for why the *objét* on Susan's coffee table is conductive, and someone points out that this *objét* is a copper statue of a cat that was made by a left-handed sculptor with hazel eyes, and it is a law of nature that all such things are conductive. This will not be a very good explanation. On some views of explanation, it is no explanation at all. It is much better to say that the *objét* is made of copper, and it is a law of nature that all copper conducts electricity.

This does not show that the law appealed to in the first putative explanation is not a law, even if the first putative explanation is a very poor explanation. Even if explanation does always involve deriving the explanandum from a law of nature, it does not follow that every generalization playing the role of the law in a bad explanation fails to be a law. The badness of the bad explanation at hand might be attributable to things other than its failure to appeal to something that is really a law. Nonetheless, there is a strong and widely shared intuition that the specific generalization about copper statues of cats made by left-handed sculptors with hazel eyes is not *quite as much of a law* as the generalization about all copper objects. The former is only a special case of the latter—in fact, it's a special case applying to a very gerrymandered set of objects. The latter seems more basic, more fundamental, than the former.

A second type of example of a dubious candidate for lawhood that is a logical consequence of the laws is provided by disjunctions of laws. Suppose that it is a law that all copper is conductive and it is a law that nothing travels faster than light; if the laws are logically closed, then it is a law that either all copper is conductive or else nothing ever travels faster than light. Does this disjunction have the explanatory power that is thought to characterize laws? Can we use it, for example, to explain why my copper figurine is either a conductor or else is traveling at a speed less than light? The intuitive answer is no: there are two reasons why my figurine is either conductive or else slower than light. One of them is that it is conductive since it is made of copper and it is a law that all copper is conductive; the second is that it moves more slowly than light since it is a law that everything does. The disjunctive law plays no role in either of these two explanations.[8]

What these examples suggest is that there are some boundaries we need to recognize, some distinctions we need to draw. Let's distinguish three different sets of propositions. First of all, there is what I will call the *Core Set*, which contains all the propositions that have the most unimpeachable claims to lawhood—the most basic or most fundamental laws, which do not appear to be hokey, arbitrary special cases of other laws. If it is a law that energy is conserved in every closed system, then presumably the proposition that energy is conserved in every closed system belongs to the Core Set. But its corollary which says that energy is conserved in every closed system that is confined to a New York subway train on a Tuesday does not. Next, let's call the logico-mathematical closure of the Core Set, the *Closed Set*. Finally, we have the *Contingent Set*, which contains all and only the logically and mathematically contingent members of the Closed Set. We've looked at reasons for calling all members of the Closed Set 'laws of nature,' reasons for restricting this appellation to members of the Contingent Set, and reasons for restricting it to the members of the Core Set—or at least for marking the important distinction between the members of the Core Set and the other members of the Contingent Set.

It seems to me that once we recognize these distinctions, there is no substantive issue left to settle—just the terminological issue of how to use the label 'law of nature.' There are three terminological conventions we could adopt, any one of which would be reasonable:

- We could call all members of the Closed Set 'laws of nature,' reserve the label 'basic laws' for the members of the Core Set, and explain the

[8] Several examples of apparent counterexamples to the logical closure of the laws are given by Lange (2000), pp. 201–7.

strangeness of calling logical truths and mathematical theorems 'laws of nature' as a pragmatic phenomenon—a violation of conversational norms. (Calling $2+2=4$ a law of nature is misleading, since it suggests falsely that it is *merely* nomologically necessary, whereas it actually enjoys a higher grade of necessity.) We could also call the members of the Contingent Set that are not also in the Core Set 'derivative laws,' to contrast with the 'basic laws.'

- We could call all members of the Contingent Set 'laws of nature,' call the members of the Core Set 'basic laws,' and other members of the Contingent Set 'derivative laws,' and refuse to call logically and mathematically necessary truths 'laws of nature,' but agree to call them 'nomologically necessary.'
- We could reserve the label 'laws of nature' for the members of the Core Set, and call all other members of the Closed Set 'nomological necessities.'

As I said, I think the choice among these is just a choice among terminological conventions. But I have a strong preference for the second convention, and I think you should too.

I prefer the second convention to the first because it seems to me that calling something a 'law of nature' ought to mean that it has a status that has something important to do with the way nature is. The truths of mathematics and logic are what they are independently of how it is with the natural world, so calling them 'laws of nature' would be misleading.

The reason why I prefer the second convention to the third is a bit more complicated. No matter which terminological choice we make, we have a distinction between the Core Set and the Closed Set. The Closed Set is deductively closed, and the members of the Core Set serve as axioms in an axiomatization of the Closed Set. Like any axiomatizable, deductively closed set of propositions, the Closed Set can be axiomatized in many different ways. For example, if the Core Set includes Newton's second law of motion as well as the law of energy conservation, then there is an alternative axiomatization of the Closed Set that includes neither of these laws, and has in their place the proposition that *force equals mass times acceleration among bodies made of metal*, the proposition that *if force is directly proportional to mass among copper bodies, then energy is always conserved in closed systems*, and the proposition that *if energy is always conserved in closed systems composed entirely of neutrons, then force equals mass times acceleration for all bodies.* For it is easily seen that the deductive closure of these three propositions is identical to the deductive closure of Newton's second law together with the law of energy conservation. These propositions can belong to an axiomatization of the Closed Set, but in an intuitive sense this would be a *less natural* axiomatization than the one provided by the Core Set. But what makes one of these axiomatizations more or less natural than another? One answer is that one axiomatization, but not the other, consists only of axioms that have a special, mind-independent, objective status; a second answer is that one axiomatization is a more sensible one to use from our point of view, for reasons that are largely pragmatic. On either answer, there is an objective matter of fact about which propositions are nomologically necessary, so there is an objective matter of fact about which propositions belong to the Closed Set. There is also, of course, an objective matter of fact about which members of the Closed Set are logico-mathematically contingent and which are necessary, so there is an objective matter of fact about the membership of the Contingent Set. Here, the agreement ends: the first view goes further and says that there is an objectively distinguished subset of the Contingent Set whose members constitute an axiomatization for the Closed Set; the second view disagrees, and says that there are many possible axiomatizations of the Closed Set, and the only thing that privileges one over the others is the pragmatic issue of which would be best for us to use.

I don't have a clue how to settle the issue between these two points of view. If the second view is correct, though, then note what follows: the distinction between the members of the Core Set and the rest of the members of the Contingent Set is not an objective, mind-independent distinction. It is a distinction drawn in terms of which of many equally legitimate logically possible axiomatizations is most expedient for us to employ (for whatever purposes we wish to axiomatize the set). It would be odd to mark this sort of distinction—which is drawn in terms of us, our purposes and our capabilities, rather than in terms of nature—by calling the things on one side of it 'laws of nature' and withholding this label from the things on the other side. Since it seems to me at least plausible that the second view of the status of the Core Set qua axiomatization of the Closed Set may be right, I would prefer to adopt a terminological convention that would be natural if the second view turned out to be right. This speaks in favor of adopting the second terminological convention.

And on the other side of the ledger, what speaks in favor of restricting the label 'laws of nature' to the members of the Core Set? Above, we saw a disadvantage of allowing consequences of the Core Set that are not themselves in the Core Set to count as laws of nature: when combined with a simple version of the covering-law model of explanation, it implies that some intuitively bad explanations are good explanations. But as I noted above, we could address this worry by adopting a more nuanced account of explanation, rather than by restricting 'law of nature' to the members of the Core Set. Furthermore, if it turns out that there is an important distinction between the members of the Core Set and the other members of the Contingent Set that we need to mark, we can always draw the distinction using the labels 'basic laws' and 'derivative laws,' terms which (unlike 'law of nature') seem neutral on the question of whether they mark a conventional distinction or a mind-independent one.

So, throughout this book I will adopt the second terminological choice. Every logico-mathematical consequence of the laws of nature will count as a law of nature in my terminology, unless it is logically or mathematically necessary. This leaves room for a distinction between basic and derivative laws of nature. I won't have anything to say about the latter distinction in this book, but I don't deny that it can be drawn.[9]

One more wrinkle needs to be acknowledged before we move on. There is an additional distinction that one might well think we should draw that I have neglected so far: among the members of the Contingent Set that are not members of the Core Set, there are bound to be some singular propositions. For example, if the Core Set includes *that all ravens are black*, then the Contingent Set will include *either Ernie is not a raven, or else he is black*—or, if the truth of this disjunction requires Ernie's existence, which is not guaranteed by the laws about ravens, then the Contingent Set will include *if Ernie exists, then either he is not a raven, or else he is black*. On the second terminological option—the one I have adopted—this proposition is a law of nature, albeit a derivative one. Some may balk at this: a law

[9] Lange (2000) adopts the third convention presented here, though he uses 'physical necessity' instead of 'nomological necessity.' I don't think this marks any substantive disagreement between me and Lange.

of nature, it seems, should be a generalization of some kind; it should be most naturally formulated as either a universal generalization or a statistical generalization. Facts about particular individuals are just not general enough to deserve the appellation 'law of nature.'

I am of two minds about this. On the one hand, it does seem counterintuitive to allow truths about particular individuals to count as laws of nature. On the other hand, it is not so clear that the distinction between propositions that are generalizations and those that are not is really a distinction between two kinds of proposition; any proposition that can be written out as a universal generalization can also be written out as a statement that refers to a particular individual,[10] and vice versa.[11] But a law of nature is a law of nature no matter what the syntactic form of the sentence you use to express it.

Here I don't want to try to settle the question of whether there is nevertheless a principled distinction that can be drawn between propositions (as opposed to sentences that express them) that are 'general enough' to be laws and those that are not.[12] Instead, I'll resolve this issue conditionally: if there is not, then every member of the Contingent Set counts as a law of nature in my usage. But if there is, then the term 'law of nature' should be reserved for members of the Contingent Set that are sufficiently general; insufficiently general members of the Contingent Set should be classified as nomologically necessary, but not as laws. Let this qualification to the claim that all contingent consequences of the laws of nature are themselves laws of nature be understood as implicit in the rest of the book. From here on out, I will ignore this complication.

2.5 At least some laws are metaphysically contingent

The laws of nature seem to possess a kind of necessity that we might call 'physical necessity' or 'natural necessity.' But they do not seem to be necessary in the strictest sense; that is, they seem to be metaphysically contingent. For one thing, the laws of nature must be discovered empirically

[10] For example, *all ravens are black* can be reformulated as *if Ernie is a raven, then he is black, and every other raven has the same color as Ernie; whereas if Ernie is not a raven (or does not exist) then all ravens are black.*

[11] For example, *Ernie is a raven* can be reformulated as *Everything that is identical to Ernie is a raven.*

[12] Earman (1978) grapples with this issue.

rather than a priori, and this is one of the traditional marks of the contingent. For another, we seem to have no trouble clearly conceiving of universes that are governed by different sets of laws, and in which some of the actual laws of nature are false. We can even figure out a lot about what things would be like in such universes. For example, in any possible universe where the gravitational force is not governed by an inverse-square law:

> **UG-IS:** Every massive body exerts an attractive force on every other, the magnitude of which is directly proportional to the product of the bodies' masses and inversely proportional to the square of the distance separating them.

but rather by an inverse-cube law:

> **UG-IC:** Every massive body exerts an attractive force on every other, the magnitude of which is directly proportional to the product of the bodies' masses and inversely proportional to the cube of the distance separating them.

there are no stable planetary orbits. Our ability to conceive of such scenarios, and reason about them, makes it plausible that the universe could have been that way: though UG-IS is true, and a law of nature, it might have been false, and UG-IC might have been a law of nature in its place. (To keep things simple, I will assume throughout the rest of this chapter that our universe is Newtonian.) This has traditionally been the standard view of laws: though they possess a special kind of necessity, they are metaphysically contingent.[13]

But this standard view is challenged by much of the contemporary literature on laws. *Necessitarians* such as Alexander Bird, Brian Ellis, Caroline Lierse, Stephen Mumford, and Chris Swoyer have argued that the facts we call 'laws of nature' are metaphysically necessary. They do not deny that laws cannot be known a priori, but they point out that Saul Kripke has taught us that a truth can be metaphysically necessary even if it is knowable only a posteriori.[14] But such Kripkean necessities always involve either identities (e.g. that Hesperus is Phosphorous, that water is H_2O), or else essential properties of things (e.g. that Nixon is human, that this

[13] See Armstrong (1983), chapter 11 and Carroll (1994), pp. 23–5.

[14] Kripke (1980).

very table is made of wood). How could laws of nature be among this class? Necessitarians answer this question with a doctrine that has come to be called *scientific essentialism* (and sometimes *dispositional essentialism*): natural properties and natural kinds have essential features, which include certain relations they stand in to one another. For example, if it is a law of nature that copper is electrically conductive, then this is because the kind *copper* stands in a certain relation to the property *conductivity* in virtue of which instances of the first always instantiate the second. In particular, the kind *copper* confers conductivity on its instances. This relation is essential to the identities of copper and conductivity; any kind in any possible world that was not thus related to conductivity just would not be copper, however much it resembled copper in other respects. Therefore, it is a metaphysically necessary truth that all samples of copper are electrically conductive: for in every possible world that contains any samples of copper at all, copper must have all of its essential features, so it must be related to conductivity in a way that guarantees the conductivity of all samples of copper there.[15]

It does not follow that when we think we are clearly conceiving of a possible world in which copper is an insulator, we are failing to conceive of any genuine possibility at all. Rather, what follows is that we are misdescribing the real possibility that we are conceiving of. We are conceiving of a metaphysically possible world in which there are instances of some natural kind that is otherwise like copper but fails to be electrically conductive, and for that reason cannot really be copper; we are mistakenly applying the name 'copper' to that kind. More generally, whenever we seem to be able to conceive of a possible world at which some actual law of nature is false, what is going on is that we are conceiving of a world where there are instances of kinds or properties that lack instances in the actual world, and we are mislabeling those kinds or properties. So, for example, there are possible worlds where all the particles lack mass but have a different property, schmass, that is like mass in all respects except that it obeys an inverse-cube gravitational law. When we think we are conceiving of a possible world where mass is governed by an inverse-cube

[15] Expositions and defenses of necessitarianism and scientific essentialism include Swoyer (1982), Bigelow, Ellis, and Lierse (1992), Ellis and Lierse (1992), Ellis (2001), and Bird (2004). An important predecessor is Shoemaker (1980), who addresses the topic of causation rather than laws. Other important predecessors include Sellars (1948) and Harre and Madden (1975).

law rather than an inverse-square law, we are really conceiving of this schmassive world, and mistaking the schmasses there for masses.[16]

One thing that makes necessitarianism somewhat plausible is that even though some scenarios where the actual laws are false seem conceivable, there also seem to be important limitations to this conceivability. The laws of nature, it seems, could have been a little different, but they could not have been *too* different. For example, consider the following wild proposition:

> **Weird-Mass:** The ratio between the impressed force on a body and that body's acceleration bears no regular relation whatever to the body's mass; the gravitational force between two bodies bears no regular relation whatever to the masses of the two bodies.

Weird-Mass would be true, for example, at any possible world where mass has the same causal-nomic role that absolute temperature has at the actual world, and vice versa. But such an alleged possible world does not seem to represent a genuine alternative possibility to the actual world; it seems like a world more or less like the actual world, in which we have switched around the names of some of the physical properties. In short, it seems that in order for a property even to count as *mass*, it would have to play a role in the functioning of the world that is at least more or less like the one that mass plays in our world. It would just be capricious to call a property in another possible world that was not even minimally mass-like in its behavior by the name 'mass.' These considerations make necessitarianism seem more plausible than it might at first.

I do not accept either scientific essentialism or necessitarianism, but I am not convinced that the traditional view is strictly correct, either. I hold that some laws of nature (in fact, very many of them) are metaphysically contingent. But some of them might be metaphysically necessary, and indeed some of them might be metaphysically necessary for the very same

[16] A necessitarian might take a stronger line, and deny that there is any metaphysically possible world at all that answers to our conception when we seem to conceive of a world where any of the actual laws of nature are false. Ellis (2005) seems to take this line, arguing that real possibilities must be discovered empirically and cannot be discovered from the armchair. But it seems that when we can clearly conceive of a situation which is free from internal contradiction, conflicts with no mathematical truths, is consistent with the essences of all individuals and properties, and denies no true identities, then there is a strong presumption in favor of its possibility. If this is denied, then it is not easy to see how we are supposed to be justified in believing that there are any metaphysical possibilities that are not actual.

reason that scientific essentialism gives. It is just that not all laws of nature are like that.

This is a relatively modest claim. But it will play an important role in some of the arguments to follow. For example, I will argue in Chapter 5 that the law-governed world-picture can be true only if the laws of nature are all inevitably true. If all laws of nature are metaphysically necessary, then of course they are all inevitably true. But since (I assume) not all laws are metaphysically necessary, we need some other explanation of why they should be inevitably true (and what exactly their inevitable truth consists in), and this explanatory need will drive my argument further. Later on, in Chapter 6, I will argue that there are possible contexts of discourse in which it is true that, had certain contingent circumstances been different, then some actual law of nature would have been false (and so, would not have been a law of nature). This observation will play a key role in the argument that leads me to the particular view of what lawhood is that I adopt in Chapter 9. If all laws of nature were metaphysically necessary, then this observation would be illusory: for surely, whatever is metaphysically necessary would still have been true under any metaphysically possible circumstances. So I need to establish that my relatively modest claim is a reasonable one to make.

Necessitarians have collectively offered a two-pronged argument for their view. The first prong of the argument concerns the special characteristics of the laws of nature, for example, their ability to support counterfactuals and their explanatory power. Necessitarians argue that their view can provide a better explanation of why laws should have these characteristics than their opponents can. The second prong concerns the nature of natural kinds and natural properties. Necessitarians argue that their view provides a better metaphysical theory of natural kinds and properties than their opponents can offer. Some of them also argue that their view can provide a better explanation of the semantics of our property-terms, and our natural-property concepts, than their opponents can provide.

In Section 2.5.1, I will argue that the first prong of the argument contributes nothing to the case for necessitarianism. For as soon as the argument is given in enough detail to make it convincing, it automatically spins off another view of laws, which can account for the special characteristics of laws as well as the necessitarian view can, but on which laws are metaphysically contingent. So, all the weight in the case for necessitarianism must be borne by the second prong. Then in Section 2.5.2, I will turn to the second prong. I will argue that even if we are wholly convinced by the second prong of the argument, and fully accept the theory of the metaphysics of natural kinds and natural properties offered by scientific essentialism, this gives us no reason to believe that all laws of nature are metaphysically contingent. In order to provide us with such a reason, the necessitarian must defend an additional assumption. In Section 2.5.3, I will argue that if the central metaphysical claims of scientific essentialism are true, then this additional assumption is very implausible. I will also show that if this additional assumption is false, then even if the metaphysics of scientific essentialism is true, then there are still many laws of nature that are metaphysically contingent.

2.5.1 The first prong: special characteristics of laws of nature

The first part of the case for necessitarianism can be summarized as follows. If laws are metaphysically necessary, then they must be counterfactually invariant: no matter how things might have been different otherwise, the laws would not have been false—for they *could* not have been false. So, we have a nice account of the counterfactual robustness of laws. But on any account of laws according to which they are metaphysically contingent, we cannot satisfactorily answer the question of why laws should support counterfactuals. If there had been an additional copper wire on my workbench, then many other contingent features of the world would have been different. Though it is a law of nature that all copper is electrically conductive, this might have been false. So why couldn't it have been false in the counterfactual scenario where there is an additional piece of wire on my workbench? Similarly, laws are supposed to explain, and there is no better way of explaining something than to show that it is necessary. If it is a law of nature that all copper conducts electricity, then it is metaphysically necessary that all copper conducts electricity. So we can answer the question of why all the copper wires on my workbench are electrically conductive by pointing out that things really could not have been otherwise. By contrast, on any view according to which the laws are metaphysically contingent, things could have been otherwise: it might have been false that all the copper wires on my workbench are electrically conductive. So, why aren't things different in that way?[17]

[17] Swoyer (1982) gives a version of this argument.

This looks to be an impressive explanatory achievement of the necessitarian view of laws, one that would be difficult to match using any account that says that laws are contingent. But more needs to be said before the explanatory achievement is complete. The explanatory hypothesis here is that the laws of nature are metaphysically necessary. But what makes them metaphysically necessary? They are metaphysically necessary because they are facts about relations among properties which are essential to their identities.[18] All right, but which relations among properties are essential to their identities? It is fair to demand an informative answer to this question. Putnam didn't just say that it is necessary that water is H_2O because natural kinds like water have essential properties, and it just so happens that being composed of H_2O molecules is one of the essential properties of water. Had he done so, he would have been arguing in a blatantly ad hoc manner. Instead, he argued for a general thesis about the essences of chemical kinds, like water. According to Putnam, they have their microstructures essentially. Water's microstructure, it turns out, is H_2O. That is why being H_2O is essential to water.[19] Similarly, Kripke didn't argue that Nixon had his actual parents essentially just because that happens to be one of the essential features of Nixon. Rather, he argued that each human being has his or her progenitors essentially; part of what it is to be a particular human being is to have certain particular progenitors. Similarly, part of what it is to be a particular artifact is to be made out of a certain particular hunk of matter. And so forth.[20] In the present case, what we need is an analogue of the principle that every chemical kind has its microstructure essentially, that every human being has his or her progenitors essentially, that every artifact has its material essentially. We need to fill in the blank in this principle: 'Every property has its . . . essentially.' Without a way of filling in the blank, we don't have a theory that implies that properties have certain of their features essentially at all; we just have an ad hoc declaration that certain relations among certain things are essential to those things. And that would hardly be better than the bald assertion that laws of nature are just necessary for some reason.

The necessitarians need to fill in the blank with a specification of a certain kind of relation among properties. But not just any kind of relation

[18] Here and throughout this section, 'properties' means *natural* properties, and what goes for them goes for natural *kinds* as well.

[19] Putnam (1975). [20] Kripke (1980).

among properties will do. One relation among properties, for example, is the relation of extensional inclusion. If extensional-inclusion relations among properties are the essential ones, then whenever the extension of one property includes the extension of another, this will be a metaphysically necessary law of nature. That will immediately eliminate the distinction between laws and accidental regularities. So the necessitarian needs to be careful about how to specify the kind of relations among properties that are the essential ones.

It won't do to identify the essential relations among properties as the nomological relations, or the relations of nomological necessitation. For that takes for granted the notion of a law of nature, which the necessitarians cannot help themselves to at this stage. Since they hold that two properties are linked by a law—that is, nomologically related—just in case they bear a relation to each other that is essential to their identities, this would amount to the proposal that the relations among properties that are essential to their identities are exactly the ones that are essential to their identities. And that tells us nothing.

So, the necessitarian account is complete only when it tells us *which* relations among properties are the essential ones, the law-making ones. The essential relations cannot just be relations of coextensionality or extensional inclusion on pain of eliminating the distinction between laws and accidental regularities; it cannot just be the nomological relations on pain of vacuous circularity. And in order for the necessitarian account to be plausible, this relation must be one that seems to have something important to do with laws of nature and their distinctive features.

Scientific essentialism aims to meet this challenge. In a nutshell, the view is that properties confer upon their instances dispositions to cause instances of other properties; these causal-dispositional relations among properties are essential to the properties they relate; the laws are just the regularities that hold necessarily since they are consequences of these essential relations. Scientific essentialism seems to me—as it does to most necessitarians—to offer the most promising way of completing a necessitarian account of laws.

But the way scientific essentialism addresses the challenge undermines the first prong of the case for necessitarianism. Recall that that prong consists of the argument that a necessitarian account of laws can provide a better explanation than any competing account of why laws of nature have their peculiar counterfactual robustness and their special explanatory power. If scientific essentialism is a meaningful doctrine, then it follows that there exists another account of laws that must be able to provide a satisfactory explanation of why laws have these special features, without positing any essences or metaphysical necessities. So either scientific essentialism is not meaningful, or else the scientific-essentialist version of necessitarianism about laws cannot be established by the popular and appealing argument I sketched at the beginning of this section. Furthermore, the way in which scientific essentialism undermines the first prong makes it plausible that any reasonable alternative version of necessitarianism would undermine it in the same way. In the rest of this section, I will be explaining how all of this goes in detail.

Why do I say that scientific essentialism undermines the first prong of the case for necessitarianism? Recall what scientific essentialism says about which relations among properties are the essential ones: F bears one of these relations to G just in case having the property F confers on a thing a disposition to cause instantiations of G.[21] Every disposition has its triggering conditions as well as its manifestations; for example, fragility is the disposition with *x is struck with significant force* as its triggering condition and *x breaks* as its manifestation. So, the complete form of a law of nature might be:[22]

> **N-Conf:** F confers on its instances the disposition to cause G in conditions C.

To say that F *confers* a disposition on its instances is not just to say that all of F's instances *do as a matter of fact have* that disposition. Suppose that it is true, but accidentally so, that every cubical object with a mass of exactly four kilograms is made of an electrical conductor. Then, every instance of the property of being a four-kilogram cube has the disposition to transmit an electric current when subjected to a difference in voltage. But no one

[21] See, for example, Swoyer (1982), pp. 214, 216–17; Ellis (2001), pp. 47–9, 217–21.

[22] Some laws might take more complicated forms than this one, and different necessitarians might have different views about what the most perspicuous way to write out a law of nature is. But I will assume for purposes of this discussion that the necessitarians' laws take the above form. I will also assume that the disposition mentioned is a surefire disposition: all instances of F that are in conditions C will indeed cause G. It might be more realistic, and it would certainly be more flexible, to allow that this disposition might be a probabilistic one. But I don't think anything in the argument of this section will turn on this simplification.

would say that this property confers this disposition on its instances, and no necessitarian would say that under these circumstances it would be a law of nature that every four-kilogram cube is a conductor. So the word 'confers' is doing real work in N-Conf; anyone who thinks that N-Conf expresses a kind of relation that properties can stand in must either take *conferring* as a substantive primitive or else give some account of it.

It might be objected that scientific essentialists need not appeal to such a notion of conferring. Instead (the objection goes) they can appeal to identity; when F stands in an essential relation to G, it does not just *confer* a disposition to cause instantiations of G on its instances; rather, the property F *just is* that disposition. So instead of N-Conf, they can take N-Ident to be the form of the relations among properties that are essential:

N-Ident: F is identical to the disposition to cause G in conditions C.

But this would lead to the implausible view that every property can figure in at most one law of nature. In Newtonian physics, mass figures in both the second law of motion and the law of universal gravitation. A necessitarian who espouses N-Ident would face a choice between saying that mass is identical to a disposition to resist acceleration when acted on by a force, thus saving the second law of motion, and saying that mass is identical to a disposition to attract other massive bodies, thus saving the law of universal gravitation.[23] Either way, one law gets left out. The only way to save the nomological status of both laws would be to insist that the disposition to resist acceleration when subjected to a force is identical to the disposition to attract other massive bodies. And this suggestion seems a non-starter; dispositions seem to be individuated by their triggering conditions and their manifestations, and these two dispositions differ with respect to both their triggering conditions and their manifestations.

It won't help to identify mass as the conjunction of the two dispositions in question. For that would leave it a matter of contingency whether anything that has one of the dispositions also has the other. Surely it is

[23] Mass is not a special case in this regard. For example, in the classical theory of electricity and magnetism, electrical charge plays roles in at least three different laws: the law relating a charge to the electric field produced by that charge, the law relating a moving charge to the magnetic field it produces, and the Lorentz force law which specifies the force felt by a charge moving through an electromagnetic field. Philosophers sometimes float the suggestion that electric charge can simply be defined as the disposition to attract opposite charges and repel like ones; this suggestion oversimplifies things by ignoring the multiple nomological roles played by charge.

a law (or at least a nomological necessity) of any Newtonian world that whatever behaves exactly as if it had a mass of five kilograms so far as the second law of motion goes also behaves exactly as if it had a mass of five kilograms so far as the law of universal gravitation goes. This would not be so if the property of having a mass of five kilograms were just the conjunctive property of having the two dispositions. It must either be that mass is identical to one of these dispositions, but having this disposition essentially confers the other disposition on its instances, or else that mass is some further property that confers both dispositions on its instances.

So in order to save both laws, our erstwhile necessitarian would have to say that mass is essentially related to two different dispositions, without being identical to both of them, and without just being identical to their conjunction. And as before, this essential relation needs to be stronger than mere coinstantiation, on pain of eliminating the difference between laws and accidental regularities. So the need for a relation between a property and a disposition other than identity or coinstantiation, a relation in virtue of which all instances of the property have the disposition, has refused to go away. It seems that the dispositional-essentialist necessitarian is stuck with N-Conf, and the relation of conferring it invokes.[24]

So, the scientific-essentialist account of which relations among properties are the essential ones, and therefore the law-making ones, appeals to the notion of a *disposition to cause*—which we might also call a *causal power* or *capacity*—as well as on the notion of a property's *conferring* such a disposition

[24] Alexander Bird seems to avoid 'conferring'-talk in his account of dispositional essentialism. He characterizes dispositional essentialism as the view that 'properties, at least those sparse properties that appear in the fundamental laws of nature, have dispositional essences.' He adds that '(t)he real essence of such a property *includes* a disposition to give some characteristic manifestation in response to a characteristic stimulus' (Bird 2004, p. 259; emphasis added). This 'includes' might be interpreted as indicating that a property's essence is a conjunction or collection of attributes, one of which is the disposition in question. If it does, then the problem considered above arises for Bird: what makes all the dispositions that are nomologically related to a given property stick together in the essence of that property? If the essence really is just a conjunction, then it would seem to be contingent that whatever has one of the dispositions also has the others—for example, that bodies with the inertial dispositions characteristic of five-kilogram objects also have the gravitational dispositions of five-kilogram objects. On the other hand, if the essence of a property includes some further element which itself entails all of the dispositions included in the property's essence—so that it is no accident that whatever has one of these dispositions has the others as well—then whatever this additional element is, it must be an attribute that confers the dispositions in the property's essence on its instances. So in the end, it seems that even Bird needs some concept to play the role of the conferring relation between a property or attribute and a disposition, in virtue of which whatever instantiates the property or attribute also has the disposition.

on its instances. Unless these concepts can be legitimately taken for granted as primitives, or else some successful account of them can be given, the scientific-essentialist completion of the necessitarian account of laws is not complete.

But what is a *disposition to cause*, i.e. a *causal power*? And what is it for a property to *confer* some causal power on its instances? Assuming that these concepts have genuine, intelligible content, it seems that this content must be spelled out in modal, counterfactual, or explanatory terms. If something has a causal power to produce effect E in circumstances C, then it presumably follows that if it were in circumstances C, it would produce E. And its possession of this capacity must play a central role in the explanation of occurrences of E that were caused via this capacity. Also, if a property F confers the power to cause G in conditions C on its instances, then it presumably follows that if (counterfactually) some object were F, and it were in conditions C, then it would have caused G, and would have done so *because* it was F and the conditions were C. Otherwise, it is not clear why 'F confers on its instances the power to cause G in C' would mean anything more than that all actual Fs as a matter of fact do have the power to cause G in C.

So, if every law of nature takes the form of N-Conf, then we *already have* an account of why laws can explain and support counterfactuals. The notions of conferring and causal powers already do all the explanatory and counterfactual-supporting work that needs to be done here. We don't need to add that this relation among F and G belongs to the essences of things, and so holds as a matter of metaphysical necessity. To do so would be explanatory and counterfactual overkill.

In short, the scientific-essentialist necessitarian faces a dilemma: either we have independent, coherent notions of causal power and conferring, or we do not. If we do not, then the necessitarian still owes us an account of *which* relations among properties are the ones that are essential to their identities.[25] If we do, then we can analyze laws of nature in terms of them,

[25] Recall that in other plausible essentialist doctrines—such as the essentialism about chemical kinds defended in Putnam (1975) and the essentialism about origins defended in Kripke (1980)—it is independently specified which features of the things alleged to have essences are the essential ones: for Putnam, the essence of a chemical kind is its microstructure, and for Kripke, the essence of a person is (or includes) their biological origin. Without such an independent specification of the property that is supposed to be essential, it isn't at all clear what an essentialist doctrine says.

and thereby account for all the special features of laws of nature that the necessitarian claims to be able to explain, without saying anything about essences or metaphysical necessity. So the power of the thesis that laws are metaphysically necessary to explain the peculiar features of laws of nature is undermined; either the thesis is too underspecified to explain what it is supposed to explain, or else all the explanatory work that needs to get done can be done without it.

But what if the necessitarian can provide some other account of which relations among properties are the essential ones, which does not refer to powers and conferring? That is, what if the erstwhile necessitarian can find some answer to the question 'Which relations among properties are the essential ones?' other than the scientific-essentialist answer?

Well, consider the alternative view on which it is the R relations among properties that are essential to them, for some R. R had better be specifiable in terms independently of the essences of properties, for reasons we have already seen. In order for this account to help us provide a plausible account of laws, we will need some reason to believe that whenever two properties are related by an R relation, a fact with the distinctive features of laws obtains. So, when two properties are related by R, it must be the case that we have a generalization that, for example, supports counterfactuals and plays an important role in the explanation of its instances. So, the view that laws are R-relations among properties already explains why laws have the distinctive features that they do; adding that R-relations are essential to the properties they relate is, again, overkill.

So the first prong of the defense of necessitarianism and scientific essentialism lends them no support. The case for these views rests on the second prong—the argument that scientific essentialism provides a better account of natural kinds and properties than do the alternatives.

2.5.2 *The second prong: the nature of natural kinds and properties*

Rather than address the case for scientific essentialism's account of the nature of natural kinds and properties directly, I shall assume for the sake of argument that that case is entirely successful, and argue that even so, it does not give us good grounds for accepting necessitarianism about laws of nature. For even if the scientific essentialist theory of the metaphysics of kinds and properties is correct, it is still more plausible than not that at least some laws of nature are metaphysically contingent truths.

The central metaphysical theses of scientific essentialism include an ontological assumption:

OA: The ontology of our world contains, in addition to particulars, natural properties and natural kinds.

an essentialist assumption:

EA: Natural kinds and properties have essences, or conditions of trans-world identity, which include certain relations they bear to one another.

and this assumption about laws of nature:

LA: A proposition states a law of nature just in case the properties and kinds referred to in that proposition stand in the appropriate essence-constituting relations to one another.

But these three suppositions are not sufficient to imply that those propositions we call laws of nature are metaphysically necessary. Recall the example of the inverse-square gravitation law UG-IS, and its apparently possible alternative UG-IC:

UG-IS: Every massive body exerts an attractive force on every other, the magnitude of which is directly proportional to the product of the bodies' masses and inversely proportional to the square of the distance separating them.

UG-IC: Every massive body exerts an attractive force on every other, the magnitude of which is directly proportional to the product of the bodies' masses and inversely proportional to the cube of the distance separating them.

OA, EA, and LA fail to imply that UG-IS is metaphysically necessary, because they do not imply that there is no possible world where UG-IC is true. In order to secure that conclusion, we must add an additional premise: that the terms 'mass,' 'force,' and 'distance' occurring in UG-IS and UG-IC are all rigid designators, picking out the very same properties in all possible worlds. Otherwise, there could be a possible world where our terms 'mass' and 'force' (and the theoretical concepts they express) pick out properties other than the ones they pick out at the actual world. Those properties, which presumably have no instances in the actual world, could bear to one another the essence-constituting relations that would make

UG-IC a law. (The point here is exactly analogous to this one: the fact that the current American president is a man may be among his essential properties, but it does not follow from this that it is metaphysically necessary that the current American president is a man, for the simple reason that 'the current American president' is not a rigid designator.) So, in order to infer necessitarianism from the basic metaphysical assumptions of scientific essentialism, one must take for granted this semantic assumption:

SA: In any proposition that states a law of nature, all terms (or concepts) that pick out natural kinds or properties do so rigidly.

Recall that UG-IC, though it conflicts with the actual laws of nature, seems to be a very clear case of an unrealized metaphysical possibility. Thus, it serves as one piece of evidence—albeit defeasible evidence—that necessitarianism is false. But note that what it is evidence for is just that—the claim that *necessitarianism* is false; that is, the claim that there are metaphysically contingent truths that are laws of nature. It is not directly evidence that the scientific-essentialist metaphysics of kinds and properties is false. We have just seen that the scientific-essentialist theory of kinds and properties—consisting of the ontological assumption OA, the essentialist assumption EA, and the assumption about laws LA—are jointly consistent with the metaphysical possibility of the falsehood of some actual laws of nature.

So it would be a mistake to say that, although the apparent possibility of UG-IC is evidence against the truth of scientific essentialism, nevertheless the considerable virtues of scientific essentialism as a theory of the nature of natural kinds and properties can give us a good reason to reject that evidence as a mere appearance of possibility. That would be a mistake because the evidence in question is not evidence for the falsehood of scientific essentialism's account of kinds and properties. It is evidence for the falsity of necessitarianism. The falsity of necessitarianism does not imply the falsity of the scientific-essentialist account of the metaphysics of kinds and properties. What it does imply is that if that account of the metaphysics of kinds and properties is correct, then nevertheless laws of nature can still be metaphysically contingent—which would require that propositions that are laws of nature can pick out kinds and properties non-rigidly.[26]

[26] The logical structure of the situation is this: widespread intuitions assure us that E is true. E is perfectly compatible with S and has no particular evidential bearing on S one way or the other—but

Here is another way to put the point: suppose we start out impressed by the intuition that some laws of nature are contingent truths—for example, say, we are impressed by the intuition that there are possible worlds where UG-IS is false and UG-IC is true. We are inclined to take this intuition as pretty strong evidence that in fact, it is metaphysically possible for UG-IS to be false and for UG-IC to be true. Then we come to learn about the virtues of the theory of kinds and properties put forward by scientific essentialism. We become convinced that this theory is more probably true than not. Does this mean we have to say that the intuition that recently impressed us so much is really just an illusory appearance of possibility? Not at all: that intuition does not conflict in the least with our new conviction in the truth of scientific essentialism's metaphysics. But now that we have a richer theoretical background to rely on, we can make that intuition speak more articulately: it tells us that some of the terms occurring in UG-IS and UG-IC (as well as the concepts those terms express) pick out their referents non-rigidly. Whatever the evidence for the truth of the scientific-essentialist theory of the metaphysics of kinds and properties is, that evidence now combines with the strong intuition of UG-IC's possibility to make a case for the semantic hypothesis that the terms referring to natural kinds and properties occurring in our statements of laws of nature are non-rigid. That is, our total evidence provides us with a strong case for the falsity of the semantic assumption SA.

Let's back up a minute and look at where we are in the dialectic. First, we saw that the virtues of the scientific-essentialist account of laws of nature, qua account of laws of nature, is not sufficient to support the conclusion that all laws of nature are metaphysically necessary. So, all of the weight in the case for necessitarianism must be carried by the other wing of the case for scientific essentialism—that is, by the case in favor of scientific essentialism qua account of the nature of natural kinds and properties. We granted for

the conjunction (E & S) logically implies N. If we took not-N for granted as part of our background information, then we would have to judge that E was incompatible with S—so, we would have to judge that the apparent truth of E is prima facie evidence against S, though a strong enough case for S might justify us in rejecting the intuition that supports E. But since, in fact, we do not know whether N is true, this is not our situation. In our situation, the apparent truth of E gives us prima facie evidence that if S is true, then so is N. If we discover a strong argument in favor of S, then we will be well justified in believing the conjunction of E, S, and N. (E is the possibility of the falsehood of some actual law of nature; S is the metaphysical core of scientific essentialism; N is the thesis that in our law-statements natural properties are picked out non-rigidly.)

the sake of argument that that account was perfectly true in all details. Then we saw that this is not enough to support the claim that all laws of nature are metaphysically necessary; in order to secure that conclusion, an additional assumption is needed, namely the semantic assumption SA. However, the appearances of possibility that make necessitarianism implausible also make the assumption SA implausible, when they are combined with the scientific-essentialist metaphysics of kinds and properties. And those appearances of possibility are not impugned in the least by the theoretical virtues of this metaphysics, since this metaphysics is perfectly consistent with them.

So where does this leave us? Even if we concede that scientific essentialism offers an account of laws of nature with considerable virtues, and that it offers us an account of the metaphysics of natural kinds and properties that is perfectly true, nevertheless we lack an argument to show that all laws of nature are metaphysically necessary. And to get such an argument, we need a defense of the semantic assumption SA. But SA is very implausible in the light of (i) what we have conceded to the scientific essentialist so far, together with (ii) certain strong and widely shared intuitions that are in no way threatened by what we have conceded to the scientific essentialist so far. So it is beginning to look as if even if the central metaphysical claims of scientific essentialism are all true, it is still more plausible than not that there are some metaphysically contingent truths that are laws of nature.

2.5.3 *Are our theoretical terms rigid?*

How might a necessitarian go about making a case for SA, against this background? It may be useful to consider the parallel example of Kripke's case for the metaphysical necessity of 'Hesperus is Phosphorous.' On the face of it, this sentence seems to state a contingent truth. It had to be discovered empirically by early astronomers. We seem to have no trouble imagining and describing in great detail scenarios in which it is false—for example, in which there are two bodies, one appearing near the western horizon just after dusk and the other appearing near the eastern horizon just before dawn, both piloted by intelligent aliens who coordinate their movements in such a way as to trick the ancient human astronomers into thinking that they are a single planet. Nevertheless, given that the identity holds, it is necessary, since it is equivalent to the necessary truth 'Venus is Venus.' Of course, this is not conclusive by itself; if the names 'Hesperus' and 'Phosphorous' have descriptive content, then the statement

'Hesperus is not identical to Phosphorous' does not really deny that any single object is self-identical; rather, it says that whatever object satisfies one description fails to satisfy a second description. For example, it might say that the brightest object normally found in the sky just before dawn is not the brightest object normally found in the sky just after sundown. To block this objection, Kripke provides a powerful case that proper names are not shorthand for descriptions; instead, they refer directly and rigidly to their referents. What the scientific-essentialist-cum-necessitarian needs to do now is provide an analogue to this part of Kripke's argument.

Take a proper name—'Moses', say—and consider a plausible candidate for the descriptive content of this name—say, 'the man who led the Israelites out of Egypt.' Can we make sense of the suggestion that this description does not really apply to Moses? It seems that we can: it is easy to understand what someone is saying when they say that Moses in fact lived centuries after the exodus from Egypt and the facts became garbled as the stories were passed down orally from generation to generation. This shows that as we understand the name 'Moses,' it is not synonymous with 'the man who led the Israelites out of Egypt'—for if it were, then we would be able to make no sense of the suggestion that Moses is not the man who led the Israelites out of Egypt, any more than we can make sense of the suggestion that Egypt is not Egypt. A similar argument can be constructed for any other plausible candidate for the descriptive content of the name 'Moses' (even a disjunctive candidate).[27]

Furthermore, it seems perfectly clear that the man Moses might well not have led the Israelites out of Egypt had he chosen not to do so. So, even if Moses really did lead the Israelites out of Egypt, it is metaphysically possible that he did not. Again, this could not be so if the name were synonymous with the description. And again, a similar argument could be given for any other plausible candidate for the descriptive content of 'Moses.'[28]

Obviously this leaves out a lot of Kripke's detailed and subtle argument for the rigidity of proper names, but it does capture the core of that argument well enough for present purposes. Our question is: can a similar

[27] This paragraph is meant to be a very abbreviated summary of Kripke's argument against what he calls 'Thesis 5' on p. 71 of his (1980); one presentation of this argument is found on pp. 87–9 of the same work.

[28] This paragraph is meant to be a very abbreviated summary of Kripke's argument against what he calls 'Thesis 6' on p. 71; one presentation of this argument can be found on pp. 74–8. (These references, again, are to Kripke (1980).)

case be made by the scientific essentialist for the truth of the semantic assumption SA? Instead of proper names like 'Hesperus' and 'Moses,' what is at issue here is the terms we use to pick out natural properties like *mass*.[29] If 'mass' is not rigid, then the most obvious alternative is that it has some descriptive content. This does not mean that it is synonymous with a particular description; it might mean that it picks out the best satisfier of a weighted list of descriptions, or even just that something must come close enough to satisfying certain descriptions at a given possible world to be a candidate for the referent of 'mass' at that world. What would be a good candidate for the descriptive content of 'mass'? Well, a good guess is that at least part of the descriptive content of 'mass' is that mass is that property that makes a body hard to push around and makes it gravitate toward other bodies. Thus, mass seems to satisfy this description:

> **Mass-Desc:** The unique quantitative natural property of a body that is such that the greater its value, the greater the impressed force needed to impart a given acceleration to the body, and the greater its value, the greater the magnitude of the gravitational force it exerts on all other bodies.

Note that although Mass-Desc is obviously based on Newton's second law of motion and the law of universal gravitation, neither one of these laws is entailed by the fact that mass satisfies Mass-Desc. For example, mass could still satisfy Mass-Desc even if gravity worked by an inverse-cube law instead of an inverse-square law.

Now let's apply Kripke's tests to Mass-Desc, considered as a candidate specification of the descriptive content of 'mass.' Can we make sense of the suggestion that mass might not really satisfy Mass-Desc? Well, to ask this is to ask whether we can make sense of a hypothesis like Weird-Mass:

> **Weird-Mass:** The ratio between the impressed force on a body and that body's acceleration bears no regular relation whatever to the body's

[29] At this point in my discussion, natural kinds will pretty much drop out of the picture, and I will focus on natural quantitative properties like mass. This is because I think the argument to follow is much more plausible when applied to the case of natural properties than when applied to the case of natural kinds like *water* and *copper*. This limitation does not weaken my argument, because my goal is only to show that *some* laws of nature are metaphysically contingent. So long as there are some laws that concern relations among properties rather than among natural kinds, it should do no harm to leave kinds out of the picture.

mass; the gravitational force between two bodies bears no regular relation whatever to the masses of the two bodies.

We saw above that this hypothesis seems to make no sense at all. Someone who seriously entertains this hypothesis, it seems, must be using the term 'mass' differently than the rest of us. The fact that being massive makes something both heavy and hard to move, it seems, is just part of what the property of mass *is*. Accordingly, if someone purported to describe a possible universe in which mass plays nothing like the role it plays in Newton's second law—for example, a world in which mass and charge, or mass and absolute temperature, have their causal and nomic roles reversed—then we would be inclined to say that they have really described a world just like the actual world, while switching around the labels we use for the physical properties.[30] Hence, the arguments that Kripke can offer for the rigidity of proper names has no analogue in the case we are considering.

So there is no obvious reason why we should believe the semantic assumption SA that is required to complete the scientific-essentialist case for necessitarianism. The alternative semantic hypothesis that readily suggests itself is that the theoretical terms like 'mass,' which purport to pick out natural quantities that figure in the laws of nature, are roughly equivalent to descriptions like Mass-Desc. In other possible worlds, the existing bodies might not possess the property that we call 'mass,' but instead possess some other property that lays the mass role, though it is governed by slightly different laws than the mass of our universe. In that case the term 'mass' picks out this other property, rather than the one it picks out in the actual world. All of this is perfectly consistent with the scientific-essentialist theses OA, EA, and LA.

I am not saying that this incipient neo-descriptivism about theoretical terms is definitely true. It might be that some other general account of the semantics of such terms is preferable. It might even be that there is no true general account of their semantics; instead, perhaps the extension of a given term in a given non-actual possible world is settled on a case-by-case basis, in a highly context-dependent way governed by considerations of

[30] The intuitions I am citing here, recall, are among those that provide some of the intuitive motivation for necessitarianism and scientific essentialism in the first place—so if we rejected them now, we would need to reconsider the case for those views from the beginning.

'family resemblances,' obeying no strict general principles. We do not need to settle this question here. What is important for the purposes at hand is only the following three points: first, that Kripke's powerful case for the rigidity of proper names does not carry over smoothly to the case of terms like 'mass'; second, that there are alternative views available on which such terms are non-rigid; and finally, that in the light of widespread intuitions in conjunction with the metaphysical doctrines of scientific essentialism that I have been assuming for the sake of argument, it is most plausible that such terms are not rigid.

2.5.4 A necessitarian rejoinder

A rejoinder is available to the necessitarian. Let us continue to suppose that the scientific-essentialist metaphysics of kinds and properties—summarized by OA, EA, and LA—is true. Let us grant for the sake of argument that SA is false, and that terms like 'mass' and 'force' are non-rigid designators with descriptive content. And let us continue assuming that our universe is Newtonian, for expositional purposes. Given all these assumptions, this proposition is true but metaphysically contingent:

> **UG-IS:** Every massive body exerts an attractive force on every other, the magnitude of which is directly proportional to the product of the bodies' masses and inversely proportional to the square of the distance separating them.

However, the following proposition is metaphysically necessary:

> **UG-IS*:** Every DTHAT(massive) body exerts an attractive DTHAT (force) on every other, the magnitude of which is directly proportional to the product of the bodies' DTHAT(masses) and inversely proportional to the square of the DTHAT(distance) separating them.

Here, 'DTHAT' is the rigidifying operator introduced by Kaplan (1989); the result of applying 'DTHAT' to any non-rigid referring phrase is a name that refers rigidly to whatever that phrase happens to refer to in the actual world. So, even if 'mass' is not a rigid designator, 'DTHAT(mass)' picks out the very same property rigidly. It follows from the scientific-essentialist assumptions OA, EA, and LA that force, mass, and acceleration are properties that are related to one another in such a way that the value of force is equal to the product of the values of mass and acceleration in every possible world where those properties have any instances at all. So, since 'DTHAT(force),' 'DTHAT(mass),' and 'DTHAT(acceleration)' all pick out the very same properties in every world where they refer at all, it follows that UG-IS* is metaphysically necessary. Similarly, by OA, EA, and LA, you get a metaphysically necessary truth whenever you take a law-statement and apply the 'DTHAT' operator to all of the property terms occurring in it. The necessitarian rejoinder is that the *real* laws of nature are these DTHAT-ed propositions, such as UG-IS*. Perhaps we usually state laws of nature by means of statements like UG-IS, but when we do so, our statements are incorrect, strictly speaking. This error does not make any difference for most practical purposes, or for most scientists' purposes. But it makes a crucial difference when we are investigating the nature of lawhood itself.

One reason why I do not find this rejoinder persuasive is that if the difference between UG-IS and UG-IS* makes no difference so far as the role these propositions play in scientific reasoning and scientific practice go, then it seems that it should make no difference so far as their nomological status goes, either. For our best reason to believe in laws of nature in the first place is that laws seem to play an important role in scientific reasoning and scientific practice. It might be objected that in scientific reasoning laws are tacitly assumed to be capable of supporting counterfactuals and explanations, and that unless they are metaphysically necessary, they can do neither, and for this reason we must conclude that despite appearances UG-IS* plays an important role in science that UG-IS cannot. But this is just a return of the argument for necessitarianism based on the virtues of its account of lawhood, which I have already replied to.

A second reason why I am not persuaded by this necessitarian rejoinder is that there is good reason to think that truths like UG-IS really are laws of nature, even if metaphysical necessities like UG-IS* are too. For truths like UG-IS behave like laws; they play the distinctive roles of laws in scientific reasoning, supporting counterfactuals and explanatory claims. Let's focus on counterfactuals. In many cases, we evaluate a counterfactual 'Had it been the case that A, then it would have been the case that C' as true on the grounds that had it been the case that A, then the laws of nature would still have held, and these together with A imply C. In typical such cases, we can reach the obviously correct judgments about these counterfactuals only if we assume, not only that metaphysical necessities like UG-IS* would still have been true if A had been, but also that contingent truths like UG-IS would still have been true if A had been.

To see why, consider a very simple example of a typical law-supported counterfactual:

> **LSC:** Had there been a solar system with one star and just one planet in it, the planet and the star would exert gravitational forces on one another in accord with Newton's law of universal gravitation.

This counterfactual, we think, is true. One quick but appealing argument for its truth goes like this: if its antecedent had been true, then the law of universal gravitation would still have been true—and this law, together with the antecedent of the counterfactual, entails its consequent.

But now, suppose that the only *real* laws of nature are the metaphysically necessary, DTHAT-ed laws like UG-IS*. In this case, the real law of gravitation, together with the antecedent of LSC, does not entail its consequent. For there are possible worlds where the mass role is played by some property other than the one that plays it here—in other words, there are metaphysically possible worlds where mass is a different property from DTHAT(mass). For example, there are possible worlds where instead of DTHAT(mass), bodies have a mass-like property governed by an inverse-cube gravitation law instead of an inverse-square law. In any such possible world, the antecedent of LSC is true but its consequent is false.

Of course, this gives us no reason to doubt the truth of LSC. Even if there are some possible worlds where the antecedent of LSC is true and its consequent is false, they are too dissimilar to the actual world to make any difference to the truth value of LSC. For they are worlds in which the mass-role is played by a different property than in the actual world (as are, presumably, the force-role and the distance-role), and other things being equal it makes a world much more similar to the actual world when the same properties play the same roles in both. To put the point more straightforwardly: if the antecedent of LSC had been true, then the same property would still have played the mass role; mass would still have been identical to DTHAT(mass). Similarly, force would still have been identical to DTHAT(force), and distance would still have been identical to DTHAT(distance), and so forth. For that reason, Newton's laws would all still have been true.

What we have just seen is that when we rely on the law of gravitation to support a simple counterfactual, we must assume not only that that law would still have been true had the antecedent of the counterfactual obtained, but also that the following metaphysically contingent principles would still have been true:

Mass-Identity: Mass is identical to DTHAT(mass).

Force-Identity: Force is identical to DTHAT(force).

Distance-Identity: Distance is identical to DTHAT(distance).

But it is easy to see that UG-IS*, together with these three identities, deductively entails UG-IS. And if each member of a set of propositions would have been true under some counterfactual supposition, then so would have every deductive consequence of that set. Therefore, the assumptions we make in routinely evaluating LSC entail that had the antecedent of LSC been true, then UG-IS would still have been true.

This example depends on nothing special about mass or force or the law of gravitation. So the point generalizes: when we take laws of nature to support counterfactual conditionals in the familiar way, we in effect count on the assumption that had a certain counterfactual supposition been true, then metaphysically contingent principles like UG-IS would still have been true, too. In other words, these contingent principles play the distinctive role of laws of nature in counterfactual reasoning. None of this impugns the status of metaphysical necessities like UG-IS* from counting as laws of nature. But it does give us a strong reason to deny that they are the only laws of nature.

3

The meta-theoretic conception of laws

3.1 Laws of nature, laws of science, laws of theories

Many philosophers have distinguished between the *laws of nature* and the *laws of science*.[1] The laws of nature are supposed to be real features of the world, governing its evolution; the laws of science, on the other hand, are propositions that current science takes to be laws of nature. The distinction is important. When philosophers put forward metaphysical theses about laws—that laws are (or need not be) true, that they supervene (or fail to supervene) on a base of non-nomic facts, that their existence requires (or does not require) the existence of universals—it is the laws *of nature* that these theses are meant to be about. On the other hand, when we make claims about the roles of laws in actual scientific practice—that scientists hold derivations from laws to be explanatory, that scientists hold laws constant in counterfactual reasoning—it is usually the laws *of science* that are at issue.[2] Drawing this distinction enables us to distinguish metaphysical, methodological, and epistemological questions about laws in a neat way: the metaphysical questions are about what kind of thing laws of nature are, the methodological questions are about how the laws of science are (or should be) related to the available evidence, and the epistemological questions are about the circumstances under which, and

[1] For example, see Friedel Weinert's introduction to his (1995).

[2] One exception is the thesis, defended by Goodman, Lange, and others, that only regularities that might be laws (as far as we now know) can be inductively confirmed. Here it must be laws of nature that are at issue: the claim is not that a regularity is inductively confirmable only if it might be a law of science for all we know—as if what is uncertain were whether present-day science takes something to be a law of nature.

the extent to which, the laws of science accurately reflect the laws of nature.[3]

A similar distinction can be drawn between the laws of nature and the *laws of a particular theory T*. Roughly, the laws of a theory T are the propositions that are laws of nature according to theory T. Thus, the laws of Newtonian mechanics include Newton's three laws of motion, the laws of special-relativistic mechanics include the conservation of relativistic 4-momentum, the laws of non-relativistic quantum mechanics include the Schrödinger equation, and the laws of modern evolutionary theory perhaps include the principle of natural selection. Whether the laws of these theories are laws of nature presumably depends on how accurate these theories are.

Some authors define a scientific theory simply as a set of putative laws.[4] Given this definition, it is a little odd to talk of the laws of a theory T; at any rate, this can't be anything more than an alternative way of talking about the things T says. Of course, we are all free to define our terms as we wish, but it seems to me that this is a very unhelpful way of defining 'scientific theory.' For example, it excludes theories that are concerned with the nomologically contingent details of natural history, such as theories about the cause of the extinction of the dinosaurs and theories about the origin of the universe. The Big Bang Theory has as much right to the title 'scientific theory' as anything. Yet, the Big Bang Theory makes claims that are nomologically contingent, given our best physical theories. For example, the laws of the general theory of relativity are compatible with the Big Bang Theory as well as the Steady State Theory. And what the Big Bang Theory adds to general relativity is not more laws, but more information about the boundary conditions of the universe.

In fact, there are many bodies of thought that are naturally classified as scientific theories which include both putative laws and putative nomologically contingent truths. For example, it is natural to think of the contents of Newton's *Principia* as comprising a grand scientific theory. This theory includes some putative laws: the three laws of motion, and the law of universal gravitation. It also includes a great deal of information about the contents and structure of the solar system: there are six planets, they orbit

[3] Non-realists of various stripes might be mistrustful of this talk of 'reflection.' To a certain extent, the views I will defend in this book endorse this mistrust. Here, I mean only to draw prima facie distinctions, which as far as we can tell yet might or might not stand up to scrutiny.

[4] For example, Putnam (1974).

the sun in stable nearly circular orbits, the planets all go around the sun in the same direction, and their orbits lie approximately in a common plane, and so forth. Newton makes it quite explicit that the laws of his theory alone are not sufficient to guarantee the stability of this system; the initial conditions had to be arranged just so in order for this system to result.[5] Thus, the laws of Newton's theory must be distinguished from the rest of the claims his theory makes.

How does a proposition P get to be a law of a theory T? The most obvious answer is that T *says that* P is a law of nature (or says something else that entails that P is a law of nature). On this view, the concept of a law of nature is a concept *used* by scientific theories in their descriptions of the natural world. The question of what is a law of nature and what is not is within the subject matter of scientific theories, on this view. This answer is at least implicitly adopted by all the major philosophical accounts of laws on the market, including the universals account of Armstrong (1983), Dretske (1977), Tooley (1977), Lewis's (1973) best-system analysis, Carroll's (1994) non-reductive realism, and the metaphysical necessitarian accounts defended by Swoyer (1982), Ellis (2001), and others. Each of these accounts maintains that there is a substantive difference between a regularity statement's being true and its being a law of nature, and that scientific theories aim to tell us not only which regularity statements are true, but also which ones are laws of nature. It makes a difference to the content of a scientific theory whether it says that a certain regularity is a law or not.

Consider an interesting consequence of this view. Newton's theory tells us a great deal that can be stated without ever using the concept of a law: for example, it tells us that there are six planets. It also tells us that it is *true* that the force on a body is proportional to the rate of change of that body's momentum. (This is a law of Newton's theory, but the proposition that it is true is distinct from the proposition that it is a law, and the former is as much a part of the content of Newton's theory as the latter.) Call this part of the content of Newton's theory its *non-nomic content*. In addition to its non-nomic content, this theory also contains a nomic content, which says which propositions are laws of nature. The non-nomic content of the theory does not entail its nomic content, nor is the converse true. (Each

[5] Cohen and Westfall (1995), pp. 339–42.

part of the theory's content does logically constrain the other, though: if the nomic content includes that P is a law, then the non-nomic content must include that P is true; if the non-nomic content includes that P is false, then the nomic content cannot include that P is a law.) So we can revise the nomic content of the theory, leaving its non-nomic content alone, to generate another theory. For example, there is a theory according to which the non-nomic claims of Newton's theory are all true, but it is *not* a law of nature (though it is true) that every massive body exerts an attractive force on every other and it *is* a law of nature that the planets all move around the sun in the same direction. Though this theory has exactly the same non-nomic content as Newton's own theory, it is a distinct theory that is logically inconsistent with Newton's. Perhaps this theory is not very interesting, or not worth taking seriously for some reason; at any event, it does not seem to have ever been taken seriously by scientists. Nonetheless, it is a theory.

A different possible answer to our question is that a proposition P gets to be a law of theory T not via T's saying that P is a law of nature, but via playing a certain distinctive role within T. On this view, it is not just because Newton's *Principia* attaches the tag 'law' to the three laws of motion and the law of universal gravitation that they count as laws of Newton's theory. It is because these propositions play a certain role within the structure of that theory, and perhaps within its applications, that is not played by the proposition that all the planets go around the sun in the same direction. On this view, unlike the first, the content of a scientific theory cannot be broken down into two pieces—first, a set of non-nomic claims; and second, a specification of which regularities are the laws of nature—neither of which entails the other. Rather, the content of a scientific theory is something that can be spelled out without using the word 'law' at all: it is simply the non-nomic content of the theory. But once a theory is specified, certain propositions will turn out to play a certain special role within it. These propositions are the laws of that theory. So, assuming that Newton's three laws of motion and his law of universal gravitation are the laws of his theory, it is not true that we could construct an alternative theory like the one described above. Since that alleged alternative is exactly like Newton's in all respects except which propositions are called 'laws' by it, the propositions that play the special role within Newton's theory also play that same special role within it.

So the laws of the alleged alternative are simply the laws of Newton's theory—the 'alternative' is just Newton's theory itself, presented in a misleading formulation that incorrectly identifies its laws.

What might this 'certain special role' played by the laws of a theory be? It would not be easy to give a complete answer to this question, but a few things can be said immediately. First, a typical application of Newton's theory involves setting up and solving a set of differential equations for a given set of initial conditions; the laws of that theory are the sources from which the differential equations are derived, whereas the nomologically contingent truths of that theory serve as sources of initial conditions when they are employed in such problems. Second, the laws of the theory often play a crucial role in establishing the reliability of a method of measuring something; for example, Newton uses the law of universal gravitation and the second law of motion to justify his method of estimating the mass ratios of the bodies in the solar system.[6] On the other hand, the nomologically contingent truths of this theory rarely, if ever, play such a role; they more typically stand in need of being justified by the results of some defensible measurement procedure, rather than playing the role of justifying measurement procedures themselves.

These observations do not add up to fully satisfactory specification of the law role. But their present purpose is only to make it initially plausible that there is such a role. This idea can be made even more plausible by reflecting on a certain fact: those who write about laws of nature in general seem to have no trouble identifying what the laws of various theories are. Everybody knows that Maxwell's equations are among the laws of classical electrodynamics, the Schrödinger equation is among the laws of non-relativistic quantum mechanics, and Einstein's field equations are among the laws of general relativity. But none of these examples has a standard name with the word 'law' in it. Moreover, canonical formulations of these theories (in textbooks, treatises, and technical literature) do not invariably make it explicit that these equations are laws of nature. What makes us so sure that these equations are the laws of the theories that they live in?

Consider a typical talented undergraduate physics student, who has just completed her course on classical mechanics. She has learned that certain

[6] This method is established in *Principia*, Book III, Corollary 2 to Proposition 8 (Newton 1999, p. 813).

propositions are called 'laws' in classical mechanics, and she has learned a lot about how they fit into the structure of that theory, and the ways they are used in solving problems. Now she is taking her first course in classical electrodynamics. Her textbook displays Maxwell's equations, but does not explicitly say that they are laws of nature according to the theory she is studying.[7] Is it plausible to think that she might react by saying, 'Well, what about these equations? Are they supposed to be laws of nature? Or are they merely consequences of the laws and the initial conditions of our universe? Perhaps the two divergence equations are laws of nature, and the two curl equations just happen to be true. Or maybe none of them are laws of nature; maybe they just summarize the way that electrical and magnetic field values happen to behave in our part of the universe. This textbook author has done a sloppy job: I don't know what the theory I'm studying says!' I don't think this is plausible at all. As the student learns to use the theory, she will come to recognize that Maxwell's equations are *doing the same sort of job* within this theory that the equations called 'laws' in classical mechanics do within that theory. She will have no trouble recognizing that these equations are laws of electrodynamics. And she will not feel that the textbook author must tell her more before she knows the content of the theory she is studying.

Classical electrodynamics might be a theory that is exhausted by its laws; that is, it might be a theory such that every logically contingent proposition that is true according to it is also one of its laws. This can make it seem strange to talk about someone's ability to tell whether a given proposition of classical electrodynamics is a law of that theory or not—for of course, they *all* are.

Nevertheless, we should not make the mistake of thinking that *being a law of classical electrodynamics* is the same thing as *being a proposition that is part of the content of classical electrodynamics*. Recall the example of the

[7] Jackson (1975) introduces the Maxwell equations without calling them laws on p. 2, though he does call them 'equations governing electromagnetic phenomena,' which might suggest that they should be thought of as laws. Later in the book, Jackson refers to the first Maxwell equation as 'Gauss's Law' (p. 33) and to the third as 'Faraday's Law' (p. 213). But these are those equations' familiar names, and in them 'Law' appears capitalized, as if it were part of a proper name; Jackson doesn't explicitly assert that they are laws of nature. Our talented physics major may remember references to 'Kepler's First Law' and to 'Galileo's Law of Free Fall' from her classical mechanics course, where she learned that those principles actually depend on initial and boundary conditions as well as the laws of classical mechanics. So if her professor used Jackson, she might be in exactly the situation I have been describing.

theory of Newton's *Principia*: it has laws, as well as putative nomologically contingent regularities about the contents and structure of the solar system. On one reasonable interpretation of it, the Big Bang Theory has as its laws the laws of general relativity, but also includes some nomologically contingent information about the boundary conditions of space-time. The Steady State Theory has at least some of the same laws as the Big Bang Theory, but places different nomologically contingent constraints on the boundary conditions. Classical electrodynamics could have been formulated in a stronger form, in which it consists of Maxwell's equations, the Lorentz force law, and a wealth of nomologically contingent information about the magnetic field of the earth. Such a theory would not be exactly the same theory as the one we call 'classical electrodynamics,' since it would encompass some geophysical theory as well. But its laws are plainly the laws of classical electrodynamics, and these laws do not exhaust its content. There is a good chance that our hypothetical student's textbook includes some such geophysical information in addition to the theory of classical electrodynamics; if it does, our student should still have no trouble telling that Maxwell's equations are among the laws of the total theory presented in the textbook, and the details about the earth's magnetic field are not.

It is plausible, though, that the theories called classical electrodynamics, quantum mechanics, quantum electrodynamics, and general relativity all consist only of their laws; that is to say, every proposition that is true according to one of these theories is also nomologically necessary according to it. Being like this might be the mark of a 'fundamental physical theory.' In any event, not all theories are like this; the theories that are like this are special. But all theories would be like this, and trivially so, if there were no distinction between *being a proposition that is part of the content of a theory* and *being a law of a theory*. So, it is not at all trivial that our hypothetical student is able to tell that Maxwell's equations are laws of electrodynamics without being told so.

Whence the student's ability to tell that Maxwell's equations are laws of classical electrodynamics, even when the textbook doesn't say so? An obvious explanation is that when someone learns a theory like classical mechanics, they thereby acquire an implicit grasp of the role played by the laws within that theory; what they have an implicit grasp of is exportable to other theories, and it is not generally very difficult to see which propositions play that role in a theory one comes to learn. We don't need our textbook authors to mark the laws explicitly for us. If this is the right explanation, then there is such a thing as the distinctive role played within a theory by the laws of that theory—though it might not be easy articulating an explicit account of what that role is.

There are other possible explanations of the student's ability to identify Maxwell's equations as laws of classical electrodynamics. For example, perhaps she performs an unconscious inference to the best explanation: 'If these equations were all true, then the best explanation by far would be that they are laws of nature. So, if classical electrodynamics were true, then these equations would almost certainly be laws of nature.' But I don't think this explanation is as satisfying as the one I offered above; for one thing, at best it seems to explain why *the student should strongly suspect that, if the theory is true, then Maxwell's equations are probably laws of nature*—whereas what needs explaining is that she can tell without much effort that these equations *are indeed laws of this theory, independently of the question of whether this theory is true.*

Another possible explanation goes as follows. When our hypothetical student learned classical mechanics, she didn't just learn a set of propositions; she learned how to apply the theory, both to real-world situations (in her labs) and to hypothetical situations (in her homework problems). Applying a theory often involves using it to figure out what would happen in various possible situations. So, for example, she will have learned to use classical mechanics to make predictions about the shape of the curve she'll get if she takes data in a certain way and plots it on a graph; she'll also learn how to make hypothetical predictions about the motions of systems that start out in initial conditions specified in the text of a homework problem. And doing all that is just a matter of evaluating counterfactual conditionals. ('If I took data in the following manner and plotted it on a graph in the following manner . . . , then the resulting curve would have the following properties . . . .' 'If the coyote sped off the edge of a cliff with an initial horizontal velocity of 50 meters per second, then it would travel N meters before hitting the bottom of the canyon.') So when she learned classical mechanics, she learned that the propositions that are called its 'laws' play certain distinctive roles in the evaluation of counterfactuals that are evaluated in applications of the theory. Then, when she learned classical electrodynamics, she learned how to apply it to the real world and to hypothetical situations, in her labs and in her homework. In learning this, she must have learned what the proper way to evaluate counterfactuals is in the course of applying this theory. And since she already learned that it is the laws of a given theory that largely determine how counterfactuals should be evaluated in the course of applying that theory, she can now interpolate, and figure out which propositions are the laws of classical electrodynamics by attending to which propositions play the same counterfactual-supporting role within applications of that theory that the laws of classical mechanics play within applications of it. So, when she figured out that Maxwell's equations are laws of classical electrodynamics, she did this by inferring that this theory *must* say that these equations are laws, since applications of this theory involve taking those equations to support counterfactuals. This explanation is very similar to the one I gave, but unlike that one it does not involve rejecting the first answer to our question (the laws of T are the propositions that T says are laws of nature) in favor of the second one (the laws of T are the propositions that play a special role within T); in fact, it embraces both answers at once, by saying that the propositions that T says are laws of nature play a certain special role within *applications of T*.[8]

But this explanation seems unsatisfying. Note that it depends on the assumption that laws support counterfactual conditionals in a way that other truths do not, so that what a theory says is a law is reflected in what that theory implies about which counterfactuals are true. I don't want to quarrel with this assumption; in fact, I will defend a more precise version of it in Chapter 5. But I do want to quarrel with a second assumption the explanation depends on: namely, that in learning to apply a scientific theory to real-world experimental situations and to hypothetical situations, we learn how that theory says we should evaluate counterfactuals. I think this assumption is doubtful at best. When we learn to apply a scientific theory—to the real world in experimental contexts, and to hypothetical situations in the case of homework problems—we *can* interpret what we are doing as evaluating counterfactuals, but we need not. For instead, we can interpret what we are doing as evaluating *indicative* conditionals. When doing an experiment, we ask what, according to our theory, *will happen* under the conditions we are going to set up in the lab; when solving a homework problem, we can address the question of what *will or did or does happen* whenever conditions are as described

[8] I am grateful to Marc Lange for pressing this objection.

in the problem. ('If I *take* data in the following manner and plot it on a graph in the following manner . . . , then the resulting curve *will* have the following properties. . . .' 'If a coyote ever *does* speed off the edge of a cliff with an initial horizontal velocity of 50 meters per second, then it *travels* N meters before hitting the bottom of the canyon.') And any piece of propositional knowledge we take ourselves to have—whether it is considered a law or just a brute fact—may be used to 'support' an indicative conditional in the way that only laws are supposed to be able to 'support' a counterfactual.[9] So, the kinds of applications of a theory one typically learns while learning that theory need not involve counterfactual conditionals; all the conditionals involved in such applications can be construed as indicative conditionals. And the difference between the laws of a theory and the other things a theory says is not reflected in which indicative conditionals are affirmed in applications of the theory. So, it seems that the role that the laws of classical mechanics play within classical mechanics, which our hypothetical student has learned to recognize, could not simply be that of supporting counterfactual conditionals. Learning the content of a theory together with the skills involved in applying it need not involve learning to use it to evaluate counterfactual conditionals as opposed to indicative conditionals—and the laws of a theory are not distinguished from its non-laws by their role in supporting indicative conditionals.[10]

We started with the question: 'How does a proposition get to be a law of a theory?' We saw that if we adopt a certain answer—namely, *not by virtue of the fact that the theory says the proposition is a law of nature,*

[9] Whenever we are sure that P is true, and we are ignorant of whether Q is true and of whether R is true, and we believe that (P and Q) entails R, we are willing to assert the indicative conditional that if Q is true, then R is true. The same doesn't go for the subjunctive counterfactual conditional that were it the case that Q, it would be the case that R.

[10] Of course, indicative conditionals that are underwritten by laws of nature can sometimes play a role in scientific explanation that conditionals underwritten by accidental regularities often cannot. But telling the difference between derivations that are explanatory (since they appeal to laws) and derivations that are non-explanatory (since the regularities they appeal to are not laws) is not part of what one typically learns in science coursework. In her courses in classical mechanics and classical electrodynamics, for example, our hypothetical student will have spent a lot of time learning how to use the theory to draw inferences from given premises; she will almost certainly not have devoted any time to learning how to classify these inferences as explanatory or non-explanatory. She may have intuitions about how to do this classification, and if she takes a philosophy of science course then she will learn to analyze and refine these intuitions. But she won't learn how to do this classification from taking conventional physics courses. Yet, it is very plausible that she will learn enough about what laws of nature are supposed to be to be able to recognize that Maxwell's equations are laws of classical electrodynamics.

but rather by virtue of the fact that the proposition plays a certain special role within the theory—then we can give a very simple and natural explanation of why we can often tell which propositions are the laws of a theory without being explicitly told. This is not the only possible explanation—so we do not have here a knock-down argument in favor of this answer to our question. But the other explanations we have looked at run into complications that we can avoid if we accept this answer. This amounts to a good plausibility argument for this answer: it doesn't show that we should accept it yet, but it does show that it deserves a hearing.

3.2 The first-order conception versus the meta-theoretic conception

On the first view considered above, scientific theories make claims about what is and what is not a law of nature. A philosophical account of laws of nature should make it clear what such claims amount to, and in virtue of what they are true when they are true. So on this view, a philosophical account of laws should tell us how to fill in the blank in the following statement:

FO1: P is a law of nature iff...

Where the blank is to be filled in by a condition that makes no reference to scientific theories.[11] Then, if we require an account of what a *law of a theory* is, we can give the following:

FO2: P is a law of theory T iff T entails that P is a law of nature.

On this way of looking at things, the question of which propositions are laws of nature and which are not is within the subject matter of science, and it is a question that at least some scientific theories should be expected to give explicit answers to. I'll call this view of the problem of laws *the first-order conception of laws*. I will call any particular philosophical account of

[11] For example, on the first-order account of laws proposed by Armstrong (1983), the blank would be filled in by: 'P is the proposition *everything that has property F also has property G*, where F-ness and G-ness are universals such that F bears the necessitation relation to G.'

laws[12] that conforms to this view a *first-order account of laws*. Most first-order accounts can be stated by filling in the blank in FO1. An exception is the non-reductive realism of Carroll (1994), according to which laws of nature cannot be illuminatingly analyzed in terms of anything more basic, but nonetheless, there is a concept of lawhood that is used in many scientific theories.

On the second view considered above, scientific theories do not make claims about what is a law and what is not. They make claims about other things—electrons, forces, genes, and so forth—and they have laws by containing propositions about the things they are about that play a special role within them. On this view, an illuminating philosophical account of laws should not start out by saying what it is for something to be a law of nature; rather, it should start out by describing the role played within a theory by the laws of that theory:

MT1: P is a law of T iff P plays role R within T.

Here, 'R' is to stand for some particular role a proposition can play within a theory. This role must not simply be that of being said or implied to be a law of nature by T, for in that case MT1 collapses into FO2. If we wish to say what it is for P to be a law of nature, we will have to add a further clause to our account. Exactly what form this further clause should take is tricky; I will return to this below. I will call this second view *the meta-theoretic conception of laws*, and any account of laws that results from specifying the role R a *meta-theoretic account of laws*.

Why call them the 'first-order conception' and 'meta-theoretic conception'? Well, suppose we think of the *first-order* scientific questions as the ones that scientific theories are intended to give direct answers to: 'What causes the moon to orbit the earth?' 'What is the mechanism of inheritance?' 'What is water made of?' 'What are the causes of cancer?', and so forth. In addition to these first-order scientific questions, there are higher-order questions, which are most aptly posed not as questions directly about the natural world, but rather as questions about scientific theories themselves: 'Is Newtonian mechanics deterministic?' 'Is modern

[12] I will always use 'theory' to refer to scientific theories, and I will refer to philosophical theories as 'accounts.' This is because I will be saying a lot about both kinds of theories/accounts, and I want to minimize the risk of confusion about which kind I am talking about on any given occasion.

chemical theory reducible to quantum mechanics?' 'Is the theory of natural selection consistent with the second law of thermodynamics?', and so forth. These higher-order questions are about theories, so we may call them 'meta-theoretic.' According to what I have called the first-order conception of laws, the primary scientific question about the laws is what they are—that is, which propositions are laws, and which are not. Furthermore, on this conception, this question is a first-order question, one to which we should expect our scientific theories to state answers. On the view I have called the meta-theoretic conception of laws, the primary question about laws is what the laws of a particular scientific theory are. This is a question about scientific theories themselves—a meta-theoretic question.

On the first-order conception of laws, laws are in a certain respect on a par with the causes of cancer. Both are things that we have a concept of which is independent of any concepts pertaining to scientific theories as such. Both are among the things that we pursue science in order to discover, and so both are among the things that we want some of our scientific theories to identify. By contrast, on the meta-theoretic conception of laws, laws are in a certain respect on a par with the postulates of a mathematical theory. It is a postulate of Euclidean geometry that two points determine a line. But it is not part of *the content of Euclidean geometry* that this proposition is a postulate (as opposed to, say, a theorem). Euclidean geometry is not a theory about postulates; it is a theory about points, lines, and planes. It says a great deal about points, lines, and planes, but it doesn't say a thing about postulates. (Though of course, standard textbooks on Euclidean geometry do say things about postulates—in particular, that the proposition that two points determine a line is a postulate of Euclidean geometry.) The proposition in question is a postulate of Euclidean geometry in virtue of the role it plays within Euclidean geometry, not in virtue of the fact that Euclidean geometry *says that* it is a postulate. So the relation between mathematical theories and postulates is not like the relation between scientific theories and the causes of cancer: one reason why we pursue science is because we want to find out what the causes of cancer are; imagine a society that decides to invest resources in mathematical research because it wants to find out what the postulates are! We pursue mathematics in order to find out interesting things about points and lines, numbers and sets, functions and limits—not in order to discover truths about the postulates.[13] Yet we do find out what the postulates are in the course of pursuing mathematics. This is because mathematical research produces mathematical theories, and as it happens, those theories tend to contain propositions that play a special role within mathematics, a role that it turns out to be useful to have a word for, the role of the postulates. On the meta-theoretic conception, laws are like postulates in this sense: we pursue science not in order to find out what the laws are, but in order to find out about other things—genes and electrons, the tides and the business cycle, and so on. Along the way, though, we do find out about laws, because scientific theories often include propositions that play special roles within those theories, a role it is worth having a name for, *the law role*. The analogy is not perfect: to be a law of a scientific theory is *not* to be a postulate of that theory. But it is a helpful analogy for bringing out the basic difference between the meta-theoretic and first-order conceptions of laws.

As far as I am aware, no one has defended (or even considered) a meta-theoretic account of laws.[14] Most of the extant accounts of laws fit the form of a first-order account, providing a completion of FO1 that is intended to provide an analysis of lawhood, or an account of the truth conditions or truthmakers of law-statements. For Armstrong, Dretske, and Tooley, it is a law of nature that P just in case P is a regularity entailed by the fact that two (or more) universals are related by a higher-order relation of nomic necessitation.[15] For Swoyer, Ellis, Lierse, and others, it is a law of nature that P just in case P states a relation among natural properties that belongs to the essence of these properties.[16] For Lewis, it is a law of nature that P just in case P is a member of the deductive system of truths that maximizes strength and simplicity while striking the best balance between them.[17] As noted

[13] The field of meta-mathematics might be an exception, but this doesn't undermine the point of the analogy I am drawing.

[14] Except me, in Roberts (2004).

[15] Armstrong (1983); Dretske (1977); Tooley (1977). On these views, the regularity P is not a law of nature; the law of nature is the higher-order connection among universals that entails the truth of P. But nonetheless, on these views, it is proper to say that it is a law of nature that P, where P is a regularity. For example, 'All copper conducts electricity' is a statement of a regularity; if the universals of Cupricity and Conductivity are related by the nomic necessitation relation, then it is a law that all copper conducts electricity. P itself is a regularity; the fact of P's being a law (which is distinct from the fact of P itself) is not a regularity, but the instantiation of the higher-order relation.

[16] See the references in note 62.

[17] Lewis (1973, 1986, 1994). In conversation, many people have asked me why I do not consider Lewis's best-system analysis a meta-theoretic account; it does, after all, analyze laws in terms of

above, Carroll argues that there is no illuminating account of the conditions under which something is a law, but nonetheless he clearly endorses the first-order conception.[18] Other philosophers have given accounts that focus not on what it is to be a law of nature, but rather on what it is to treat something as a law of nature. Thus, Lange's project is not to characterize what a law of nature is, but rather to characterize the 'root commitment' that we undertake when we attribute lawhood to a proposition.[19] Rescher and, more recently, Ward have given projectivist accounts of laws, which take lawhood to be a property that we somehow endow laws with in our reasoning about the world, rather than a mind-independent property that propositions can have in themselves.[20] In these works, Lange, Rescher, and Ward do not offer a completion of the formula FO1. Nonetheless, for them the primary nomological concept is that of a law of nature, rather than that of a law of a theory; their focus is on what we do when we treat a proposition as a law of nature, rather than on what role a proposition must play within a theory in order for it to be a law of that theory.

The meta-theoretic conception of laws is not itself a full-fledged philosophical account of laws; there are many possible meta-theoretic accounts of laws, corresponding to different ways of specifying the law role.[21] In this book, I am going to articulate and defend a meta-theoretic account of laws, which I call the *measurability account of laws*, or MAL. It will be spelled out in Chapter 9. In the remainder of this chapter, I will be concerned not with any particular meta-theoretic account, but with the meta-theoretic conception as such.

theories—at least, if we think of theories as systems of propositions. The answer is that Lewis does not define the notion of a *law of a system*; Lewis's systems simply have members, they do not have laws. For Lewis, a law of nature at a world is a member of the best system true at that world. The notion of a law of a theory does not come up at all in Lewis's account.

[18] Carroll (1994). In more recent work (2007), Carroll argues for a particular analysis of lawhood, though it is not a reductive analysis. This new account of laws is still a first-order account.

[19] Lange (2000).

[20] Rescher (1970), pp. 105–20; Ward (2002).

[21] Throughout this book, I use 'conception' and 'account' to refer to more general and more specific philosophical doctrines, respectively. These terms don't mark any boundary that it would be worthwhile to try to define precisely. The main use to which I put the two terms is to distinguish between *the meta-theoretic conception of laws*—which is the general approach to laws that explains laws of nature in terms of laws of theories rather than the other way around—and particular *meta-theoretic accounts of laws*—which are specific versions of the meta-theoretic conception that include a specification of the law role. This is just a local terminological decision intended to avoid confusion in this book; I don't mean to be making any general terminological recommendations.

3.3 What is a law *of nature?*

By filling in the value of R in MT1, we specify what it is to be a law of a theory. But we are not interested only in laws of theories; we are also interested in laws *of nature*. Can a meta-theoretic account of laws provide an account of what it is to be a law of nature?

3.3.1 The first proposal: laws of nature as laws of true theories

One obvious way to do so would be to supplement MT1 with the following:

MT2a: P is a law of nature iff P is a law of some true theory.

This seems plausible enough; we take something to be a law just when we take it to be a law of a true theory. For example, we deny that Newton's law of universal gravitation is a law of nature because the theory of which it is a law turned out not to be true. And to the extent that we are confident that the general theory of relativity is a true theory, we think that its laws are laws of nature.

Surely we do not want to allow P to count as a law of nature if P is not even true.[22] Furthermore, even if P is true, we do not want to let it count as a law of nature just by virtue of being a law of some theory unless that theory itself is true. For example, suppose that Kepler's second so-called law of planetary motion is a law of a theory that Kepler held, and this theory has turned out to be false. In the theory that replaced Kepler's theory, his second law turns out to be true, but only as a matter of nomological contingency, owing to the initial conditions of the solar system.[23] Under these circumstances, we do not want to count Kepler's second law as a law of nature. This suggests that it is a necessary condition for a proposition to be a law of nature that it be a law of some true theory. Moreover, this *seems* to be a sufficient condition as well: if we know that T is a true theory, and P is a law of T, then what more do we have to find out in order to establish that P is a law of nature? Perhaps P gets to count

[22] See Chapter 2, Section 2.3.

[23] Obviously, this simplifies the actual situation somewhat: in Newton's theory, Kepler's second law of planetary motion is not even true; it is only a good approximation. But for the purposes of this example, this detail is not important.

as a law of nature only if it is a law of some true theory that satisfies some additional requirement. But what could this additional requirement be?

All of this adds up to a nice case for MT2a. But unfortunately, MT2a leads to a consequence that is positively disastrous. There are compelling reasons to think that, if there are such things as laws of nature at all, then there are (or at least, could be) uninstantiated laws. Furthermore, there are (or at least, could be) uninstantiated laws such that it is compossible with all the laws for them to be instantiated; call these *contingently uninstantiated laws*.[24] For example, if Newtonian mechanics is true and it is a law that force = mass × acceleration, then there could be some value of mass, M, such that no object anywhere in the universe ever has a mass as great as M. To make the example definite, suppose that M is greater than the total mass of all the matter in the universe. But then one special case of Newton's second law—the case where the mass of the body in question is greater than M—will have no instances. It is not nomologically impossible for there to be instances of this case; the total mass of the universe could have been much greater than it actually is, and it could have contained bodies whose masses are greater than M. (At least, there is nothing in Newtonian physics that rules this out.) It is just that, given the way things happen to be in the actual world, there are no such bodies. But if MT2a is right, then this cannot be so: if there are no instances of the special case of Newton's second law applying to masses greater than M, then the laws of nature guarantee that there are no masses greater than M.

To see why, suppose that N2 is a law of nature:

$$\text{N2} : \text{f} = m\text{a}$$

for the reason that Newtonian mechanics—which I'll call 'NM' for short—is a true theory, and N2 is a law of NM. Now consider another theory, NM*, that is just like Newtonian mechanics, except that in place of N2 it has N2*:

$$\text{N2*} : \text{f} = \Phi(m)\text{a}$$

where:

$$\Phi(m) = \begin{pmatrix} m & \text{if } m < M \\ 2m - \text{M} & \text{otherwise} \end{pmatrix}$$

[24] If you don't agree that there are compelling reasons to think that there could be contingently uninstantiated laws, then see the following section.

Note that $\Phi(m)$ is a continuous, uniformly increasing function of m that is equal to m for values less than M and begins to deviate from m at higher values. N2* is thus in an intuitive way very similar to N2; both say that the acceleration of a body depends on the net impressed force it feels, in such a way that as the mass increases, the amount of force required to cause a given amount of acceleration increases in a continuous manner. The two propositions differ only in the details of the mathematical relation between net impressed force and acceleration for a body of a given mass. It seems clear that there could be such a theory as NM*—just like NM, except with N2* in place of N2—and that the two theories would differ only on a point of mathematical detail. Whatever the law role turns out to be, it is plausible that N2* would play it in NM*, since N2*'s place within NM* is analogous to N2's place in NM, and otherwise the two theories are so similar.

First say it, then qualify it to death: I said that NM* was 'just like' NM, except that it has N2* in place of N2. Of course, this can't be strictly true: making one change in a theory is bound to introduce other changes as well. Many regularities that are logical consequences of the truth of NM and that depend on N2 for their derivation (such as, for example, the law of conservation of momentum) will not be consequences of NM*, and conversely. In addition, there is no unique way of generating a theory by subtracting one of its laws and replacing it with a different law. For example, suppose that P is a proposition that is entailed by NM. Then the biconditional *P iff N2* is a consequence of NM. One alternative to NM which has N2* in place of N2 has P as one of its consequences, and does not have the biconditional as a consequence; another has the biconditional as one of its consequences, but not P. The instruction to generate NM by starting with NM, deleting N2, and putting N2* in its place does not determine which of these two alternatives to NM we should end up with. So to be more careful, I should say: start out with a natural axiomatization of NM, in which each of NM's basic laws appears as a separate axiom. N2 will presumably be among these axioms; remove it, and put N2* in its place.[25]

[25] If N2 is not one of the axioms, but is instead a consequence of more basic laws that do appear as axioms, then find the smallest subset of these more basic laws such that if you remove that subset, the remaining axioms will not entail N2. Then make the least radical modification of these axioms that you can which will make them (together with the remaining axioms) have N2* rather than N2 as a consequence.

The result is a theory which, in an intuitive sense, differs from NM only locally: we have surgically modified the mathematical relation between mass, force, and acceleration, while leaving the rest of the theory alone to as great a degree as possible. (And if you would like the modification to be even more local, then we can make it so by redefining $\Phi(m)$ in such a way that it differed from m by a smaller amount and only for a narrower range of values.) Now, whatever the law role turns out to be, it seems plausible that a sufficiently local modification of a law of one theory should result in a theory in which the modified law plays the law role; whether a proposition plays the law role within a theory should be sensitive to the details of the theory, but it is implausible that it should be so sensitive that even a very tiny modification to an equation which leaves everything else alone as much as possible should turn a law of a theory into a non-law.[26] The general point here, which seems plausible enough, is that there is an alternative to NM which agrees with NM on all instantiated cases, but is such that it and NM differ on what their laws say about some uninstantiated values of mass.[27]

Ex hypothesi, NM is true. Therefore, NM* is true, since NM and NM* differ only in what they say about the behavior of bodies with masses greater than M, of which there are none. So if MT2a is right, it follows that N2 and N2* are *both* laws of nature—since each of them is a law of a (different) true theory. But N2 and N2* jointly entail that there is no body with a mass greater than M. So the laws of nature preclude the existence of any such body.

There doesn't appear to be anything special about this example. The general point is that for a given true theory T, and a given uninstantiated law L of T, there is some theory that agrees with T on all instantiated cases, but has a law L* that differs with L on the uninstantiated cases—that is, L* predicts that if L were instantiated then something incompatible with what L predicts would happen. So L and L* jointly entail that L is not instantiated. For the case of laws expressible as mathematical relations among physical quantities, this is particularly plausible. In any case, where

[26] For example, the common intuition that Maxwell's equations are among the laws of classical electrodynamics does not seem to depend on all of the precise mathematical details of those equations; if a 4π somewhere were a 2π instead, it is hard to see how that should change the fact that these equations are laws of the theory they figure in.

[27] I am grateful to Bernard Gert for making me see how important these qualifications are.

one of the laws of T has an uninstantiated case, one of the most basic or fundamental laws of T must have an uninstantiated case. Write T out in a form which includes each of its most basic or fundamental laws as a separate postulate. Now find the basic law with an uninstantiated case. This law states that one quantity's value is a certain mathematical function of certain others. Fiddle with this function in a way that it yields a different value for the uninstantiated case, but the same value for all actually instantiated cases. Leave the rest of the basic postulates of the theory alone. If the resulting equation does not play the law role within the resulting modified theory, then the question of which equations play the law role within a theory must turn on minute mathematical details of those equations, which is just not plausible.[28]

So it seems that for any true theory with an uninstantiated law, there is another true theory with a uninstantiated law that makes an incompatible prediction about what would happen if the first law were instantiated. Given MT2a, it follows that every uninstantiated law of nature is nomologically necessarily uninstantiated. To the extent that we think it possible that there are uninstantiated laws that are uninstantiated as a matter of nomological contingency, we have a reason to reject MT2a.

3.3.2 The importance of contingently uninstantiated laws

You might think that the common intuition that there could be contingently uninstantiated laws is a negotiable intuition, one that could be reasonably rejected in the face of a sufficiently good argument for something incompatible with it. But this is not so. For if we give up the idea

[28] Objection: perhaps the fact that equation L plays the law role within T depends on the fact that L together with another equation M (also posited by T) deductively entails another equation Q which has some very special feature. (For example, maybe L is the second law of motion, M is the third law of motion, and Q is the law of the conservation of momentum; maybe the 'special feature' of Q is the fact that it takes the form of a conservation law.) If we replace L by an alternative L*, then L* and M need no longer entail Q. (For example, if we replace N2 by N2* as in the above example, then the resulting theory NM* need not entail the conservation of momentum, or any conservation equation at all.) This is so even if L* differs from L only for a small range of values of the independent variables figuring in it, and all of those values are in fact uninstantiated.

However, in a case like this, we could generate our alternative theory T* by fiddling both with L* and with M*, again only for cases of values of quantities figuring as independent variables that are in fact uninstantiated. If we coordinate this fiddling so that, for the uninstantiated values of the quantities in question, L* and M* jointly entail Q, then the objection is overcome: the resulting theory has laws that make different predictions from the original theory's laws about what would happen in cases that in the actual world never arise.

that there could be contingently uninstantiated laws, then we give up the very distinction between laws of nature and nomologically contingent regularities. Either every true regularity is a law, or none is.

To see why, suppose that there are no contingently uninstantiated laws of nature, and there is at least one law of nature $\forall x(Fx \supset Gx)$. Suppose that as a matter of fact, $\forall x(Hx \supset Jx)$. Now, $\forall x(Fx \supset Gx)$ entails $\forall x((Hx \,\&\, \neg Jx) \supset (Fx \supset Gx))$, so the latter is a law.[29] It is also an uninstantiated law. So by the hypothesis that there are no contingently uninstantiated laws, it is a law that $\neg\exists x(Hx \,\&\, \neg Jx)$; that is, it is a law that $\forall x(Hx \supset Jx)$. But the latter was an arbitrarily chosen true regularity. Hence all true regularities are laws. Discharging our two initial suppositions, we get the conclusion that if there are no contingently uninstantiated laws, then if any regularity is a law, then all true regularities are laws.

A corollary is that if there are necessarily no contingently uninstantiated laws, then necessarily either every regularity is a law or none is—so there is no distinction between laws and accidental regularities. But if there is no distinction between laws and accidental regularities, then the very idea of a law loses its point. So if we are going to continue using the concept of a law of nature at all, we had better insist on its being at least possible that there are contingently uninstantiated laws.

But MT2a does seem to rule out the possibility of contingently uninstantiated laws. For it is not implausible that every law of every true theory will be like Newton's second law was assumed to be in the example above: that is, for every true theory T and every proposition P that is an uninstantiated law of T, there is a second theory T* that agrees with T on everything except that in place of P it has a proposition P* that agrees with P on all instantiated cases but differs from P on some uninstantiated cases, and P* is a law of T*. The construction of P* and T* for the case where T is Newtonian mechanics and P is the second law of motion made it very

[29] Recall that throughout this book, I am using the term 'law' in such a way that every logically contingent proposition entailed by the laws is itself a law. Some authors deny this. They would prefer to use a term such as 'the nomologically necessities' to refer to the deductive closure of the laws. To translate into their idiom, every use of 'law of nature' in the present discussion should be replaced by 'logically contingent nomological necessity.' Then, the claim I am arguing for in this subsection is translated into: if there are no logically contingent, nomologically necessary regularities that are uninstantiated and are uninstantiated as a matter of nomological contingency, then either all true regularities are nomologically necessary or none are. (The complexity of this translation is one reason why I prefer my way of using the term 'law.')

plausible that this is so (since it did not appear to depend on any idiosyncrasy of this particular example), though this is not a knock-down argument. But the implausibility here is enough to make MT2a very unattractive. An advocate of the meta-theoretic conception of laws had better look for another account of laws of nature.

3.3.3 Monotonicity and God's own theory

There is some reason to worry that the problem just encountered is not only a problem for MT2a, but is a problem for MT1 as well (and thus a problem for the meta-theoretic conception of laws as such). For it seems plausible that the relation between a theory and its laws is monotonic, in the following sense:

> **Monotonicity**: If P is a law of T, and T* entails T, then P is also a law of T*.

The idea is that if you have a theory, and it has some laws, then if you later expand your theory by adding more content to it, then nothing that was a law of it before stops being a law. Thus, if we accept Newtonian mechanics, and then augment it by adding Maxwell's electrodynamics, leaving all the claims of the original Newtonian theory in place, then all of the laws of the original Newtonian theory will still be laws of the final, augmented theory. It seems very plausible that this should hold as a general principle. But if it does, then a very curious consequence follows.

For suppose that Monotonicity holds in general. Now consider the theory that consists of all and only the true non-nomological propositions; call it *God's Own Theory*, or 'GOT' for short. GOT entails every true theory, so by Monotonicity, every law of every true theory is a law of GOT. Back in Section 3.3.1, we saw that it is very plausible that for every uninstantiated law L, there is some true theory one of whose laws disagrees with L about what would happen if L were instantiated—in other words, one of whose laws, together with L, entails that L is uninstantiated. So, for every uninstantiated law L of GOT, there is a law M of some true theory such that M and L jointly entail that L is uninstantiated. Since every law of every true theory is a law of GOT, it follows that M is a law of GOT, so the laws of GOT entail that L is uninstantiated; L is *non-contingently* uninstantiated according to GOT. But L could have been any uninstantiated law of GOT; therefore, there are no contingently uninstantiated laws of GOT. By the argument of Section 3.3.2, it follows that either every true regularity is a law of GOT, or else there are no laws of GOT.

This seems an outrageous conclusion. Why couldn't a being who knew everything about the world recognize a distinction between the laws and the accidental regularities? On one common interpretation of the modern notion of a law of nature, it is as if (and perhaps it is true that) God created the world by setting up the laws of nature and setting the initial conditions. If this is so, then surely God recognizes the distinction between the laws and the regularities that depend on the initial conditions. But if God is omniscient, then surely his theory of the universe is GOT, within which no regularities are distinguished as the laws, since all of them play the law role in it.

In fact, we don't need to resort to theological speculation to make the point: consider a community of scientists who have managed to discover the whole truth about the universe. Their theory would be GOT; but surely their theory would be a scientific theory like any other, and some propositions but not others would play the law role within it? Of course, this community is a rather extreme idealization—it is the community of scientists at the famous Peircean limit of inquiry. We cannot expect everything that is true of our own theories to be true of theirs. But if we can in principle asymptotically approach GOT as time approaches infinity, then it seems there must be a continuous series of theories connecting our theory with GOT; somewhere along this series there will have to stop being a meaningful distinction between the laws of a theory and the nomologically contingent regularities of a theory, which would seem to be a dramatically discontinuous break.

All of this can be made to seem like a *reductio ad absurdum* against the meta-theoretic conception of laws. But it is not, for two reasons. The first is that a defender of the meta-theoretic conception can deny that Monotonicity holds in all cases. As a universal principle, Monotonicity seems intuitively plausible, but we have seen no compelling reason why it should be accepted. And the intuition that speaks on its behalf does not come with very high credentials: the trouble case arises when we consider a theory that is far stronger than any theory that human scientists have ever proposed—a theory that provides a complete road-map of the entire space-time continuum, down to the last grain of sand. Our intuitions concerning theories and their laws are honed on much more modest examples. The example of Newtonian mechanics and its augmentation by Maxwell's electrodynamics is a case where we have strong intuitions, and there it is very plausible that there is no violation of Monotonicity. But the difference between the two theories in that example is nothing like the difference between one of our theories and GOT.

In addition, there is some reason to doubt that Monotonicity is true in general. Consider the case of Galileo's so-called law of free fall. Let us formulate it in a way that renders it plausibly true in a Newtonian world (or, for that matter, the actual one): 'Any body of sufficient heaviness will fall with an approximately constant acceleration, approximately equal to 9.8 meters per second per second, when dropped near the surface of the earth,' where 'sufficient heaviness,' 'approximately,' and 'near' are made precise in some way that renders this statement both true and non-trivial. Suppose that Galileo held (or at least, could have held) some collection of true beliefs which comprise a pre-Newtonian theory within which his law of free fall plays the law role. (Without a detailed account of what the law role is, it isn't possible to say for certain whether there is any such theory that Galileo might have held. But it is at least not implausible that there is one.) We may suppose that the complete theory of Newton's *Principia* entails this hypothesized Galilean theory—including its law of free fall. But the latter is *not* a law of Newton's theory: given Newton's theory, it depends not only on the laws but also on the contingent details concerning the mass and diameter of the earth. Hence, if there is a 'Galilean' theory comprised of consequences of Newton's theory and within which Galileo's so-called law plays the law role, then we have here a counterexample to Monotonicity. This particular example is sketchy and conjectural, but it illustrates a familiar pattern: the laws of one theory[30] turn out not to be consequences of the laws of a successor theory alone; instead they are consequences of the laws of the successor theory *together with* hypotheses about initial and boundary conditions.[31] This gives the friend of the meta-theoretic conception some reason to doubt that Monotonicity is true in general.

[30] Or at least, propositions that say that the laws of one theory are approximately true.

[31] For example, the approximate truth of Newton's laws in our local environment follows from the laws of general relativity together with the proposition that the gravitational fields in our environment are weak and the relative velocities are small.

The second reason why there is no *reductio* here is that we have not reached an *absurdum*. Why couldn't it be the case that every true regularity is a law relative to GOT?[32] The central motivating idea behind the meta-theoretic conception is that lawhood is a matter of a proposition's playing a certain role within a scientific theory. Whatever that role is, it is presumably distinguished by its importance in scientific practice. Scientific practice is a practice engaged in by creatures who do not have a complete road-map of the space-time continuum at their disposal. The special feature that distinguishes the laws from the accidental regularities is a feature that has to do with the way a theory is used by creatures who do not have a God's-eye view of the universe, and who have to resort to empirical means—involving the testimony of their senses together with the guidance of accepted theory—to find their way around. A theory such as the GOT is not a theory that such creatures will ever be in a position to use. No surprise, then, if a distinction (such as that between laws and non-laws) that is important because of the role it plays in the practices of such creatures will not be a significant distinction in the context of a theory like GOT.

3.3.4 Are there laws of nature simpliciter*?*

We still haven't solved our problem: how to make sense of the notion of a law *of nature*, as opposed to the notion of a law *of some theory*? Even if the primary nomological concept is the concept of a law of a theory, it would be painful to eliminate the idea of a law of nature altogether. We sometimes wonder whether something is a law of nature, even if we have no particular theory in mind; we take the laws of nature to bear a special relation to counterfactuals and explanation; perhaps most importantly, to junk the idea of a law of nature (as opposed to the idea of a law of a theory) would be to junk the idea that we live in a law-governed cosmos, something that we should be reluctant to do.

However, given the troubles that MT2a gets into, it is hard to see how the meta-theoretic conception could make room for the concept of a law

[32] The meta-theoretic account of laws that I will defend in this book—the MAL—actually implies that GOT has *no* laws. Like the claim being considered in the text, this obliterates the distinction between the laws and the nomologically contingent regularities relative to GOT. So the present discussion is relevant to the MAL. I take up this issue below in Chapter 8, Section 8.7.3, and Chapter 9, Section 9.7.

of nature. If the laws of nature are not just the laws of the true theories, then what could they be?

To see the problem, consider again the example of Newtonian mechanics and the alternative theory T* that was discussed above. Suppose again that both Newtonian mechanics and T* are true theories of our world. Suppose that earth scientists accept Newtonian mechanics, while the scientists of a distant planet accept T*. It is hard to imagine how the aliens would ever have come up with T* and taken it seriously. But perhaps their scientific culture is such that non-differentiable functions like $\Phi(m)$ seem more natural to them than they do to us. Perhaps the ancient natural philosophers of the distant planet arrived at an elaborate theory of the cosmos in which such functions played a crucial role, and their modern theories evolved more or less continuously from these ancient theories, until finally they arrived at T*. We will be inclined to say that N2 is a law of nature, and there is much to be said for this view: after all, N2 plays the law role within a true theory. The aliens will be inclined to call N2* a law of nature, and a parallel case can be made for their claim. Is one of us wrong? Well, in virtue of what *could* one of us be wrong? Perhaps the natural world contains facts about what is a law and what is not, and at most one planet's scientists have arrived at the true theory of what the laws of nature are—but this move is not available to a defender of the meta-theoretic conception; it is a capitulation to the first-order conception. Perhaps the earthling theory is right and the alien theory wrong in virtue of its greater simplicity. But the aliens might not agree with this assessment, and why should we take our standards of simplicity to be privileged?

3.3.5 Law-statements have a contextual semantics

It is tempting to say that both the earth scientists and the alien scientists would be right—but if this means that both N2 and N2* are laws of nature, then we are in trouble. For the same reasoning would lead to the conclusion that every pair of putative laws that agree on instantiated cases but disagree on uninstantiated cases would both be laws of nature. Perhaps there aren't enough alien civilizations in the universe for both members of each such pair to appear in a theory accepted by somebody somewhere. But why should it matter if anyone has ever actually come up with all these theories? Someone somewhere *could* have come up with each of these theories, and surely what the laws of nature are cannot depend on the contingencies of which theories have been written down and which have not. So if we grant that both N2 and N2* are laws of nature, then we are on a slippery slope that leads to the abolition of all accidental regularities, and thus to the undermining of the very point of the distinction between laws and non-laws.

But there is a way for a friend of the meta-theoretic conception to avoid this disaster. What we want to do is grant that in the hypothetical scenario just described, both the earthling scientists and the alien scientists are right in what they say about the laws of nature, but resist saying that both N2 and N2* are laws of nature. This we can do, if we say that in the context of earthling scientific discourse, 'N2 is a law of nature' is true, whereas in the context of the aliens' scientific discourse, 'N2* is a law of nature' is true, and in no context is 'N2 and N2* are both laws of nature' true. In short, the meta-theoretic conception should be combined with a contextual account of the semantics of law-statements. On such a view, there is no such thing as a *law of nature, full stop*—where this means, something that can be truly called a law of nature in any context of utterance whatsoever. Nonetheless, in many contexts, some statements of the form 'P is a law of nature (and not merely a law of the theory T)' are true.

The obvious objection here is that whatever else the laws of nature may be, they are surely objective, and a contextual account of law-statements would deny laws their objectivity. But a contextual account does not make laws non-objective simply by making the truth conditions of law-statements context-dependent. Context-independence is not the same thing as objectivity, for it can be a perfectly objective matter of fact that some context-dependent sentence is true in the context where it is uttered. For example, 'The last dinosaur died at least two weeks ago' has context-dependent truth conditions since it is true at some times and false at others, but one can use it to state a perfectly objective matter of fact. If a contextual account of law-statements renders laws objectionably non-objective, it must be for some other reason.

Someone might say that a contextual account of law-statements is unacceptable because the laws of nature objectively bear special relations to counterfactuals and scientific explanation, and these special relations have nothing to do with anything context-dependent, and a contextual account of law-statements cannot be compatible with this fact. But even if this alleged fact is indeed a fact, I don't see why a contextual semantics for law-statements can't be perfectly consistent with it. Suppose that which counterfactuals are true, and which explanations are good ones, varies from context of utterance to context of utterance. If the truth conditions of law-statements also vary from context to context, then it could be that these ways of varying line up in such a way that in any given context, the special relations among the true law-statements, the true counterfactuals, and the good explanations all hold. Then, the proposition that laws bear a special relation to counterfactuals and to explanations will be true in all contexts of utterance, even though the laws of nature, the true counterfactuals, and the good explanations themselves vary from context to context. Whether this is so depends on the details of the contextual account of laws of nature, as well as on the details of the special relations that hold among laws, counterfactuals, and explanations.[33] So even if there is a context-independent relation among laws, counterfactuals, and explanations, that is not enough to show that the truth conditions of law-statements are not context-dependent.

Another way to articulate the worry that a contextual account of law-statements would be incompatible with the objectivity of laws is this: modern science seems to give us a picture of our world as a law-governed one. What exactly this amounts to is not easy to articulate, but it seems to be a very important idea about the nature of the world itself, independently of us. But if a contextual account of law-statements is true, then the existence of laws of nature is not, after all, an interesting fact about the world itself. Rather, it is simply a fact about our language that it includes a certain context-dependent predicate. So adopting a contextual account of law-statements deprives the idea of the law-governed world of much of what makes it exciting. Perhaps this is not a very powerful argument against the *truth* of a contextual account, but it does seem to make such an account seem profoundly disappointing. And if such an account of law-statements does turn out to be true, then the moral seems to be that the concept of a law of nature does not have anything like the scientific and metaphysical significance that it seems to have. Perhaps the study of laws and lawhood should not be considered in any way central to science or philosophy of science; perhaps it should just be regarded as one special topic in the semantics of natural language.

[33] The view of laws that I will defend in Chapter 9 implies that this is true, with respect to counterfactuals at least.

I think this is an important thing to worry about. But in the end, I think this worry can be overcome. Even on the kind of contextual account of law-statements that I will defend in this book, the idea that we live in a law-governed world, properly understood, is important and profound, with many implications both for philosophy and for science. But this is a matter I will not confront again until the final chapter of this book.

3.3.6 The second proposal: law-statements as elliptical

The meta-theoretic conception of laws requires a contextual account of laws of nature—that is, an account that attributes context-dependent truth conditions to statements of the form 'P is a law of nature' (as opposed to, 'P is a law of theory T'). How should such an account go?

The most obvious way to go is to say that whenever we call something a law of nature, we are speaking elliptically. What we really mean is that it is a law of some theory, which we need not explicitly identify in this context:

> **MT2b**: Every token of 'It is a law (of nature) that P' is elliptical for 'It is a law of T that P,' for some particular theory T.

This blocks the argument given above which seemed to show that there can be no contingently uninstantiated laws. For that argument concluded that *the laws of nature* ruled out the existence of instances for the uninstantiated values of mass by deriving this from the conjunction of a law of one theory and a law of another theory. In order for this argument to go through, we must take one token of 'law of nature' to be elliptical for 'law of NM,' and another to be elliptical for 'law of NM*.' And if we do this, then the argument is a simple fallacy of equivocation.

MT2b cannot be the whole story, however. For when Newton said that it was a law of nature that every body exerts an instantaneous attractive force on every other, the magnitude of which is directly proportional to the product of their masses and inversely proportional to the distance separating them, we take him to have said something false. Yet, if all he had meant by this assertion was that the stated regularity is a law relative to his own physical theory, then it would presumably have been true. We can take care of this problem if we take law-statements to mean that a proposition is a law of some particular unnamed theory, *and that theory is true*:

> **MT2c**: Every token of 'It is a law (of nature) that P' is elliptical for 'It is a law of T that P, and T is true' for some particular theory T.

However, this proposal faces other problems. Sometimes we conjecture that some proposition is a law of nature without having any particular scientific theory in mind. Such a conjecture seems to be meaningful, and it seems that it must be true or false. But on the ellipsis proposal I am now considering, it has no truth value. Conjecturing that P is a law of nature, when there is no salient theory T such that 'law of nature' is elliptical for 'law of T,' amounts to saying that P is a law of theory____, with nothing to fill in the blank. Nothing is said by such a statement, so it cannot be either true or false.

Of course, one could accept this consequence. Perhaps when we say that P is a law of nature, and we do not have any theory T in mind such that what we really mean is that P is a law of T, then we are under an illusion when we think that we have said something with a truth value. On this view, conjecturing that P is a law of nature, period, without any particular theory in mind, is like saying, 'The anonymous official leaked the scandalous documents to the press for self-serving reasons,' when there is in fact no anonymous official that is picked out by the context. Of course, in cases like this, it can seem to us that our conjecture has a definite truth condition, and so it must have a definite truth value, and we can even have great reasons to believe that this is so, when it is not. Perhaps something similar is going on in a case where we conjecture that something is a law of nature and we have no particular theory in mind.

But this is not very plausible. Consider Bob, who is largely ignorant of science. Bob comments to one of his friends while watching an episode of *Star Trek*: 'I don't think anything like this could ever really happen. For one thing, it is a law of nature that nothing can travel faster than the speed of light. Anyway, I heard that somewhere.' When Bob says that it is a law of nature that nothing can travel faster than light, what he said seems to have a definite truth value: if current physics is pretty much right, then what he said was true. On the proposal I am now considering, Bob's utterance must have been elliptical for 'It is a law of theory T that nothing travels faster than light, and T is true,' for some value of T. But the proposition that nothing travels faster than light is a law *of the theory of relativity*, which poor Bob has no inkling of. So Bob could not be speaking elliptically, using '... is a law of nature' as shorthand for '... is a law of the theory of relativity, which is true.' He must be, but he couldn't be. Therefore the ellipsis view is false.

3.3.7 The third proposal: 'law of nature' as an indexical

What we want to say is that every token utterance of 'P is a law of nature' has the same truth condition as 'P is a law of T, and T is true,' for some theory T. The case of Bob shows us that we must not suppose that 'P is a law of nature' is simply an *abbreviation*, which the speaker could cash out by specifying the theory T, but need not go to the trouble of doing so since it is clear in the context which theory T is. Instead, what we should say is this:

> **MT2d**: 'P is a law of nature' is true in context k iff there is a theory T such that T is true, T is salient in k, and P is a law of T.

Whereas the ellipsis proposal made law-statements out to be eliminable abbreviations, this one makes them out to be indexical statements: their semantic values are governed by a function from contexts of utterance to truth conditions.[34]

Given MT2d, one need not be able to identify the salient theory T; it is enough for there to be a salient theory. (Just as in general, one need not to be able to identify, in non-indexical terms, the referent of an indexical one is in a position to use.) In the case of Bob, the salient theory is the one accepted by the relevant experts in Bob's linguistic community.[35] Bob's utterance concerns the physics of high-speed travel; in Bob's community, the theory addressing such physics that is accepted by the relevant experts is the theory of relativity. Hence, when Bob says it is a law of nature that nothing travels faster than light, his assertion is true just in case it is a law of relativity theory that nothing goes faster than light and that theory is true. This seems to be just a special case of the well-known linguistic division of labor.[36]

MT2d thus looks very promising. But it is not complete as it stands, since it doesn't tell us what makes a theory salient in a given context

[34] In my (1999), I discussed the merits of an account that makes law-statements out to be indexicals. That proposal was a variant of Lewis's best-system analysis (Lewis 1973), and is very different from the view discussed here. But I think that much of what I said there about the virtues of the idea that the law-predicate is an indexical of some sort carries over to the present proposal.

[35] But why does *anyone* have to accept a theory according to which it is a law that nothing travels faster than light, in order for Bob's utterance to be true? Because otherwise, the case of Bob would be the case of Serendipides, which I will consider below, in Section 3.3.10.

[36] Burge (1979).

of utterance. The case of Bob suggests one way of spelling this out: a theory is salient in the context just in case it concerns the phenomena referred to by the law-statement, and it is accepted by the relevant experts in the speaker's community. But what about a case in which the relevant experts are in disagreement about which theory ought to be accepted? For example, consider a debate in 1907 between Ed, an enthusiast of the new special theory of relativity, and Ned, a doctrinaire Newtonian. Ed says, 'It is a law of nature that the speed of light in a vacuum is the same in all inertial frames of reference'; Ned replies, 'No, that is not a law of nature.' The relevant experts do not all agree on a common theory concerning the relativity of the speed of light. So there is no true theory accepted by all the relevant experts, relative to which it is a law that light has the same speed in all inertial frames. Nor is any such true theory accepted by the majority of the relevant experts. (It is only 1907, after all.) So if a theory must be accepted by all, or a majority, of the relevant experts, then MT2d makes Ed's statement false, and Ned's true.[37] Yet, we want to say that Ed's statement is true, and Ned's is false. In order to get this result, we must not require that in order to be salient, a theory must be accepted by at least a majority of the relevant experts in the speaker's community. The most we can plausibly require is that the theory be accepted by someone in the speaker's community; neither a consensus nor a majority of expert opinion is required. It should be added that there need not be any single expert in the community who understands and believes the whole of T; if T is a large and complex enough body of theory that no single scientist grasps the whole of it, though specialists grasp and accept each of its parts, then that is sufficient for it to be salient in the context.

So, in order for 'P is a law of nature' to be true in a given context, P must be a law of a theory T which is (i) true and (ii) accepted by someone in the speaker's epistemic community (or accepted collectively by some sub-community of that epistemic community). One more thing needs to be added: this theory T must be the *total body* of true theoretical beliefs held in the speaker's epistemic community. To see why, recall that in order to avoid the disastrous elimination of contingently uninstantiated laws (which leads to the disastrous elimination of the very distinction between laws and

[37] However, if Ned had said, 'No, that is not a law of nature, for it is not even true,' then he would have said something false according to MT2d (assuming that it is true that the speed of light is Lorentz-invariant).

accidental regularities), a meta-theoretic account of laws must reject the principle of Monotonicity. This means it must allow for the possibility that some theory T is strictly stronger than some other theory T', and not every law of T' is a law of T. Now, suppose that T and T' are as described, that both are true, and that in a context k, the speakers belong to an epistemic community that unanimously accepts T. Then surely, we want to say that in this context it is true that P is a law just in case P is a law of T; if it is one of the propositions that is a law of T' but not of T, then it should not count as a law in the context k. (Otherwise, we might as well just accept Monotonicity; for otherwise, any law of any theory entailed by the salient theory T counts as a law of nature; under these circumstances, why not just say that the laws of T include all the laws of all the theories entailed by T? But that would amount to accepting Monotonicity.) So what we want to say is that the salient theory in context k is not just any old true theory that is accepted in k; rather, it is the strongest true theory accepted in k. In other words, it is *the true part of the total body of theory accepted by the members of this community*.

However, we must not identify the salient theory T as the theory comprised of *all* the theoretical commitments of the members of the speaker's epistemic community. For one thing, *that* theory is almost certain to be logically inconsistent. For another, 'P is a law of nature' can be true in a context k only if P is a law of some *true* theory that is salient in k. Suppose we believe Newtonian mechanics, and Newtonian mechanics is true, but we also hold some false theoretical belief that is irrelevant to the laws of Newtonian mechanics—for example, that the earth is less than 6,000 years old. It seems that when we assert in this context that the laws of Newtonian mechanics are laws of nature, what we say is true. But none of our law-statements in this context could be true if the salient theory included our false belief about the age of the earth. Hence, we should restrict the salient theory to the body of true theoretical commitments of members of the speaker's community.

3.3.8 Laws in other possible worlds

All of that is fine so long as we are considering contexts in which law-statements are used only to make claims about what the laws of the actual world are. But law-statements also occur in descriptions of alternative possibilities: 'Consider a possible world in which it is a law of nature that all x-particles acquire spin-up when they enter a y-field.'[38] They also occur within the antecedents and consequents of counterfactual conditionals: 'If Bode's law were a law of nature, then either Pluto would not exist or else it would have a different orbit'; 'If phenomenological thermodynamics were a true fundamental theory, then it would be a law of nature that entropy never decreases in any closed system (and so Brownian motion as we observe it would be physically impossible).' Sometimes, negations of true law-statements occur within counterfactuals: 'If it were not a law of nature that no material particle can travel faster than light, then physicists would have gotten an electron to go faster than light by now.'[39]

In each of these cases, something is being said about which propositions are laws of nature in some non-actual, hypothetical situation. MT2d tells us only what the truth conditions of token assertions of the form 'It is a law of nature that P' are. Such assertions are about what is a law of nature *in the world where the assertion is made.* So as it stands, MT2d cannot tell us what the truth conditions of examples like the ones considered just above are. For that, we need an account of when a given law-statement is true at a given possible world as uttered in a given context, where the context in question might not be located in the world in question. The natural way of adapting MT2d for this purpose is:

> **MT2**: 'P is a law of nature' is true at world w in context k iff there is a theory T such that T is salient in k, T is true at w, and P is a law of T.

As the absence of a letter 'e' at the end of its name suggests, MT2 is my final proposal. It is not complete yet, though, because we still need to say what makes a theory salient in a context where laws at other possible worlds are under discussion.

I have argued that the truth conditions of law-statements depend on a contextual parameter: the salient theory. I have also argued that in a context k, the salient theory is that theory which comprises all the true theoretical commitments undertaken by all members of the epistemic community that includes the speakers. What I want to suggest now is that this is only the *default* way in which the context determines the salient theory, and this default can be canceled. One way in which this default can be canceled

[38] This example comes from a thought-experiment proposed by Carroll (1994).

[39] This example is borrowed from Lange (2000), who uses it for a different purpose.

is by a speaker's saying something that focuses everyone's attention on some other theory, making it the most salient theory for purposes of the conversation. For example, suppose we are in a context in which we all believe that quantum mechanics is true, and quantum mechanics *is* true, and suppose that someone says:

> **M1**: There are possible worlds where Newtonian mechanics is true; at all those worlds, it is a law of nature that momentum is always conserved.

Intuitively, this statement should come out true. Moreover, if someone says:

> **C1**: Had Newtonian mechanics been true, it would have been a law of nature that momentum is always conserved,

their utterance should count as true. In each of these cases, the speaker has singled out the theory of Newtonian mechanics for special attention, and thereby made it the salient theory (even though that theory is, *ex hypothesi*, false at the actual world). It is crucial that this shift in the salient theory occurs, for if it did not then both of the statements in question would have been false in our present context (which is obviously not how it is). For the default salient theory in our present context is *ex hypothesi* quantum mechanics; the strict conservation of momentum is not a law of quantum mechanics, so in any context where quantum mechanics is the salient theory, the statement 'It is a law of nature that momentum is always conserved' is false at *every* possible world, so M1 would be false, and C1 would be a counterfactual with a necessarily false antecedent (which is surely not how its speaker intended it to be taken). But since the utterance of M1 or C1 makes Newtonian mechanics become the salient theory, M1 and C1 both are true in our present context. For example, let w be a world where Newtonian mechanics is true; since the strict conservation of momentum is a law relative to Newtonian mechanics, MT2 implies that relative to any context where Newtonian mechanics is the salient theory, it is true at w that it is a law of nature that momentum is always conserved. So once our present context becomes modified by having its default salient theory canceled, and Newtonian mechanics made salient, it is true in our present context that there are lots of possible worlds where Newtonian mechanics is true, and in all of those worlds it is true that it is a law of nature that momentum is always conserved. This is just what it takes to make M1 true, and C1 significant, in our present context.

In other cases, though, the default salient theory must be canceled even though there is no unique theory that gets singled out as its replacement. For example, keep supposing that we are in a context where the default salient theory is quantum mechanics, and imagine that someone utters one of these statements:

M2: It is possible for it to be a law of nature that all copper is liquid.

C2: If it had been a law of nature that all copper is liquid, then there would have been no bronze statues.

Intuitively, each of these statements should count as true in our present context. But neither of them is true in any context where the salient theory is quantum mechanics, for the very same reason that (as we just saw) neither M1 nor C1 would be true in such a context. The utterance of either M2 or C2 seems to require a shift in the salient theory, just as the utterance of either M1 or C1 does. But which theory becomes the new salient theory, when someone utters M2 or C2? Presumably, there are many possible scientific theories relative to which it is a law that all copper is liquid; which one of them gets to become the new salient theory in our context?

It seems that none of them should. When M2 or C2 gets uttered, our context becomes indeterminate, in that there is no definite matter of fact about which theory is the salient one. What is definite is that whichever theory is salient, it is one relative to which it is a law that all copper is liquid. M2 and C2 both get to count as true because (presumably) they would get to count as true no matter which of these theories was the salient one. By contrast, C3:

C3: If it had been a law of nature that all copper is liquid, then it would have been a law of nature that there is plenty of solid copper in the world.

would come out false no matter which of the many theories whose laws include the proposition that all copper is liquid, so C3 is definitely false. However, C4:

C4: If it had been a law of nature that all copper is liquid, then it would have been a law of nature that all silver is liquid too.

would be false in contexts where some such theories are salient, and true in contexts where others are (since presumably, there are some theories relative to which it is a law that all copper is liquid and a law that all silver is liquid, and there are some theories relative to which the first proposition is a law but the second is not). So unless something else about what is going on in our present conversational context serves to narrow down the range of theories that might be salient, C4 is neither definitely true nor definitely false in our present context (which seems like the right thing to say).

All of these ways in which the default gets canceled, and the salient theory shifts around, conform to the general pragmatic maxim that other things being equal, the context should be allowed to shift in ways that render any statements that have been made non-trivially true.[40] Supposing again that we are in a context in which we all believe that quantum mechanics is true, and quantum mechanics *is* true, an utterance of C1 would be a counterfactual conditional with a necessarily false antecedent unless the context shifted in such a way to allow its antecedent to count as true (relative to our present context) at some possible worlds; an utterance of M1 would just be false unless the context shifted in such a way. So, these shifts naturally take place.

Summing up: when we are talking about which propositions are and are not laws of nature in the actual world, the salient theory is the total body of true theory that is accepted in our extended epistemic community. But when we are talking about other possible worlds and their own laws of nature, things are different. There are three ways in which we might talk about other possible worlds where the laws are different—where, for example, some actual non-law P is a law of nature: we might simply stipulate a possible world where P is a law of nature; we might assert the possibility that P is a law of nature; we might assert a counterfactual whose antecedent can be true only at a world where P is a law of nature. In each case, in order for what we are saying to remain true and significant, the context must shift in such a way that the salient theory becomes one relative to which P is a law. In some cases, enough will be said in the context to pick out the new salient theory uniquely—for example, when

[40] For example, the phrase 'the cat' usually refers to the unique cat who is present or visible, if there is one. But when you are over at my house, playing with my cat Tina, and you suddenly exclaim, 'Oh no! I forgot to feed the cat before I left home!' this default is canceled, and your use of 'the cat' refers to your own poor cat, who is at your house starving, rather than to well-fed Tina, whom you did not forget to feed simply because it was never on your agenda to feed her. Here, the referent of 'the cat' shifts in the way that makes your utterance true. A classic discussion of this kind of phenomenon is Lewis (1979b).

someone says 'Consider a possible world where Newtonian mechanics is true.' In other cases, the new salient theory will be only as determinate as it has to be in order to make what we have said about the other possible worlds we are considering true, with the result that some of what we go on to say about those other possible worlds might be neither determinately true nor determinately false—not because of any indeterminacy in the worlds themselves, but because of an indeterminacy in the truth conditions for law-statements in the context we now inhabit.

Putting all of this together into a proposal:

> **MT3**: The default salient theory in a context k is that theory which comprises all the true theoretical commitments of the members of the extended epistemic community of the speakers. But this default is canceled, and another theory becomes the salient one, whenever this is necessary in order for (i) someone's statement about the laws of some non-actual world to be true, or (ii) someone's modal statement about laws of nature to be true, or (iii) the antecedent of someone's counterfactual-conditional statement to be true at any possible world. When that happens, if a particular scientific theory has been singled out for attention, it becomes the salient theory; otherwise, if there is a unique theory T such that the modal or counterfactual statement that has been asserted would be true if T were salient, then T becomes the salient theory; otherwise, it becomes indeterminate what the salient theory is, but determinate that the salient theory is one that renders the asserted modal statements or counterfactual antecedents true.

That is quite a mouthful, but the key point can be summarized very simply: when we are talking about the laws of other possible worlds, the salient theory shifts in whatever way is necessary to make what we say both true and significant.

The whole meta-theoretic conception of laws is on the table now; it consists of the conjunction of MT1, MT2, and MT3. Now let's turn to considering some objections.

3.3.9 The problem of laws without theories, part 1: empirical law-candidates

MT2 says that in any context where it is true that P is a law of nature, there is some true salient theory T in which P plays the law role. This claim must face an important objection. Not only the scientifically ignorant (like Bob the *Star Trek* commentator) make statements and conjectures about the laws of nature when they have no particular theory in mind. Sometimes, a scientist will hypothesize that something is a law of nature, even when no one has yet articulated a theory of which it might be a law. For example, Boyle's famous experiments with the air-pump led him to propose his famous gas law: at the time, this law was only an empirically discovered regularity, fitting into no broader theory within which it could play the law role. Thus, MT2 seems to imply that Boyle spoke falsely when he called his law a law of nature.[41]

A related difficulty concerns Bohr's model of the hydrogen atom. Bohr in effect proposed that it is a law of nature that the energies of electrons in a hydrogen atom can only take a certain discrete set of values. We now take this to be a law of nature, but this is because it is a consequence of laws of quantum mechanics, a theory that Bohr was not privy to at the time he proposed his model of the atom. In fact, Bohr's regularity was part of a theory of the atom that was known to be false (since it is incompatible with the long-term stability of hydrogen atoms). It seems that there is no true theory within which Bohr's regularity plays the law role that was accepted by any scientist at the time. So, if Bohr had said in 1920 that his regularity was a law of nature, then MT2 seems to imply that he would have spoken falsely. And this seems implausible.

In the Boyle case, no theory at all has been articulated within which the regularity in question plays any role at all; in the Bohr case, the relevant regularity does fit into a theory, and might even play the law role within that theory, but that theory is false. The worry is that in cases like these, the empirical regularity might actually be a law of nature, in which case we want to count the scientist's conjecture as true. But the meta-theoretic conception of laws seems to make that conjecture false automatically. What is common to each case is that we have a conjecture that a certain empirically confirmed regularity is a law, in the absence of a true theory of which it is a law. I will call such conjectures *empirical law candidates*. The objection to MT2 here is that it seems to make all attributions of lawhood to empirical law candidates false, whereas it seems very plausible to say that such an attribution could be true.

[41] Actually, Boyle didn't call his law a 'law'; in fact, he objected to the idea that non-human nature obeys laws. But it would be a cheap move to defend the meta-theoretic conception from this worry by appealing to this convenient fact.

I will use the Boyle and Bohr cases as my main examples, taking it for granted that their law-statements were true. Perhaps these cases are not clean examples, since Boyle's and Bohr's putative laws are not really laws of nature. But the Boyle and Bohr cases are well-known examples that are good approximations to the kind of case I am worried about. Here I will indulge in the useful fiction that their law-statements in fact succeeded in stating things that are laws of currently accepted theories. A fictional example could easily make the same point, at the cost of being unfamiliar.

One way to deal with these cases is to note that it seems natural for us to say retrospectively that Boyle's and Bohr's law-statements were true, because today, in our present context, there are salient theories within which their propositions play the law role, and we take these theories to be true. At least, we take these theories to be true *whenever we take Boyle's and Bohr's law-statements to be true*. To the extent that we are skeptical or tentative of current scientific theories, we are skeptical or tentative about the truth of the law-statements in question. And to the extent that we are sympathetic to anti-realist treatments of these theories, we are also sympathetic to anti-realist treatments of those law-statements. The problem arises because in some contexts, it seems right to say that Boyle and Bohr spoke truly when they made their respective law-statements; in these contexts, there are salient theories, which we take to be true, within which their statements play the law role. So, although the statements made by Boyle and Bohr were false in the contexts in which they were made, they are true in our context. Since we evaluate these statements in our own context, we reach the intuitive judgment that they are true.

But this might not seem like enough. If Boyle had said, 'Humans have walked on the moon,' then what he said would have been false when he said it, though the very same sentence would be true in our own context. This would not create any illusory appearance that Boyle had spoken truly. Why should things be any different in the case of a law-statement? Why should the fact that Boyle's law-statements are true in our context create any illusion that he spoke truly at the time even if he did not? It simply seems that Boyle *spoke truly*; it does not merely seem that the same sentence he uttered would be true if uttered in our own context. Perhaps it is relevant that the context-dependence of tensed statements is a well-known phenomenon, even among people who never explicitly think about context-dependence, whereas the context-dependence of law-statements is esoteric; maybe there is no illusory appearance of Boyle's having said something true in the human-on-the-moon case simply because we just can't help noticing that Boyle would have said something false in his own context if he had said that humans had been to the moon, whereas it is easy to fail to notice this in the nomological case. But I don't know what to say here, and won't pursue the matter further.

One way to deal with this problem is to interpret MT2 tenselessly—that is, as referring to the theory that includes all and only the true theoretical commitments that the members of the speaker's community *ever* accept, and not just the ones that are accepted at the time of utterance. On this interpretation of MT2, if Boyle's and Bohr's epistemic communities went on to develop and accept true theories within which their regularities played the law role, this would be enough to make their law-statements true. On this view, the semantics of Boyle's and Bohr's law-statements were not fully determinate at the time they made them: their truth conditions depended in part on things that happened later. This is a special case of a more general phenomenon: the semantic values of our expressions sometimes fail to supervene on our past and present history; sometimes, they depend on what is going to happen later. Mark Wilson has argued that this phenomenon is widespread.[42]

I think this maneuver has considerable appeal. But it also has a significant disadvantage: it suggests that if humanity had been wiped out by a plague, after Boyle announced his law but before the modern kinetic theory of gases had been developed, then his law-statement would have been false—though it is true in the actual world. This seems wrong, because it seems to make the truth or falsity of Boyle's statement depend on the future history of humanity. And Boyle was not, after all, issuing any predictions about future human history.

There are at least two ways in which a defender of MT2 can interpret the statements of Boyle and Bohr in a way that makes them out to have said things that were both true (in their own contexts) and independent of the future course of history. On the first interpretation, when Boyle and Bohr called their respective empirical law candidates 'laws of nature,' they were not using this expression in its strict sense, but in a looser, honorific sense. In effect, they were saying: 'Here is a striking and simple regularity that we

[42] Wilson (1982).

have great evidence to believe holds quite generally. Let us dignify it with a dignified name.' There would be nothing wrong with saying something like this. It would involve using the term 'law' in a loose sense, but this would not be a crime. We know that scientists and other people do often use 'law' in such a loose sense—there is the law of large numbers, Leibniz's law, the law of diminishing returns, and so-called law of causality, none of which is a serious candidate for lawhood in the strict sense.

Another possibility is that each man was in effect conjecturing that there was a true theory to be found, that perhaps would be found soon, within which his law functioned as a law. On this interpretation, each was effectively using 'this regularity is a law of nature' as elliptical for 'there is a true theory to be found, which we are in hot pursuit of, within which this regularity plays the role of a law.' Thoughts like this not uncommonly play a heuristic role in the development of scientific theory: when a striking empirical regularity has been noted, it is desired to find a general theory that explains it, by virtue of its being a consequence of that theory's laws. What is desired in this case is not simply a theory that *says that* the regularity in question is a law. Theories like that are cheap. What is desired is a theory with a certain sort of generality and unity, within which the regularity (or, something that implies it, or something that implies it given certain prevailing conditions) *functions as* a law—plays the theoretical role distinctive of laws. Thus, Newton sought a theory that Galileo's and Kepler's so-called 'laws' would fall out of, and Schrödinger, Heisenberg, and others sought a theory whose laws would imply the quantum-related regularities noted by Planck, Bohr, Einstein, and others. Calling an empirical regularity a 'law' might sometimes function as a way of marking it as a target explanandum, which we hope to explain by deriving it from the laws (proper) of a new theory.

We have seen four strategies by which a defender of MT2 can accommodate the intuition that when scientists conjecture that some empirical law candidate is a law of nature, they speak truly. The first strategy is to point out that we naturally interpret these conjectures as true, because they are true in the context we find ourselves in, even though they were false in the contexts in which they were originally made. The second is to say that the salient theory is the theory that the relevant experts in the speaker's community eventually accepts, and since this community is temporally extended, which theory that is might not yet be settled at the time of the speaker's utterance. The third is to say that such conjectures really only apply an honorific to the empirical law candidate, marking it as worthy of special attention. The fourth is to say that the scientist is conjecturing that the empirical law candidate is a law of a true theory that we may be able to discover soon, together with a recommendation that we seek such a theory. On this interpretation, calling an empirical law candidate a 'law of nature' is a heuristic guide to finding a new theory: we desire a theory within which something that plays the law role explains why this regularity obtains.

On none of these four interpretations is any attribution of lawhood to an empirical law candidate true (i) given a strict reading of the phrase 'law of nature,' (ii) in the context where it was made, and (iii) in a way that is independent of the future course of human history. But such an attribution of lawhood can be true subject to any two of these three qualifications on at least one of the four interpretations. It seems to me that this gives us the resources to explain our intuition that such attributions can be true.

Which of the four interpretations is the right one? I doubt that there is a single correct answer. In some cases where it seems to us that an attribution of lawhood to an empirical law candidate is true, this is because we are evaluating the attribution in our own context instead of the context in which it was made; in some cases, the most natural way to interpret such an attribution involves a temporally externalist semantics (*à la* Wilson); in some cases, the attributor seems to have said something true simply because the empirical law candidate is indeed a striking regularity deserving of special attention; in some cases, the attribution seems true because it was vindicated by the discovery of a theory whose laws explain the regularity. In some cases, the intuition may be explained in an overdetermined way by two or more of the four strategies. The right explanation of our intuitions about a particular case depends on the details of the case.

3.3.10 The problem of laws without theories, part 2: the case of Serendipides

There is a different sort of case that MT2 cannot handle so easily. Serendipides, a little-known Ionian philosopher from the fifth century BCE, once wrote: 'It is a law of nature that no ponderable body shall ever travel with greater swiftness than that of light.'[43] He made this remark in passing in the course of a treatise explaining how all bodies are composed of tiny droplets

[43] My thanks to Professor George P. Burdell for his help with the translation.

of castor oil. This treatise did not successfully articulate any true theory within which his alleged law played anything like the law role. In fact, Serendipides did not articulate any theory in which his alleged law plays any significant theoretical role whatsoever.

It seems to us as if what Serendipides wrote was true (about the speed of light, not about the castor oil). Yet, if MT2 is correct, then it was certainly false in the context in which Serendipides wrote it. The second, third, and fourth strategies for accommodating empirical law candidates are clearly inapplicable to the case of Serendipides; it seems that the only option for the meta-theoretic conception is to say that Serendipides's remark seems true to us only because it would be true if uttered in our present context. This is counterintuitive. It seems that Serendipides's claim was not at all justified; it was merely a lucky guess. But lucky guesses can be true after all, and the Serendipides guess seems a prime example. Here I think a friend of the meta-theoretic conception must bite the bullet. But the difficulty here is not really that painful; 'grin and bear it' might be more apt than 'bite the bullet.' After all, we do have an explanation of why it seems to us as if Serendipides spoke truly—for he would have spoken truly had he made his claim in our own context. Furthermore, the concept of a law of nature is one that plays its distinctive roles primarily in the context of scientific discussions; *ex hypothesi*, Serendipides's remark is not made or applied in any such context. Our intuitions about the truth values of law-statements made outside their primary context should not carry much weight in our theorizing about such statements.

In conclusion, although we do find it intuitive to think true many conjectures of the form 'P is a law of nature,' where P is an empirical law candidate that does not yet have a home in any articulated theory in which it plays the law role, this is not a decisive objection to the meta-theoretic conception of laws or to MT2. But of course, this fact alone gives us no positive reason to accept the meta-theoretic conception.

3.3.11 Undiscovered laws of nature

Consider sentence UL:

UL: There are laws of nature that haven't been discovered yet.

UL is undoubtedly true. If we interpret it at face value, and assume MT2, then UL is true in our present context just in case there is a theory T and a proposition P such that T is true, T is salient in our present context, P plays the law role in T, and it has not yet been discovered that P is true. This might be so if T is some theory we all accept and P is a logical consequence of the laws of T that no one has managed to work out yet. But this is clearly not all that we mean when we assert UL: it isn't just that there are laws that are consequences of laws we already know but that we haven't managed to derive from the known laws yet; in addition, there are undiscovered laws that are not part of any theory anyone has ever yet come up with. That is, UL* is true:

> UL*: There are laws of nature that are not part of the content of any theory that has been discovered yet.

MT2 implies that UL* is true only if there is a theory T that is salient in our present context even though no one has ever thought of it before. This seems impossible: how can a theory be salient in our present context if no one has ever even thought that theory up yet? And this seems like a big problem for MT2, and indeed for the whole meta-theoretic approach to laws.

Here's how I think a friend of the meta-theoretic approach should deal with this issue. Consider sentence UTT:

> UTT: There are undiscovered true theories, some of which posit unknown laws.

From a common-sense point of view, before the meta-theoretic conception is on the table, UTT seems a sensible thing to say (though perhaps an overly wordy thing to say). In fact, it seems to amount to pretty much the same thing as UL*; its evident truth is arguably what makes us confident that UL* is true. On the meta-theoretic conception, UTT almost certainly is true: it is true just in case there are theories no one has discovered yet, which are true, and within which some propositions (that are true but as of yet unknown) play the law role. From a meta-theoretic perspective, UTT seems to say articulately exactly what UL* is trying to say: namely, that we don't know everything about the universe yet, that there are new truths to discover, that some of those truths are such that if we did discover them then we would recognize them to be laws. So, in saving the truth of UTT, the meta-theoretic conception seems to me to do justice to the intuition that UL* is true.[44]

3.4 Some examples of meta-theoretic accounts

3.4.1 What is a 'role within a theory'?

There are potentially infinitely many different philosophical accounts of laws that endorse the meta-theoretic conception of laws. What they all have in common is that they endorse MT1, MT2, and MT3. They differ from one another in how they identify the law role—the R that occurs in the schema MT1. All meta-theoretic accounts must agree that whether a proposition plays the law role R within a theory T must supervene on the non-nomic content of T. So a meta-theoretic account cannot say, for example, that P plays R in T just in case T says that P is a law of nature; this would fit the form of MT1 but it would represent a collapse back into the first-order conception of laws.

What belongs to the 'non-nomic content' of T? The rough-and-ready answer is: all of T that you can formulate without using the term 'law of nature,' or any of its cognates, such as 'nomological necessity' and 'nomological possibility.' We should add that the non-nomic content of T must not contain propositions that can be stated only by using other concepts that are obviously very closely related to that of a law of nature—for example, the concept of a causal power, that of a necessitation relation between universals, or the counterfactual conditional.

To see why, consider for a moment a simplified version of the Armstrong-Dretske-Tooley view of laws, according to which it is a law of nature that all Fs are Gs just in case the universal F bears a necessitation relation to the

[44] An anonymous referee pointed out that one might hold the view that there could be laws of nature that cannot be encapsulated within any theory at all. It seems to me that anyone who endorses the meta-theoretic conception of laws must bite the bullet and deny this possibility. But I am not sure how great a cost this is. One might endorse the meta-theoretic conception of laws as an explication of the law-governed world-picture, as I articulated that picture back in Chapter 1—which includes the idea that the laws of nature are in principle within the ken of science (which they would presumably not be if some laws could not even be articulated by a scientific theory). Thus, one could leave open the possibility that a first-order account of laws is correct—but only if laws as such might in principle exceed our epistemic grasp. In fact, this is one way of stating the conclusion of Chapter 4.

universal G. This is a clear case of a first-order account of laws: it holds that universals and their relations to one another are out there in the world, independent of us and our theories, that laws of nature are instances of universals being related by a certain kind of relation, and that the central aims of science include discovering what universals there are and which ones stand in this special relation to one another—in other words (according to this account), one of the central aims of science is to discover which propositions are the laws of nature. But now, suppose that we allowed the 'non-nomic content' of a theory T to include everything that T says about universals, and about necessitation relations among universals. Then we could easily formulate this simple first-order account of laws as a meta-theoretic account, by defining the law role R as follows:

> The proposition P plays R in T just in case P is of the form *F stands in the necessitation relation to* G and T says or entails that P is true.

But this simplified version of the Armstrong-Dretske-Tooley account clearly should not be allowed to count as a meta-theoretic account—it is the very paradigm of a first-order account of laws! In order to avoid having to admit that this account can after all be formulated as a meta-theoretic account, we must not allow the non-nomic content of a theory T to include what T has to say about the necessitation relations holding among universals. This doesn't seem at all ad hoc: one of the core ideas of the meta-theoretic conception of laws is that science is not in the business of formulating theories that tell us, literally and explicitly, what the laws are. If this is right, then surely science is also not in the business of formulating theories that tell us, literally and explicitly, which universals bear necessitation relations to which others. And more generally, if scientific theories aren't in the business of explicitly specifying the extension of lawhood, they shouldn't be in the business of explicitly specifying anything else in terms of which lawhood can be plausibly analyzed—for if they were, then they would effectively provide information about which propositions are laws. First-order theorists of laws have made plausible cases for analyses of lawhood in terms of nomological necessity, counterfactual conditionals, and causal powers;[45] these accounts are as plausible as they are to a large

[45] For an account of lawhood in terms of counterfactuals, see Lange (2000); Harre and Madden (1975) give an account of laws in terms of causal powers.

extent because it is plausible that the concept of a law is closely related to the concepts of a true counterfactual and a causal power. So, what makes these accounts at least initially plausible by the same token rules out their raw materials from having any place in the non-nomic content of a scientific theory—telling us about which counterfactuals are true and which kinds of things have which causal powers comes dangerously close to telling us what the laws of nature are, so the non-nomic content of a theory can't tell us that. And this, in turn, heads off the objection that by fixing up the law role R just right, we can re-formulate any of these first-order accounts of laws as meta-theoretic accounts—the law role R cannot, for example, be the role played in a theory T by all and only the propositions entailed by T that tells us which counterfactuals are true, or which kinds of things have which causal powers, for *that* role fails to supervene on the non-nomic content of T.

So, the non-nomic content of a theory cannot include anything the theory says about counterfactuals, causal powers, necessitation relations among universals, or anything else that shares the modal character of laws. What can it include? Well, to begin with, it can include every proposition implied by the theory that concerns only the occurrent properties and relations among objects, and regularities (whether strict or statistical) among these. More generally, it can include any proposition entailed by the theory that does not depend for its truth on logically contingent counterfactuals, or on the natural modalities (such as causal necessity and physical possibility).

But the non-nomic content of a theory need not be restricted to propositions it entails. A scientific theory T should not, for present purposes, be thought of simply as a set of propositions, or a set of abstract models. The things that have laws are scientific theories as they are formulated, tested, and applied by scientists. So theories come with a family of practical methods for hooking them up with the world—methods of empirically determining the values of the quantities that the theory posits, for example. Newtonian mechanics in isolation from all empirical methods of determining masses, positions, or times would be an interesting abstract object to perform logical and mathematical investigations on, but it would not be an empirical theory of the natural universe. Since it is only empirical theories of the natural universe that clearly posit laws of nature, we should allow that a theory may include such additional elements. This might make it difficult to individuate particular theories in some cases—when we acquire a new way of observing electrons without any change in the theoretical propositions about electrons that we believe, have we adopted a new theory? Or are we still using the same old theory? In cases like this, it seems to me that there may be no determinate answer. In this case, theory-identity is vague.[46] And so, whether proposition P is a law of theory T might be a vague matter as well—since P might play the law role within some of the possible precisifications of T but not others. None of this seems disturbing or even surprising. Once we make it sufficiently precise which theory we are talking about, it should be sufficiently precise which propositions are its laws—but sufficient precision here might be more demanding than sufficient precision in some other contexts.

What I mean by *a role played within a theory T* is just something shared in common by some set of propositions entailed by T, where which propositions share this something-in-common supervenes on the non-nomic content of T. The non-nomic content of T can include practices and methods associated with the application of T as well as the non-nomological propositions that T entails. There are clearly many different such 'roles,' and so there are many different possible meta-theoretic accounts of laws. Let's look at a few of them.

3.4.2 Two regularity meta-theoretic accounts

According to the much-maligned *naive regularity account* of laws, it is a law of nature that P just in case P is a true universal generalization, in which only purely qualitative (i.e., non-gruesome) predicates occur. Whatever its other faults, the naive regularity account might have the virtue of being the simplest possible philosophical account of laws that not all reasonable people would immediately reject out of hand. Indeed, contemporary discussions of the philosophical problem of laws often begin with the naive regularity account, on the assumption that it will strike most readers as 'the obvious answer.'

The naive regularity account is a first-order account, but there is a meta-theoretic account that parallels it, and is perhaps the most obvious and simplest meta-theoretic account of laws. We might call it the *naive*

[46] Of course, this does not automatically imply that theories are 'vague entities,' whatever that might mean. It could just be that our names for particular theories are not nailed down with complete precision, so that there is no hard fact of the matter about which of a few different theories is the one called by a given name.

regularity meta-theoretic account, or 'NRM account' for short. It fills in the schema MT1 in this way:

> **MT1-NRM**: P is a law of T iff: (i) T entails P; and (ii) P is a universal generalization in which only purely qualitative predicates occur.

The similarity to the naive regularity account is obvious, but the two accounts of laws are not equivalent.[47] One way to see why is to note that one of the disastrous consequences of the naive regularity account is not a consequence of the NRM account. What I have in mind is the collapse of the distinction between laws of nature and accidental regularities: surely there are some universal regularities that just happen to be true, but are not consequences of the laws of nature. Standard examples include that all moas die before reaching the age of fifty, and that all spheres of solid gold are less than a mile in diameter. According to the naive regularity account of laws, these are, if true, laws of nature. But the NRM account disagrees. Suppose it is indeed true that all moas die before reaching the age of fifty; unless that generalization is implied by some true scientific theory that is salient in our present context, 'It is a law of nature that all moas die before reaching the age of fifty' is false in our present context—or to put it more simply: it is not a law of nature that all moas die before reaching the age of fifty. (So I say, truly, in this context.) So on the NRM account, it is not enough for something to be a true regularity for it to count as a law of nature; in order for it to count as a law of nature in a given context, it must be a consequence of a true salient theory in that context.

So the NRM account of laws is free of one of the shortcomings of the first-order naive regularity account. But that is not to say that it is at all attractive! It suffers from difficulties enough. For example, it does not allow for there to be such things as *accidental regularities according to a theory*. On the theory of Newton's *Principia*, recall, it is true but not a law that all of the planets go around the sun in the same direction. According to the NRM account, this cannot be: if it is true that all planets go around

[47] As I have formulated them, neither the naive regularity account nor the NRM account satisfies the requirement that every logically contingent consequence of a law must itself be a law, since a universal generalization has consequences that are not themselves universal generalizations. This can be fixed by adding a simple closure clause to each account. But it hardly seems worth the effort; neither account has much going for it.

the sun in the same direction according to Newton's theory, then this regularity must be among the laws of that theory. For this reason (among many others that it would be tedious to list), we should not accept this meta-theoretic account of laws. But it serves as a useful illustration of what a meta-theoretic account of laws could be like, and how a meta-theoretic account will typically differ from any first-order account of laws—even one that is superficially quite similar to it.

In general, for any philosophical account of laws of a reductive Humean bent—any account that purports to reduce the laws of nature to the non-nomological facts—there will be a corresponding meta-theoretic account, that parallels it in the way that the NRM account parallels the naive regularity account. For example, consider David Lewis's best-system analysis, or BSA: it says that the laws of nature are the generalizations that appear as theorems in the best deductively closed system of truths, where the best such system is the one that achieves the best combination of simplicity and information content. The parallel meta-theoretic account, which we might call the *best-system meta-theoretic account*, or BSM account, fills in the schema MT1 in this way:

> **MT1-BSM**: P is a law of T iff P is a member of the best system of non-nomological propositions entailed by T.

Here, instead of looking at all the deductively closed systems that are true, we look at all the deductively closed systems that are included within the consequences of the theory T. This makes room for there to be accidental regularities of a theory, in the same way that the first-order BSA makes room for accidental regularities full-stop: a theory T might entail that every F is a G, though this regularity does not find a place within the best system of propositions entailed by T.

But like the NRM account, the BSM account faces important difficulties. In particular, the problems I raised for the BSA in Sections 1.3 and 1.6 do not seem to depend on the BSA's being a first-order account; they seem to arise equally for the BSM.

3.4.3 The inductive-regularity meta-theoretic account

The two meta-theoretic regularity accounts considered above both identify the law role R as something that supervenes on the propositional content of a theory. In this section, I'll present a simple example of a meta-theoretic account that allows the law role to depend on aspects of a theory other than its propositional content.

One of the traditional ways of trying to sophisticate the naive regularity account of laws is to identify the laws as the regularities that are discoverable in a certain way. In particular, the thought goes, laws are regularities that can be discovered by an inductive inference from empirically discovered instances, without any need for an exhaustive enumeration of the instances. This thought lends itself naturally to a particular meta-theoretic account of laws.

Suppose that we have a scientific theory T, which has a rich propositional content including many universal and statistical regularities, and is also associated with a family of empirical methods for ascertaining the values of physical quantities that are referred to in its propositional content. Some of the regularities implied by T have *instances* that can be empirically confirmed using the empirical methods associated with T. But what is an instance? Well, for a universal regularity of the form *All Fs are Gs*, an instance is an F that is a G, and for a statistical regularity of the form *the probability of Fx conditional on Gx is p*, an instance is likewise an F that is a G.[48] What is it for such an instance to be confirmable using the empirical methods associated with T? This is just for those methods to include methods that can be used to ascertain empirically whether something is an F, and whether it is a G.

Now, the idea that a law of a theory is a regularity of that theory that has been discovered empirically via inductive inferences, and not via confirming all of its instances one by one, can be expressed by the following fleshing-out of the schema MT1:

MT1-IRM:

- P is a *basic law* of T iff: (i) T entails P; (ii) P has instances all of which are in principle empirically confirmable using the practical methods associated with T; (iii) T does not entail that there are no instances of P other than those that are themselves entailed by T.

[48] This is too simple to be a general account of what instances are. A full account of instancehood would deal with the question of whether an instance of P must also be an instance of every generalization that is logically equivalent to P, and with the infamous problem of whether a white tennis shoe is an instance of *All ravens are black*. I don't want to get bogged down in this issue here, though: I am just trying to provide an illustrative example of a meta-theoretic account. Anyone who wanted to defend the account I am using for an example in earnest would have to fill in more details than I am providing here.

- P is a *law of T* iff P is a conceptually contingent proposition that is entailed by the basic laws of T.

This implies that the laws of T are included among the regularities entailed by T, but it allows that not every regularity entailed by T is among T's laws. There are two different ways in which a regularity R can be entailed by T and yet fail to count as a law of T according to MT1-IRM, and both of them are ways in which R might belong to the content of T without having been arrived at inductively by the framers of T.

First, T might entail a regularity R by means of entailing a complete list of R's instances, and entailing that R has no more instances. For example, if T is the theory of Newton's *Principia*, then it entails that there are exactly six planets, and that each planet goes around the sun counter-clockwise (as viewed from above the earth's north pole). This regularity does not count as a law of T, since it does not satisfy clause (iii): T entails that there are no more instances of this regularity than the six instances that T itself entails. This regularity is not discovered inductively, by means of empirically confirming some of its instances without confirming all of them; it has been discovered deductively by means of discovering every single one of its instances.

Second, R's instances might fail to be empirically confirmable via the practical methods associated with T. So, for example, let 'Big S' be a name that we have introduced stipulatively as a rigid name of whatever speed happens to be the least upper bound on the speeds that ravens ever achieve; in other words, 'Big S' is synonymous with 'DTHAT: the speed s such that either: (i) at some time some raven will travel at speed s and at no time will any raven travel at any speed greater than s; or (ii) at no time will any raven travel at speed s, but for every speed s' less than s, at some time some raven travels at s'.' If our theory T implies that there is a universal speed limit (such as the speed of light), then it thereby implies that there is some upper bound on the speeds that ravens will ever achieve, without specifying that upper bound.[49] So, in this case, T will entail that 'Big S' refers to some particular speed, and it will also imply that *every raven always travels at a speed no greater than Big S.* This latter regularity has not been confirmed inductively; it has been discovered more or less a priori by means of the trick of introducing

[49] We can accommodate the frame-relativity of speed by stipulating that throughout, 'speed' is short for 'speed in the Earth's rest-frame.'

the name 'Big S.' So we should hope to exclude it from counting as a law of T, if we think that laws are regularities that can and must be discovered inductively. And indeed, it is excluded by MT1-IRM: the instances of this regularity are not such that the practical methods associated with T will suffice to confirm them. An instance would be a raven who is flying at a speed less than Big S; since the value of Big S cannot be ascertained by means of any observation procedure, we cannot discover by means of any such procedure whether a given raven is flying at a speed less than Big S.[50]

MT1-IRM thus provides the core of a meta-theoretic account of laws according to which the laws of theory T are those regularities implied by T which, in a reasonably intuitive sense, must have been arrived at via inductive inference from particular empirically discovered instances of them by the scientists who accept T. Let's call this account the *inductive regularity meta-theoretic account*, or the IRM account for short. It is interesting to note that the IRM account has the consequence that God's Own Theory (which was introduced back in Section 3.3.3) has no laws at all, since it includes every instance of every regularity as well as the fact that there are no more instances. Since there are other, weaker, true theories that do have laws according to the IRM account, it follows that the IRM account rejects Monotonicity. The meta-theoretic account that I will endorse in Chapter 9 shares these features.

This is not the only way in which the meta-theoretic account I will defend resembles the IRM account. That account—the Measurability Account of Laws, or the MAL—can be roughly summarized by saying that the laws of a theory T are all those regularities (whether strict or statistical) implied by T that (i) represent correlations between the values of magnitudes that are measurable via the empirical methods associated with T, and (ii) do not fall into one of a short list of categories of regularities that must be excluded. These categories of regularities that must be excluded all happen to consist of regularities that are plausibly thought of as having been discovered by some means other than induction from observed instances.[51]

[50] Of course, we can indirectly discover that a given raven is flying at a speed that is less than Big S by observing another raven that is flying faster than it. But not every instance of our regularity can be empirically confirmed in this way, even in principle: when we come across the fastest raven ever at her peak of swiftness, this indirect method will be useless.

[51] One excluded class consists of those regularities that express the reliability of testimony from certain experts; another excluded class consists of regularities that are implied by T because T implies all of their instances; a third class consist of regularities that are implied by T only because of what T tells

So the MAL appears to be very close in spirit to the IRM account; you might think of the MAL as a more sophisticated attempt to capture the idea that the IRM is based on. However, this is not at all the way that I will motivate the MAL. In Chapters 5 through 8, I will develop a very different line of thought that leads naturally to the MAL. This line of thought begins with reflections on the relations between laws and counterfactuals. It may be that an entirely different line of thought that begins with reflection on the relation between laws and induction can lead to the same conclusion; the similarity between the MAL and the IRM certainly suggests this. But this is an avenue I won't explore further in this book.

3.5 The virtues of the meta-theoretic conception

Why should we take the meta-theoretic conception seriously? I have mentioned one reason: we do not usually need to be told what the laws of a given scientific theory are. Provided with an exposition of the non-nomological content of a theory, and an introduction to its use and application, we can just tell which propositions ought to be called its laws. The way we seem to do this is by recognizing which propositions play the same role as propositions that are called laws in other theories we are already familiar with. This creates the strong impression that to be a law of a theory is not simply to be called a law by that theory; it is to play a distinctive role within that theory.

Another reason has to do with the ways in which laws are proposed and invoked in giving theoretical explanations of empirical regularities. It is a victory for science when a theory is developed which, in terms of a relatively small and simple set of laws, accounts for a wide range of empirical regularities. But such victories are not cheap: you cannot just write up the empirical regularities you want to explain in the most compact form you can think of, and append 'It is a law that' to the front of them in order to achieve a theoretical explanation. This is one way of taking the point of the infamous thirty-third footnote of Hempel and Oppenheim's 'Studies

us about the values of certain measurable quantities. In none of these cases is the regularity supported solely by means of induction from an observed subset of its instances. The details are found below in Section 8.6.

in the Logic of Explanation': Newton's theory seems to explain Galileo's law of free fall and Kepler's laws of planetary motion by deducing them (or approximations to them) from his laws.[52] The same thing could not have been achieved by simply taking the conjunction of these regularities and calling it a law. But there is a kind of theoretical understanding that we get from Newton's theory that we would not get from a theory that simply listed the regularities to be explained. What accounts for the difference?

Friedman and Kitcher have offered the answer that we get genuine explanation of empirical regularities only when we can explain them using a theory that *unifies* these regularities.[53] Each offers a different account of how to measure the degree of unification provided by a theory. Without going into the details of their specific proposals, it is not hard to see that there is something to their basic idea: not just any list of regularities counts as explaining a set of empirically confirmed generalizations. That list must somehow cohere into a theory that is unified and unifying, in some sense that is not easy to make explicit but not difficult to recognize when you see it.

One of the main functions laws of nature are supposed to play in science is that of providing the starting points of explanations. If you show how something follows from the laws of nature, then there is a sense in which you have explained it (though this might not answer every explanation-seeking why-question you want to ask about it). Suppose we have found a great deal of confirming evidence for the regularities R1, R2, and R3. On the first-order conception of laws, there is no reason why we could not formulate a theory that says that R1, R2, and R3 are all laws of nature, and stops there. But unless this theory turns out to be unified and unifying (which only happens rarely), we will not take this to be a satisfactory explanation. You might say that the reason for this is that we will not have sufficient evidence to be justified in believing that R1, R2, and R3 are laws of nature. But this is a mere epistemological problem. If for some reason, we *just believed* that R1, R2, and R3 were all laws, it still seems as if we would not feel that we had a satisfactory explanation of why R1, R2, R3, and all their consequences were true. You might say that this is because we will still want to know why R1, R2, and R3 are laws; our explanatory thirst will not have been fully quenched. But this is always

[52] Hempel and Oppenheim (1965), p. 273.

[53] Friedman (1974); Kitcher (1981).

true whenever a law-positing theory is used to explain something: at some point, explanations come to a stop at an unexplained explainer. Newton would have liked to know why the law of universal gravitation is a law; this did not prevent him from thinking that the fact that it is a law explains why its empirical consequences are true. So why is it that we will not in general take the theory that R1, R2, and R3 are laws of nature to provide a satisfactory explanation of why all their empirical consequences hold?

One answer is that laws, simply by being laws, do not automatically provide explanations of their consequences. To explain why a certain regularity is found in the phenomena, we must not only derive it from putative laws, we must also locate those laws within a unifying theory. But in this case, it is not clear why lawhood itself should be thought to be doing any of the explanatory work. Unification alone is an explanatory virtue; the lawhood of the laws posited by a unifying theory seems to be a superfluous extra ingredient. Yet, if we are going to take seriously the idea of a law-governed world at all, it seems very important to hold onto the idea that lawhood has something important to do with explanatory power.

A more attractive answer is that only if a set of propositions cohere together to make a unified and unifying theory will those propositions be *laws*, and thus serve as suitable starting points for explanation. In other words, you cannot generate a genuine explanatory theory simply by *postulating that* some proposition is a law of nature. What you need to do is articulate a theory with certain virtues, within the context of which some propositions cohere together in a unified and unifying way. No theory provides theoretical explanation unless it achieves this sort of virtue, which is a feature of the theory as a whole. But lawhood is a property of propositions that do play a role in theoretical explanations. Not all the propositions of an explanatory theory need to be laws, of course, but laws as such are things that do play a role in theoretical explanations. Hence, lawhood is not a property a proposition can have all by itself; rather, it is a matter of belonging to the right sort of theory in the right sort of way.

Both of the reasons we have seen suggest strongly that the meta-theoretic conception of laws is worth taking seriously, but neither constitutes a conclusive argument in its favor. In the next chapter, I will try to do better, by arguing that if the first-order conception of laws is correct, then laws are not epistemically accessible to empirical science at all, but that if the meta-theoretic conception is correct, then they are. In other words, the

Lawhood Thesis and the Discoverability Thesis can both be true only if the meta-theoretic conception of laws is correct. This gives us a powerful reason for accepting the meta-theoretic conception. For if empirical science is unable to discover laws, then we can know nothing at all about them, and we have no reason to recognize them in our thinking about the natural world.

3.6 Weighing the virtues and shortcomings of the meta-theoretic conception

At the end of the day, in order to decide whether it is reasonable to adopt the meta-theoretic conception, we will need to consider both what speaks for it and what speaks against it. In this concluding section of the present chapter, I will perform a brief survey of these. This survey will be partly anticipatory of things to come, for my argument for the meta-theoretic conception is far from complete at this point.

Let me start with what speaks against the meta-theoretic conception. It denies that there are any laws of nature *simpliciter*—where a law of nature *simpliciter* is a proposition that is truly called a law of nature in any context of utterance whatsoever. The truth conditions, and the truth values, of law-statements depend on the context of utterance. This is surprising, and perhaps counterintuitive. But the reasons we have seen for denying this consequence of the meta-theoretic conception are far from conclusive. First of all, there are doubts about whether laws could have their presumed special relations to counterfactuals and scientific explanations if law-statements have a contextual semantics. But this is no objection, if the truth conditions of counterfactuals and explanatory claims themselves are context-dependent, and the context-dependencies all match up in the right way. Below (in Chapters 5 through 8), I will argue that at least for the case of counterfactuals, the context-dependencies do match up in just the right way to preserve the special relation between laws of nature and counterfactuals (in scientific contexts, at least). In this book I will not attempt to offer an account of scientific explanation. But to the extent that the relation between laws and explanation is closely related to the relation between laws and counterfactuals, it is not implausible that success with the latter will carry over to the former.

Second, there are doubts about whether a context-dependent account of law-statements can do justice to the pervasive idea that we live in a world governed by laws. As noted above, this is not an argument against the truth of the meta-theoretic conception—unless it can be supplemented with a non-question-begging argument that we do live in a universe governed by laws. Nonetheless, I will argue in the final chapter of this book that the meta-theoretic conception of laws can be combined with the idea that we live in a law-governed universe, though that idea will be somewhat transformed in the process.

The meta-theoretic conception of laws requires us to give up some of our intuitions about the truth values of various actual and hypothetical law-statements. These include both law-statements involving empirical law-candidates that have not yet been incorporated into any general theory, as well as law-statements made without empirical grounds in the absence of any significant theoretical context whatsoever (as in the case of Serendipides). In these cases, the defender of the meta-theoretic conception of laws can explain our intuitions about the truth values of such statements by supposing that we reach these intuitions by imagining the statements to have been made in the context of a conversation with us, rather than by evaluating their truth values in their own contexts. If there is a remaining intuition that such statements had the truth values we intuitively assign them even in their own proper contexts, then the meta-theoretic conception can accommodate these intuitions only by engaging in some creative reinterpretation of the statements themselves. This is a non-negligible cost of accepting the meta-theoretic conception. But as noted above, the cost is limited: it involves only rejecting some of our judgments about particular law-statements that seem to have little if anything to do with the use of law-statements in real scientific practice. I will have a little more to say about this intuitive cost below.

Now let me turn to what can be said in favor of the meta-theoretic conception. First, there is the argument of Section 3.1, that those who know a little physics are typically able to recognize the laws of a physical theory without being told explicitly what they are. This is easily explained on the hypothesis that the laws of a theory are not the propositions the theory explicitly calls 'laws,' but rather the propositions that play a certain role in that theory, and a little training in physics can endow one with the practical ability to recognize where that role is being played (even if it does not enable one to explicitly specify the role in question).

Second, there is the argument to be presented in Chapter 4. This argument establishes on the basis of plausible premises that if the first-order conception is true, then the laws of nature are in principle epistemically inaccessible to empirical natural science, but that they are not in principle inaccessible if the meta-theoretic conception is true. Finally, there is the argument of Chapters 5 through 8. If successful, this argument shows that laws can have the privileged relationship to counterfactuals that they are widely held to enjoy if and only if a particular meta-theoretic conception of laws—the MAL—is true.

Consider how the two arguments just mentioned play off against the intuitive costs of accepting the meta-theoretic conception mentioned above. It seems as if we cannot hold on to all of our intuitions here; something has to give. We cannot hold on to both:

(1) All of our intuitions about the truth values of law-statements made in certain contexts where no theory incorporating the putative law is in sight

and:

(2) Our intuition that laws of nature are in principle discoverable by the methods of empirical natural science, and our intuition that laws bear a special relation to counterfactuals.

If we want to hang on to all of (1), we must reject the meta-theoretic conception in favor of the first-order conception; if we want to hang on to all of (2), we must reject the first-order conception in favor of the meta-theoretic conception. It seems to me that the choice here is not really very difficult. Our intuition that laws are empirically discoverable, and our intuition that laws bear a special relation to counterfactuals, are pretty much non-negotiable: give up the empirical-discoverability intuition, and we make laws irrelevant to science; give up the relation-to-counterfactuals intuition, and we give up much of what is supposed to be distinctive of laws. On the other hand, to reject our intuitions about whether various actual and possible people spoke truly when they made various law-statements under conditions of theoretical ignorance is to say something surprising, but it does not involve abandoning anything crucial to our notion of a law of nature. We should give up (1), and hang on to (2).

There is more than one way to describe the choice we make here. On what seems to be the standard contemporary analytic view of the methodology of philosophy, the way to describe it is this: 'Our ultimate data points come from our pre-theoretical intuitions. Other things being equal, the best theory is the one that saves as many of the most important data points as possible. Since (2) is comprised of intuitions that are more central than the intuitions that comprise (1), the theory that saves (2) and abandons (1) does a better job of saving important phenomena than the theory that saves (1) and abandons (2).'

The other way of describing the choice is the one I find more congenial. The situation is this: we find ourselves *in media res* using a concept that we express by the term 'law of nature.' No one bothered to give this concept a precise definition before it came to be used widely. And in fact, there is no precise concept such that it is a determinate matter of fact that *it* is the concept we have been using. For virtually all of the uses we have found for the concept, it has not been necessary to nail the concept down precisely, and so we have not done so. We have a situation of *semantic indecision*: there are many possible precise meanings that could be assigned to the predicate 'is a law of nature,' and we have not chosen between them (mainly because we have not needed to). Now, we come to discover that on no precisification of the meaning of this predicate will everything that we want to say with it be true. We face a choice: not a choice between competing theories about what the objective matter of fact about the nature of laws of nature is, but a choice about how we are going to use the term 'law of nature.'

One option is not to make a choice—to leave the semantics undecided. There is no principled objection to taking that option, except that if we do, we won't be able to answer all the questions about the nature of the universe we live in that we want to answer. Those questions require, for the formulation and for their answers, precise concepts that the day-to-day business of empirical science has no use for.

Given that we want to make a choice, what we have to do in order to make it well is to figure out what the most important jobs we want the concept to do are, and what must be true in order for the concept to do those jobs. In the case at hand, we want our law-concept to mark a distinction that the empirical natural sciences are good for investigating. (Otherwise, we will have a concept marking a distinction that creatures such as ourselves cannot ever know how to apply, and that would be no good to us.) We also want our law-concept to have something important to do with counterfactuals—for their link with counterfactuals is at the heart of most of what we deem special about the things we call 'laws.' The way we classify as true or false various statements about laws made by people in various situations of theoretical ignorance is much less important. For these reasons, a meta-theoretic conception of laws supplies a much better precisification of our law-concept than any first-order conception of laws can.

Whichever way the choice among conceptions of laws is described, the foregoing argument obviously depends crucially on the arguments to be given in subsequent chapters. So let's get on with it.

4

An epistemological argument for the meta-theoretic conception of laws

4.1 The Discoverability Thesis, the Governing Thesis, and the first-order conception

It is worthwhile to bother giving a philosophical account of laws of nature at all only if the concept of a law of nature really does play an important role in empirical science. There are some philosophers who deny that it does, including van Fraassen and Giere.[1] They think that the very idea of a law of nature is a metaphysical holdover from a bygone age, which some philosophers still get excited about even though it has long since lost all of its relevance to real science. I think they're wrong about this, and so do all of the defenders of first-order accounts of laws.

Other philosophers think that, although there are such things as laws, they do not govern the universe in any but a thin metaphorical sense.[2] I also disagree with these philosophers, and it seems that the majority of philosophers who take laws of nature seriously do as well.[3]

But my aim in this chapter is not to argue that there are laws, or that the concept of a law is important to science, or that there is a genuine sense in which laws govern the universe. It is to argue that *if* we believe these three things, *then* we should accept the meta-theoretic conception of laws and reject the first-order conception. In short, the Lawhood Thesis, the

[1] van Fraassen (1989); Giere (1999).

[2] See Lewis (1994).

[3] Including Armstrong (1983), Carroll (1994), Dretske (1977), Lange (2000), Chapter 1 of Maudlin (2007), Swoyer (1982), and Tooley (1977), among many others.

Discoverability Thesis, and the Governing Thesis can all be true only if the meta-theoretic conception is right.

So here I'm just going to take it as a premise that laws of nature are within the subject matter of empirical science—that science can discover laws; in other words, that scientific inquiry can lead to justified beliefs about which propositions are laws. I will also take it for granted that laws are not just cosmic regularities in the universe; that they are in some good sense compulsory as well. I aim to show on the basis of these premises that the first-order conception of laws is subject to a devastating problem which does not afflict the meta-theoretic conception.

4.2 The main argument

Suppose that the first-order conception of laws is correct. Then, one of the questions we can expect our scientific theories to answer is, 'Which propositions are laws of nature?' It will be part of the content of a typical scientific theory that certain propositions are laws, and perhaps also that certain other propositions are not laws.

So, consider a scientific theory T, which says that one or more propositions are laws of nature. Let L be one of the propositions that T says is a law of nature. We can rewrite T as follows:

T: It is a law that L, and X

where 'X' is just whatever else T says, over and above that L is a law. Now, consider another theory, T*:

T*: L is true, but L is not a law, and X.

If the first-order conception of laws is correct, then T and T* are both genuine theories, and they are logically inconsistent with each other. So at most one of them can be true.

How might empirical evidence be used to choose between T and T*? There are two cases to consider. First, suppose that the view of laws considered back in Section 1.3 is correct: the laws of nature do not really govern the universe on this view; they are simply the regularities that comprise the cosmic order of the universe. On this view, L's being a law is a matter of its being true, and of there being a whole system of true regularities into which it fits in the right way. So, we might be able to use empirical evidence to justify preferring T to T*, or vice versa—by finding evidence that there is a set of particularly harmonious regularities into which L does or does not fit. But if the view that laws are just cosmic regularities is correct, then the laws do not govern the universe in any sense other than a figurative one. (See Sections 1.2–1.3.)

On the other hand, if the laws of nature do govern the universe in some genuine sense, then we cannot discover that L is or is not a law simply by discovering that it does or does not fit into a particularly harmonious system of regularities. In this case, the only difference the lawhood of L makes to the actual, observable course of nature will be the difference that the *truth* of L makes. L's lawhood, in other words, is screened off by its truth.

In this case, T and T* are radically empirically equivalent, in the following sense: it is a necessary truth that, if either T or T* is true, then there is a possible world (or if you like, a possible course of history) in which the other one is true, and in which all of the available empirical evidence, at every moment in history, is exactly the same as it is in the actual world.

I claim that it follows from this that it is impossible for empirical evidence to give us any good reason to believe one of these two theories rather than the other. (This is the key move in the argument. It is also the one that critics are most likely to attack. In the following sections, I will consider a wide range of objections to it. But first, I want to get the rest of the argument on the table.)

But that means that it is impossible for there to be any empirical evidence that favors T over T*, or vice versa. T is an arbitrary theory that posits at least one law, and L is an arbitrary law posited by T. So this result generalizes, yielding the conclusion that if the first-order conception is correct, then empirical evidence can never favor one theory over another, when the only difference between the two is that one of them calls a certain proposition a law and the other calls it an accidental regularity.

In other words, though scientific evidence might favor the hypothesis that some proposition is true, it can never give us a good reason to go beyond that and say that the proposition is a law of nature. Lawhood, insofar as it outruns mere truth, is beyond the epistemic scope of science.

On the other hand, suppose that the meta-theoretic conception of laws is correct. In that case, T and T* are not genuine rival theories. To see why, consider their common part, which I'll call T-Common:

T-Common: L is true, and X.

To make things simple, let's suppose that L is the only proposition that T explicitly calls a law of nature, and also that T does not explicitly deny that anything else is a law of nature.[4] In that case, T-Common is completely non-nomological: it doesn't tell us anything about which truths are laws and which ones are nomologically contingent.

So T-Common is the kind of thing that counts as a scientific theory, according to the meta-theoretic conception: it says a lot about what goes on in the world, but it does not say or entail that anything is a law of nature (or that anything is true but not a law of nature). Nonetheless, T-Common might have laws. For there might be propositions that play the law role with respect to it.

Suppose for the moment that L plays the law role within T-Common. In this case, a reasonable way to give an informal statement of T-Common would be to state what I originally called T: 'L is a law of nature, and X.' If you say that, then you specify the content of T-Common, and at the same time you make an illuminating meta-level comment about T-Common, namely that L is one of its laws. So T is analogous to a presentation of Euclidean geometry that starts out by saying, 'It is a postulate that two points determine a line.' Such a presentation says more than Euclidean geometry says—because, recall, Euclidean geometry doesn't say anything about postulates—it just says stuff about points and lines and so forth. But the extra bit that this presentation says is both true and pertinent. It's an important and correct meta-level comment on the theory that is being presented.

Let's continue supposing that L plays the law role within T-Common. What should we say about T*? Well, T* attempts to do what T does—it specifies the content of T-Common, and it makes a relevant meta-level comment about T-Common—but the meta-level comment it makes is false. So T* exhibits a special kind of incoherence. It simultaneously does

[4] In the more complicated case where T posits a number of laws, then we should formulate T-Common as: 'L+ is true, and X,' where L+ is the conjunction of all T's laws—including both the ones T* says are laws (if there are any) and the ones that T* says are true non-laws. From here on, the argument will proceed as in the text.

two things: first, it specifies the content of a theory; and second, it makes a meta-level comment about that theory, but the second part is incompatible with the first part. It gives a meta-level comment about the theory it is specifying, where that meta-level comment could not be true if the content of the theory is as specified.

So, if L plays the law role within T-Common, then T is a fine way of informally presenting T-Common, but T* is incoherent. So we do not have two incompatible theories that we must decide between on empirical grounds. We just have one theory, T-Common. T* is not a well-defined empirical theory that is a competitor to T; it is just a mess. At best, it is a confused and misleading attempt to specify T-Common.

We have been supposing that L does play the law role within T-Common. If it does not, then everything I just said goes in reverse: T* is a natural and illuminating way of presenting T-Common, and T is at best a confused and misleading attempt to do so.

In neither case do we face the epistemic disaster engendered by the first-order conception. So, if the meta-theoretic conception is right, then there is no threat to the idea that science is able to discover laws of nature. On the meta-theoretic conception, empirical evidence can be used to confirm scientific theories whose content is entirely non-nomological. Those theories do not say that various things are laws of nature, but those theories have laws, in the sense that various propositions play the law role within them. Furthermore, whenever we believe a true theory T, it would be true in our context that the laws of T are laws of nature. So, to the extent that we are justified in believing a theory T, we are justified in saying that its laws are laws of nature. The threat to the empirical discoverability of laws of nature thus evaporates when we reject the first-order conception in favor of the meta-theoretic conception.

Summing up: if the first-order conception of laws is correct, then unless the laws are just cosmic regularities that do not literally govern the universe, lawhood is not empirically discoverable. So if the Lawhood and Governing Theses are correct, then the Discoverability Thesis is correct only if the meta-theoretic conception of laws is correct.[5] Therefore, the law-governed world-picture is correct only if the meta-theoretic conception of laws is.

[5] These were introduced back in Section 1.7.

In one sense, that concludes the argument. But in another sense, it does not. The key move happened when I said that T and T* are empirically equivalent, and therefore no empirical evidence can give us a good reason to believe one of them rather than the other. This move is liable to make many philosophers suspicious, and there are a variety of objections that might be made against it. Perhaps the main burden of the argument lies in replying to these objections. I will be doing that for the remainder of this chapter.[6]

4.3 The objection from bad company

The argument of Section 4.2 bears a striking similarity to a number of historically influential, and infamous, arguments purporting to draw metaphysical consequences from epistemological premises. These arguments have a common characteristic form: 'All of our evidence concerning Xs consists of information about Ys; but information about Ys could not possibly justify belief in anything more than Zs; therefore, Xs are nothing more than Zs.' In this way, phenomenalists have argued that physical objects are nothing more than patterns in sense data, since otherwise our sensations would be impotent to tell us anything about them; logical behaviorists have argued that mental states are nothing more than behavioral dispositions, since otherwise our observations of our fellow humans would be unable to give us any knowledge about their mental states; instrumentalists have argued that unobservable posits of theoretical science are nothing more than handy devices for making predictions about the observable, since otherwise observational data would be unable to confirm hypotheses about them. Now I have argued that laws can be nothing more than non-nomic propositions that play a certain role within the structure of a scientific theory, since otherwise our evidence would be unable to confirm hypotheses about them. My argument is evidently in bad company.

This is not itself a refutation of my argument. What it does is make it reasonable to presume that there must be something wrong with my

[6] The argument above is a descendant of an argument John Earman and I gave in Earman and Roberts (2005b) for the thesis of Humean Supervenience. The conclusion of the present argument is formulated rather differently: it is that unless laws do not literally govern the universe, the meta-theoretic conception must be correct. But I will argue in Chapter 10, below, that the meta-theoretic conception entails Humean Supervenience.

argument. For my argument appears to work in pretty much the same way as the bad old arguments for phenomenalism, logical behaviorism, and instrumentalism; since nowadays we assume that those views are all wrong, there must be something wrong with the epistemological arguments that seem to support them, and whatever it is that's wrong with them is presumably wrong with my argument as well, since it works in such a similar way. In short, by now we should have learned that we play a dangerous game when we try to tailor our metaphysics to suit our epistemology.[7]

I think this is a serious worry, and it deserves a response. My response is that each of those bad old arguments had something wrong with it that we can identify, and that my argument does not share in common with it; each of them relied on an implausible, overreaching epistemological premise that my argument does not rely on. In particular, each of them relies on a premise that places a strong restriction on what can count as evidence; my argument places a much weaker and more plausible restriction on what can count as evidence.

What can count as a piece of empirical evidence is any fact that we can *observe* to be the case. What can be observed to be the case? I take it that making an observation is reaching a non-inferential judgment, at the prompting of some sensation or other, in a way that is usually reliable under normal circumstances. Our ability to make such a judgment can be (and in fact, always is) dependent on our possession of some other knowledge. Some of this knowledge might be explicitly propositional: I can observe that Heather is wearing her favorite hat only if I know that Heather's favorite hat is her dark brown one. Some of this knowledge might not be explicitly propositional: I can observe that there is a cat on top of the refrigerator only if I know how to tell cats and refrigerators when I see them. Thus, observation can require both practical and propositional knowledge: in other words, observing is an acquired skill, and observation is theory-laden.

The fact that I must already have certain knowledge in order to make a certain observation does not render the judgment I reach in observation inferential: I have to know that Heather's favorite hat is the dark brown one in order to observe that she is wearing her favorite hat, but I do not *infer* that she is wearing her favorite hat from the fact that her favorite

[7] See Carroll (1994), p. 55.

hat is the dark brown one. It might be objected that really, in this case, I infer that Heather is wearing her favorite hat from the two premises (1) that her favorite hat is the dark brown one, and (2) that she is wearing her dark brown hat—and only the second of these premises is something that I *observe* to be the case. But why should we stop there? Surely I can observe that Heather is wearing her dark brown hat only if I know that hats are garments worn on the head; so all I *really* observe is that Heather is wearing a dark brown garment on her head, and I *infer* from this, together with the premise about what hats are, that she is wearing a dark brown hat. Again, surely I can observe that Heather is wearing a dark brown garment on her head only if I know that that thing on her head is a garment rather than a part of her body, which I know only because I know what sorts of things are parts of human bodies. If we keep this up, we are eventually going to conclude that nothing is observed at all, or that what is observed is restricted either to our own sense contents or to the facing surfaces of nearby objects and their directly sensible properties. But we have learned to resist that line of thought, and we should resist it. The reasonable thing to say is that, even if I can't observe that Heather is wearing a hat without knowing that a hat is a garment worn on the head, nonetheless I can count as observing—rather than inferring—that Heather is wearing a hat. And if so, then it would be arbitrary to insist that it is different when I claim to observe that Heather is wearing her favorite hat—that this must be an inference from my knowledge about which hat is Heather's favorite together with something else that I do observe. What makes the difference between non-inferential observational judgment and inferential judgment is a matter of whether I actually draw an inference in reaching my judgment. And I need not draw any inference when I judge, as a spontaneous response to promptings from my eyes, that Heather is wearing her favorite hat, *even if* I would not be able to spontaneously reach this judgment, or reach it in a way that would normally be reliable, if I didn't know which hat was Heather's favorite.[8]

Once we grant that observation is a learned skill, that observation can be (and typically is) theory-laden (in the sense that you can only make a given observation if you have some background propositional knowledge)

[8] I think I am simply echoing Wilfrid Sellars's 'Empiricism and the Philosophy of Mind' here (Sellars 1997). But the point is not uniquely Sellarsian; it is a consequence of 'direct realism.'

and that what is characteristic of observations is their non-inferentiality and their being reliable in normal circumstances, there is no bar to allowing observations made with sophisticated scientific instruments to count as observations in the fullest sense. To insist that observations must involve no mediating equipment other than the sense organs that Mother Nature gave us would be to grant an arbitrary epistemological privilege to what is an accident of biological evolution.[9]

Given this understanding of observation, it is unwarranted to restrict the available evidence concerning physical objects to our awareness of our own sense data; we can observe physical objects directly. It is unwarranted to restrict the available empirical evidence concerning the mental states of other humans to our observations of their bodily movements: I can see, for example, that Heather did not find my joke amusing. It is likewise unwarranted to restrict the available empirical evidence relevant to the confirmation of scientific theories to the events we can detect via unaided sensation, *sans* background theory or artificial instrumentation: in the standard example, physicists with the right training can see that there is a mu meson in a bubble chamber. So the bad old arguments for phenomenalism, for logical behaviorism, and for instrumentalism are committed to implausibly strong premises that place artificial restrictions on what can count as observational evidence.

Is my argument against the first-order conception of laws based on a similar overly restrictive premise about what can count as evidence? The only assumptions about what can and cannot count as observational evidence that I made are that *we cannot observe that some proposition is a law*, and that *we cannot observe that some proposition, though true, is not a law*. Is there any reason to doubt either assumption? Are there any plausible scenarios in which someone might, at the prompting of her sensations, form a judgment to the effect that some proposition is a law, or that some proposition is a true non-law, in a way that involves drawing no inferences, and involves a mechanism that would be generally reliable when conditions are normal?

It seems to me that there simply are no such plausible scenarios. It is not just that Mother Nature has not endowed us with a lawhood-detecting sense

[9] Here, I think I am simply echoing Maxwell (1962), as well as an entire generation of critical response to van Fraassen's Constructive Empiricism (van Fraassen 1980); Churchland and Hooker (1995).

organ; there is no plausible possibility of building an artificial one, either.[10] Note that if there were such an artificial lawhood-detector, it would have to be reliable in a way that was *more than merely nomologically necessary*: for if it were enough to build a lawhood-detector that was reliable in all possible worlds with the same laws as the actual world, then it would be a trivial task to build one. Just program a computer to automatically output a list of the laws of our world, whatever they happen to be: in any possible world with the same laws as our actual world, someone who relied on this computer would always reach true judgments about what is a law and what is not. This method of 'detecting laws' would be nomologically necessarily reliable, even if the programmer programmed the machine randomly and just happened to get the right laws of our world by a lucky accident. In this case, we would not be willing to say that we have a device that lets us observe lawhood. So the requirements that a lawhood-detector would have to meet must be stronger than nomologically necessary reliability. It would have to be reliable even across possible worlds where the laws are quite different from the actual laws. But if the first-order account of laws is correct, then lawhood can vary from world to world even as everything we actually observe remains the same; no lawhood-detector could be reliable across possible worlds if that is the way things are.

As Carroll notes, it is dangerous to adopt metaphysical conclusions on the basis of epistemological premises.[11] This is because of the danger that the epistemological premises are wrong; after all, epistemology shows no signs of being about to close in on its Final Theory. But if this observation led us to issue a ban on all arguments with metaphysical conclusions and epistemological premises, it would leave metaphysics in a desperate state. In metaphysics, it isn't easy to find good premises anywhere; metaphysics

[10] Objection: 'It is not implausible that we can in some cases *just see* that some action being performed before us is morally wrong. But there is no plausible account of how to build a moral-wrongness detector, either. So this argument proves too much.' Reply: suppose that it is indeed possible to observe that some action is morally wrong. We can account for this in the following way: normal humans have a background of beliefs including the belief that *actions of kind K are morally wrong*, where actions of kind K are detectable via ordinary perception. If this is so, then there is no problem explaining how someone might reliably, spontaneously reach the judgment that, say, those kids tormenting that other kid are doing something wrong, without doing any moral calculation or drawing any conscious moral inference. There is no analogue of this in the case of laws of nature: it is just not plausible that there is any true, or approximately true, principle of the form *Propositions of kind K are laws of nature*, where it is observable that a proposition is of kind K.

[11] Carroll (1994), p. 55.

needs all the help with premises it can get. The fact that our epistemological knowledge is far from certain is not a good reason to forbid the use of any epistemological premises in metaphysics; if it were, then by parallel reasoning, we should forbid the use in metaphysics of any premises from any fields of knowledge other than logic and mathematics—including metaphysics itself! Nonetheless, we don't want to rest any metaphysical weight on epistemological premises that we have some positive reason to think shaky. The epistemological premises on which the infamous, classic arguments for phenomenalism, logical behaviorism, and instrumentalism rest are manifestly shaky. The epistemological premises of my argument for the meta-theoretic conception are not.

4.4 The objection from inference to the best explanation

The objection from inference to the best explanation runs as follows: even if two theories are empirically equivalent, in the sense that they have exactly the same implications concerning what we will observe, nonetheless the available empirical evidence might give more support to one of them if one of them provides a *better explanation* of that evidence. Applied to the case of the theories T and T*, the argument might go like this:

> **IBE1:** According to T, L and all of its consequences are true because L is a law of nature. According to T*, L is true, but this is for no reason at all; it is just an accident that L and all of its consequences are true. But we provide a better explanation of a range of facts when we say that they are all consequences of a law of nature than we do when we say that they are all consequences of some accidental fact. Therefore, if the empirical evidence includes many consequences of L, then T provides a better explanation of our evidence than T* does, so we are epistemically justified in preferring T to T* (in spite of the fact that they are empirically equivalent).

But that couldn't be quite right; it proves too much. Nothing in it depends on what T is or what L is. So if it were cogent, it would show that whenever our empirical evidence includes many facts that are consequences of L, we are always justified in preferring a theory that says L is a law over one that is exactly the same except that it says that L is true but not a law. But this is patently false. There have been many theories in the history of science that were well confirmed in their day according to which certain propositions are true but are not laws of nature. For example, the theory presented in Newton's *Principia* implies that all of the planets in the solar system go around the sun in the same direction, and that this fact is not a law since it depends on the initial conditions of the solar system. If IBE1 were a sound argument, then it would show that nobody should have believed the theory Newton presented. They should have preferred an alternative theory according to which it is a law of nature that all the planets go around the sun in the same direction. But this just seems wrong: to go beyond Newton's theory and say that it is a law that all the planets go around in the same direction would be nomological overkill.

So in order to make out a case that the choice between T and T* can be decided by means of an inference to the best explanation, a more nuanced approach is needed. We need a way of evaluating the goodness of explanations that sometimes, but not always, tilts the balance in favor of a theory that says that some proposition is a law, over an empirically equivalent rival that says that the same proposition is true but not a law.

There are two dangers we want to avoid. We want to avoid believing in too many inexplicable accidents. We also want to avoid positing too many laws of nature, or positing laws that are too complex, because other things being equal, we get a better, more unified explanation from a smaller and simpler set of laws. These two desiderata are in tension with each other: with a set of laws that is too impoverished, we fail to avoid the danger of too many inexplicable accidents; with a set of laws that is too rich, we fail to avoid the danger of too many laws. We have a balancing act to perform.

So a better way to make out the claim that the question of whether to accept T or T* can be settled on explanatory grounds is this:

IBE2: If T and T* both fit well with the existing empirical evidence, then we are epistemically justified in preferring the one that provides the better explanation of that evidence, where goodness of explanation is measured according to the following criteria: a theory provides a good explanation of the known empirical facts to the extent that it (i) posits a small and simple set of laws; (ii) minimizes the number of striking coincidences and inexplicable accidents in the world; and (iii) strikes a good balance between these.

You may notice a striking similarity between IBE2 and David Lewis's best-system analysis of laws of nature. But you don't have to be sympathetic to Lewis's way of analyzing the concept of a law in order to agree with this characterization of how explanatory inference can help us distinguish the laws from the nomically contingent truths. If you accept the first-order conception of laws, then whichever particular philosophical theory of laws you prefer, Lewis's or Armstrong's or Carroll's or someone else's, IBE2 is a very attractive description of the inference to the best explanation we use to decide what to believe about the laws of nature. Such an inference to the best explanation would make it possible to resist my argument against the first-order conception, because either T or T* will turn out to supply the better explanation of our evidence according to the criteria in IBE2. So the question of which we should believe is not underdetermined by the available evidence.

I think that IBE2, or something like it, provides the most promising way for an advocate of the first-order conception of laws to resist the argument of Section 4.2. But I am skeptical of IBE2, for two reasons.

The first reason is that it is difficult to square with actual scientific practice. Note that the criteria of goodness of explanations provided by IBE2 leaves an awful lot of wiggle room. Reasonable people can differ on how to individuate and count inexplicable accidents, how to evaluate the simplicity of a proposed set of laws, and how to balance these against each other. To the extent that we expect there to be disagreements about how to interpret and apply these criteria, we should expect there to be disagreements about whether T or T* should be accepted.

But there do not seem to be many controversies in the history of science in which the two sides favor theories that have the form of T and T*. Perhaps the controversy over Bode's law is an example,[12] but I am not aware of any others. Controversies between rival theories always seem to involve theories that differ on a lot more than whether a single proposition,

[12] But that controversy might be better described as a controversy about whether Bode's law can be derived from more fundamental laws, without relying on contingent features of the disk from which the solar system formed. If so, the controversy over whether Bode's law is a law does not have the form of the controversy between T and T*. See Graner and Bubrulle (1994).

which all sides agree is true, is also a law of nature. If the question of whether to accept T or T* had to be decided by means of IBE2, then the history of science should be rife with such controversies.

Of course, this objection is not conclusive. Perhaps scientists really do decide which hypotheses concerning laws to accept on the basis of the kind of explanatory inference exhibited in IBE2; perhaps controversies of the kind I have been discussing have not broken out because there is much more consensus than I have recognized among scientists about how to interpret and apply the criteria of goodness of explanations cited in IBE2. In any event, one might argue, the really important question is not whether scientists actually do consciously carry out such explanatory inferences, but rather whether such inferences could epistemically justify us in accepting either T or T* in preference to the other.

But there is also a second reason why I am skeptical. IBE2 provides a powerful methodological rule that offers significant guidance in deciding which theories to accept on the basis of given bodies of evidence. If we are justified in believing the theories that this rule directs us to believe, then it seems we must be justified in believing that this rule is reliable: that it is more likely than not to give us good advice about which theories to accept. The claim that this rule is reliable is not a truth of logic; in that sense, it is synthetic. Moreover, it is contingent, for there are possible worlds where applying the rule IBE2 offers us would lead us astray—for example, worlds where the set of laws of nature is exceedingly rich and complex, and worlds where there are a lot of strange coincidental regularities that don't follow from the laws of nature. So how are we supposed to be able to know that we can trust this methodological rule?

One very attractive answer is a naturalistic one: we are supposed to be able to know that we can trust the rule IBE2 gives us on empirical grounds. This is the only way we can be justified in accepting any contingently reliable methodological principle. Our methodological knowledge is of a piece with the rest of our empirical knowledge. The only alternative to this kind of naturalism appears to be the view that we can have synthetic a priori knowledge of methodological principles that are only contingently reliable—which means that scientific methodology depends on a priori knowledge of truths that are both synthetic and contingent. It seems to me that that is a view that we should avoid if it is at all possible.

Of course, in order to use empirical evidence to support the hypothesis that one methodological rule is reliable, we are going to have to rely on other methodological principles. And in order to use empirical evidence to support the hypothesis that those methodological principles are reliable, we are going to have to rely on some other methodological principles. But this doesn't have to lead to either a vicious regress or a vicious circle. What it shows is only that our total body of empirical knowledge is a tissue of mutually supporting elements, rather than a hierarchical structure resting on a foundation.

There is no worry about vitiating circularity here unless it turns out that the only way in which we can use empirical evidence to support the claim that a given methodological rule is reliable is to use that very methodological rule in order to support the claim that the results we have used that rule to obtain are true. That is, unless the only way in which we can empirically support the claim that methodological rule R is reliable is by means of an argument that goes like this:

> Our evidence supports H1 via R; and we have reason to believe that H1 is true, because our evidence supports it (via R);
>
> Our evidence supports H2 via R; and we have reason to believe that H2 is true, because our evidence supports it (via R);
>
> (Etc.)
>
> So, we have a great deal of empirical evidence that R is a reliable methodological rule.

That way of empirically justifying the use of rule R would obviously be worthless. If there were no better way of empirically justifying the use of rule R, then no reasonable naturalist would be willing to grant that we are justified in using R.

But this is exactly the situation that does obtain with respect to the methodological rule given by IBE2. Recall that we started focusing attention on IBE2 precisely because, given the first-order conception of laws, it seemed to provide the only real hope of evading an argument for skepticism about which true propositions are not only true but also laws. In order to get any useful empirical feedback on whether this rule is reliable or not, we would need to have some independent empirical way of getting information about which among the true propositions are not merely true but also laws. But there seems to be no independent check available. Any other way of confirming a putative law would face the same underdetermination problem, and the only way of getting around this problem seems to be to appeal to an inference to the best explanation—but this would just mean using IBE2 again.

This might seem a petty objection: after all, the only way we can empirically test the reliability of our senses is by using our senses to check the conclusions about the world we have reached on the basis of our senses; doesn't this have the same form as the objection I have raised to using IBE2 to check the reliability of IBE2? Yet I don't want to suggest that we are unjustified in trusting our senses to be reliable (within limits). Am I unfairly holding IBE2 to a higher standard than I am willing to hold our senses to?

I don't think I am. I can perform a genuine test of my vision—a test that might actually discredit my vision as unreliable—by looking at an apple once, turning away, and then looking in the same direction in which I seemed to see an apple again. Or, I can reach out my hands to see if I can feel the apple. (If I go to see my ophthalmologist, she and I can collaboratively perform more sophisticated tests.) In cases like these, I use one perceptually based belief to check the accuracy of another one; there is no logical guarantee at all that the two perceptually based beliefs will be in agreement. Things are different with IBE2. To apply IBE2, you have to make use of all of the available empirical evidence; there is a kind of 'requirement of total evidence' built into it. You can't judiciously pick some subset of the existing evidence, apply IBE2 to it, and justly claim that you have reasoned responsibly to your conclusion. If we use IBE2 to check the result of some particular application of IBE2, we are either using the same body of empirical evidence, or we are using a larger body of available evidence (since new evidence has come in since we made the first application of IBE2, the one we want to test). In neither case is there any possibility of IBE2 failing the test. In the first case, we are applying the same rule to the same set of evidence, so a failure of the test would indicate only that we had misapplied the rule at least once. In the second case, if the second application of IBE2 yields a different result than the first one did, this doesn't give us any reason at all to think that IBE2 has been shown unreliable. IBE2 is an ampliative inference procedure; such procedures often yield different conclusions when applied to different bodies of evidence. In fact, it is not really unusual that after we acquire more empirical evidence, our ampliative inferential procedures will lead to different conclusions than they did before, when we had less evidence to work with. That's part of why it's a good thing to seek more empirical evidence. In no case, then, can we use IBE2 to check the accuracy of an earlier result of applying IBE2 so that it has a chance of showing the earlier result to be wrong in a way that discredits IBE2. In this way, IBE2 contrasts sharply with our senses. We don't have to adopt a double standard in order to reach different judgments of the two.

So, the only empirical evidence we could ever have for the reliability of IBE2 would consist of cases in which IBE2 led to a true conclusion. But the only reason we will ever have for believing that IBE2 has led to a true conclusion in some case is that we have confirmed that conclusion using IBE2. So there seems to be no way of empirically confirming that IBE2 is a reliable methodological rule that is not blatantly and viciously circular.

Where does this leave us? The only way left to defend the reliability of IBE2 seems to be to try to argue that we can have a priori knowledge of its reliability, even though it is both synthetic and contingent that IBE2 is reliable. So unless we are prepared to pay the price of countenancing that kind of synthetic a priori knowledge, it seems that we have no way of resisting the underdetermination argument I gave earlier. Therefore, if the first-order conception of laws is true, then we face a choice between skepticism about laws, on the one hand, and an epistemology that embraces synthetic a priori knowledge of metaphysically contingent truths, on the other.[13] The meta-level conception of laws offers us another option. This gives us a good reason to embrace it.

4.5 The objection from Bayesianism

It might be suggested that on a Bayesian view of confirmation, it is possible for T to be more highly confirmed than T*, or vice versa, and that this undermines the epistemic argument for the meta-theoretic conception, by

[13] Note that this is much stronger than what Kant affirmed: he thought all our knowledge of the empirical world rested on synthetic a priori knowledge, but he thought this knowledge was of necessary truths.

blocking the inference to the conclusion that we cannot be justified by empirical evidence in believing one of these theories rather than the other. I will argue in this section that this is not so.[14]

Bayesian confirmation theory holds that the confirmation and disconfirmation of scientific hypotheses by empirical evidence is a matter of the degrees of belief of a rational subject going up or down as a result of conditionalizing on the evidence. The process of conditionalization is described by Bayes's theorem:

$$\textbf{Bayes's Theorem: } P(H|E) = \frac{P(H)P(E|H)}{P(E)}$$

Here P is a probability function representing the degrees of belief of a rational subject before an evidence statement E is discovered and taken into account, and H is the hypothesis getting confirmed or disconfirmed. Thus $P(H)$ is the *prior probability* of H—the subject's degree of belief in H prior to the consideration of the new evidence E; $P(H|E)$ is the *posterior probability* of H—the subject's new degree of belief in H after E has been taken account of (which for a Bayesian means: after the subject's degrees of belief have been updated by conditionalizing on E); $P(E)$ is the subject's degree of belief in E prior to the empirical discovery that E is true; $P(E|H)$ is called the *likelihood*. E is generally thought of as a single evidence statement, such as a report of the outcome of a single experiment; but it makes no difference if we allow E to be the conjunction of a whole body of empirical evidence statements.

The question is: can an appeal to Bayesian confirmation show that it is possible for the empirical evidence to lend differential support to T and T*—that is, to support T more highly than T*, or T* more highly than T? I'll focus on the question of whether such an appeal can show that the first disjunct is possible; everything said here can be adapted to the question of whether the second disjunct is possible simply by everywhere reversing T and T*.

Bayesianism can provide a way of confirming T to a greater degree than T* only if there can be some body of empirical evidence E such that:

$$P(T|E) > P(T^*|E)$$

[14] Nothing I say in this section should be taken as either an affirmation or a criticism of Bayesian confirmation theory itself. I remain strictly neutral on the substantive questions of confirmation theory. I aim only to show that Bayesian confirmation theory cannot be used to refute the argument of Section 4.2.

which by Bayes's theorem is equivalent to:

$$P(T)P(E|T) > P(T^*)P(E|T^*) \tag{4.1}$$

This might be so if the likelihoods on both sides of inequality 4.1 are equal and $P(T) > P(T^*)$. But in this case, the only reason why T ends up being better confirmed than T* is that the subject in question started out with a higher degree of belief in T than in T*. In other words, the subject in question started out with a prejudice in favor of T, and this is solely responsible for the confirmational outcome: if we switch the priors of T and T*, we reverse this outcome, so everything depends on which theory enjoys the greater degree of belief before any evidence is considered. It might be objected that the fact that the prior of T is greater than that of T* might not simply reflect initial prejudices; for it might be that at the time when the evidence E is considered, $P(T)$ and $P(T^*)$ are products of previous conditionalization on evidence discovered earlier, which favored T over T*. But this only pushes the problem back: we can redefine 'E' as a conjunction of evidence statements including the ones already taken account of earlier, and redefine $P(T)$ and $P(T^*)$ as the subject's degrees of belief before considering the earlier evidence; then inequality 4.1 must hold if all the evidence taken into account so far supports T better than it supports T*, and if the likelihoods $P(E|T)$ and $P(E|T^*)$ are still equal, then the confirmational advantage of T over T* is still traceable to priors that reflect degrees of belief antecedent to considerations of any evidence. So, in order for a Bayesian response to the argument of Section 4.2 to succeed, it must be that there exists some body of possible evidence statements E such that:

$$P(E|T) > P(E|T^*) \tag{4.2}$$

In order to give a successful Bayesian reply to the epistemological argument for the meta-theoretic conception, it is necessary to show that there can be a body of evidence statements E that satisfies inequality 4.2.

In one particularly simple case of empirical hypothesis-testing, a hypothesis H either entails an evidence statement E, or entails its negation ¬E. In such cases, $P(E|H)$ equals one or zero. But since T and T* agree perfectly on which non-nomological propositions are true, and only non-nomological propositions can be evidence statements, it follows that T entails E just in case T* does, and T entails ¬E just in case T* does. So in any such case, inequality 4.2 is false: both sides of the inequality will be equal to one or both will be equal to zero; in either case, the two sides are equal. This shows that for no body of evidence E that is either entailed by T (or by T*), and for no body of evidence E that is logically inconsistent with T (or with T*), can inequality 4.2 be satisfied. No such evidence could be the evidence that favors T over T*.

If there is a body of evidence E that does satisfy inequality 4.2—that is, a body of evidence that favors T over T* from a Bayesian point of view—then, it must not be entailed by T, or entail ¬T*. It must lend T a degree of probability that falls short of complete certainty. What could such an E be like? Perhaps it could be such that T, together with some auxiliary hypothesis A, entails E, where A itself enjoys a high probability, and A together with T* does not entail E. In this case:

$$
\begin{aligned}
&P(E|T \cdot A) = 1\\
&P(A) \gg 0\\
&P(A) < 1\\
&P(E|T^* \cdot A) < 1
\end{aligned}
$$

Under these conditions:

$$
\begin{aligned}
P(E|T) &= P(E|T \cdot A)P(A) + P(E|T \cdot \neg A)P(\neg A)\\
&= P(A) + P(E|T \cdot \neg A)P(\neg A)
\end{aligned}
$$

and:

$$P(E|T^*) = P(E|T^* \cdot A)P(A) + P(E|T^* \cdot \neg A)P(\neg A)$$

so inequality 4.2 is satisfied just in case:

$$
\begin{aligned}
P(A) + P(E|T \cdot \neg A)P(\neg A) > P(E|T^* \cdot A)P(A)\\
+ P(E|T^* \cdot \neg A)P(\neg A) \qquad (4.3)
\end{aligned}
$$

which might well be true. It is guaranteed to be true if the conditional probability of E given A is independent of whether T is true and whether T* is true, which is often the case with crucial auxiliary hypotheses used to generate testable predictions from scientific theories.[15] For in that case, inequality 4.3 is equivalent to:

$$P(A) + P(E|\neg A)P(\neg A) > P(E|A)P(A) + P(E|\neg A)P(\neg A)$$

that is:

$$P(A) > P(E|A)P(A)$$

which must be true since $P(E|A) < 1$.

But this doesn't much help the cause of the Bayesian reply to the argument of Section 4.2. In order for the auxiliary hypothesis A to do the trick, it must be the case that A entails $(T \supset E)$, but does not entail $(T^* \supset E)$. This means that A is equivalent to some conjunction:

$$B \cdot (T \supset E)$$

where B does not entail either $(T \supset E)$ or $(T^* \supset E)$. It follows that A is equivalent to:

$$(B \cdot E) \vee (B \cdot \neg T)$$

Since $T = (X \cdot L \textit{ is a law})$, we have this equivalence:

$$A \leftrightarrow \{(B \cdot E) \vee (B \cdot \neg X) \vee (B \cdot \neg L) \vee (B \cdot L \cdot L \textit{ is not a law})\} \quad (4.4)$$

Now consider an alternative auxiliary hypothesis, A*:

$$A^* = B \cdot (T^* \supset E)$$

where this B is the same one as before. If we change the example so that it is A*, rather than A, that has the large prior probability, then we will reverse the verdict of the calculation above: It will turn out that E confirms T* more highly than it confirms T. (For it will be T* rather than T that, together with a very probable auxiliary, entails E.)[16] Going through the

[15] For example, the hypothesis that germs cause puerperal fever can be tested by inducing the personnel in a hospital suffering from a high incidence of that dreaded disease to wash their hands in a solution of chlorinated lime before examining patients; this test depends on the auxiliary hypotheses that chlorinated lime will kill germs. Here let T be the hypothesis that germs cause puerperal fever, A be the auxiliary hypothesis that chlorinated lime kills germs, and E be the statement that the rate of puerperal fever will go down in the hospital after the hand-washing practice is adopted. If A is false—if chlorinated lime has no harmful effect on germs—then it seems that the probability of E is independent of whether T is true or not. So in this case, it seems that $P(E|\neg A) = P(E|T \cdot \neg A) = P(E|T^* \cdot \neg A)$ (where T* is any alternative hypothesis to T).

[16] Recall that B does not entail $(T \supset E)$.

same reasoning that led to 4.4 but with A* and T* in place of A and T, we get this equivalence:

$$A^* \leftrightarrow \{(B \cdot E) \vee (B \cdot \neg X) \vee (B \cdot \neg L) \vee (B \cdot L \textit{ is a law})\} \qquad (4.5)$$

Now, in order for the fact that A together with T entails E but A together with T* does not entail E to show that from a Bayesian point of view, there can be empirical evidence that favors T over T* in a way that is independent of any loading of the priors in T's favor, then it must be possible for P(A) to be higher than P(A*), for reasons that do not depend on any loading of the priors in T's favor. But an examination of 4.4 and 4.5 shows immediately that $P(A) > P(A^*)$ if and only if:

$$P(B \cdot L \cdot L \textit{ is not a law}) > P(B \cdot L \textit{ is a law})$$

But the propositions here have the same logical forms as T and T* themselves (they result from substituting B for X in T* and T respectively). So, A has the high probability that it needs in order for the Bayesian reply under consideration to work only if empirical evidence has already distinguished between two theories that disagree on nothing except whether some proposition that is true according to both of them is a law or not. In other words, we can use the fact that E might be entailed by a highly probable auxiliary A together with T, but is not entailed by A together with T*, to show that evidence can differentially confirm two theories that are related to each other in the way T and T* are only if we take it for granted that empirical evidence can differentially confirm two theories that are related to one another in exactly the same way. That is to say, the Bayesian reply to the argument of Section 4.2 that we are considering can succeed only by presupposing that the conclusion of that argument is false.

What we have learned so far is this: a successful Bayesian reply to the epistemological argument for the meta-theoretic conception must show that it is possible for there to be an evidence statement or conjunction of evidence statements E such that $P(E|T) > P(E^*|T)$, even if the priors have not been loaded by assigning unequal probabilities to two theories that differ only over the question of whether some proposition is a law or a true non-law. The needed evidence E cannot be a proposition that is entailed by T but not T*, it cannot be a proposition that entails ¬T* but not ¬T, and it cannot be a proposition that is entailed by some highly confirmed auxiliary hypothesis A together with T but not by A together with T*.

How else can E be evidentially relevant to the controversy between T and T*? There is only one conspicuous possibility: that T and T*, either alone or together with some set of well-confirmed auxiliaries, assign different chances or objective probabilities to E.

If T and T* themselves say something about the objective probability of E, then it is easy to see how inequality 4.2 could be satisfied. Assuming Lewis's Principal Principle,[17] the degrees of belief of a rational subject who knows the objective probabilities of chancy events will follow those objective probabilities. If T says, or entails, that the objective probability of E is 0.657, then the personal probability $P(E|T)$ had better be 0.657. So, if T and T* both entail something about the objective probability of E, then inequality 4.2 will be satisfied just in case the objective probability that T assigns to E is greater than the one that T* assigns to E.

But this cannot be the case. The only difference between the content of T and that of T* is in how they distribute lawhood over propositions; they entail all the same non-nomological propositions. T and T* might disagree about whether it is a *law* that the objective probability of E is 0.657, but if one of them entails that this probability of E *is* 0.657, the other does as well. Similarly, for any auxiliary hypothesis A you like, $(T \cdot A)$ and $(T^* \cdot A)$ might differ in whether their laws entail that the objective probability of E is 0.657, and on whether this value of E's probability is (nomologically) contingent on other states of affairs, but if one of them entails that this probability *is* 0.657, they both do. This hurts the prospects for a Bayesian reply to the argument of Section 4.2 in two ways: first, it eliminates one way in which it might be the case that inequality 4.3 holds; second, and more importantly, it means that if the common content of T and T*—that is, T-Common—entails any specification of the objective probability of E, either by itself or together with some highly confirmed auxiliary hypotheses, then inequality 4.2 *cannot* hold.

So, if inequality 4.2 is satisfied, and this is not due to loading of the priors, then E must have different conditional probabilities given T and T*, even though E bears the same entailment and consistency relations to both T and T*, and T and T* both imply exactly the same information regarding E's objective probability, and all of this will remain true even if

[17] Or some functionally similar surrogate, such as the 'New Principle.' See Lewis (1994) for discussion of both the Principal Principle and the New Principle.

we strengthen T and T* by conjoining both with any highly confirmed auxiliary hypothesis. This makes it very hard to see how inequality 4.2 could be satisfied. And inequality 4.2 is, recall, essential to a successful Bayesian reply to the argument of Section 4.2.

Here is another way to see the same point. Suppose that there is no biasing of the priors in favor of T or T*; that is, P(T) = P(T*). It follows from the definition of conditional probability, inequality 4.2 is satisfied just in case:

$$P(T \cdot E) > P(T^* \cdot E) \tag{4.6}$$

This means that in order for inequality 4.2 to be satisfied, the prior of $(T \cdot E)$ must be greater than that of $(T^* \cdot E)$, even though T and T* are consistent with all of the same evidence statements, and with all of the same highly confirmed auxiliary hypotheses, and T and T* (together with any highly confirmed auxiliary you like) make exactly the same difference to the chance or other objective probability of E. In the light of this, it seems that the truth of inequality 4.6 can only reflect the fact that the rational subject whose prior degrees of belief are modeled by the probability function P simply *finds the conjunction of E and T more plausible than the conjunction of E and T**, in advance and independently of any consideration of what the empirical evidence is. Thus the priors are loaded—if not in favor of T over T*, then at least in favor of $(T \cdot E)$ over $(T^* \cdot E)$. In the end, it seems that there is no way for Bayesian confirmation theory to enable the empirical evidence itself—without help from the initial prejudices of the Bayesian rational subject—to favor T over T*.

4.6 The objection from contextualist epistemology

Epistemological contextualism is the thesis that the truth conditions of knowledge ascriptions vary from context to context. Many different versions of the thesis have been defended in recent years.[18] They all maintain that in different contexts, the requirements for knowledge are variably strict. On many versions, knowledge requires that the knower be able to rule out all relevant alternative possibilities to the proposition known, and which

[18] For example, DeRose (1995); Lewis (1996); Neta (2003).

alternatives are relevant varies from context to context. A number of authors who advocate this sort of contextualist epistemology have employed it in refutations of various versions of skepticism. The skeptic argues that for any proposition P of a certain kind (e.g., propositions about the external world), we cannot know that P since we cannot rule out some proposition Q that is logically inconsistent with P (e.g., the proposition that one is a disembodied victim of a Cartesian demon). The contextualist reply is that in non-philosophical contexts—the contexts in which we unhesitatingly say things like 'I know that my keys are on the dresser'—it is true that we cannot rule out the skeptic's proposition Q. But this does not show that our familiar ordinary knowledge-ascriptions are false. For in the everyday contexts where we say such things, Q is not a relevant alternative. There are contexts in which Q is a relevant alternative, for example contexts in which we are talking about epistemology and worrying about how to reply to a skeptic. In these contexts, what the skeptic says is right: we do not know anything incompatible with the skeptic's proposition Q, since we cannot rule out Q on the basis of the evidence available to us. But this in no way threatens the truth of ordinary knowledge-ascriptions; those ascriptions are made in non-philosophical contexts, in which the skeptic's Q is not a relevant alternative, and so in which Q need not be ruled out in order for one to know that P.

There is a striking structural similarity between the typical skeptic's argument and the argument of Section 4.2. The skeptic argues that one cannot know P, since one cannot rule out Q, and Q is inconsistent with P; I argued that if the first-order conception of laws is correct, then one cannot be justified in believing T, since one cannot have evidence that favors T over T*, and T* is inconsistent with T. In each case, we have a claim to a certain epistemic status with respect to one proposition threatened by the inability to achieve the same epistemic status with respect to the negation of a second proposition, which is inconsistent with the first. Since the two arguments are similar in this way, it is inviting to think that what undermines the one will also undermine the other. But I don't think this suggestion withstands scrutiny.

Could there be any contexts in which exactly one of T and T* is a relevant possibility for purposes of evaluating knowledge-ascriptions? We have good reason to doubt this, if the first-order conception of laws is correct. On the first-order conception, there is a matter of fact about whether L is a law, and what this fact is is something that we expect our scientific theories to tell us. For science is, among other things, in the business of telling us which propositions are laws and which propositions are not. T and T* offer competing answers to this question. Which answer is the right one is something that some good scientific theory should tell us. So it is hard to see how it could be that T and T* are not both relevant possibilities, in any context in which we are interested in what science has enabled us to know. Note the contrast here with typical skeptical hypotheses, such as that we are all victims of a Cartesian demon. When I am inquiring about where my keys are, I am concerned to find out, for example, whether my keys are on my dresser or in my coat pocket. I am not inquiring about whether I really have keys at all, or about whether the material world even exists. So independently of our desire to answer the skeptic, we can motivate the idea that the hypothesis that I am a victimized disembodied Cartesian soul who has no keys at all is not a relevant possibility in the context in which I am inquiring about the location of my keys. It is not one of the propositions that I am trying to decide between. By contrast, according to the first-order conception, whenever we are engaged in scientific inquiry, one of the primary questions we want to answer is, 'Which propositions are laws of nature?' One partial answer is, 'They include L,' and another is, 'They do not include L.' It is hard to see how both could fail to be among the relevant possibilities in the context, given that they are competing answers to the very question that is the subject of inquiry.

4.7 The objection from the threat of inductive skepticism

Another objection (which has been put to me in conversation many times by many philosophers) goes like this: the argument of Section 4.2 assumed that when two theories are underdetermined by all the available empirical evidence, then the evidence cannot give us any reason to prefer one to the other. But this assumption leads straight to wholesale inductive skepticism. Granted, it is hard to see how to refute many an argument for wholesale inductive skepticism, including Hume's and all of the variants on it that philosophers have produced. But still, no one believes that inductive skepticism is true.[19] Since the epistemological argument for the meta-theoretic conception of laws, if successful, leads to an argument for inductive skepticism, we are rationally obligated to accept its conclusion only insofar as we are also rationally obligated to embrace wholesale inductive skepticism. Ergo, it is not unreasonable to remain unmoved by this argument, even if one cannot say exactly where it goes wrong.

This is a serious objection; if I cannot give an adequate response to it, then the argument of Section 4.2 does indeed have, at best, the status of Hume's argument for inductive skepticism: an argument that poses an interesting puzzle, but not the sort of argument that its author can seriously expect to convince his audience of the truth of its conclusion. Fortunately, things are not really as bad as that.

Let's begin by sharpening up the objection a bit. The objection does not say—and it is not true—that my argument against the discoverability of laws given the first-order conception *is* an argument for wholesale inductive skepticism. Furthermore, it is not a variant on Hume's argument against the justification of induction; it has nothing like the same logical form as Hume's argument. The problem here, if there is one, is that my argument relies on an implicit premise that implies wholesale inductive skepticism; so, no one should accept all the premises of my argument unless they are prepared to accept wholesale inductive skepticism.

What is the offending premise? It might seem to be this:

> **SUP:** For any two incompatible theories T1 and T2, and any possible body of empirical evidence E, if E is consistent with both T1 and T2, or if E is inconsistent with both of them, then E cannot provide any epistemic justification for believing one of these theories rather than the other.

('SUP' stands for 'Simple Underdetermination Principle.') SUP surely does lead directly to wholesale inductive skepticism. For whenever there is a non-demonstrative inference leading from a set of evidence statements E to some conclusion T, this same evidence will be consistent with some other theory that is incompatible with T. (That is just what it means for the inference to be non-demonstrative.) So, given SUP, it follows that this evidence cannot give us any epistemic justification for believing T

[19] With the possible exception of some Popperians.

rather than the second theory that is also consistent with E. But this is just what wholesale inductive skepticism says: no non-demonstrative inference from a given set of premises can justify believing the conclusion of that inference rather than an alternative that is also logically consistent with its premises. So, if my argument depends on SUP as a premise, then no one can consistently accept my argument and reject inductive skepticism.

But my argument does not really depend on SUP as a premise. The crucial move in my argument depends only on the following premise, which is strictly weaker than SUP:

> **RUP:** For any pair of mutually inconsistent theories T1 and T2, if every possible body of evidence that is consistent with T1 is also consistent with T2 and vice versa, then no body of empirical evidence can provide any epistemic justification for believing one of them rather than the other.

('RUP' stands for 'Radical Underdetermination Principle.') SUP can be symbolized like this:

S: $\forall x \forall y(Ixy \supset \forall z((Czx \equiv Czy) \supset Nxyz))$

and RUP like this:

R: $\forall x \forall y(Ixy \supset (\forall z(Czx \equiv Czy) \supset \forall w Nxyw))$

where Ixy = 'x and y are mutually inconsistent theories,' Cxy = 'x is a body of evidence that is consistent with y,' and Nxyz = 'z gives us no epistemic justification for believing either x or y rather than the other.' It is easily verified that S entails R but not vice versa. Since as we have seen, SUP is equivalent to wholesale inductive skepticism, the crucial premise of my argument does not entail wholesale inductive skepticism (since it does not entail SUP).

But still, it might be wondered whether there are any decent reasons to believe RUP that are not equally decent as reasons to believe SUP. If there are none, then you can have a good reason to accept my premise RUP only insofar as you have a good reason to accept wholesale inductive skepticism. If this is so, then I am almost as badly off as I would be if my argument took wholesale inductive skepticism as a premise.

What I need to do, then, is provide a reason why we should believe RUP that is not a reason to believe SUP. The reason I have to offer is this. Consider a methodological rule or practice that tells us that under certain conditions, we should accept a theory T1 and reject a second theory T2 even though *all possible* empirical evidence fits the two theories equally well. Let's call any such methodological rule or practice *anti-RUP*—for if any such rule or practice is legitimate, then RUP must be false. Note that any anti-RUP rule or practice directs us to adopt a procedure whose reliability cannot, in principle, be checked against the empirical evidence. No matter how much empirical evidence we had, it would be impossible for us ever to find a clue that an anti-RUP rule or practice was not perfectly reliable—even if in fact it were grossly unreliable, *always* telling us to accept the wrong candidate in any pair of radically underdetermined theories it was ever applied to. If there is no way, in principle, for the empirical evidence to tell us that a methodological rule or practice is not perfectly reliable, even in circumstances where that rule or practice is as unreliable as it could possibly be, then to rely on that rule or practice is to rely on a synthetic a priori contingent assumption—the assumption that this rule tends to lead us to infer to the right theory. I take it that other things being equal, we should prefer an account of the epistemology and methodology of science that does not require or depend on supposed synthetic a priori knowledge of contingent truths to one that does. (This premise was also invoked in my response to the objection from inference to the best explanation back in Section 4.4.) So, we should reject all anti-RUP methodological rules and practices. That is, we should embrace RUP.

This argument does not show that we should accept SUP (and thus, inductive skepticism). For most of the ampliative inferences we rely on do not depend on any anti-RUP methodological rules or practices. The ampliative inferences we draw in everyday life, for example, lead to conclusions whose negations are incompatible with some possible bodies of empirical evidence—for example, 'All dogs bark,' 'That coin is going to land heads-up every time it is flipped,' 'Eating that particular vegetable will always result in gastric distress.' Since we can empirically check whether particular conclusions of such inferences are correct—without relying on the very same inferential procedure we used to reach these conclusions in the first place—we can empirically test the reliability of the inferences, and thus test the reliability of the rules or practices that endorse them. If we are drawing our ampliative inferences in a way that is in fact unreliable, we have a chance of finding out that we are doing so. If after much employment of our inductive methods, we have seen no reason to think they are systematically unreliable, then we have at least some empirical reason to think that they are probably mostly reliable; they have been given ample opportunity to show their unreliability (if it exists), and they have not done so. So, ampliative inferential procedures like that are not ruled out by RUP.

Hence, we have a good reason to adopt RUP that is not also a reason to adopt SUP. Since my argument depends only on RUP and not on the stronger SUP, accepting its premises does not commit one to inductive skepticism.

4.8 Conclusion

Where do things stand now? The argument of Section 4.2 has not fallen to any of the objections I have considered, but things are not the same as they were before. In order to reply to two of the objections, I had to invoke an additional premise that was not among the premises of the original argument.

The additional premise, which we might call 'the minimal naturalist requirement,' says that scientific methodology does not appeal to a priori knowledge of propositions that are metaphysically contingent. To adopt this requirement is (at least) to require that every ampliative inference procedure that can be legitimately used in empirical natural science must be such that its reliability can be empirically tested. The additional premise can do its job even if we adopt a very liberal notion of what counts as empirical testability of the reliability of a procedure: all that is required in order for the procedure's reliability to be testable is that if the ampliative inference procedure in question is radically unreliable, leading from true premises to false conclusions almost all of the time, then it must be possible to discover empirical evidence that the procedure is not generally reliable. In Section 4.4, we saw that the rule IBE2 is not like this: IBE2 might be a radically misleading rule in our universe; if our only epistemic access to the nomological truths is given to us by IBE2, then even if IBE2 is radically misleading, there is no way we can ever discover that it is anything less than perfectly reliable. In Section 4.7, we saw that the same is true of any ampliative inference procedure that violates the Radical Underdetermination Principle (RUP). If an inferential rule or procedure is not testable in this way, then the empirical evidence could never make us any the wiser even if the rule or procedure led to a radically false conclusion every single time it was applied. Nothing in the empirical evidence, then, gives us any reason to think that the rule or procedure is reliable. To regard relying on a rule like that in scientific inquiry as justified is to take scientific methodology to depend on the support of a priori principles that are not only synthetic but also metaphysically contingent.[20] But other things being equal, we should prefer an account of scientific methodology that does not appeal to a priori knowledge of contingent truths.

Not all philosophers will accept this premise. I find it plausible on its face that we should prefer an account of scientific methodology that does not involve this kind of synthetic a priori knowledge to one that does, so long as one is available; I have argued that if we say both that laws of nature are empirically discoverable and that the first-order conception of laws is correct, then we cannot consistently accept a non-aprioristic methodology. On the other hand, if we adopt the meta-theoretic conception, then even if we maintain that science is capable of discovering laws, this does not force us to adopt an aprioristic methodology. I think this gives us a very strong reason to adopt the meta-theoretic conception. But not everyone will agree with me that we should prefer a naturalistic methodology to an aprioristic one. For one thing, not everyone will agree that eschewing synthetic a priori knowledge of contingent truths is something we should want to do; for another, not everyone who agrees with me that it would be nice to be able to do that thinks that it is a realistic goal. (Certainly, I have not shown here that there exists any non-aprioristic methodology that

[20] Objection: 'But we do that anyway, if we think that scientists are justified in assuming that we are not victims of a Cartesian demon, or brains in a mad scientist's vat. For, all of the available empirical evidence gives us no reason at all to think that we are in neither predicament. And the claim that we are in neither predicament is surely both synthetic and metaphysically contingent.' Reply: We don't have to assume that science rests on synthetic a priori knowledge to the effect that such skeptical-nightmare scenarios are false. There are at least two other ways in which we could explain why scientists are justified in believing things that are incompatible with such scenarios, which cannot be used to explain why scientists are justified in believing in the reliability of an inferential procedure that can decide the question between T and T*. The first is externalism about empirical evidence: the empirical evidence available in the actual world includes every proposition that we can see to be true; these include, for example, that we have bodies, and that we are surrounded by various physical objects. Victims of skeptical-nightmare scenarios lack this empirical evidence (even though they don't know they lack it, and can't be blamed for not knowing this). The second is epistemological contextualism: skeptical nightmare scenarios are not relevant alternatives in scientific contexts. As explained above in Section 4.6, this move can't be used to dismiss T*.

can do everything we need the methodology of science to do. All I have done is present a reason why we definitely cannot consistently combine any such methodology with a first-order account of laws, which is not also a reason why we cannot consistently combine such a methodology with a meta-theoretic account of laws; obviously this falls far short of the goal of demonstrating that science as we know it can be based on a non-aprioristic methodology.) So it is not obviously rationally forbidden to reject the minimal naturalist requirement, and no one who rejects it will be rationally compelled by my argument.

So the argument of this chapter is not a knock-down argument for the meta-theoretic conception. But it does underline the price that must be paid for adopting the first-order conception of laws: there is some reason to think that the world contains laws as conceived by the first-order conception, and that they have an important role to play in science over and above the role of merely true propositions, *only if* science relies on alleged synthetic a priori contingent truths in its methodology. So one can be a well-motivated first-order theorist of laws only if one is willing to accept synthetic a priori knowledge of contingent truths, and their employment in scientific methodology. To me, this is too high a price to pay.

Given the minimal naturalist requirement, the argument of this chapter establishes the first main claim of this book: if there are laws of nature, and they literally govern the universe, and it is possible in principle for science to discover them—that is, if the Lawhood Thesis, the Governing Thesis, and the Discoverability Thesis are all true[21]—then the correct account of lawhood must be a meta-theoretic account.

[21] These theses were introduced back in Chapter 1, Section 1.7.

5

Laws, governing, and counterfactuals

5.1 Where we are now

Back in Chapter 1, I argued that the law-governed world-picture is captured by the following short list of theses:

The Lawhood Thesis: There is a distinct class of true propositions fittingly called *the laws of nature*; alternatively, there is a property fittingly called *lawhood* that some but not all true propositions (and no false propositions) have.

The Discoverability Thesis: Science is in principle capable of discovering which propositions are the laws of nature—i.e., which true propositions have the property of lawhood.

The Governing Thesis: The laws of nature govern the universe, in some robust, non-figurative sense of 'govern.' It is not just that everything behaves *as if* it were governed by laws; the evolution of the universe *really is* governed by laws.

The Science-Says-So Thesis: We can be justified in believing that the laws of nature govern the universe (in whatever sense of 'govern' makes the Governing Thesis come out true) without appealing to any extra-scientific sources of epistemic justification.

In the preceding chapter, I argued that the Lawhood Thesis, the Discoverability Thesis, and the Governing Thesis can all three be true only if the correct account of lawhood is a meta-theoretic account. In this and the following four chapters, I will argue that the Governing Thesis and the Science-Says-So Thesis can both be true only if a particular meta-theoretic account of laws is correct. In this chapter, I will begin by addressing the question of just what the universe would have to be like in order for the Governing Thesis to be true.[1]

5.2 What would things have to be like in order for the laws of nature to govern the universe?

The Governing Thesis says that the laws of nature really do govern the universe in some serious sense; it is not just that everything in nature behaves as if it were governed by laws. What would it mean for this to be true?

If the laws of nature govern the universe, they do not govern it in the way that the laws of the land govern the citizens. They do not forbid violations by way of imposing or licensing sanctions against them. But they do forbid violations, in another way: there *can be* no violations of them. A violation of a law of nature is the same thing as a state of affairs inconsistent with the truth of that law; there can be no violations of the laws; hence, nothing can come to pass that is inconsistent with the truth of the laws. In other words, the laws are *inevitably* true.

Moreover, the laws *have always been* inevitably true; they did not at some point become inevitably true, the way it became inevitably true at some point that this book would not be published earlier than 2008. From here on out, whenever I talk about 'inevitability,' I will mean this kind of eternal inevitability that characterizes the laws of nature. Something is inevitably true in my sense just in case it has always been inevitably true.[2]

It is not as if the laws of nature *just happen* to be inevitably true. It is not as if there is this one feature a proposition can have, *lawhood*, and this other one, *inevitable truth*, and it just so happens that every proposition that has the one also has the other. The point of the Governing Thesis is not that the propositions that happen to be laws of nature also happen to be the ones that

[1] This chapter owes a great deal to ideas worked out by Marc Lange in his (2000) and (2005). In fact, it wouldn't be an exaggeration to say that most of this chapter consists of reshufflings of Lange's ideas. In the following chapters, however, I am going to put these ideas to work in ways that Lange would not agree with.

[2] Some people think that the laws of nature can change over time. For example, perhaps the laws underwent some evolution during the first brief period after the Big Bang, before they settled down into their current form. (See Balashov (1992) for discussion of this view.) On this view, the laws of nature have not always been inevitably true, though perhaps they are inevitably true now. In order to accommodate this view, we might introduce some kind of time-indexing into the account of inevitable truth I am about to offer. But I won't pursue that line of thought in this book.

govern the universe. Rather, being a law is what enables a proposition to govern the universe, so it is what makes a proposition inevitably true. Lawhood is not merely correlated with inevitable truth, it *confers* inevitable truth. The laws of nature are inevitably true, *precisely because* they are laws of nature.

It might seem that by saying this, we make little, if any, progress. We have exchanged the thesis that the laws of nature govern the universe for the thesis that the laws of nature are eternally inevitably true precisely because they are the laws of nature. Is this new thesis any clearer than the one we started with? Well, I think the step we have taken is helpful. For the idea of inevitability can be plausibly cashed out in terms of counterfactual conditionals, and by transforming the Governing Thesis into a thesis about counterfactuals, I think we can make some headway toward figuring out what it would take for it to be true, and whether or not it is true.

5.3 Lawhood, inevitability, counterfactuals

My question is: what would things have to be like in order for lawhood to confer inevitability—that is, for the laws of nature to be inevitably true on account of their being laws of nature? It's fair to ask what kind of answer I expect to get. Someone might ask this question hoping to get a good metaphysical theory of what the *truthmaker* of 'lawhood confers inevitability' is; someone might ask the question hoping to get an answer that is spelled out using only crystal-clear, epistemologically and metaphysically unproblematic concepts. I'm not hoping for either of those. The more modest kind of answer I want is a condition that is plausibly equivalent to 'lawhood confers inevitability,' and that is more inferentially tractable than it. That is, I want to trade in 'lawhood confers inevitability' for a proposition whereof we can more easily find and recognize good arguments in which it occurs as a premise or a conclusion. The proposition I am going to arrive at is spelled out in terms of counterfactuals. Metaphysically and epistemologically, counterfactuals are perhaps no better understood than conferring inevitability is. But we have a much more developed framework for evaluating arguments that have to do with counterfactuals than we do for arguments that deal with conferring inevitability. So my hope is that by finding a condition—spelled out in terms of counterfactuals rather than either inevitability or governing—which is plausibly equivalent to 'lawhood confers inevitability' (and thereby plausibly equivalent to 'the laws of nature govern the universe'), we can get some traction on the question of whether the law-governed world-picture is accurate.

But spelling things out in terms of counterfactuals can help us get better inferential traction only if we already know something about how counterfactuals work. It turns out that in order to make progress on our main question, we don't actually need to know very much about counterfactuals, but we do need to count on a few basic assumptions about them. Before proceeding, I should explain what those are.

I will always write as if counterfactuals are truth-valued, and context-variable: they have truth values relative to contexts. But this is not essential; if you prefer to think of counterfactuals as lacking truth values, and only being assertible or not assertible in a context, you can replace 'assertible' for 'true' throughout. So the assumptions we will need to count on do not really include the assumption that counterfactuals have truth values; but they do include the assumption that whatever kind of semantic value counterfactuals have, these can be context-dependent. For example, in a context of discourse where Michael's great love of chocolate is the most salient fact about him, it might be true/assertible that if Michael were here with us at this ice cream parlor now, he would be happy, since they have such great chocolate ice cream; on the other hand, in a context of discourse where it is more salient that it is now 11:00 pm and Michael always gets upset if he doesn't get to go to sleep before 9:00, it will be true/assertible that if Michael were here with us now, he would not be happy.

I won't make any assumptions about what the right account of the semantics of counterfactuals are (though in subsequent chapters I will sometimes talk about David Lewis's possible-worlds semantics for counterfactuals when discussing his views). But I will make a few simple assumptions about the logic of counterfactuals, which I take to be fairly obvious and uncontroversial; I will introduce these as they come up.

I'll work up to answering the main question in stages: before addressing the question of what things would have to be like in order for lawhood to confer inevitability, I propose to address the simpler question of what things would have to be like in order for some class of propositions to be inevitably true. And before addressing that one, I propose to address the even simpler one of what things would have to be like in order for a single proposition to be inevitably true.

5.4 What is it for a proposition to be inevitably true?

What are we saying, when we say that a proposition P is (eternally) inevitably true? A natural answer to this question is that we are saying that not only is P true, but P would still have been true, no matter what else had happened, and no matter what else were the case. In other words, if things had been different in any way, then P would still have been true.

That thought takes the form of a universally quantified counterfactual conditional:[3]

(1): $\forall Q\ (Q \mathbin{\Box\!\!\rightarrow} \text{(still) } P)$

where the quantifier ranges over propositions. Is (1) really equivalent to the inevitable truth of P? The answer is plausibly 'Yes.' Suppose that (1) is false; then there is some proposition—say, Q—such that had Q been true, P might have been false. That is to say, there is some way that P might have not turned out to be true. In other words, P's truth is '*evitable.*' Conversely, if P's truth is 'evitable,' then there is something that could have happened or could have been the case, such that if it had happened or had been the case, then P might not have been true. So there is a counterinstance to (1). (1) looks to be the right way to spell out the idea that P is inevitably true.

But actually, (1) won't do as it stands. Suppose that Q is a proposition that is logically consistent, but logically inconsistent with P. If $Q \mathbin{\Box\!\!\rightarrow} P$ is true, then by an uncontroversial principle in the logic of counterfactuals[4] it follows that:

$$Q \mathbin{\Box\!\!\rightarrow} (Q \cdot P)$$

which has a logically consistent antecedent and a logically inconsistent consequent. No such counterfactual can be true. So (1) entails that the only

[3] I am using David Lewis's symbol $\Box\!\!\rightarrow$ to formalize counterfactual conditionals. $A \mathbin{\Box\!\!\rightarrow} C$ should be read as: 'If it had been the case that A, then it would have been the case that C.' So 'I woke up when my alarm went off $\Box\!\!\rightarrow$ I did not miss my bus' should be rendered in plain English as 'If it had been the case that I woke up when my alarm went off, then it would have been the case that I did not miss my bus'—or more colloquially, 'Had I woken up when my alarm went off, I would not have missed my bus.' '$A \mathbin{\Box\!\!\rightarrow}$ (still) P' should be read as 'If it were the case that A, then it would still have been the case that P.' This has the same content as '$A \mathbin{\Box\!\!\rightarrow} P$', but it sounds more natural in a case where we take it for granted that P is actually true. If we all know that I arrived at the meeting late, it would sound a little strange to say 'Had I woken up when my alarm went off, I would have arrived at the meeting late,' but more natural to say 'Had I woken up when my alarm went off, I would *still* have been late.'

[4] Namely: for any propositions A, B, and C: If $A \mathbin{\Box\!\!\rightarrow} B$ and $A, B \vdash C$, then $A \mathbin{\Box\!\!\rightarrow} C$.

inevitably true propositions are the logically necessary truths. We need a broader notion of inevitability than this, if we want to apply it to the laws of nature.

The solution to this problem is to recognize that inevitability, like God's omnipotence, must be subject to the constraints of logical possibility—and its being subject to this constraint does not eviscerate it. So we should modify (1) as follows:

(2): ∀Q (if Q is logically consistent with P, then Q □→ (still) P)

(2) has a whiff of triviality about it. 'Surely,' you might say, 'so long as P actually is true, it would still have been true under any circumstances that are consistent with it?' But this isn't so. Let P be the proposition that I am completely dry right now. The proposition that I have just come in from the pouring rain is logically consistent with P. But as it happens, today I forgot to bring both my raincoat and my umbrella, so if I had just come in from the pouring rain, I would not be completely dry. So this value of P does not satisfy (2). And the reason why it fails to satisfy (2) seems to be the reason why we would say that it is not inevitably true. So (2) seems to be a good explication of what we mean when we say that a proposition P is inevitably true.

But there is yet another worry. Counterfactuals are notoriously context-variable: the same one can be true in one context and false in another, even within the same possible world, and even when all of the pronouns, indexicals, and so on have the same extensions in both contexts. Suppose we are driving across the country, and suddenly we both notice that the fuel tank is almost empty. You (the passenger) say to me (the driver), 'If we weren't on a stretch of highway where gas stations are plentiful, we would be in real trouble now.' I reply, 'No, if I had not known that we would be driving along a stretch of highway with lots of gas stations today, I would have made sure to buy more fuel this morning. So if we were not on a stretch of highway where gas stations are plentiful, we would not be in trouble, because we would have started out with a full tank, and therefore we would still have plenty of fuel.' Which of us is right? That depends on the context of the conversation. If what is most important for purposes of the conversation is the amount of fuel we started out with this morning, then you are right. In that case, when we consider a hypothetical counterfactual scenario in which the stretch of highway we are on has very few gas stations, we hold constant the actual fact about how much gas we started out with. But if what is most important for purposes of our conversation is whether my poor judgment has almost landed us in a heap of trouble, then I am right. For in that case, when we consider the same hypothetical counterfactual situation, what we hold constant is my characteristic behavior patterns, which in that case would have involved my making sure we had plenty of fuel before we began the trip.

Why is this a worry? Well, (2) implies a whole bunch of counterfactuals; if any of them are context-variable, then (2) itself is context-variable (unless it is just false in every context). But (2) is our proposal for explicating 'P is inevitably true,' so now it seems that that statement is context-variable as well. This seems counterintuitive; inevitable truth doesn't seem like the kind of feature you can give to a proposition or take from it just by switching to a different context.

This worry might be based on a mistake about what context-variable expressions are like. When we assertorically produce a token of a context-variable sentence type in a context, we assert a proposition; when we switch to a different context, we change which propositions are expressed by which sentences, but we don't thereby change which propositions are true (except, of course, for propositions about ourselves and which context we are in). I say, 'He is a Methodist,' while pointing at George W. Bush; a little later I say, 'He is a Baptist,' while pointing at Bill Clinton. Both utterances are true; the apparent conflict between them is not a real conflict because there has been a context shift between the utterances. This context shift didn't change anybody's denominational affiliation. The propositions expressed by my two utterances both stayed true throughout the proceedings; what changed was only which proposition is expressed by my utterances of a given sentence type. Similarly, if we switch from a context in which a given counterfactual is true to one in which it is false, we haven't altered the truth value of any proposition; we've just changed which proposition is expressed by which counterfactual sentence. If the counterfactual in question is one of the ones implied by (2), then the sentence 'P is inevitably true' may have been true in the first context, but it is false in the second one. But this doesn't mean that we have deprived P of a special property, the property of *inevitable truth*, by switching from one context to another. All it means is that the sentence 'P is inevitably true' expresses different propositions in the two contexts; the proposition it expresses in the first context may be true, but the proposition it expresses in the second context is false.

Does this adequately diagnose and dismiss the worry? It's not so clear. If the worry is driven by the thought that a shift in context can change the truth value of a context-sensitive sentence, but shifts in the context cannot change what is inevitable and what is not, then the worry has been dispatched: a shift in the context corresponds to a shift in what the standards of inevitability are, rather than a shift in what is inevitable according to some fixed standard. But the worry might be driven by a different thought. Counterfactuals are context-sensitive because which counterfactuals are correctly affirmed is sensitive to local details of the context, such as what the purpose of the conversation is. But it is not obviously true that which inevitability ascriptions are correct in a given context is sensitive to such local details of the context. In other words, the standards of truth for counterfactuals are shifty in a way that the standards of inevitability might not be. In fact, there is some plausibility to the view that inevitability is not the sort of thing that has shifty standards at all; something is either inevitable or it isn't, period.

For example, if our conversation happens to be focused on the way in which a certain mechanism is wired up, then it is true in our context that if Joe pushed the red button there would have been an explosion; if our conversation happens to be focused on Joe's competence and safety consciousness, then it is true in our context that if Joe pushed the red button there would have been no explosion, since Joe would first have made sure that the red button wasn't connected to the explosives. Which counterfactual is true in our present context depends completely on the point of this particular conversation: are we discoursing on the properties of this particular configuration of machinery, or are we discoursing on Joe's admirable qualities? In the first context, the details of the actual configuration of the mechanism might be so important that it gets held constant for the purposes of evaluating a great range of counterfactuals; in the second context, the fact that Joe would never push a button that would set off an explosion may be so important that it gets held constant in a great range of counterfactuals. But in the first context, would we say that it is inevitable that the mechanism is configured in the way that it is? In the second context, would we say that it is inevitable that Joe is as competent and safety conscious as he is? It is at the very least not obvious that we would say this, or that we would speak truly if we did.

What this suggests is that perhaps the counterfactuals whose truth makes some proposition inevitably true must not be the kind of counterfactuals that are sensitive to the details of the purpose of the present conversation. Perhaps there are many counterfactuals that are context-sensitive in that way, but perhaps there are also many that are not, and the counterfactuals that matter for inevitability are of the second kind. If this is right, then instead of saying that P is inevitably true just in case (2) is true, what we should really say is that P is inevitably true just in case (2*) is true:

(2*): ∀Q (if Q is logically consistent with P, then the counterfactual (Q $\Box\!\!\rightarrow$ (still) P) is true no matter what the details of the conversational context)

But on the other hand, maybe inevitability ascriptions really are context-sensitive, surprising as this may seem at first. What it is for P to be inevitably true is just for P to be true and for it to be the case that no matter what else had been true (so long as the 'what-else' was logically consistent with P), P would still have been true. That is, what it is for P to be inevitably true is for (2) to be true. But since counterfactuals are context-variable, so is (2). In the contexts where (2) is true, it is true that P is inevitably true; in the contexts where (2) is false, it is false that P is inevitably true. It might be surprising that inevitability ascriptions can be context-variable in this way. But it is also surprising when one first discovers that counterfactuals are context-variable. We have by now gotten used to the context-variability of counterfactuals, so we no longer regard it as surprising. In view of the tight link between inevitability and counterfactuals, and the context-variability of the latter, we should be prepared to accept the context-variability of the former. Our intuitions may balk here, but this is a case where our intuitions will have to give way to reason.

So we have two possible views here: the first view is that P is inevitable just in case (2) is true, and this means that inevitability ascriptions may turn out to be context-variable in a surprising way. The second view is that inevitability-ascriptions are not shifty in the way that counterfactuals are, so P is inevitable only if (2*) is true. Which view is right? Right now I won't try to settle this question. Eventually, I'll return to the issue, but for now it will be possible to plow ahead leaving this particular question unsettled. The preliminary conclusion we have reached is that what it is for a proposition P to be inevitably true is either for (2) to be true or for (2*) to be true. I'm going to proceed on the assumption that (2) is the right explication of inevitable truth, and pause now and then to add the qualifications that must be added if (2*) is the right explication instead.

5.5 What is it for a whole class of propositions to be inevitably true?

What is it for an entire class of propositions to be inevitably true? We're supposing that (2) is the right way to spell out what must be the case in order for a single proposition to be inevitably true. It might seem that extending this view into a view of what it takes for an entire class of propositions to be true is straightforward. For a class of propositions consisting of P1, P2, etc., the whole class is inevitably true just in case each of its members is inevitably true. Thus:

∀Q (if Q is logically consistent with P1, then Q □→ (still) P1)

∀Q (if Q is logically consistent with P2, then Q □→ (still) P2)

etc.

But this can't be right. Consider the proposition that either P1 is false or else P2 is false; call this proposition A. A is consistent with P1, and it is also consistent with P2. So if the whole class is inevitably true, then we get the result that A □→ P1, and A □→ P2. It follows[5] that:

A □→ (A · P1 · P2)

But in this counterfactual, the antecedent is logically consistent and the consequent is not. This counterfactual cannot be true. Hence, we reach the result that no set of propositions with more than one member can be inevitably true, an undesirable result.[6]

[5] Assuming two more obvious principles in the logic of counterfactuals, namely:

For any propositions B, C, and D: {B □→ C, B □→ D} ⊢ B□→ (C · D); and

For any proposition B: B □→ B.

[6] This argument is due to Lange (2000), pp. 100–3.

The resolution to this problem is similar to the resolution of a problem we saw earlier: inevitability is subject to the limitations of logical consistency—and this goes for the inevitability of a class of propositions as well as for a single proposition. What we must say is that the class **K** is inevitably true *as a class* just in case all of its members are true, and:

(3): ∀Q ∀P (if Q is consistent with **K** and **K** logically entails P, then Q □→ (still) P)

That is, every member of **K** and all of their logical consequences would still have been true, under any counterfactual supposition that is consistent with all the members of **K**. Under this condition, the members of **K** are collectively as stable under counterfactual suppositions as they logically could be; **K** is *maximally counterfactually stable*. There is no way in which **K** could be more stable as a class under counterfactual suppositions than it is—for, trivially, all of its members logically could still all have been true only under counterfactual suppositions that are logically consistent with them all.

This notion of maximal counterfactual stability, and this way of motivating it, was introduced by Marc Lange (2000; 2005). Lange uses this notion to explicate the relation between laws and counterfactuals, and the sense in which laws of nature are necessary. The way I characterized inevitable truth is pretty much equivalent to the way Lange characterizes necessary truth: the truths that are necessary (in some sense of necessity) are the ones that would still have been true, no matter what other possible proposition (in the sense of possibility corresponding to this sense of necessity) had been true. Thus, the necessary truths (for any given sense of necessity) comprise a set that is maximally counterfactually stable.

I don't have any substantive disagreement with Lange on any of this, but I prefer to say that it is the notion of inevitability rather than the more general notion of necessity that is helpfully explicated using the concept of maximal counterfactual stability. For there are widely recognized types of necessity that cannot be illuminated in terms of maximal counterfactual stability. These include logical necessity, which cannot be illuminated in this way since the definition of maximal counterfactual stability takes for granted the notions of logical consistency and logical entailment, which are themselves interdefinable with logical necessity and possibility. They also include doxastic and epistemic necessity. Suppose that it so happens that

Thunderclap won the tenth race only because he was doped; in his undoped state, poor Thunderclap would not have a chance against the other horses that ran in that race. Suppose I know that Thunderclap won, and I don't know anything at all about which horses were doped and which were not. Then it is epistemically necessary (for me) that Thunderclap won, and epistemically possible (for me) that Thunderclap was not doped; yet the counterfactual 'Thunderclap was not doped □→ Thunderclap won' is not true. Nor am I even inclined to believe that it is true; if you asked me about it, I would tell you I have no idea whether it is true or not. This shows that the epistemically necessary propositions do not comprise a maximally counterfactually stable set—even from the point of view to which the epistemic necessity is relativized. Maximal counterfactual stability is a useful tool for explicating non-logical types of necessity that are objective rather than doxastic or epistemic; 'inevitable truth' seems an apt description of that kind of necessity, though not so apt for other kinds.

I have been assuming that we accept (2) as the right explication of the statement that P is inevitably true. If we go for (2*) instead, we need to make a modification to (3); in its place we should accept (3*):

(3*): ∀Q ∀P (if Q is consistent with K and K logically entails P, then the counterfactual (Q □→ (still) P) is true no matter what the details of the conversational context)

Now we can turn to the question of what things have to be like in order for lawhood to confer inevitability.

5.6 What is it for lawhood to confer inevitability?

It might seem that in order for lawhood to confer inevitability, it is necessary and sufficient that the whole class of laws of nature is inevitable as a class—or perhaps, that it is a necessary truth that the whole class of laws of nature is inevitable. But this isn't quite the right answer.

Suppose that lawhood confers inevitability. Suppose also that it is a law of nature that no particle travels faster than the speed of light, c. Now consider the following counterfactual:

C1: If it were not a law of nature that no particle travels faster than c, then no particle would travel faster than c.

Should we say that C1 is true? Well, the intuitive answer is that it is false: given all the energy and resources that physicists have put into building better and better particle accelerators, it seems pretty clear that they would have gotten a subatomic particle to go faster than c by now if it weren't for those meddlesome laws of nature always getting in the way. (This wonderful example is due to Lange, who uses it to make a similar point.[7]) And this verdict seems consistent with the idea that lawhood confers inevitability. In fact, it seems to be just the verdict we must accept if we accept that idea: if lawhood is what confers inevitability on the actual laws—that is, if the actual laws are inevitably true precisely *because* they are the laws of nature—then when we are considering a counterfactual scenario in which one of the actual laws is not a law, it seems that we should not carry the inevitability of that law with us to that counterfactual scenario. If it were not a law that no massive particle ever goes faster than light, then the very reason why it is inevitable that no particle ever goes that fast would not be there—so why should it still be inevitable?

Now consider this counterfactual:

> C2: If I had eaten waffles for breakfast this morning, then it would still have been a law of nature that no massive particle travels faster than c.

If lawhood confers inevitability, then it seems that we should count this counterfactual as true. Suppose the contrary: then, had I eaten waffles for breakfast this morning, it might not have been a law of nature that no particle goes faster than c; in that case, there would have been no reason why it should have been inevitable that no particle ever goes that fast; and in that case, some particle might have gone faster than c. But if lawhood confers inevitability, then it cannot be true that had I eaten waffles for breakfast, some law might have been false.

So we have reached verdicts about counterfactuals C1 and C2, on the assumption that lawhood does indeed confer inevitability: C1 is false and C2 is true. These verdicts, however, are different from the verdicts we should have reached had we assumed that the actual laws of nature are inevitable as a class, or if we had assumed that it is a necessary truth that the laws of nature are inevitable as a class. Consider first C1: its antecedent

[7] Lange (2000), pp. 47–8.

is logically consistent with the truth of all the actual laws of nature—it denies only the *lawhood* of one of the actual laws, not it's *truth*—and its consequent follows from the truth of all the actual laws. So, given the maximal counterfactual stability of the actual laws, C1 should be true. Now consider C2: its consequent is not a consequence of the propositions that are laws of nature in the actual world. (Those propositions could all be true, even if some of them were not laws.) So the principle that the actual laws are inevitable as a class—i.e., maximally counterfactually stable—does not imply that this counterfactual is true. It may be true for all that; but its truth is not vouchsafed by the inevitable truth of the laws of nature as a class, or even from its being a necessary truth that the laws are inevitably true as a class.

What all of this shows is that the claim that lawhood confers inevitability is not equivalent to the claim that the actual laws of nature are inevitably true as a class—or even to the claim that the latter is a necessary truth. We must not explicate the claim that lawhood confers inevitability like this:

> (4): ∀Q ∀P (if Q is consistent with the set of propositions that are laws of nature, and that set logically entails P, then Q □→ (still) P)

What should we say instead?

The problem raised by counterfactuals like C1 is that, although we want the thesis that lawhood confers inevitability not to entail that such counterfactuals are true, (4) does entail that they are true since their antecedents satisfy the restriction (4) imposes on Q. The antecedent of C1 is consistent with the set of propositions that are laws of nature; it's just not consistent with the lawhood of all those propositions. So, the stronger requirement we need to place on Q is that it be consistent with the *lawhood* of all the propositions that are laws.

The problem raised by counterfactuals like C2 is that, although we want the thesis that lawhood confers inevitability to entail such counterfactuals, (4) does not. It does not because the consequent of such a conditional does not satisfy the restriction (4) places on P. (4) requires that P be logically entailed by the set of propositions that are laws; the consequent of C2 is not entailed by that set of propositions, but it is entailed by their lawhood. So, we need to weaken the restriction on P, so that it requires only that P is entailed by the *lawhood* of all the propositions that are laws.

So here is what happens to (4) when we make the revisions needed to take care of the problems raised by C1 and C2:

(5): ∀Q ∀P (if Q is consistent with the lawhood of all of the propositions that are laws of nature, and the lawhood of those propositions logically entails P, then Q □→ (still) P)

This formulation of (5) is not as perspicuous as we might like it to be. The requirement that Q be 'consistent with the lawhood of all of the propositions that are laws of nature' is easy to interpret as the requirement that Q be consistent with the proposition that all of the laws are laws, which is a trivial truth. So, this restriction on Q seems to have no teeth. But on the intended interpretation of (5), this restriction has teeth: the requirement is that Q is consistent with the lawhood of every proposition that happens to be a law *in the actual world.* This is not a trivial requirement, since in some other possible worlds different propositions are laws of nature, so the proposition that Q is required to be consistent with is not one that is true in every possible world. To make this clearer, it will be helpful to introduce a little terminology:

A proposition is an *@-LAW* just in case it is a law of nature in the actual world.

In this definition, 'the actual world' is a rigid indexical: as used in any possible world w, it refers rigidly to w. So, '@-LAW' and 'law of nature' have the same extension. But the two terms work differently when they occur in counterfactuals. 'If some law of nature were not a law of nature, then . . .' is a counterfactual with a necessarily false antecedent; but 'If some @-LAW were not a law of nature, then . . .' is not: its antecedent is true in any possible world w where for some proposition P, P is a law of nature at the world where the counterfactual is uttered but P is not a law at w.

With this definition in hand, we can reformulate (5):

(5): ∀Q ∀P (if Q is consistent with the lawhood of all of the @-LAWs, and the lawhood of all the @-LAWs entails P, then Q □→ (still) P)

(5) seems in the spirit of the thesis that lawhood confers inevitability, and it does not suffer from the problems posed by C1 and C2. But (5) is not quite right as it stands; there are more problem cases that we need to take account of.

Gauss's law states that at every spatial point at every time, the divergence of the electric field **E** is directly proportional to the electrical charge density ρ:

$$\mathrm{div}(\mathbf{E}) = 4\pi\rho$$

Suppose for the sake of argument that Gauss's law is in fact a law of nature. (That is, Gauss's law is an @-LAW.) Suppose also that the laws of nature are not logically inconsistent with the proposition that ρ takes a constant value everywhere in space and time. This is not implausible; the laws of classical electrodynamics (of which Gauss's law is an example) are consistent with there being no electric charges anywhere in the universe, in which case ρ has the constant value zero everywhere at all times. Now, consider the following counterfactual:

> **C3:** Had it been a law of nature that ρ is a constant in time and space, then the electric field **E** would have a constant divergence.

(5) implies that C3 is true. For, the antecedent of C3 is logically consistent with the lawhood of every member of @-LAWS, but the lawhood of Gauss's law entails that if ρ is a constant, then so is the divergence of **E**; so, by (5), if the antecedent of C3 were true, then so would be the consequent of C3.

But this result is not very plausible at all. If it were a law of nature that ρ is a constant, then the laws of nature governing electrodynamical phenomena would have to be very different from the way they actually are. For one thing, a charged body would not be free to move through a vacuum,[8] since by moving it would make the local charge density change at points as it moved into and out of them. A world where this was so would be very different indeed from the world described by classical electrodynamics. Who can guess how much the other laws of electrodynamics might be different from the way they are in the actual world? So, given the counterfactual supposition made by the antecedent of C3, there seems no reason at all to be confident that the consequent of C3 would also be true. This seems to indicate that we should reject (5).

But the reason we have here to reject (5) is not at all a reason to reject the thesis that lawhood confers inevitability. We can agree that in any possible

[8] Or, for that matter, through any medium that does not have the same charge density as the body itself.

world, the laws of nature at that world are inevitably true in virtue of their being the laws at that world. But that doesn't mean that all of the actual laws would still have been laws even if there had also been some additional laws, whose lawhood would necessitate some radical differences in the total set of laws, though we cannot say just what those radical differences would be. In other words, even if the laws are inevitably true because they are the laws, still, all bets are off once you start speculating about hypothetical situations in which the laws must be different in who knows what ways.

So the case of C3 shows that we have a reason to reject (5) that is not a reason to reject the thesis that lawhood confers inevitability. So (5) must not be the right way to explicate the thesis that lawhood confers inevitability.

How can we modify (5) to fix this problem? Well, C3 is implied by (5) because its antecedent satisfies the restrictions (5) places on Q: it is logically consistent with the lawhood of all of the propositions that are actually laws. It is problematic, though, because it is not consistent with there not being any *other* laws besides the actual laws. So to fix the problem, what we need to do is strengthen the requirements on Q: we need to require that Q be consistent with the lawhood of *exactly* the propositions that are actually laws: Q must entail neither than any actual law is a non-law, nor than any actual non-law is a law. This yields:

> **(6)**: ∀Q ∀P (if Q is consistent with the lawhood of all and only the @-LAWs, and the lawhood of all the @-LAWs logically entails P, then Q □→ (still) P)

There is a striking asymmetry in (6): the restriction on Q requires consistency with the lawhood of *all and only* the actual laws, whereas the restriction on P requires entailment by the lawhood of *all* the actual laws. It is natural to think that this symmetry should be ironed out. And there is a further kind of problem case that motivates that very revision.

Suppose, again, that it is a law of nature that no particle travels faster than c. Also suppose that as a matter of fact many particles travel at speeds quite close to c.[9] Now consider this counterfactual:

> **C4**: If no particle ever did travel faster than c/2, then it would still not be a law of nature that no particle travels faster than c/2.

[9] A disadvantage of this example is that, since speeds other than c are relative to a frame of reference, the statement just made in the text is not really well formed. To make it well formed, we could stipulate

C4 is not implied by (6), for its consequent does not satisfy the restriction (6) places on P: it is not entailed by the lawhood of all of the actual laws of nature. For none of the actual laws of nature says or entails that it is *not also* a law of nature that no particle travels faster than c/2. Yet C4 is plausibly a consequence of the thesis that lawhood confers inevitability. For if lawhood confers inevitability, then in order for things to have been different in such a way that some actual non-law was a law, they would have to have been different in such a way that some actually 'evitable' truth was inevitable. But for things to have been different in such a way that some proposition was inevitably true, it is surely not sufficient for them to have been different in such a way that that proposition *just was* true. In order for things to have been different in such a way that something that is actually not inevitable was inevitable, there would surely have to have been a difference in how the inevitability-maker is distributed—that is, a difference in the extension of lawhood. What this shows is that we should modify (6) by weakening the restriction on P: it is sufficient for P to be entailed by the fact that *all and only* the members of @-LAWS are laws; P need not be entailed by the weaker fact that *all* the members of @-LAWS are laws. This yields NP:

> **NP:** ∀Q ∀P (if Q is consistent with the lawhood of all and only the @-LAWs, and the lawhood of all and only the @-LAWs logically entails P, then Q □→ (still) P)

This gives the right verdict on C4: it is true. For the antecedent of C4 satisfies the restriction NP places on Q: it is logically consistent with the lawhood of all and only the propositions that are actually laws. And the consequent of C4 satisfies the restriction NP places on the variable P: it is entailed by the proposition that all *and only* the propositions that are laws of the actual world are laws.

'NP' stands for 'nomological preservation.' It says that the nomological facts—that is, the facts about which propositions are laws of nature and which ones are not—are preserved under every counterfactual supposition

that 'speed' is to mean speed relative to a certain specified frame of reference. Alternatively, we could change the example so that it concerns relative speeds between particles, rather than speeds simpliciter; it is a law that no particle ever travels relative to any other particle at a speed greater than c, but many pairs of particles have moved relatively to one another at relative speeds that are very close to c. I'll ignore this complication in the text, since nothing important to the way the example works depends on it.

that is logically consistent with them all. These nomological facts comprise a maximally counterfactually stable set: they are inevitably true as a class.

NP seems to be exactly the right counterfactual principle for explicating the idea that lawhood confers inevitability. It says that the nomological facts are inevitably true; since the nomological facts entail that all of the actual laws of nature are true, NP says that something is inevitably true, in virtue of which all of the laws are true. So the laws of nature themselves are not simply inevitably true as a class (a thought which leaves out the idea that the laws are inevitable *because they are the laws*); they have to be true because they are consequences of a class of inevitably true propositions, namely the nomological facts. This means that the laws would not necessarily have still been true if a different set of propositions had been the laws. But no matter how things might have differed from the way they actually are, so long as they differed in a way that is logically compatible with the laws' being exactly the propositions that actually are laws, the nomological truths would still have been true, and so the laws would still have been true. This captures exactly the thought that the laws of nature have a kind of inevitable truth that is grounded in the fact that they are the laws of nature: their truth follows from their lawhood, which is itself inevitable.

Thus far in this section, I have been proceeding on the assumption that (2) was the right way to cash out the idea that a single proposition is inevitably true. If, bothered by worries about context-variability, we are inclined to go for (2*) rather than (2), then parallel reasoning should lead us to modified versions of (4) through (6), up to the following modified version of NP:

> **NP***: ∀Q ∀P (if Q is consistent with the lawhood of all and only the members of @-LAWS, and the lawhood of all and only the members of @-LAWS logically entails P, then the counterfactual (Q □→ (still) P) is true, no matter what the conversational context is).

Note that if NP* is true, then so is NP: in fact, if NP* is true, then NP is true in all possible contexts of utterance. So if we take NP* to be the correct explication of the thesis that lawhood confers inevitability, and thus the correct explication of the Governing Thesis, then we could express our view equally well by saying that the Governing Thesis is explicated by the thesis that NP is true in all possible contexts of utterance. I will return to the question of which explication of the Governing Thesis we should take below in Section 5.8, and in Chapter 6.

5.7 NP and 'supporting counterfactuals'

One of the most widespread ideas in the philosophical literature on laws of nature is that laws are distinguished from accidental regularities (i.e. true general propositions that are not laws of nature) in that laws 'support counterfactuals' in a way that accidental regularities do not.[10] Although I motivated NP as an explication of the idea that lawhood confers inevitable truth, and thereby as an explication of the Governing Thesis, it is also a plausible way of spelling out the slogan 'laws support counterfactuals.'

The paradigm case of a counterfactual getting 'supported' by a law goes like this: it is a law that all Fs are Gs; object o is such that it is nomologically possible for it to be an F, but in fact it isn't an F; it seems to follow that if o were an F, then it would also be a G. This is a case with a particularly simple form, but the idea can be generalized to take account of laws that do not take the form $\forall x(Fx \supset Gx)$, and to take account of counterfactuals that are supported by laws of this form but are not substitution instances of $Fx \mathbin{\Box\!\!\rightarrow} Gx$. In the simple paradigm case, the antecedent of the counterfactual is nomologically possible, and together with the supporting law it entails the consequent. This seems to be what is really crucial to the way the simple paradigm case works: the antecedent could be true consistently with the laws, so if it were true, then the laws would still have been what they are, so everything entailed by the antecedent together with those laws is true. More formally:

(8): If A is consistent with the lawhood of all and only the members of @-LAWS, and A together with the proposition that all and only the members of @-LAWS are laws entails C, then A $\mathbin{\Box\!\!\rightarrow}$ C.

This is equivalent to:

SC: If A is consistent with the lawhood of all and only the members of @-LAWS, and (A $\supset$ C) is entailed by the lawhood of all and only the members of @-LAWS, then A $\mathbin{\Box\!\!\rightarrow}$ C.

[10] See, for example, Goodman (1954); Chisholm (1946); Rescher (1970); Lewis (1973a); Dretske (1977).

This principle SC is (except for a difference in notation) the principle called by the same name by John Carroll.[11] Carroll identifies SC as a conceptually necessary truth linking the concept of a law to the concept of a counterfactual.

If we assume two simple and non-controversial principles from the logic of counterfactuals, it is easy to prove that SC is equivalent to NP. The assumptions are:

Trivial: For every logically consistent P: P $\Box\!\!\rightarrow$ P.

Two-Premise Closure: For every logically consistent P, and for every Q, R, S: If P $\Box\!\!\rightarrow$ Q, P $\Box\!\!\rightarrow$ R, and $\{Q, R\} \vdash S$, then P $\Box\!\!\rightarrow$ S.

(These assumptions are true given Lewis's or Stalnaker's semantics for counterfactuals, for example. For the closest P-world (or, all the closest P-worlds) must be worlds where P is true, and any world at all where two proposition that logically entail a third are both true must be a world where the third is true as well.) Proof: suppose that NP is true. Let A be consistent with the lawhood of all and only the @-LAWs, and let C be any proposition such that the lawhood of all and only the @-LAWs entails $(A \supset C)$. Then A satisfies the requirements on Q set by NP, and $(A \supset C)$ satisfies the requirements on P set by NP. So by NP, A $\Box\!\!\rightarrow$ $(A \supset C)$. By Trivial, A $\Box\!\!\rightarrow$ A, and so by Two-Premise Closure, A $\Box\!\!\rightarrow$ C. Therefore, NP entails SC. Now, suppose that SC is true. Let Q be consistent with the lawhood of all and only the @-LAWs, and let P be any proposition that is entailed by the lawhood of all and only the @-LAWs. Then, since P entails $(Q \supset P)$, $(Q \supset P)$ is entailed by the lawhood of all and only the @-LAWs. So by SC, Q $\Box\!\!\rightarrow$ $(Q \supset P)$. By Trivial, Q $\Box\!\!\rightarrow$ Q, and so by Two-Premise Closure, it follows that Q $\Box\!\!\rightarrow$ P. Therefore, SC entails NP.

So NP is equivalent to SC, and SC explicates the slogan that laws support counterfactuals. Thus, the condition that must be satisfied in order for the Governing Thesis to be true is the same condition that must be satisfied in order for laws to support counterfactuals.

This is not really a surprise, since the idea that laws govern the universe seems closely allied to the intuition that laws support counterfactuals. Perhaps laws support counterfactuals *because* they govern the universe; perhaps what we mean when we say that laws govern the universe is

[11] Carroll (1994), p. 20.

that they support counterfactuals. Either way, there is a close connection between the two ideas, and so it should not be surprising if it turns out that the condition that must be fulfilled in order for one of them to be true is the same as the condition that must be fulfilled in order for the other to be true.

5.8 The worry about context-variability

I have been seeking a condition, spelled out in terms of counterfactuals, that plausibly articulates what things would have to be like in order for lawhood to confer inevitability. The condition I have come up with is NP. I argued back in Section 5.2 that the idea that lawhood confers inevitability is a plausible rendering of the Governing Thesis. So, I have tentatively reached the conclusion that what it takes for the Governing Thesis to be true is, precisely, that NP is true.

But back in Section 5.4, we saw a reason to worry about using any principle spelled out in terms of counterfactuals—such as NP—to explicate either the idea that lawhood confers inevitability or the Governing Thesis itself. For the truth values of counterfactuals can vary from context to context. If any of the counterfactuals that are within the scope of NP are among the context-variable ones, then NP itself is context-variable. So, if we accept NP as an explication of the thesis that lawhood confers inevitability, then we get the conclusion that inevitability-ascriptions are context-variable. And if we use this thesis, in turn, to explicate the Governing Thesis, we get the result that the Governing Thesis is context-variable. Since the Governing Thesis is an essential part of the law-governed world-picture, it follows that that world-picture cannot be accurate in all contexts, even if it is accurate in some contexts.

This seems like a problem. And the problem here is not merely that the Governing Thesis (and so, the law-governed world-picture) turns out to be context-variable; it is that the truth value of the Governing Thesis turns out to depend on pragmatic features of the context in the same ways that the truth values of counterfactuals can depend on those features. Recall the example of the almost-empty fuel tank: which counterfactual is true in the context depends on which aspects of the actual situation are most important for the purposes of the conversation. If the important thing, for purposes of the conversation, is how much gas we had when we started out, then it is true that if there weren't a lot of gas stations around we would be in big trouble; but if the important thing is whether the driver has acted irresponsibly, then the contrary counterfactual is true. So the truth values of counterfactuals can vary depending on what the point at issue in the conversation is—that is, on what the speakers are trying to establish about the actual world by engaging in the conversation, what they take the important questions at issue to be. If the counterfactuals implied by NP are like this, then whether NP is true in a given context or not depends on what questions are important for purposes of the conversation at hand.

Suppose that you and I are having the almost-empty-fuel-tank conversation, and we are both aware of all the relevant actual-world facts; these are taken for granted in the background. If we agree to affirm one counterfactual or the other, what we thereby agree on is something that merely expresses what we were interested in establishing in that conversation.[12] If it is like that for the counterfactuals implied by NP, then the truth of NP in a given context is just a matter of that conversation's having a certain point. But when we affirm the Governing Thesis, it just doesn't seem like we are affirming something whose truth or falsity is a matter of what the point of our present conversation is. On the contrary, it seems like we are affirming something deep and important about the nature of the universe.

One way out of this difficulty is to say that the Governing Thesis should not be explicated by means of NP, but rather by means of NP*. Whereas NP just says that a whole bunch of counterfactuals are true—something that can be true or false depending on what context we are in—NP* says that a whole bunch of counterfactuals are true no matter what context we are in. NP*, then, is not shifty in the way that NP might be. So if we use NP* to explicate the Governing Thesis, we don't have to worry about context-variability.

However, I am going to argue in the next chapter that NP* is not a necessary truth. There are possible contexts of discourse in which NP is false. I do not know whether any such contexts ever arise in the actual

[12] We can support this claim by considering what would happen if you and I persisted in asserting mutually contrary counterfactuals—'We would so have been in big trouble!' 'We would not have been in big trouble!'—even after we had established that we both agreed on all the relevant actual-world facts. In that case, we would clearly be in disagreement about what the point of the conversation had been all along, and this is what we would then start arguing about. Settling which counterfactual was true in the context would just be a matter of settling what the point of our conversation had been.

world, but there are possible worlds in which they do. If we are in a world where such contexts arise, then NP* is false in the actual world, so if the Governing Thesis is equivalent to NP*, then the Governing Thesis is false. On the other hand, if we happen to live in a possible world where none of these contexts arise, then *the fact that we do* is not something that can be discovered by means of empirical-scientific inquiry (as I will argue in the next chapter). So, the Science-Says-So Thesis—which says that by engaging in empirical-scientific inquiry, we can come to learn that the Governing Thesis is true—is false. Either way, the law-governed world-picture is not accurate—either because laws don't really govern the universe, or because empirical science is impotent to tell us that they do. Unless we are prepared to reject the law-governed world-picture, then, we had better not explicate the Governing Thesis by means of NP*.

So we're stuck with NP as our explication of the Governing Thesis, and the truth of NP can depend not only on which possible world we live in, but on pragmatic features of the context as well. How bad does this make things for the law-governed world-picture?

5.9 A solution, and a look ahead

Well, NP and the Governing Thesis can still be true in many contexts of discourse. So in those contexts, the law-governed world-picture might still be accurate. But the worry is that NP's being true in a given context might turn out to be nothing more than a fact about the pragmatic features of that context, such as what the speakers take to be the point of the conversation. NP will presumably be true in any context where the most salient feature of the actual world is that it has exactly the laws of nature that it does. But, for *any* set of true propositions Γ, in any context where the most salient feature of the actual world is that the truths in Γ are all true, Γ will presumably be maximally counterfactually stable. So there doesn't seem to be anything special about the laws of nature that is indicated by the fact that NP is true in the contexts where it is true. And this seems to be a reason to worry: the law-governed world-picture, and the Governing Thesis in particular, are intended to express the idea that there *is* something very special indeed about the laws of nature—something more than that in our present conversation we treat them as the most salient aspect of the actual world.

So if NP is true in our present context of discourse, then that fact by itself doesn't signal anything special about the laws of nature themselves. What more could we say that would signal this? Well, if NP were not *just* true in our present context, but it were also true in a broad and interesting class of contexts that can be picked out otherwise than as *the set of contexts in which the laws of nature are the most salient feature of the actual world*, then that would be something. For example, suppose it turns out that NP is true in every *scientific* context—where a 'scientific context' is one in which the point of the conversation is to exposit, apply, or expand empirical-scientific knowledge. Since we haven't just defined the 'scientific contexts' as *the contexts where the laws of nature are the most salient aspect of the natural world for purposes of counterfactual reasoning*, it is an interesting, non-trivial fact (assuming it is a fact) that NP is true in all scientific contexts. If this is so, then it does indicate something special about the laws of nature. Moreover, this would help to vindicate the spirit of the law-governed world-picture: for it implies that whenever we are engaged in scientific discourse, NP is true in the context, and so it is true in the context that lawhood confers inevitability. There would then be no consistent way of pursuing or applying scientific knowledge while simultaneously denying that lawhood confers inevitability. Science would indeed present us with a picture of a law-governed universe.

This would be one way to save the Governing Thesis from collapsing into something uninteresting. I don't know whether it is the only way to do so. But it turns out not to matter whether it is the only way to do so. For as I will argue in Chapter 7, the Science-Says-So Thesis is true if and only if NP is true in every possible scientific context. Thus, the Governing Thesis is both true and avoids collapsing into triviality *if* NP is true in all possible scientific contexts, and the Science-Says-So Thesis is true *if and only if* NP is true in all possible scientific contexts. Hence, the truth of NP in every possible scientific context is a necessary and sufficient condition of the truth of the conjunction of the Governing Thesis and the Science-Says-So Thesis.

6

When would the laws have been different?

6.1 Where we are now

In Chapter 5, I argued that what it takes for the Governing Thesis to be true is for NP to be true:

> **NP:** $\forall Q\ \forall P$ (if Q is consistent with the lawhood of all and only the @-LAWs, and the lawhood of all and only the @-LAWs logically entails P, then Q $\Box\!\!\rightarrow$ (still) P)

(where the @-LAWs are those propositions that are laws of nature in the world where NP is asserted). NP can be put by saying that the nomological truths—that is, the true propositions about what is a law of nature and what isn't—are maximally counterfactually stable: they would all still have been true under any counterfactual supposition that is logically consistent with them all. That is as counterfactually invariant as they could (logically) possibly be.

But then a worry presented itself: NP is a generalization that says that a whole class of counterfactuals are true. But counterfactuals are notoriously context-variable. So it seems that NP itself might be context-variable in the same ways and for the same reasons that counterfactuals are. But it is counterintuitive that the Governing Thesis could be context-variable in the same ways and for the same reasons that counterfactuals are.[1] In fact, if it turns out that the Governing Thesis is context-variable in the same ways and for the same reasons that counterfactuals are, then even if the letter of the Governing Thesis is true (in some contexts), the spirit of the law-governed world-picture is compromised, for those who

[1] See Section 5.8.

affirm the law-governed world-picture are not trying to affirm something whose truth is context-dependent in the same ways that counterfactuals are.

What this suggests is that if would-be advocates of the law-governed world-picture are not confused—if they are not attempting to attribute a context-neutral feature to the universe by means of a principle that is context-variable—then the Governing Thesis must have a context-independent truth value. By the argument of Sections 5.2 through 5.6, this can be so only if NP has a context-independent truth value. And if the law-governed world-picture is not just wrong, then the Governing Thesis (and so, NP) must be true. This seems to lead to this conclusion: if the law-governed world-picture is neither based on a confusion nor just plain wrong, then NP must be true in every possible context of utterance.[2]

However, I am going to argue in this chapter that NP is not true in every possible context of utterance. I am going to do this by describing some possible scenarios in which there is a conversational context in which it is plain that NP is false. This seems to pose a big threat to the law-governed world-picture.

But there is a way to get around this problem. The gist is that although NP is not true in all possible contexts, it might be true in all possible *scientific* contexts of discourse, and that would be enough to vindicate the law-governed world-picture (or so I will argue). In the last section of the chapter, I will consider some famous putative counterexamples to NP that seem to show that it is not even true in all scientific contexts. I will argue that these counterexamples fail. So the possibility is still open that NP is true in all possible scientific contexts.

6.2 The God Cases

One kind of context in which NP can be false is what I will call a *God Case*. I will present two God Cases in this section.

[2] In other words, the thesis NP*, defined in Section 5.6, must be true.

6.2.1 *A monotheistic God Case*

Imagine that the following story is true:

> The natural universe was created by an intelligent and benevolent deity whose purpose in creating it was to provide a suitable habitat for intelligent life. In the act of creation, the deity determined, by a free choice, the laws of nature and the initial conditions. As it turned out, the laws of nature preclude the existence of any complex life in environments where the temperature is over 500 kelvins. There are possible universes that the deity could have created in which the laws are exactly what they actually are, and it is always everywhere hotter than 500 kelvins. But the deity refrained from creating any of those universes. By a judicious choice of initial conditions, the deity provided for the existence of many regions with more temperate climates, in many of which intelligent life evolved and flourishes.

Now imagine a conversation between Bert and Ernie, both of whom believe the above true story. The conversation is about how there ended up being a universe hospitable to intelligent life; it takes place in a seminar on the topic of Natural Theology. Bert says, 'It's lucky for us that we were provided with regions of moderate temperature in which to live. We would not be able to live at all if the entire universe were hotter than 500 kelvins!' Ernie replies, 'Well Bert, we are indeed lucky to have been provided for so well, but what you just said misses the point. If the entire universe had been everywhere and always hotter than 500 degrees, then the laws of nature would have been different, in such a way as to allow intelligent life to flourish under such conditions. For the laws of nature, as well as the initial conditions, were all designed by the deity for the purpose of providing us with a good environment. We are lucky that the deity cares so much for us, but to put the point the way you just did suggests that the determination of the laws of nature was beyond the deity's control—that the divine planning had to be done within the confines set by the laws of nature. This underestimates the powers of the deity.'

In effect, Bert asserts the following counterfactual:

> **Bert's counterfactual:** The universe is always everywhere hotter than 500 kelvins □→ there is no intelligent life anywhere in the universe.

and Ernie asserts this one:

> **Ernie's counterfactual:** The universe is always everywhere hotter than 500 kelvins □→ the laws of nature permit the flourishing of intelligent life at temperatures greater than 500 kelvins.

The common antecedent of these two counterfactuals is consistent with the lawhood of all and only the actual laws, *ex hypothesi*. This common antecedent, together with the actual laws of nature, entails that the consequent of Bert's counterfactual is true, and the consequent of Ernie's counterfactual is false. So, NP entails that Bert's counterfactual is true and Ernie's is false.

But these verdicts are just wrong. For the reasons that Ernie gives, his counterfactual is true, and Bert's is false. Therefore, NP is false in the context of the conversation between Bert and Ernie.

The reason why Ernie's counterfactual is true is that the context is a theological one: the point of the conversation is to engage in exposition of theological matters, and to engage in theological reasoning. When considering counterfactual scenarios in which things are different, but not in a way inconsistent with all of the actual theological facts, those facts should be held constant. So, in the counterfactual situation that Bert and Ernie are talking about, it is true (just as it is in the actual situation) that the laws and the initial conditions were both up to the deity, and the deity's purpose in making a universe was to provide a suitable place for intelligent life to live. Being no slouch as an engineer, the deity would certainly have selected a set of laws and a set of initial conditions that together conspired to make the universe just such a place.

Things would be different if Bert and Ernie had had their conversation in a different sort of context. If they were collaborating on their science homework instead of engaging in theological disputation, and one of the problems their teacher had set for them was to work out the biological consequences of the hypothesis that the universe is always everywhere hotter than 500 kelvins, then Bert's counterfactual would be the right answer, and Ernie's would be a mistake. For in that case, the actual truths that they would need to hold constant when working out the consequences of the counterfactual hypothesis of a hot universe would be the truths they have been learning about in their science class, such as the laws of nature. Hence, what this God Case shows is not that *there are possible worlds at which NP is false*; rather, what it shows is that *there are possible contexts in which NP is false.*

Whatever the other merits or faults of this story may be, it is logically consistent and evidently perfectly coherent. So it is at least logically and conceptually possible for NP to be false in some context.

6.2.2 A polytheistic God Case

For what it is worth, there are polytheistic God Cases as well. Here is my favorite. Imagine that the following story is true:

> The laws and initial conditions of the universe were selected by a committee of gods. Zeus wanted it to be a law of nature that the gravitational force obeys an inverse-square law, whereas Hera wanted the gravitational law to be an inverse-cube law. Zeus wanted the whole thing to be designed in such a way that there would be a large population of ancient moas, whereas Hera wanted things to be arranged in such a way that every moa would die before reaching its fiftieth birthday.[3] A compromise was struck: inverse-square law; no moas older than fifty. A different compromise could have been reached—there could have been an inverse-cube law and a large population of ancient moas. But some compromise had to be reached, because neither Zeus nor Hera was willing to let the other get everything they wanted, and neither of them had enough authority on the committee to overrule the other.

Now imagine a conversation in which the participants are engaged in lamentations about how their destinies are influenced by petty squabbles among the gods. In the context of this conversation, the following counterfactual is clearly true:

Moa-cube counterfactual: There is a large population of ancient moas $\Box\!\!\rightarrow$ the gravitational force obeys an inverse-cube law.

The moa-cube counterfactual, like Ernie's, is inconsistent with NP. So in the context in which it is uttered, NP is false.

6.2.3 Some reactions to the God Cases

In my experience, nobody ever believes that the God Cases really show what I say they show upon first hearing them. There are a variety of ways in which you might reply to them, and many of these replies are very attractive at first. But I don't think any reply is successful. I'll go through

[3] In a famous example due to Karl Popper, it is a true universal regularity but not a law of nature that no moa ever lives to be older than fifty years (Popper 1959).

every reply to them I've heard anyone give, and a few that I haven't heard anyone give, and try to convince you that none of these replies works.

Not the real laws 'The God Cases do not really show that there are contexts where NP is false. Even if the cases you have described are possible, there is no violation of NP in either case. For in those cases, the real laws of nature are not the principles you are calling "laws of nature." The real laws of nature are things like, *that whatever the deity wills to be true is true, that the deity desires that there be a universe inhabited by intelligent life*, and things like that. And those propositions are all maximally counterfactually invariant in the God Cases; so NP is true in those cases.'[4]

According to the objection, the real laws of nature in the God Cases are all principles concerning the powers and dispositions of the gods; in what follows I'll call such principles *theological principles*. What reason do we have to believe that in the God Cases, the laws of nature are all theological principles? You might simply say that the true theological principles in these cases are the propositions that are maximally counterfactually stable, and therefore they are the laws of nature in these cases. But this would be ad hoc and question-begging. It amounts to insisting that NP is true, and inferring from this that whatever principles would have to be the laws in order for NP to be true in the God Cases are the laws in the God Cases. Do we have any independent reason to think that the real laws of nature in the God Cases are the theological principles?

One reason someone might give for thinking so appeals to the idea that the laws of nature at a possible world are just whatever propositions are true in that world and are beyond the power of any agent to violate. In the God Cases, the one set of propositions that no agent can violate—not even the deity or deities themselves—is the set of propositions that ascribe powers and dispositions to the deity or deities. Hence these are the laws in the possible worlds that figure in the God Cases. Let's call this *the inviolability principle*.

But the inviolability principle is not very plausible. For one thing, it seems to imply that in any possible world where the conservation of mass is a law, the proposition that states exactly how much mass there is in

[4] This objection was raised in conversation by Marc Lange.

the universe is also a law, since no agent would ever be able to bring it about that there is some other amount of mass in the universe. Yet, even if mass-conservation is a law of nature, surely the amount of mass in the universe could be nomologically contingent.

There is another important liability of the inviolability principle as well—and it shares this liability with any view that says that in the God Cases, the theological principles are the real laws of nature. Accepting this claim means denying the very possibility that the laws of nature were created by a deity or other supernatural being by a choice, other choices having been metaphysically possible. For, suppose that a deity does bring about the laws of nature by fiat—then, the deity could have chosen to create other laws, and so the laws are not such that it is impossible that the deity brings about violations of them. (Perhaps it is impossible for the deity to bring about violations of the laws once they have been made the laws—but if the deity's choice in creating the laws was not the only possible choice, then it is metaphysically possible for the deity to have chosen other laws.) Hence, according to the inviolability principle, the laws of nature are not the laws of nature. This is a contradiction, so we have a *reductio* on the supposition that the laws of nature are the product of a freely acting supernatural being. If the inviolability principle is true—or if, for any reason, the real laws of nature in the God Cases are all theological principles—then it is impossible for there to be any laws of nature that are the product of a freely acting creator.

This is somewhat ironic. There is a long tradition of arguing that there could be no laws of nature unless they *were* the handiwork of a divine legislator, whose legislative actions were free. Adherents of this tradition include Descartes, Leibniz, Newton, Richard Swinburne, and, most recently, John Foster.[5] The claim that in the God Cases the real laws of nature are the theological principles turns this tradition on its head, implying that there could be no laws of nature that *were* the handiwork of a divine legislator.

The concept of a law of nature is a scientific concept; if we believe that the empirical natural sciences are autonomous of theology, then we should not build any theological presuppositions into our analysis of this concept. So we should accept neither the traditional view that there can be no laws

[5] Foster (2004).

of nature without a divine lawmaker, nor the inverted view that there can be no laws of nature *with* a divine lawmaker.

Further problems for this reply to the God Cases can be seen by considering that many distinguished figures in the history of modern science—including Descartes, Newton, and perhaps Galileo—held that the actual world is like the world of the monotheistic God Case in the relevant respects. They did not identify the laws of nature with principles about the attributes and powers of God, but rather with the sorts of things that we ordinarily think of as putative laws of nature. For example, Newton held that in creating the universe, God selected both the laws of nature and the initial conditions of the universe in such a way that the harmonious system of planetary orbits resulted. Thus, in the 'General Scholium' of the third book of his *Principia* he writes:

> The six primary planets revolve about the sun in circles concentric with the sun, with the same direction of motion, and very nearly in the same plane. Ten moons revolve about the earth, Jupiter, and Saturn, in concentric circles, with the same direction of motion, very nearly in the planes of the orbits of the planets. And all these regular motions do not have their origin from mechanical causes, since comets go freely in very eccentric orbits and into all parts of the heavens.... This most elegant arrangement of the sun, planets and comets could not have arisen without the design and dominion of an intelligent and powerful being. And if the fixed stars are the centers of similar systems, they will all be constructed according to a similar design and subject to the dominion of *One*...
>
> (Newton 1999, p. 940)

The fact that there are immense distances among the systems of the fixed stars is not guaranteed by the Newtonian laws; on Newton's view, they are a consequence of the nomologically contingent initial conditions, set up by God so that evolution under the actual laws would lead to the stability of the world system. That is, given God's interest in creating a stable world system, he fine-tuned the initial conditions to go together with the laws in such a way as to lead to such a system. Had God chosen to impose different laws on the universe, then his plan to create a stable world system would have required him to tune the initial conditions differently. And conversely: had he imposed very different initial conditions on the universe—conditions that would not have led to a stable and harmonious world system under the actual laws—then he would have to have imposed different laws on it.

So it is not much of a reach to suppose that when he was in the midst of one of his more theological discussions, Newton would have been happy to affirm (or at least, would have been committed to affirming) that if the initial conditions had been sufficiently different, the laws would have been different as well. So Newton's own views committed him to a picture not essentially different from the monotheistic God Case. Should we say that on Newton's own view, the *real* laws of nature are not the three laws of motion, the law of universal gravitation, and so forth, but rather certain theological principles? This would be a bizarre thing to say. The laws of nature, after all, are laws *of nature*; they pertain to the natural, created world, not to the supernatural or the divine. The laws Newton was talking about were laws imposed by a divine legislator, and Newton's usage of 'laws' stands in a direct ancestral relation to contemporary scientific usage of it. So it is not plausible to suppose that Newton was not talking about what *we* talk about when we talk about laws (though of course, we disagree with him about which propositions *are* the laws). If the things I called 'laws of nature' in the monotheistic God Cases are not the *real* laws of nature in that case, then Newton was deeply confused: in affirming his views about which propositions are laws of nature, he affirmed something logically or conceptually incoherent. Unless we are prepared to attribute such incoherence to Newton, we had better not say that in the God Case scenarios, the laws of nature are really theological principles.

Not the right kind of possibility 'All that your descriptions of the God Cases show is that it is logically possible, and perhaps conceptually coherent, that NP is false in some possible scenario. But they do not show that such cases are metaphysically possible. If the actual laws are not in fact the product of a supernatural creator, then perhaps it belongs to the essence of lawhood that laws cannot be the product of such a creator. In that case, the God Cases would be metaphysically impossible. So, for all these cases show, it might be metaphysically necessary that NP is true in every context of utterance.'

What this objection alleges is right: all I can claim to have shown is that it is coherently conceivable that there are counterexamples to NP. The God Cases fail to refute the thesis that it is metaphysically necessary that NP is true in every context. But this is irrelevant. Even if the God

Cases are metaphysically impossible, they still show that if the Governing Thesis requires the truth of NP in all contexts, then the law-governed world-picture cannot be right.

The reason is that even if the God Cases are metaphysically impossible, empirical natural-scientific inquiry cannot show that they are impossible—or even that they are not actually true. Whether the laws of nature are the handiwork of a purposive supernatural creator is not a question that the empirical natural sciences can address.[6] But part of the law-governed world-picture is the Science-Says-So Thesis: the idea is not just that our universe is governed by laws of nature, but that this is something that the empirical sciences have discovered. If the truth of the Governing Thesis depends on the non-existence of a supernatural designer, then it is not within the scope of empirical natural science. The idea of a law-governed universe will then be an extra-scientific idea, imposed on the results of scientific inquiry. This is one of the things that the law-governed world-picture, as I described it back in Chapter 1, is meant to exclude.

Someone might reply that still, science could give us a good reason to accept the conditional that *if* there is no supernatural designer at work behind the scenes, *then* we live in a law-governed universe. This would make the idea of a law-governed universe part of an atheistic interpretation of modern science, rather than part of the content of modern science itself. But there are at least two reasons to resist this view. One is that the idea that we live in a law-governed universe has animated the thinking of theistic and non-theistic scientists alike; Descartes, Newton, and Leibinz hold the universe to be law-governed as much as Laplace and Hawking do. The conception of a law-governed universe seems to belong to the modern-scientific way of thinking about the world, which is plausibly neither theistic nor atheistic but rather autonomous of theology altogether. If we give the reply under consideration, we must either consign the idea of a law-governed universe to the extra-scientific realm, or else reject the autonomy of science from theology.

[6] It won't work to point to empirical evidence of tremendous evil in the world, and run the problem-of-evil argument against the existence of God; for God Cases don't require there to be a supremely good creator, or even a creator who cares very much about humanity. All they require is that the laws of nature are the product of a purposive creator or creators. This is what the polytheistic God Case adds to the argument.

The second reason is that if we take this view of the matter, then we are at a loss to explain *why we should believe* that NP is true in all possible contexts. Perhaps it is; but what good reason do we have to think so? The truth or falsity of NP is not the sort of question that lends itself to experimentation or empirical investigation, since what things would be like in non-actual circumstances is not the kind of thing we can observe, even with the most powerful instruments. If lawhood has an essence, and that essence is incompatible with being the product of a divine designer, then we could hardly discover this through empirical investigation. If the laws of nature were logically or metaphysically necessary truths, then of course the nomological facts would be maximally counterfactually stable, but the laws of nature are contingent—or at least, some of them are.[7] The only alternative seems to be that NP itself is a logically or conceptually necessary truth. But the fact that the God Cases are coherently conceivable demonstrates that NP is neither logically nor conceptually necessary.

Of course, we could all agree to make NP true in any context where we are discoursing, just by adopting the convention that we shall hold constant the actual nomological facts whenever we engage in counterfactual reasoning—but then NP, and the Governing Thesis, would just be true by conventions we have adopted; they would tell us nothing about the nature of the universe. Perhaps it is a psychological fact about us already that we always do hold the actual nomological facts constant when engaging in counterfactual reasoning—but in that case, the truth of NP (and hence that of the Governing Thesis) would be a reflection of our psychology, rather than an important truth about how it is with the universe.

So if we insisted that the Governing Thesis requires the truth of NP in all metaphysically possible contexts, and dismissed the God Cases as conceivabilities that are not real possibilities, then we would face a forced choice between two unattractive alternatives: on the first, the Governing Thesis is an article of faith for which we can find no supporting evidence; on the second, we adopt a deflationary view that deprives the Governing Thesis of all its interest as a claim about the way the universe is.

For these reasons, the mere fact that the God Cases are coherently conceivable is enough for them to raise trouble for the Governing Thesis, *if* the Governing Thesis is understood as requiring that NP is true in every

[7] See Chapter 2, Section 2.5.

context. Even if these cases are not metaphysically possible, that doesn't help matters.

Not in the scope of NP It might be objected that the God Cases are not counterexamples to NP, since they are not in the scope of NP. Properly construed (the objection runs), NP should apply only to counterfactuals with antecedents that are *metaphysically compossible* with the lawhood of exactly the actual laws. Mere logical consistency is not enough.

But I formulated NP in terms of logical consistency rather than metaphysical compossibility on purpose; I'll say something about why below, in Section 6.4. Furthermore, the objection is not really to the point here. In the monotheistic God Case, it is not at all clear that the antecedent of Ernie's counterfactual is not compossible with the lawhood of the actual laws. In that case, it is assumed that God chose the laws and the initial conditions *freely*; God's freedom might require the metaphysical contingency of his actions. In that case, the antecedent of Ernie's conditional is not only logically consistent with the lawhood of the actual laws; it is metaphysically compossible as well. It is metaphysically possible that God decided to create a universe hostile to life; but the fact that he chose not to do so is important enough in the context of the theological context between Bert and Ernie that it still trumps the laws in the evaluation of their counterfactuals.

Lange's test In his article 'When Would the Natural Laws Have Been Broken?'[8] Marc Lange considers a number of putative counterexamples to NP, and argues that they are not genuine counterexamples. The putative counterexamples he considers are not much like the God Cases, but it is worth looking into whether Lange's strategy for dealing with the putative counterexamples he considers would also work on the God cases.

Here is an example similar to the ones Lange considers. Our friend Julia is an astronaut on an expedition to Pluto. Looking at our copy of her itinerary, we note that she just passed Saturn five minutes ago. I say, 'Too bad Julia isn't here right now; I would love to hear her tell us about what Saturn looks like up close.' You reply, 'Since we know that she was passing Saturn five minutes ago, she could only be here now if she had traveled the distance from Saturn to North Carolina in five minutes or less. That is to

[8] Lange (1993b).

say, if Julia were here now, she would have just traveled faster than light. If she were in any state to talk, I bet she would have more interesting things to tell us than what Saturn looks like!' The first of the two counterfactuals you have asserted:

Julia-1: Julia is here now □→ Julia just traveled faster than light

appears to violate NP: it is consistent with the lawhood of all the actual laws that Julia is here right now (since it wasn't nomologically necessary that she take her space trip in the first place), but it is not consistent with the actual laws for Julia to have traveled faster than light.

Lange's reply to this sort of apparent counterexample to NP can be motivated by an example like the following one, which has nothing to do with laws: suppose that it is 11:00 pm and we are at the ice cream parlor. We get to talking about our friend Michael, whom we know to have a great love of chocolate ice cream. I say, 'If Michael were here, he would order the chocolate ice cream.' Then you point out to me that it is 11:00 in the evening, and Michael generally finishes dinner and has his dessert at 8:30. 'If Michael were here,' you say, 'he would have already eaten a large helping of chocolate ice cream, and he would not want any more.' I reply, 'Well, of course you're right, but *what I meant* was that if Michael were here with us and had not yet had dessert, then he would order the chocolate ice cream.' Suppose that I am being sincere: when I made my first counterfactual assertion, I really did mean what I just said I meant. It would not have been unreasonable for me to say what I said, expecting that in the context you would understand that I was suppressing part of the antecedent for the sake of brevity. That is, though I seemed to be asserting the following counterfactual:

Michael-1: Michael is here □→ Michael gets the chocolate ice cream

I was speaking elliptically, and the counterfactual I meant to assert was:

Michael-2: (Michael is here and has not had dessert yet) □→ Michael gets the chocolate ice cream

Michael-1 is evidently incompatible with Michael-3:

Michael-3: Michael is here □→ Michael has already had dessert and does not want any more and so won't order any ice cream so in asserting Michael-1, I seem to be committed to rejecting Michael-3. But I am not actually committed to rejecting Michael-3; for what I really meant to assert was Michael-2, which is perfectly compatible with Michael-3.

Now, back to Julia. Perhaps in asserting the counterfactual Julia-1, you were speaking elliptically. Perhaps all you really meant to assert was:

> **Julia-2:** (Julia was passing by Saturn five minutes ago, and Saturn is more than five light-minutes from here, and Julia is here now) □→ Julia just traveled faster than light

but you asserted the briefer counterfactual Julia-1 because it was shorter and easier to say, and you expected me to catch on that you were speaking elliptically. In that case, in asserting Julia-1, you only appear to be saying something in conflict with NP. For what you really meant to be asserting was Julia-2, which is perfectly compatible with NP. (It is compatible with NP because its antecedent is not logically consistent with the lawhood of the actual laws.) So, when we find what you said plausible, we do not thereby find a reason to reject NP. Your plausible utterance is only an apparent counterexample to NP; taken literally, it is inconsistent with NP, but when it is understood properly as an elliptical expression of Julia-2, it is seen to be perfectly compatible with NP.

Suppose that we find your assertion, which is apparently an assertion of Julia-1, to be very plausible, and we take it for granted that what you asserted is true. How can we figure out whether this commits us to rejecting NP or not? If your assertion was elliptical for Julia-2, then its truth is not incompatible with NP, so we don't have here a case of evidence against NP. On the other hand, if your assertion was not elliptical, then insofar as we find it plausibly true, we have evidence against NP. So, whether we have a genuine counterexample to NP here depends on whether your assertion was elliptical or not. But how can we tell whether your counterfactual assertion had an elliptical antecedent or not?

It's important to see why this is an important question, and why it is a hard one to answer. The context of utterance can make contributions to the truth conditions of a counterfactual assertion in more than one way. One way is by determining which features of the actual situation should be 'held constant' for purposes of evaluating the counterfactual.[9] Another is by determining whether it should be understood in the context that the antecedent that was actually uttered was elliptical for a stronger antecedent. For example, suppose that I am inclined to say that if it were raining then I would be wet, and the reason why I am inclined to say this is because it is particularly salient in the present context that I left my umbrella at home. There are two possibilities here: one is that since it is salient in the context that I left my umbrella at home, that fact should be held constant for purposes of evaluating the counterfactual. The other is that since it is salient in the context that I left my umbrella at home, and since the counterfactual in question is obviously related to my having or lacking an umbrella, everyone will understand that what I really meant was that if it were raining and I had (still) left my umbrella at home, then I would be wet.

This difference doesn't seem to make much of a difference when all we want to know is whether some counterfactual is true in some context. And perhaps for that very reason, it can be very hard to tell which way the context is making a difference to the truth conditions of this counterfactual. But this kind of difference makes all the difference for the question of whether your apparent utterance of Julia-1, if true, is a counterexample to NP. If the fact that Julia was passing by Saturn five minutes ago and Saturn is more then five light-minutes from earth should be held constant for purposes of evaluating the counterfactual, then the truth of your assertion is incompatible with NP. But if that fact is an elliptically suppressed part of the antecedent of the counterfactual you are asserting, then the truth of your assertion is compatible with NP.

Lange proposes a plausible test we can use to see which way the context is making a difference. Suppose someone asserts a counterfactual of the form (A $\Box\!\!\rightarrow$ C). Imagine immediately asking them why they think this counterfactual is true; suppose they answer, *because B*. Suppose this is a plausible answer, since A and B, together with other background assumptions that are in play, imply C. Now, immediately, before the context has enough time to shift in terms of which features of the actual world should be held constant for purposes of evaluating counterfactuals,

[9] Or, if you prefer: by determining which similarity metric should be used for picking out the closest possible world where the antecedent of the counterfactual is true.

ask the speaker whether B would still be true, if A were. Suppose the answer is yes: then, the context is such that when we consider a counterfactual with antecedent A, we should hold B constant.[10] The counterfactual assertion need not be understood as elliptical. On the other hand, suppose the answer is no: then, the context is such that when we consider a counterfactual with antecedent A, we should not hold B constant.[11] So, the counterfactual assertion must have been elliptical. The counterfactual the speaker really asserted was not 'A □→ C,' but rather 'A&B □→ C.'

So, in the Julia case, you say 'If Julia were here now, then she would have just traveled faster than light.' Why's that? 'Because five minutes ago she was passing by Saturn, and Saturn is more than five light-minutes away.' Okay, but if Julia were here now, then would it be the case that five minutes ago she was someplace more than five light-minutes away? Presumably the answer is no: if Julia were here now, then she would have to have been much more nearby five minutes ago. This shows that the counterfactual you asserted was elliptical: you were not holding constant the actual fact that Julia was more than five light-minutes away five minutes ago; rather, that fact was part of the antecedent of the counterfactual you meant to assert, a part that you could reasonably leave out in this context since you could reasonably expect your audience to be able to 'fill in the blank.'

For this reason, the plausibility of Julia-1 is not really a threat to NP. An assertion of Julia-1 in the context I described above seems plausibly true to us, not because the counterfactual it literally asserts is plausibly true, but because in the context an assertion of that counterfactual is naturally taken as an elliptical expression of the counterfactual Julia-2, which is perfectly compatible with NP. By means of this strategy, Lange is able to undermine many apparent counterexamples to NP.

However, the counterexamples to NP posed by the God Cases cannot be undermined in this way. Suppose Ernie asserts his counterfactual, which is in violation of NP. His assertion is extremely plausible in the context. We wonder whether it is so plausible because it is really true in the context, or whether it only seems plausible because in the context, it is naturally taken as elliptical for a different counterexample, which does not conflict

[10] Or: the similarity metric in play in this context is such that B is true in all the closest A-worlds.

[11] Or: the similarity metric in play is such that B is not true in all the closest A-worlds.

with NP. So we apply Lange's test. Why does Ernie's counterfactual seem true? Because the deity wanted to create a universe fit for habitation by intelligent life. 'If the universe had been always everywhere hotter than 500 kelvins, then would the deity still have wanted to create a universe fit for habitation by intelligent life?' In the context at hand, the answer seems to be: 'Of course! The temperature of the universe is under divine control; if it were different, then that would be because the deity had made it different, and it would not have forced a change in the deity's plans!'

6.3 Other counterexamples to NP

We don't have to turn to examples involving theological speculation to get counterexamples to NP; other kinds of counterexample can be constructed, following the same general pattern as the God Cases.

That general pattern goes like this:

(a) There is some non-scientific or extra-scientific truth EST.

(b) There is a certain kind of non-nomological fact—the F-facts—such that the F-facts can be different in different possible worlds.

(c) The propositions that are actual laws of nature are called the @-LAWs, and the propositions that are actually the F-facts are called the @-Fs.

(d) EST entails that whatever the laws of nature are, and whatever the F-Facts are, they stand in a certain relation R to one another. So in particular, given that the laws are the @-LAWs, and the F-Facts are the @-Fs, EST entails that R(the @-LAWs, the @-Fs).

(e) We consider a context in which the topic of the conversation is the subject matter of whatever field of study EST belongs to; we suppose that the participants are firmly convinced of EST (and again, EST is true).

(f) We construct a counterfactual supposition A with the following properties: (i) A is logically consistent with the proposition that the @-LAWs are the laws of nature; (ii) A does not entail that the @-LAWs are the laws of nature; (iii) A entails that the @-LAWs do not bear the relation R to the F-Facts; but (iv) A does *not* entail that *the laws of nature* do not bear R to the F-Facts.

(g) So, if A were true, it follows logically that either EST would be false, or else the laws of nature would not be the @-LAWs.

(h) But since, in the context we have constructed, the topic of the conversation is not empirical science, or which propositions happen to be laws of nature, but rather the field of study to which EST belongs, and EST is especially salient in the context, it follows that in this context, if A were true, then EST would still be true and the laws of nature would not be the @-LAWs.

Here's how this schema is filled out in the monotheistic God Case:

1. By hypothesis, the @-LAWs are consistent with the universe being always everywhere hotter than 500 kelvins—but they entail that if the universe is always everywhere that hot, then there is no intelligent life anywhere.

2. The extra-scientific truth EST mentioned in (a) is the truth that an all-powerful deity created the universe for the purpose of making a suitable habitat for intelligent life. By hypothesis, this is a theological truth in this example.

3. The F-facts mentioned in (b) are the initial conditions of the universe.

4. The relation R mentioned in (d) is the relation that a set of possible laws bears to a possible set of initial conditions just in case those laws and those conditions would lead to a universe in which intelligent life can exist. EST entails that whatever the laws are, and whatever the initial conditions are, they must be adjusted to one another in such a way that the universe contains intelligent life, so (d) is satisfied.

5. The context of the example is one in which the topic under discussion is theology, so (e) is satisfied.

6. A is the proposition that the universe is always everywhere hotter than 500 kelvins. A is thus logically consistent with the proposition that the laws of nature are the @-LAWs, by 1. A does not entail that the @-LAWs are the laws of nature, though, since a universe that is everywhere hotter than 500 kelvins is consistent with many different possible sets of laws.

A also entails that the @-LAWs do not bear the relation R to the F-Facts: for if A is true, then if the @-LAWS are all true, then the F-Facts (the initial conditions) together with the laws must lead to a universe always everywhere hotter than 500 kelvins; therefore, since the @-LAWs are true, it follows (by 1) that there is no intelligent life; thus the initial conditions and the @-LAWS are not such that together they would lead to a universe with intelligent life. Therefore, if A is true, then the @-LAWs and the F-Facts do not stand in the relation R.

However, A does not entail that the laws of nature do not bear the relation R to the F-Facts. For, since A is consistent with the existence of intelligent life, it is consistent with there being some set of laws that, together with the initial conditions, lead to the existence of intelligent life.

So, (f) is satisfied.

7. So if A were true, then either EST would be false, or else the @-LAWs would not be the laws of nature. That is: if the universe were always everywhere hotter than 500 kelvins, then either the universe would not have been designed and created by an all-powerful deity for the purpose of making a habitat for intelligent life, or else the laws of nature (unlike the @-LAWs) would have allowed for life to flourish in environments hotter than 500 kelvins. (g) is satisfied.

8. By 5, the context in question is one of theological disputation. In this context, EST is more salient than the lawhood of all and only the @-LAWs. So, it would be correct to say here that if A had been true, then EST would still have been true, and so the laws of nature would have been different from what they actually are.

6.4 A moral-theoretic counterexample to NP

Now let's look at a different way of filling out the schema. Suppose that a conversation about ethics is going on. In particular, the conversation is focused on the question of what it takes for a person to be morally responsible for its being the case that P at time t. Many views are possible here. On one view, an agent is responsible for its being the case that P at time t only if, at some time t′ that is earlier than t, the agent performed a bodily motion M such that the laws of nature guarantee that if any agent performs M at t′, then *the chance that it will be the case that P at t* is greater after t′ than it was before t′.[12] In other words, you are responsible for something's being the case only if you moved your body in a way that, given the laws of nature, increased the chance of its being the case. Call this *the chance-raising view of responsibility*. I don't want to worry here about whether this view is right or not. Presumably, it is far too crude to be right[13]—but suppose for the sake of argument that it is right; we'll worry about what follows if it isn't right later. The chance-raising view of moral responsibility will be the value of EST in our new instance of the schema of the preceding section. The role of the F-facts will be played by the facts about which people are morally responsible for what. Since the chance-raising view implies that these facts are related to the laws of nature in a certain way, line (d) of the schema is satisfied.

It will be useful to have a contrasting position in view. Another possible view about moral responsibility is that you are morally responsible for its being the case that P at t only if *either* you performed a bodily motion that raised the chance of P at t *or* you knew that you could have performed a bodily motion that would have lowered the chance that P at t but you refrained from doing so. On this view, you can be morally responsible for its being the case that P at t, even you did not perform any bodily motion that raised the chance of P at t. Call this view *the more severe view of moral responsibility*, since it counts us morally responsible for many more things than the chance-raising view does.

Now, we need to construct our example of a counterfactual supposition to play the role of A in the schema. Suppose that the actual accepted laws of radioactive decay are in fact laws of nature; one consequence is that

[12] There are two kinds of time-relativization going on here: what has a chance is a proposition about what is the case at a given time, so there is *the chance that it will be the case that P at t*—for example, the chance that it will be raining in Greensboro, North Carolina, at noon next Saturday. But this chance itself can be different at different times. For example, suppose that atmospheric trends undergo a dramatic shift on Wednesday. Then the chance *that it will be raining at noon next Saturday* might be greater after Wednesday than it was before Wednesday. So, there are times that are involved in the proposition to which a chance is assigned (in this case, noon next Saturday); and then there are times at which a chance is assigned (in this case, before Wednesday and after Wednesday). In the text, t is the time involved in the proposition to which a chance is assigned; t′ is a time at which that chance is assigned.

[13] But note that this view does not say that raising the chance of P at t is *sufficient* for being responsible for P at t; it only calls this a necessary condition. So it is not nearly as crude as it might have been.

the chance that a given atom of a radioactive isotope such as uranium-238 will undergo spontaneous decay during any given interval of time depends only on the length of that interval; that is, an atom of a given isotope is equally likely to undergo spontaneous decay at any moment in its pre-decay life, and there is nothing that can be done to make it more likely to decay spontaneously at one time rather than another. Suppose that we have access to a laser that will rip apart any atom of uranium-238 that its beam is trained on. When an atom gets lasered, it undergoes decay to be sure, but it does not undergo *spontaneous* decay.[14] Now, suppose that a given atom of uranium-238—call this atom α—which has been sitting on a tiny pedestal in a lab, does in fact spontaneously decay at time t. At time t, Sue has been sitting in the lab all day, trying to decide whether to zap α with her laser or not. Now we can construct our counterfactual supposition A:

> A: Sue was morally responsible for the fact that α spontaneously decayed at time t.

Since the actual laws of nature guarantee that there is nothing at all Sue could have done that would have raised the chance that α spontaneously decayed at time t, the following three propositions form an inconsistent triad:

- A
- the chance raising view of responsibility (which is our value of EST)
- the lawhood of all and only the actual laws

so line (g) of the schema is satisfied. Yet, A is logically consistent with the lawhood of exactly the actual laws. For the lawhood of exactly the actual laws is logically consistent with the more severe view of moral responsibility, and on the more severe view of moral responsibility, Sue is morally responsible for A's spontaneously decaying at time t. This is because at any time, Sue could have zapped α with her laser, which would have instantly reduced the chance of α spontaneously decaying at t to zero. And on the more severe view of responsibility, Sue is responsible for α's

[14] If this seems like cheating, we can augment the example by supposing that laser-induced decay leads to different by-products than spontaneous decay does. We can then modify A, below, to read that Sue was morally responsible for the fact that α decayed and left those by-products that are typical of spontaneous decay.

decaying at time t if she could have done something that would have reduced the chance of that to zero but refrained.

Now, suppose that the case of Sue is being used as an example in the course of a philosophical discussion about the nature of moral responsibility. The participants in the conversation have all lately been brought around, partly by means of considering examples like the case of Sue, to the view that the chance-raising view is the right view, and *ex hypothesi* it *is* the right view. 'So now, what should we say about the case of Sue and her laser?' someone asks. 'In particular, what would things have been like if Sue *had been* morally responsible for the spontaneous decay of α at time t?' What is the answer? By logic, it follows that either the chance-raising view of moral responsibility would have been wrong, or else the laws of nature would have been different from what they are. But which disjunct would have been true? In the context at hand, the important truths are the truths of moral theory. The laws of radioactive decay aren't really that important; they have been brought up only so that we can think about how the various possible theories of moral responsibility would apply in the actual world. If it turned out the laws were very different from what we thought they were, we wouldn't care a whit, for purposes of our conversation about moral theory. On the other hand, the chance-raising view of responsibility is extremely salient here: at this point in the discussion, we have all accepted that view as the correct view of moral responsibility, and we are now applying that view to see what it says about a particular case. So in this context, it seems that the right thing to say is that if A were true, then the chance-raising view of responsibility would still be true, so the laws of nature would have to be different. This is a counterexample to NP, since, again, A is logically consistent with the lawhood of all and only the actual laws. It is not logically consistent with the lawhood of exactly the actual laws *together with* the chance-raising view, but it is logically consistent with the lawhood of exactly those laws together with the more severe view of moral responsibility.

This counterexample to NP, like the God Case counterexamples, passes Lange's test. One of the participants in our discussion of moral theory says, 'Had Sue been responsible for α's spontaneous decay at t, then the laws of nature would have been different'; when asked why, she replies: 'Because Sue can be morally responsible for α's decay at t only if she performed some bodily motion that, given the laws of nature, raised the chance of that decay; but the propositions that happen to be laws in the actual world rule out the possibility of any such bodily motion.' Now we ask Lange's follow-up question: 'If Sue had been responsible for α's spontaneous decay at t, then would it still have been the case that responsibility requires chance-raising, and that the propositions that are the laws of the actual world rule out chance-raising in this case?' The answer here seems to be 'yes': the fact that the propositions that are the actual laws of nature rule out bodily motions that increase the chances of spontaneous decays is a logical feature of those propositions, so it would not have been any different even if Sue had been responsible. And since what we're talking about here is the nature of moral responsibility, and we do not take the facts about what constitutes moral responsibility to be in any way dependent on what the laws of nature happen to be, we should hold the actual nature of moral responsibility constant here, rather than the actual laws of nature.

But what if, in fact, the chance-raising view of responsibility is not true? Does this affect the argument at all? Well, one thing to note is that it seems likely that on other views of moral responsibility that advert to the laws of nature at some point, a similar counterexample to NP can be constructed; the example doesn't really depend crucially on the details of the chance-raising view—it just depends on the fact that the chance-raising view imposes certain relations between the non-nomological facts about who is responsible for what and the laws of nature. Thus, it fed right into the general schema of Section 6.3. Furthermore, if the Governing Thesis requires the truth of NP in all possible contexts, and the law-governed world-picture requires that empirical science is capable of justifying us in believing that the Governing Thesis is true, then the law-governed world-picture requires that empirical science is capable of finding out whether the right view of moral responsibility is like the chance-raising view in the relevant respects. And that is not believable.

Someone might object that in this counterexample, the antecedent is not *metaphysically compossible* with the lawhood of exactly the laws, on the grounds that the truths of moral theory are necessary truths—and, the objector might add, we should have used metaphysical compossibility rather than logical consistency in NP from the start.

But if we say that, we face a big problem. Suppose for the sake of argument that the truths of moral theory are indeed metaphysically necessary. And suppose for the sake of argument that the chance-raising account of responsibility is true. We want NP to be true in various scientific contexts where we need to apply it—and it won't be true in certain scientific contexts if we make the recommended revision (formulating NP in terms of metaphysical compossibility rather than logical consistency). For example: consider a context where we're applying science to assess some particular claims about who is responsible for what, holding fixed just as much moral theory as we need. (So this is very different from the context considered above, in which we found a counterexample to NP: there, the topic under discussion was moral theory itself; here, the topic is the contingent facts about who is actually morally responsible for what, and we are taking for granted both a bit of moral theory and a bit of empirical-scientific knowledge in order to apply them to the question before us.) Suppose that in the circumstances, the laws entail that if α had spontaneously decayed, then a chain reaction would have started. So, if Sue had been responsible for the spontaneous decay of α, she would have been responsible for something that started a chain reaction. This seems like an example of the kind of counterfactual we want NP to imply: it is a case where we are interested in learning how things would have been different, though the laws had been exactly what they actually are. If we require metaphysical compossibility of the antecedent with the lawhood of exactly the actual laws, rather than just logical consistency, then NP won't apply in a case like this. For, given everything we have stipulated about this case, Sue's being responsible for the spontaneous decay of α is not metaphysically compossible with the laws.

6.5 Scientific contexts and non-scientific contexts

The reason why we were worried about the possibility of counterexamples to NP is that NP seems to be just what must be true in order for the Governing Thesis to be true, and if the Governing Thesis is true, then it seems that it cannot be as context-dependent as counterfactuals often are: its truth or falsity in a given context cannot simply be a reflection of which features of the actual situation are most important to the speakers in that context. And that, in turn, seems to require that the truth of NP in a given context be more than a reflection of the speakers' interests. This requirement would be met if it were a necessary truth that NP is true in every context of utterance. But we have seen a few examples of possible cases in which NP is false in some context.

So where does this land us? Do the counterexamples we have seen show that we have to reject the law-governed world-picture? Not necessarily. Another possibility is that the law-governed world-picture does not really require that the Governing Thesis be true in every possible context of utterance, so it doesn't really require that NP be true in every possible context of utterance. What would compromise the law-governed world-picture is not just any old context-variability in NP, but rather the kind of radical context-dependence that many counterfactuals exhibit. Recall the example of the almost-empty-fuel-tank from Section 5.4: in that case, once all the actual-world facts about the situation are fixed, the truth or falsity of a certain counterfactual depends entirely on what the purpose of the conversation was—that is, on what facts about the actual situation the conversation was primarily concerned with. If it turns out that NP is true in all and only those contexts where the focus of the conversation is the nomological facts in the actual world, then the truth of NP in a given context indicates nothing more than what the purpose of the conversation in that context is. This would make NP, and with it the thesis that lawhood confers inevitability, and with it the Governing Thesis, into expressions of the point of our present conversation, rather than descriptions of important features of the world that are independent of the point of our present conversation. That is what we want to avoid, if we want to defend the law-governed world-picture as a view of the universe worth taking seriously. In order to avoid it, we don't need to insist that NP is true in every possible context whatsoever. All we need to insist on is that NP remains true across a broad range of possible contexts, where that range can be picked out independently of which features of the actual world the conversationalists happen to be focused on, and where that range is such that whatever is true across all contexts in it can reasonably be thought to indicate something important about the nature of the universe.

For example, suppose that NP is true in every possible *scientific* context. What this means depends on how we distinguish scientific contexts from non-scientific ones. We might stipulate that in order for a context to count as a 'scientific' one, it must be one in which the actual laws of nature are the supremely salient contingent feature of the actual world for purposes of evaluating counterfactuals. If we made this stipulation, then it would follow without too much trouble that NP is indeed true in every possible scientific context.[15] But this would be a hollow victory: the claim that NP is true in all scientific contexts would amount to no more than the claim that the nomological truths are all counterfactually stable in those contexts where they are the supremely salient (for purposes of evaluating counterfactuals) features of the actual world—but necessarily and trivially, *every* set of truths is counterfactually stable in those contexts where they are the supremely salient (for purposes of evaluating counterfactuals) features of the actual world, so this wouldn't tell us anything interesting about the laws of nature *per se*. However, we need not make such a stipulation (and it's a pretty unmotivated stipulation anyway). We can instead stipulate that by 'scientific context' we shall mean any context in which the primary aim of the conversation is to exposit, apply, or extend empirical, natural-scientific knowledge. In any such context, empirical-scientific reasoning is being employed, or else results of such reasoning are being appealed to. So empirical-scientific reasoning is being counted on to justify some claim.

This way of picking out the 'scientific contexts' does not amount to characterizing them as the contexts in which the actual laws of nature are the supremely salient features of the actual world, so that they must be maximally counterfactually stable. So if NP turns out to be true in all such contexts, this is not just the trivial truth that the nomological facts are maximally counterfactually stable in all those contexts where the nomological facts are considered the most salient features of the actual world for purposes of counterfactual reasoning.

If NP is true in all possible scientific contexts, then so is the Governing Thesis. If this is so, then the truth of the Governing Thesis is not an idea that we glean from some extra-scientific source and then superimpose on the results of scientific inquiry; rather, it is something that we are automatically committed to affirming whenever we are engaging in scientific inquiry or

[15] Here's how the argument would go if we took Lewis's framework for granted: since the actual laws are the most salient contingent feature of the actual world, the closest possible worlds to the actual world are all worlds with the same laws of nature as the actual world—in Lewis's terminology, the worlds with the same laws as the actual world form a *sphere* around the actual world (Lewis 1973a). If a counterfactual antecedent A is consistent with the lawhood of the actual laws, then A must be true in some world in this sphere. The A-worlds in this sphere must include all of the A-worlds that are closest to the actual world. So whatever A is, so long as A is compossible with the lawhood of exactly the actual laws, it is true that if it had been the case that A, then the laws of nature would have been exactly what they are in the actual world. QED.

appealing to its results. So the threat to the law-governed world-picture that we have recently encountered can be overcome.

The counterexamples to NP that we have seen so far all arise in non-scientific contexts: the God Case counterexamples arise in theological contexts; the moral-responsibility counterfactual arises in the context of a conversation about moral theory; and more generally, any counterexample to NP that results from the general schema I laid out in Section 6.3 must take place in a non-scientific context—a context where the extra-scientific truth EST is more salient for purposes of the conversation than are the facts about which propositions happen to be laws of nature in the actual world. So, although we have seen reasons to believe that NP is not true in every possible context of utterance, we have as yet seen no good reason to think that NP is ever false in a scientific context.

In this chapter, I won't offer a general argument for the claim that NP is true in every possible scientific context; I will, however, argue that this is plausible in Chapters 8 and 9. But before closing this chapter, I should consider some objections to this claim.

6.6 Scientific God Cases?

John Carroll raised the following objection (in conversation): might not there be a possible context that is just like that of Bert and Ernie, except that it is a scientific context rather than a theological one? In such a context, the story about the universe having been created by a deity whose purpose was to provide a suitable environment for intelligent life is itself a scientific hypothesis, well supported by empirical evidence. A minority of philosophers and scientists seems to believe that this is the situation we are actually in, since the apparent fine-tuning of the universe fuels a scientific version of the design argument. But for the purposes of Carroll's objection, all that is important is that there is some possible world where our counterparts have good scientific evidence for theism. So imagine, for example, that electron microscopy reveals the string of characters 'Made by God' apparently stamped on all large molecules, or that deep-space imaging reveals religious messages in all human languages 'written' in the pattern of radiation that reaches our radio telescopes, or that some very powerful empirical fine-tuning argument is discovered which is found to be impervious to all objections. In such a case, Bert and Ernie could have the conversation I reported back in Section 6.2.1 in a scientific context, since the (*ex hypothesi*) true theological story they both believe is in fact a piece of scientific knowledge. And that seems to show that we have a possible counterexample to NP even in a scientific context. If this is right, then the God Cases prove more than I intended for them to prove!

I think we can get around this problem by being careful about how to characterize 'scientific' contexts. Above, I characterized them as contexts in which the primary aim of the conversation is to exposit, apply, or extend empirical natural-scientific knowledge. I will say more about how to flesh this out later on, in Chapter 7. But the important point here is a simple negative point: in order to count as scientific in the relevant sense, a context must be one in which the conversationalists are *not* drawing on any *extra-scientific* source of evidence or epistemic justification. What makes a source extra-scientific is that it is not included among those sources of evidence or epistemic justification that must be relied on in modern natural-scientific research. Testimony, or taking someone else's word for it, is a source of evidence that is often relied on in natural science. But when it is, it is always relied on in one of two ways. First, we may take someone's testimony about something's having been established on non-testimonial grounds—for example, we may take testimony about an empirical observation, the result of an experiment, or the result of a calculation. Second, we may take someone's testimony as a report of introspection, as in certain sorts of psychological experiments or physiological studies (when querying subjects about their symptoms, for example). But in scientific research, testimony is not used as a source of evidence or justification in other ways. For example, the fact that Joe said that neutrinos have mass does not qualify as evidence for the hypothesis that neutrinos have mass, no matter how highly we think of Joe, unless we have some reason to believe that Joe made his claim on the basis of observations and legitimate theoretical reasoning. We cannot simply take Joe's word as a *basic* source of scientific evidence about matters outside the realm of what Joe can introspect; what his word can do (apart from reporting his introspections) is simply to convey epistemic justification gleaned from other sources.

Now, there are two ways in which a scientific case for theism might work: in the first way, empirical observation reveals some sort of message sent to us by the creator, and the case for theism depends on the thought that we should believe the theistic hypothesis because God has told us that it is true. This is presumably what is going on in the possible case where radio-telescopic observations reveal religious messages 'written in the sky.' In the second way, we do not rely on the literal receipt of any such message from the deity; instead, empirical evidence simply confirms the hypothesis of a creator, in the same way it confirms other hypotheses. This is presumably what would be going on in the case of a successful version of the design argument.

In the first case, it seems to be possible for us to be justified not only in believing that the universe was created by a deity, but also in particular beliefs about what the creator's purposes in creating the universe were. For, whatever message the deity uses to convey to us the knowledge of its existence can also tell us what the purposes were. Or, it could lend credence to certain religious texts or traditions (e.g. by using the same name for the creator, or by otherwise using similar language) which tell us about what those purposes were. So, we would be justified in accepting Ernie's counterfactual; we would thereby be justified in rejecting NP. But then, we are not in a scientific context, since we are relying on divine testimony as a basic source of evidence.

In the second case, we would accept a theistic hypothesis in a scientific context. But it is not clear how we could be justified in believing anything about what the purposes of the creator were. For example, contemporary versions of the design argument allege that without an intelligent creator it would be enormously lucky that the values of the fundamental constants were all found within that narrow range of possible values that allows for the evolution of intelligent life. But the reason why that narrow range of values allows for the evolution of intelligent life is that it allows for the existence of large quantities of condensed matter, and so it allows for the formation of stars, galaxies, and heavy elements. What entitles us to assume that out of all this amazing cosmic furniture, it is us that the creator was aiming for? Since we have no way of directly observing the creator's behavior, or studying his or her psychology, other than by looking at the physical universe that exists, and since this universe leaves it wide open just what purpose it was designed to serve, we cannot justify any particular belief about what this purpose was on the basis of the empirical evidence alone. Without some direct communication from the creator, it seems, we cannot discover the reason that motivated him or her. But the case for the truth of Ernie's counterfactual depends crucially on an assumption about the creator's motives. So in a context where we adopt the theistic hypothesis on purely scientific grounds, we cannot be justified in asserting Ernie's counterfactual.

In short, we can meet Carroll's objection by posing a dilemma: in any possible case where we have empirical knowledge of the existence of a creator, either this knowledge depends essentially on divine testimony or it does not. If it does, then the context is not a *scientific* one in the relevant sense; if it does not, then we cannot have sufficient justification for asserting a counterexample that violates NP.

6.7 Lewisian non-backtracking counterexamples

David Lewis has famously argued that if our universe is deterministic, then counterfactuals of a certain type—namely *non-backtracking counterfactuals*—do not generally respect the requirement that the actual laws of nature be held constant for purposes of counterfactual reasoning. When we are evaluating such counterfactuals, it is typically the case that the nearest possible world where the antecedent is true is a world where not all the actual laws of nature are true.[16] This means that such counterfactuals violate NP. Since Lewis's argument is not restricted to non- or extra-scientific contexts such as those of theological discussions, NP is frequently violated in scientific contexts if he is right.[17]

6.7.1 Determinism and backtracking

Suppose that the laws of our world are deterministic in the Laplacean sense: given the complete state of the universe at one time, the laws are

[16] On Lewis's view, a counterfactual A $\Box\!\!\rightarrow$ C is true just in case C is true in one or more possible worlds where A is true that are more similar ('closer') to the actual world than any world where A is true and C is false. The degrees of similarity of various possible worlds to the actual world are determined by a 'similarity metric' that is picked out by the context of utterance. The context-variability of the similarity metric is Lewis's device for representing the context-variability of the truth conditions of counterfactuals. See Lewis (1973a).

[17] Throughout this section, I am going to write as if Lewis's possible-worlds semantics for counterfactuals is right. This is not because I am committed to Lewis's semantics; it is just because it is easier to confront Lewis's arguments by agreeing to work within his preferred framework.

compatible with only one state of the universe at any other time (whether it is earlier or later than the first time). It follows that in every context of utterance in which NP is true, *Backtracking* is true:

> **Backtracking:** For any proposition A that is false but true in some world with the same laws as the actual world, the nearest A-world is one in which the state of the universe differs from the actual one at every time, including times in the distant past.

The proof is simple: if A is as described, then NP implies:

> (i) A □→ every @-LAW is a law of nature.[18]

For any time t, let 'DTHAT:(State at t)' rigidly denote the state that the universe is actually in at t. Since A is counterfactual, it follows that:

> (ii) A □→ for some time t*, the state of the universe at t* is different from DTHAT:(State at t*).

Since the actual laws are *ex hypothesi* Laplacean deterministic, the truth of these laws, together with the proposition that the state of the universe at some time t* is different from DTHAT:(State at t*), entail that at every time t, the state of the universe at t is different from DTHAT:(State at t). For suppose otherwise: then it is possible for the actual laws all to be true, for the state of the universe at t* to be different from DTHAT:(State at t*), and for the state of the universe at some other time t′ to be DTHAT:(State at t′). But it is also possible for the actual laws all to be true, for the state of the universe at t* to be DTHAT:(State at t*), and for the state of the universe at t′ to be DTHAT:(State at t′) (since this is how it is in the actual world). That means that the actual laws plus the state of the universe at time t′ are jointly consistent with multiple possible states at time t*, which is inconsistent with the Laplacean determinism of the actual laws. So, by (i), (ii), and Two-Premise Closure,[19] it follows that: A □→ (the state of the universe is different from its actual state at every time). QED.

Therefore, in any world with deterministic laws, in any context where Backtracking is false, NP is false too. This gives us an easy recipe for finding possible contexts in which NP is false: just find contexts in deterministic

[18] Recall that the @-LAWs are those propositions that are laws of nature at the actual world.

[19] If A □→ B, A □→ C, and {B, C} ⊢ D, then A □→ D.

worlds where Backtracking is false. If there are any possible deterministic worlds in which any science is done, and any scientific contexts within those worlds where Backtracking is false, then NP is not true in all possible scientific contexts. Since, for all we know, our own world may be deterministic, this even raises the possibility that there are actual scientific contexts in which NP is false; perhaps NP is false in *every* actual scientific context.

The crucial question is: is Backtracking false in any scientific contexts? Lewis gives a number of reasons for thinking that, in fact, Backtracking is false in almost every context. I will survey these reasons in the next three subsections.

6.7.2 Backward-directed counterfactuals

To keep things simple, suppose for the present discussion that the actual world is deterministic. Suppose that at noon today I drank a tall glass of water. Had I not drunk the water at noon, things would have been different later. I would have been more thirsty than I was, for example; perhaps I would have been dehydrated. Would things have been different earlier?

In an obvious sense, they would have. Right before noon, I would not have been about to drink a tall glass of water; at 11:00 am, it would not have been true of me that I was going to drink a tall glass of water in one hour; etc. But these would not have been intrinsic differences in how things were before noon; they would not be temporally local differences. The interesting question is whether the *intrinsic* state of the universe at times earlier than noon would have been different.

Again, it seems that they would have. Had I not drunk the water at noon, then something would have been different earlier. Perhaps I would not have been thirsty just before noon; perhaps at 11:55 I would have become engrossed in some task that would have distracted me from my thirst; perhaps someone would have stolen all my drinking water a little before noon. At any rate, *something* would certainly be different; otherwise, I would have drunk the water! This answer is plausible on its face; it becomes only more plausible when we remember that (we are taking it for granted that) the world is deterministic in the Laplacean sense.

But many philosophers have found it implausible to suppose that things would have been different before noon, had I not drunk the tall glass of water at noon. As Lewis expresses the point, what goes on at one time depends counterfactually on what goes on at earlier times, but it does not depend counterfactually on what goes on at later times (except perhaps under unusual circumstances, e.g. in time-travel scenarios)—at least, this is so in *standard* contexts of utterance. In other words, according to Lewis, *forward-directed counterfactuals*—counterfactuals in which the antecedent says that things are different at earlier times and the consequent says that things are different at later times—are very often clearly true, whereas *backward-directed counterfactuals*—in which the antecedent says that things are different at later times and the consequent says that things are different at earlier times—are rarely, if ever, clearly true.[20]

But why should we believe this? Why should we not be happy to say that if I had not drunk a tall glass of water at noon, then things would have been different earlier? One possible answer is that counterfactual dependence entails causal dependence. So, since what goes on at one time never depends causally on what goes on at later times, it cannot depend counterfactually on what goes at later times either. Actually, we need not put the point this strongly; perhaps there can be cases of backwards-in-time causation, but we do not believe that my drinking or failing to drink a tall glass of water at noon has any causal influence on events preceding it. This answer makes a very strong presupposition, though, when it assumes that counterfactual dependence is sufficient for causal dependence. Lewis's theory of causation[21] implies that this assumption is true. But this very feature of Lewis's theory leads it into all sorts of well-known difficulties involving overdetermination, pre-emption, and the like.[22] So we have reasons to doubt the sufficiency of counterfactual dependence for causal dependence that are independent of our present concerns. And at any rate, there is no intuitive strangeness about affirming that what happens at 11:00 am counterfactually depends on what happens at noon without causally depending on it: had I not drunk a tall glass of water at noon, then something different would have been going on at 11:00 am—not because my failure to drink a glass of water at noon would retroactively cause

[20] Lewis (1979a) uses the term *backtracking counterfactuals* for what I here call 'backward-directed counterfactuals.' I use a different term because I want to keep it clear that backward-directed counterfactuals are not what the thesis I have called *Backtracking* is about. As we will see below, Backtracking seems to have important implications for both forward-directed and backward-directed counterfactuals.

[21] Lewis (1973b).

[22] See the 'Postscripts' to the reprinted version of Lewis (1973b) in Lewis (1986).

something to happen at 11:00 am, but simply because I could not have been doing something other than drinking a glass of water at noon without there having been some course of events preceding noon that differs from the actual course of events.

A different reason why one might object to the counterfactual dependence of earlier events on my drinking a tall glass of water at noon is that it is very hard to say *exactly what* would have been different before noon had I not been drinking a tall glass of water at noon. Would I have had a glass of water at 11:50, quenching the thirst that in the actual course of events prompted me to drink water at noon? Would I have been distracted by some emergency? Would all the glasses have been dirty for some reason? Or what? It is not clearly true that things would have been different in any of these ways. But how could it be that things would have been different earlier had I not drunk a tall glass of water at noon, without its being that things would have been different in some particular way?

Lewis appears to be giving a similar argument when he writes:

> Today I am typing words on a page. Suppose today were different. Suppose I were typing different words. Then plainly tomorrow would be different also; for instance, different words would appear on the page. Would yesterday also be different? If so, how? Invited to answer, you will perhaps come up with something. But I do not think there is anything you can say about how yesterday would be that will be clearly and uncontroversially true.
>
> The way the future is depends counterfactually on the way the present is. If the present were different, the future would be different; and there are counterfactual conditionals, many of them as unquestionably true as counterfactuals ever get, that tell us a good deal about how the future would be different if the present were different in various ways. Likewise the present depends counterfactually on the past, and in general the way things are later depends on the way things were earlier.
>
> Not so in reverse. Seldom, if ever, can we find a clearly true counterfactual about how the past would be different if the present were somehow different. Such a counterfactual, unless clearly false, normally is not clear one way or the other. It is at best doubtful whether the past depends counterfactually on the present, whether the present depends on the future, and in general whether the way things are earlier depends on the way things will be later.
>
> (Lewis 1979a, p. 455)

What Lewis claims here—that there are typically no clearly true counterfactuals about how what happens earlier would be different if what happens later were different, whereas there are many clearly true counterfactuals that go in the reverse direction—seems false. For example, the following counterfactuals are clearly true:

> C5: If I had not drunk a tall glass of water at noon, then *something* about the state of the universe would have been different at each moment earlier than noon.
>
> C6: If Lewis had typed different words today, then *something* about the state of the universe would have been different at each moment earlier than today.

Of course, these counterfactuals are not very informative. From the way Lewis discusses his typing example, it seems that what he has in mind is that there are no clearly and uncontroversially true counterfactuals that tell us exactly what things would have been different earlier and how they would have been different had things been different later, whereas there are many such counterfactuals going in the other temporal direction that are 'as unquestionably true as counterfactuals ever get.'

But even if this were true, it would give us no reason to doubt that Backtracking is true in the context at hand. For it is possible for C5 to be true in a given context, even if none of the following counterfactuals is true in that context:

- Had I not drunk a tall glass of water at noon, I would have quenched my thirst by drinking a tall glass of water at 11:50 am.
- Had I not drunk a tall glass of water at noon, someone would have stolen all my drinking water at 11:50 am.
- Had I not drunk a tall glass of water at noon, I would have been distracted from my thirst by the fact that my house was on fire at noon.

and so forth. In short, it can be clearly true that if things had been different at noon, then they would also have been different at every time earlier than noon, even if there is no particular way things could have been different such that it is clearly true that they would have been different in that way. (Similarly, it can be clearly true that if I were taller than I am, then I would (still) be taller than my mother, even if there is no particular number of centimeters such that it is clearly true that I would be that many centimeters taller than my mother.)

There are other examples that seem to show that what Lewis alleges is not true. There are plenty of cases of clearly true counterfactuals that say that things would have been different earlier in some particular way had things been different later. For example, 'Had Jimmy Carter pushed the button, he would first have made sure that it wasn't hooked up to launch a nuclear assault.' We count this counterfactual clearly true, focusing on Carter's propensity to be a humanitarian and a peacemaker, which we hold fixed in our counterfactual reasoning. Of course, the truth of this counterfactual depends on the fact that in the context, Carter's humanitarian proclivities are singled out as particularly salient; but for this, it would not be clear how things would have been different earlier had he pushed the button. But the very same thing is true in the case of a forward-directed counterfactual: 'If Colonel Jack T. Ripper had had access to the button and pushed it, then there would have been a nuclear holocaust' is clearly true—at least, it is clearly true in a context where it is clear that we should hold fixed the fact that the button in question is wired in such a way that it would launch the missiles if pressed, that the missiles bear nuclear warheads, and so on. In the absence of some such fact about the context, it is not at all clear exactly how things would have been different later if Ripper had pushed the button—it is clear only that later on, things would have been different in some way or other. There seems to be no asymmetry here between past-directed and future-directed counterfactuals. So Backtracking should look no more suspicious than the innocent-seeming principle that had things been different at time t, they would also have been different at every time later than t.

6.7.3 A syntactic peculiarity of backward-directed counterfactuals

Lewis argues, however, that we are happy to count backward-directed counterfactuals as clearly true only in a very special sort of 'non-standard' context. As evidence for this claim, he points out what he takes to be a syntactic peculiarity of such counterfactuals: they usually seem more natural and more assertible when they are formulated as 'would have to have' conditionals rather than 'would have' conditionals. Thus, in each of the following pairs of conditionals, the second one seems much more natural than the first:

- If the glass had shattered, it would have been struck first. If the glass had shattered, it would have to have been struck first.

- If there had been a clap of thunder, then there would have been a flash of lightning slightly earlier. If there had been a clap of thunder, then there would have to have been a flash of lightning slightly earlier.
- If I had not drunk a tall glass of water at noon, then I would have quenched my thirst earlier, or been distracted by an emergency, or something like that. If I had not drunk a tall glass of water at noon, then I would have to have quenched my thirst earlier, or been distracted by an emergency, or something like that.
- If Carter had pushed the button, he would have made sure it was disconnected first. If Carter had pushed the button, he would have to have made sure it was disconnected first.

Lewis's view is that the 'would have to have' construction yields a sentence with the same content as the 'would have' construction, which means that the fact that the former seems so much more natural than the latter requires some explanation. We also need to explain why a similar phenomenon does not occur in the case of forward-directed counterfactuals. Lewis seems to be able to offer a natural explanation: typically, backward-directed counterfactuals are clearly true only in special contexts, whereas forward-directed counterfactuals are often clearly true even in standard contexts. The point of the complicated 'would have to have' construction is to signal that we have (perhaps temporarily) left a standard context and entered one of the anomalous non-standard ones where Backtracking is true. Hence, we have no need of this syntactic device when stating forward-directed counterfactuals.[23]

Lange has argued that Lewis is mistaken about this; a 'would have to have' conditional does not in general have the same content as the corresponding 'would have' conditional.[24] One example he gives is that of a person whose profession involves lighting fuses, and whose general habit is to light fuses using matches. On a given occasion when he failed to light a fuse he was supposed to light, it is not true that had he lit the fuse, he would have *had* to light it with a match. If that were true, the fact that he had run out of matches would be a good excuse for his failure. But if he had had an acetylene torch, it would not be true that had he lit the fuse, he would have to have used a match—for he could equally

[23] Lewis (1979a), p. 58. [24] Lange (2000), pp. 68–73.

well have used the torch. Nonetheless, it might still be true that had he lit the fuse, he *would* have used a match—if he is so ingrained in his habit of using matches that it would not have occurred to him to use the torch. He *could* have used the torch; it's just that he *would* not have done so. Lange's account of 'would have to have' conditionals is that they are true just in case the consequent is true in all of the closest worlds where the antecedent is true, as well as in all of the nearly closest worlds where the antecedent is true.[25] So in the case of the fuse-lighter, the closest possible worlds where he lights the fuse are worlds where he uses a match, but there are some other worlds that are almost as close where he lights the fuse using a torch.

I agree with Lange that 'would have to have' conditionals are not in general equivalent in content to their 'would have' counterparts. But I would suggest a different account: they are simply counterfactuals, and they have the same truth conditions other counterfactuals have, but their consequents are modal claims. The counterfactual 'Had it been that A, then it would have to have been that C' is just another way of saying, 'Had it been that A, then it would have been necessary that C.' This occurrence of 'necessary,' like almost all uses of that term in ordinary language, indicates a restricted modality, and which restricted modality is indicated depends on the context. In the case of the fuse-lighter, we would say that he has to use a match—that it is necessary that he use a match—if no alternative to his using a match is compatible with the circumstances that can reasonably be thought to be under his control in the context. If he had an acetylene torch with him, and just did not think about using it since he is so inflexible in his habit of using matches, then we would not be willing to say that he *had* to use a match. Since this would not change if contrary to fact he had lit the fuse, we are not willing to say that had he lit the fuse, he would have to have used a match. (This proposal agrees with Lange's verdict on the fuse-lighter example, and it agrees with his rejection of Lewis's account of 'would have to have' conditionals, but it differs from Lange's in calling upon the contextually determined restricted modality, rather than the contextually determined similarity metric over possible worlds, to do the crucial bit of work. These two contextual parameters are clearly related to one another, but they are not interchangeable.)

[25] Lange (2000), p. 70.

This still leaves us with a phenomenon to explain: the fact that so many 'would have to have' conditionals seem so much more natural than the corresponding 'would have' conditionals, even in circumstances where both are true. It seems to me that a good explanation is readily available. In the first place, it seems to me that Lewis has overstated the evidence: it is not true that in all cases where we are inclined to count a backward-directed counterfactual as true, the corresponding 'would have to have' conditional is more natural. For example, it seems true that if Carter had pushed the button, then he *would have* made sure it was disconnected from the missiles first; it does not sound more natural to say that he *would have to have* made sure it was disconnected from the missiles first. It is because of what kind of guy he is that he would have made sure the button was disconnected first, not because he would have *had* to do so! (Of course, Lange's fuse-lighter provides a similar example.) Second, in the cases where the 'would have to have' conditional is more natural than the 'would have' conditional, we believe both conditionals, and the 'would have to have' conditional states our reason for believing the 'would have' conditional. Had there been a clap of thunder, then there would have to have been a flash of lightning slightly earlier; here, the relevant brand of restricted necessity indicated by 'have to' is nomological necessity. We believe that the laws require all thunder claps to be preceded by lightning flashes. Moreover, this is the reason why we believe that there would have been a lightning flash had there been a thunder clap. So whereas in stating the 'would have' conditional, we make a counterfactual assertion that seems open to challenge, we pre-emptively meet this challenge in asserting the 'would have to have' conditional. For this reason, the 'would have to have' conditional leaves us feeling more secure: fewer lingering doubts about the truth of what has been said are left hanging. I do not know whether this is the true explanation of why 'would have to have' conditionals often seem so much more natural than the corresponding 'would have' conditionals. But its availability shows that Lewis's explanation is not our only option; the phenomenon he cites does not give a decisive reason for thinking that the context must shift in an unusual way in order for a backward-directed counterfactual to be true.

6.7.4 Forward-directed counterfactuals

So far, I have been looking at arguments to the effect that Backtracking must be false in some contexts because the backward-directed counterfactuals it implies are not true. A very different way of arguing against Backtracking involves arguing that in contexts where it is true, some garden-variety forward-directed counterfactuals cannot be true, or cannot be known to be true. But, the argument continues, there are many contexts in which we can know that these counterfactuals are true. Hence, in such contexts Backtracking is false. (And so, if the actual laws are deterministic, then NP must be false as well.)

Consider again the example of the glass of water. Suppose I am inclined to think that C7 is true:

> **C7:** If I had not drunk a tall glass of water at noon today, then I would have been thirsty a little later, and I would have drunk a glass of water sometime before 12:30.

That seems plausible enough. But what makes it plausible? If Backtracking is true in the present context, then the nearest possible world where I do not drink the water at noon today—call this world w—differs from the actual world on the total state of the universe at every moment going all the way back to the Big Bang. Any change in the conditions at the Big Bang, even a very small change, might lead to enormous and multifarious differences some fifteen billion years later. Perhaps there is no way to surgically tinker with the Big Bang in a way that would, under the evolution prescribed by the actual laws (which we are still supposing to be deterministic), lead to my not drinking the water at noon today without also leading to big changes in other things that are relevant to the evaluation of C7. For example, perhaps every such tinkering would lead either to my not even being alive today at noon, or to humans having evolved in such a way that we must eat solid ice instead of drinking liquid water, or to there being a devastating water shortage today, or to my being imprisoned and denied access to water, or to some such scenario. How can we be sure that there is a possible set of initial conditions for our world that would lead to my not drinking a glass of water at noon, but would leave unchanged such actual facts as my being alive, my proclivities to thirst, the availability of potable water to me, and everything else that makes me confident that I would drink a glass of water by 12:30 if I did not drink one at noon? The task of establishing the existence of such possible initial conditions is surely computationally intractable. So perhaps I could never be justified in believing in them. But in that case, it seems that I cannot be justified in believing that C7 is true, even under the circumstances in which anyone would readily assent to it.

The upshot here is that it seems that in any context where Backtracking is true, we cannot know (or even be justified in believing) that even the most commonplace and obvious counterfactual conditionals are true. Lewis uses this kind of consideration to argue that Backtracking cannot be true in the sorts of contexts in which we ordinarily evaluate counterfactuals: he writes that under the assumption of determinism, if the nearest world where the antecedent of a counterfactual true is one where there are no violations of the actual laws, then 'it would make counterfactuals useless; we know far too little to figure out which of them are true under a resolution of vagueness that validates very much backtracking.'[26] Since for all we know our world could be deterministic, this seems to give us a powerful reason to affirm the existence of possible contexts, and maybe even actual contexts, in which NP is false. Indeed, it seems to suggest that NP is false in almost all the contexts we ever find ourselves in—including scientific contexts.

This is a much more serious problem for Backtracking and NP than the worries concerning backward-directed counterfactuals above. But I do not think it is decisive. The key to getting around the problem is to consider a point about modal epistemology. What is at issue here is our entitlement to assume the existence of a certain possibility: the possibility that the antecedent of a counterfactual is true, and the actual laws of nature hold, and the other contingent features of the actual situation that we employ as auxiliary assumptions in the reasoning we use in evaluating the counterfactual are all true. Demonstrating the existence of a possible world where all of this is true would evidently require constructing such a world—finding a global solution to the equations of motion given by the laws of nature that represents a possible world in which the putative possibility is actual.[27] This is much more than we generally require of someone

[26] Lewis (1979a), p. 46; Lewis attributes this point to Jonathan Bennett.

[27] Perhaps less would be required: perhaps it would be enough to prove an existence theorem establishing the existence of a solution to the equations of motion for boundary conditions corresponding to the truth of the counterfactual antecedent and all the other features of the world we consider relevant to the counterfactual. This is still a tall order. Never mind coming up with a proof of the theorem: the first step would be to translate the antecedent and the conditions we want held constant into a boundary condition, something we have no idea how to do for so simple a proposition as 'JTR did not drink a tall glass of water at noon today.'

in order to justify their claim that something is possible. Ordinarily, we treat propositions as possible until we have seen some reason to think that they are impossible, such as a logical contradiction, empirical evidence for an identity or an essential property, a violation of a well-motivated metaphysical principle, and so on.

There is no reason to proceed differently here. When I consider the counterfactual C7, and decide to affirm it, I assume that there is a possible world where all the actual laws are true, where I do not drink a tall glass of water at noon, and where everything else that I consider relevant to my hypothetical reasoning (e.g., that human biology is pretty much what it is, that the customs and practices in my culture are pretty much as they are, that I exist, that earlier in the day I did whatever I did to make myself thirsty by noon, that the water-management situation is pretty much what it is in the actual world, that I am not in prison, and so on) is all true as well. In fact, I take it for granted that there are many possible worlds like that. In each of them, the total state of the universe is different in some way from the way it actually is, at every moment of past history. But I assume that none of these differences makes a difference to the things I am currently interested in—or that if they are, then some other little difference cancels out the effect. Furthermore, I assume that among all these possible worlds, the ones where I have a drink by 12:30 are the ones that are most similar to the actual world in the respects that I am focusing on just now. I can offer no demonstration that any of this is so. But there is no apparent reason to think that it is not so. The possibilities I affirm seem to stand innocent until evidence of their guilt is produced.

If this reply strikes you as insufficient, consider that the situation is not that different with ordinary counterfactuals in contexts where Backtracking is false (for whatever reason). If I affirmed C7 in a context like that, I would be implicitly committing myself to a possible world where I do not drink a glass of water at noon, and in which all of the actual features of the world that are relevant to the reasoning I use in evaluating the counterfactual are true. But who knows how many undiscovered a posteriori metaphysical necessities might be relevant here? Perhaps my essential properties, the essential properties of glasses, the essential properties of water and all of its subatomic constituents, all conspire to rule out many possibilities in a way we are not aware of at this stage of inquiry? Clearly though, it would be absurd to insist that we cannot be justified in believing that C7 is true just because there is much we do not yet know about what the set of metaphysically possible worlds contains. It seems to me that it would be almost as absurd to insist that we cannot know that C7 is true because there is much we do not know about what the set of nomologically possible worlds contains.

6.7.5 Summing up

In any context where the laws of nature are Laplacean-deterministic, NP entails Backtracking. So, assuming that the laws are Laplacean-deterministic, NP must be false in any context where Backtracking is false. So if Backtracking is false in any scientific contexts, then we have a reason to believe that NP is not true in all possible scientific contexts.

I have considered three arguments for the claim that Backtracking is false in some scientific contexts. The first goes like this: in any context where Backtracking is true, there are true backward-directed counterfactuals; but typically (even in scientific contexts), no backward-directed counterfactuals are true; hence, typically (even in scientific contexts), Backtracking is false. This argument fails because it is not true that there are typically no true backward-directed counterfactuals. That appears to be so only because it is hard to find true backward-directed counterfactuals with very precise consequents. But Backtracking does not entail that there are any true backward-directed counterfactuals with very precise consequents; it entails only that there are some true backward-directed counterfactuals.

The second argument alleged that the backward-directed counterfactuals that Backtracking entails are typically marked by a syntactic peculiarity, and this peculiarity is best explained by the hypothesis that such counterfactuals can be true only in non-standard contexts. The peculiar syntax serves as a cue to switch from a standard context to a non-standard one. Most scientific contexts are standard contexts, so backward-directed counterfactuals are not true in them. Hence, Backtracking is not true in them either. This argument fails for at least two reasons. First, it is not true that all backward-directed counterfactuals are marked by the syntactic peculiarity. Second, the alleged 'syntactic peculiarity' is no such thing—it is a syntactically straightforward way of asserting, not an ordinary backward-directed counterfactual, but a backward-directed counterfactual with a modal statement as its consequent.

The third argument purports to show that if Laplacean determinism is true, then if Backtracking is true, then we cannot know the truth values of even the simplest and most obvious forward-directed counterfactuals. But this argument turns out to depend on imposing very high standards on knowledge of possibility-ascriptions. If it were appropriate to impose these high standards, then we would never know whether any non-trivial counterfactual were true, whether Backtracking was true or not. So if there is any problem here at all, it is not a special problem for Backtracking.

None of the three arguments is convincing. So, I conclude, so far we have seen no reason to suspect that Backtracking is ever false in a scientific context—and so, we have as yet no reason to think that NP is ever false in a scientific context.

6.8 Where things stand now

NP is not true in all possible contexts: we have seen examples of possible contexts in which it is false. But all of these examples involve counterfactuals asserted in non-scientific contexts. We have seen no reason to suppose that NP is ever false in a scientific context. If NP is true in every possible scientific context, then we can use it as our explication of the Governing Thesis without worrying about the difficulties concerning the context-variability of counterfactuals discussed above. If NP is true in every possible scientific context, and we are currently discoursing in a scientific context, then we can truly say that NP is true, that therefore lawhood confers eternally inevitable truth, and that therefore the laws govern the universe in a genuine sense. What we thereby say is context-dependent, but not in such a way that what we say is just an expression or reflection of which features of the actual situation happen to be important to us for purposes of our present conversation. NP is true—the nomological facts are maximally counterfactually stable, and so inevitably true—in *any* context, like our present context, in which the topic of discussion is in the subject matter of the natural sciences and the reasoning appealed to in order to justify claims is scientific. There is no standpoint from which you can engage in or appeal to scientific reasoning and coherently deny NP. So if NP is true in every possible scientific context, then this would vindicate the law-governed world-picture. And in Chapter 7, I will argue that this is the only way in which the law-governed world-picture can be vindicated. To say all of this is not to affirm the law-governed world-picture, or even the Governing Thesis. It is just to identify what things must be like in order for the law-governed world-picture to be correct—and to note that, for all we have seen so far, that world-picture still has a fighting chance.

7

How could science show that the laws govern?

7.1 Why the law-governed world-picture must include the Science-Says-So Thesis

'The law-governed world-picture' is the name I am using for a bundle of general ideas that seem to be part of the common sense of our scientific culture. This bundle might actually be part of our scientific knowledge, or it might be an optional interpretation of that knowledge, or it might be an illegitimate projection of philosophical notions onto that knowledge; whichever of these it is, it is recognizable as part of the world-view commonly associated with modern science.

This bundle of general ideas is primarily concerned with the way the natural universe is. But it is also partly concerned with our knowledge of the natural universe. If it is part of the scientifically informed common sense of our culture that the universe is governed by laws of nature, then it is also part of the scientifically informed common sense of our culture that *scientific inquiry is capable of revealing to us* that it is so governed.

The part of the law-governed world-picture that is concerned with what our universe is like independently of us is captured by what I have been calling the Lawhood Thesis and the Governing Thesis. These two theses together are not sufficient to capture the whole of the law-governed world-picture, though. For suppose that both of these theses are true: that leaves open certain logical possibilities that the law-governed world-picture excludes. One is that, although we know that our universe is governed by laws of nature, we are unable to form any justified beliefs about *which* propositions are the laws of nature (except insofar as we know that any proposition known to be false must not be a law of nature). This possibility is excluded by the Discoverability Thesis, which says that we can form justified beliefs about which propositions are (not only true, but also) laws of nature, and that empirical scientific investigation is the method that lets us do this.

But the Lawhood Thesis, the Governing Thesis, and the Discoverability Thesis together still leave open some logical possibilities that the law-governed world-picture excludes. One of these is that, although there are laws of nature, and we can be justified in believing hypotheses about which propositions are the laws of nature, and these laws do in fact govern our universe, there is no way in which we can ever be justified in forming the opinion that these laws *govern* the universe—as opposed to, say, just being cosmic regularities to which the universe happens to conform;[1] if we form this opinion, then we do so as a completely unjustified leap of faith. If this is so, then some important reasoning that goes on within science—which I discussed back in Section 1.6—is on shaky ground, since that reasoning seems to depend on the assumption that laws of nature govern the universe in some genuine sense, and are not mere cosmic regularities. For this reason, the law-governed world-picture should be construed as rejecting this possibility.

A second logical possibility left open by the conjunction of the Lawhood, Governing, and Discoverability Theses is that we can indeed be justified in believing that the laws of nature govern our universe, but the source of this justification is extra-scientific. In other words, engaging in scientific inquiry is *not enough* to win us justification for believing that the laws govern the universe, but some other kind of epistemic activity, which we can pursue *in addition to* empirical natural science, *is* up to the job. What might this other kind of epistemic activity be? Perhaps it involves consulting the doctrines of revealed religion: perhaps these doctrines assure us that the deity's relation to the created universe is such that there must be laws of nature set up to govern creation, since otherwise God would need directly to govern each individual event and process on a case-by-case basis—something incompatible with his dignity, goodness, and reasonableness. On the other hand, perhaps it involves a priori speculative metaphysics, or the mystical insight of very wise persons, or of those

[1] I discussed the important difference between these two ideas back in Sections 1.2 and 1.3.

with abnormal intuitive powers. But the ways of thinking about the universe and its laws that seem to have become part of the scientifically informed common sense of our age rule out all such possibilities. The law-governedness of our universe is something that we need not go 'beyond science' in order to discover. We do not know that we live in a law-governed universe because of revelations, or mystical insights, or esoteric a priori metaphysical investigations: our knowledge of the law-governed character of our universe (assuming that we have such knowledge) is of a piece with the rest of our empirical, natural-scientific knowledge.

Both of these possibilities—the possibility that the law-governed character of the universe is unknowable, and the possibility that it is knowable but only by extra-scientific means—are ruled out by what I have called the Science-Says-So Thesis. In fact, that thesis is pretty much equivalent to the denial of both of these possibilities. This is why it is an indispensable part of what I have been calling the law-governed world-picture.

7.2 What is 'extra-scientific'?

What the Science-Says-So Thesis requires is that it is possible to be justified in believing the Governing Thesis without appealing to any extra-scientific sources of epistemic justification. But what is an 'extra-scientific' source of epistemic justification? It is tempting to suppose that the answer is: any *non-scientific* source of justification—that is, any source of justification other than confirmation by empirical evidence according to the canons employed in the empirical natural sciences. But this would be a mistake. Our knowledge of pure logical and mathematical truths is not based on confirmation by empirical evidence, so this answer would imply that logical and mathematical reasoning count as 'extra-scientific' sources of epistemic justification. So, if we could come to know that our universe is governed by laws of nature, but this knowledge depended on appeal to logical and mathematical reasoning, then it would follow that the Science-Says-So Thesis was false. That would be an unwanted consequence: in demanding that our justification for believing in a law-governed universe not depend on 'extra-scientific' sources, we did not mean to demand that it must not involve logical or mathematical reasoning! What we meant to demand was only that our justification for believing in a law-governed universe must not require appeal to sources of justification that *go beyond those appealed to in science.* Logic and mathematics are not empirical sciences, but they are not *extra*-scientific either, since appeal to them must be made in the course of pursuing scientific inquiry.

So, in the Science-Says-So Thesis, we should understand 'extra-scientific sources of epistemic justification' to refer to sources of epistemic justification that do not need to be appealed to in the course of pursuing empirical, natural-scientific inquiry. The result is that the Science-Says-So Thesis requires that a community of inquirers who studied the world using empirical natural sciences, and appealed to all the tools of reasoning and sources of knowledge that this required of them, but did not pursue knowledge of the universe by any other means in addition to these, would be capable of coming to be justified in believing that the universe is governed by laws of nature. And this is exactly what we need that thesis to say, in order for it to do its job—that of rounding out our formulation of the law-governed world-picture.

The Science-Says-So Thesis would be satisfied if the Governing Thesis were itself an empirical hypothesis that was capable of being confirmed by empirical evidence, in the same ways that more familiar examples of empirical hypotheses (e.g., that the boiling point of water at standard pressure is 100 degrees Celsius, that the orbit of Venus lies inside that of Earth, that aspirin can prevent heart attacks, and so forth) can be confirmed by empirical evidence. But this is not the only possibility. The Science-Says-So Thesis is also satisfied if the Governing Thesis is a consequence of propositions that we are justified in believing on grounds that are not empirical, but that are among those appealed to by scientific inquiry—like logical and mathematical reasoning.

Are there any other sources of epistemic justification that are neither empirical nor extra-scientific, in addition to logical and mathematical reasoning? I think it is clear that there must be. For example, surely the justification of our empirical-scientific beliefs depends on the justification of our belief that there exists an external world, and our most general beliefs about its nature. If I am not justified in believing that I am not a victim of a Cartesian demon, or a brain in a mad scientist's vat, then I am not justified in believing that water contains hydrogen, no matter how many experiments I have personally performed that seemed to confirm that it does. I assume that skepticism about the external world can be avoided somehow, but this is not the right place to take a stand on how the trick is to be done. However it is done, the source of our assurance of the existence of an external world is surely not an extra-scientific source of knowledge, even if such knowledge is not 'scientific' in the strictest sense. For any community of inquirers that pursued scientific knowledge would have to rely on this source, just as they rely on logic and mathematics.

For example, perhaps we have some a priori source of basic metaphysical knowledge which constitutes our ground for believing in an external world (such as Descartes held). In that case, this source must be relied on (at least implicitly) in all empirical-scientific inquiry; it is not, therefore, an extra-scientific source of knowledge—even though the things it tells us (for example, that there exists an external world) could not be established by testing them against the empirical evidence, as if they were ordinary empirical hypotheses.

On the other hand, the answer to the skeptic might take a somewhat less exciting form: some epistemological contextualists maintain that we are justified in believing that there is an external world simply because the proposition that there is no such world is not a relevant alternative in the context at hand.[2] In this case, anything that we know in those contexts in which we do empirical science simply because the alternative is not a relevant alternative in those contexts is non-extra-scientific knowledge.

If empirical-scientific inquiry essentially depends on the results of some branch of metaphysics—the 'metaphysical foundations of empirical science,' let's call it—including, for example, the 'Principle of the Uniformity of Nature,' the 'Same-Cause Same-Effect' principle, and so forth, then these principles are among the things that we know in a way that is not extra-scientific. And in general, any source of knowledge that we cannot do science without relying on is a source of knowledge that is not extra-scientific. If such sources of knowledge can justify us in believing that laws of nature govern our universe, then the Science-Says-So Thesis is satisfied.

[2] See DeRose (1995) and Lewis (1996).

So, what sources of knowledge *would* count as extra-scientific knowledge? One paradigm case is theology. Whether there exists a god seems to me to be a question that is beyond the ken of empirical science; if I am right about this, then if knowledge that the universe is governed by laws requires either knowledge that there is a god or knowledge that there is no god, then the Science-Says-So Thesis is not true. Some philosophers—some living, some dead—will of course disagree with me here. Descartes famously argued that all of our justification for our beliefs about the physical world are dependent on our knowledge of the existence of an all-powerful and benevolent god; on this view, our knowledge of the existence of this god and of his attributes of all-powerfulness and benevolence do not count as extra-scientific. If Descartes is right about this, then I am wrong to say that the Science-Says-So Thesis will automatically be violated if it turns out that our justification for believing that the universe is governed by laws of nature depends on our justification for believing in the existence of God (and in some of his attributes). But this does not show that Descartes would have rejected the Science-Says-So Thesis; he would presumably agree with me that our justification for believing in a law-governed universe does not depend on extra-scientific sources of epistemic justification, he would just disagree with me about what we can learn from the sources of epistemic justification that aren't extra-scientific. And it seems likely that Descartes would grant that there are some sources of epistemic justification for certain theological beliefs that *are* extra-scientific, and on which our knowledge that the universe is governed by laws of nature does not depend—for example, scriptural revelation of particular matters of faith that cannot be discerned by the natural light of reason. In our own century, John Foster (2004) has argued on very non-Cartesian grounds that we can coherently understand our universe as law-governed only by adopting a view of laws that assumes the existence of a god. Like Descartes, I think he disagrees with me not on the Science-Says-So Thesis, but only on the extent of what we can know on grounds that are not extra-scientific. For his view of laws is supported by appeal to a theory of how inductive inferences are justified, which makes their justification depend on that of an inference-to-the-best-explanation whose conclusion is an explanatory hypothesis, the explanatory power of which can ultimately be explicated only by reference to God. So for Foster, like Descartes, we have some sources of epistemic justification for theological beliefs that are not extra-scientific, since science cannot be done without relying on them. But perhaps, for Foster, like Descartes, there are presumably some sources of epistemic justification for theological beliefs that are extra-scientific—such as scripture and church tradition.

A second paradigm source of extra-scientific epistemic justification is speculative metaphysics.[3] As I mentioned above, it may be that there is such a thing as *the metaphysical foundations of science*: a body of metaphysical knowledge on which our empirical scientific knowledge rests—perhaps including such things as the Principle of the Uniformity of Nature. If so, then this body of knowledge does not count as extra-scientific, and so if the Governing Thesis is a consequence of principles that we know in this way, then the Science-Says-So Thesis is satisfied. What would be an example of the kind of metaphysical reasoning that *is* extra-scientific? Well, perhaps a paradigm case would be an answer to the question of whether there exist *tropes*—token property-instances, inhering in particulars but distinct from them. Perhaps our scientific knowledge depends on the principle that nature is in some sense uniform, but it is not at all plausible that it depends on the theory of tropes (or, for that matter, any other solution to the metaphysical problem of properties). So if we have some way of coming to be justified in believing either that there are such things as tropes or that there are not, then this is extra-scientific justification.

So, the Science-Says-So Thesis requires two things: first, that we can be justified in believing the Lawhood Thesis and the Governing Thesis; second, that this justification need not make appeal to extra-scientific sources of epistemic justification—where an 'extra-scientific' source is one that need not be appealed to in the course of empirical-scientific inquiry. In addition to the standard methods of empirical testing and confirmation used in the sciences, there are other sources of epistemic justification that are not extra-scientific, and it is possible that these include some of the sources of metaphysical knowledge. But there are clear cases of extra-scientific sources of epistemic justification. (Perhaps I should say: there are clear cases of alleged sources of epistemic justification that are extra-scientific.) So the second requirement of the Science-Says-So Thesis is not superfluous; it excludes some possibilities that the first requirement doesn't.

[3] To be clear: I don't mean to claim here that speculative metaphysics is a source of justification; only that if it is, then it is a source of extra-scientific justification. Same thing goes for theology.

7.3 How can the Science-Says-So Thesis be true?

If the Science-Says-So Thesis is true, then we can be non-extra-scientifically justified in believing the Governing Thesis—which, in the light of Chapter 5, means that we can be non-extra-scientifically justified in believing the thesis NP.[4] There are three possible ways in which this might be so: it might be that NP is a logico-mathematical truth; it might be that NP is an empirical hypothesis capable of being supported by confirming empirical evidence, in the way (or one of the ways) in which empirical hypotheses are typically confirmed in science; it might be that NP is neither a logico-mathematical truth, nor empirically confirmable, but nevertheless justifiable on grounds that are not extra-scientific. Let's consider these possibilities in turn.

7.3.1 NP a logico-mathematical truth?

We can reject the first possibility. For we saw in Chapter 6 that there are possible contexts in which NP is false. For example, in the Monotheistic God Case, the context of the theological discussion between Bert and Ernie is one in which NP is false. But whatever is logically and mathematically necessary must be as true in that context as in any other. Hence, NP is not a logico-mathematical truth.

7.3.2 NP an empirical hypothesis?

Is it possible that NP is a generalization we are capable of discovering by finding empirical evidence that confirms it? This is a very strange suggestion. NP is not much at all like more familiar generalizations that can be confirmed by empirical evidence—such as the particular generalizations that we take to be laws of nature. In fact, there are two things about NP that make it very different from such paradigm cases.

The first way in which NP differs from more familiar empirical hypotheses is that its entire content consists of what it says about counterfactual situations, rather than in what it says about the actual world. NP could be true or false consistently with every actual fact about the actual course of nature. And no matter how the actual course of nature went, NP would

[4] NP was introduced back in Section 5.6.

still be consistent with it. This is all so because, again, NP says nothing at all about what actually happens—its content is exhausted by what it implies about which counterfactuals are true—and all that we can ever observe (even by means of theory-laden, instrumentation-enabled observation techniques) is what actually comes to pass. Ordinary empirically confirmable hypotheses are not much like this: 'All gold is electrically conductive,' 'Water has a boiling point of 100 degrees Celsius,' 'Energy is always conserved in a closed system,' 'The extinction of the dinosaurs was caused by the impact of a comet with the earth,' and so forth all make claims about what is the case; none gives information that is only about which counterfactuals are true.

This peculiarity of NP certainly seems to suggest that it is not the sort of thing that can be confirmed empirically. After all, in order for it to be empirically confirmable, it must be empirically *testable*, and it is empirically testable only if it makes some logically contingent *predictions* about the *actual course of events*, which is precisely what it does not do. But it would be hasty to conclude immediately from this that NP is not empirically confirmable. After all, we think we can have empirical evidence for believing particular non-trivial counterfactuals. Consider a couple of examples:

Salt Case: If I taste a small sample from the pile of white powder in the shaker before me, and find that it is salty, then I am justified in believing that *if I were to shake a small amount of this powder into a glass of pure water, then it would dissolve*—even if I have resolved never to actually do such a thing.

New-Planet Case: If an astronomer discovers a planet orbiting another sun, and determines that its mass is twice that of Earth and that its radius is also twice that of Earth, then she is justified in believing that *if we were to travel to the surface of that planet, we would find ourselves one-half as heavy there as we are accustomed to being on Earth*—even though we shall never have the opportunity to weigh ourselves on the surface of this new planet.

In these cases, and in many others, it seems that someone is perfectly well justified in believing a certain non-trivial counterfactual, and that their evidence for this counterfactual is empirical. So it cannot be that hypotheses about which counterfactuals are true are entirely beyond the reach of empirical testing and confirmation.

But in each of these cases—and, plausibly, in any other case where someone has empirical justification for believing a counterfactual—the justification depends on a more or less precise, more or less explicitly articulated principle that licenses inferences from non-counterfactual facts about the actual world to counterfactual conditionals—a bridge principle, so to speak, linking the actual-factual and counter-factual realms. Plausible first approximations of the principles used in the above cases are as follows:

> **Salt Case Bridge Principle**: If x is a sample of salt, then if a portion of x were to be placed in pure water, that portion would dissolve.
>
> **New-Planet Case Bridge Principle**: If one planet has twice the mass and twice the radius of another, and a body on the second planet has weight W, then if that body were on the first planet, it would weigh $W/2$.

These are not the *only* background premises that are relied on in these cases; for example, in the Salt Case I must also rely on the premise that if a white powder found in a shaker tastes salty then it is very probably salt. The 'Bridge Principles' above, by contrast, are *actual-to-counterfactual bridge principles*: they are what we rely on when we draw inferences from statements about the actual state of affairs to counterfactual conclusions. Since empirical observation is necessarily limited to what is actually the case, some such bridge principle must be relied on (tacitly if not explicitly) whenever we come to be justified on the basis of observation in believing or affirming a counterfactual.

So, the fact that NP's entire content consists of what it says about which counterfactuals are true does not automatically mean that it is not capable of being tested or supported by empirical evidence. With the help of actual-to-counterfactual bridge principles playing the role of auxiliary hypotheses, empirical tests of counterfactuals—and of generalizations about counterfactuals—can be performed. Is it possible to confirm NP by means of empirical evidence with the assistance of such bridge principles?

This brings us to the second way in which NP differs from more familiar types of empirical hypotheses—and unlike the first, this second difference distinguishes NP from empirically supported counterfactuals such as the four presented above. NP is not itself a particular counterfactual conditional. It affirms the truth of a whole class of non-trivial counterfactuals, but it does not—at least by itself—specify which counterfactuals belong to that class. Let's call the non-trivial counterfactuals that must be true in the actual world if NP is true[5] *the @-Nomological Counterfactuals*, or the '@-Counterfactuals' for short. Which counterfactuals are among the @-Counterfactuals depends on which propositions are the laws of the actual world—or as I have been calling them, the @-LAWs. NP does not say anything about which propositions are the @-LAWs, though, so it doesn't specify which non-trivial counterfactuals must be true if it is true.

So in order to test NP empirically by means of empirically determining that particular counterfactuals are true, it seems that we would first need to find out which counterfactuals are the @-Counterfactuals—for these are the ones that have to be true in order for NP to be true. That's not quite right—we wouldn't necessarily need to learn what *all* the @-Counterfactuals are; if we could get pretty good evidence that a certain interesting class of counterfactuals are among the @-Counterfactuals, then by empirically determining that they were all true, we might be able to provide some empirical support for NP. So what we need to do is learn what we can about which counterfactuals are the @-Counterfactuals. To do that, what we must do is find out what we can about which propositions are among the @-LAWs. Suppose we manage to pull this off—we arrive at a pretty well-confirmed theory that, while perhaps not a complete specification of the laws of nature of the actual world, at least provides us with a significant amount of information about them. With this in hand, how can we proceed to seek empirical evidence for NP?

Well, suppose, for example, that our well-confirmed theory tells us that it is a law that all copper objects conduct electricity, and also that there is no law of nature that rules out my owning a table made entirely of copper. Then one of the @-Counterfactuals is: *If I owned a table made entirely of copper, then I would own a table that conducted electricity*. Can we find out empirically whether this counterfactual is true? It seems obvious that we can. Indeed, *ex hypothesi*, we have already found out empirically that it is a law of nature that all copper conducts electricity, and we have already found out empirically that there is no law of nature that would prevent me from owning a table made entirely of copper, and this seems

[5] Strictly speaking, I should say here: 'the non-trivial counterfactuals that must be true in the actual world *in context k* if NP is true *in k*.' Since the context-relativity of non-trivial counterfactuals and NP plays no direct role in the present discussion, I suppress this explicit relativization to context in the text. Let it be understood as implicit throughout.

enough to guarantee that the counterfactual in question is true. But wait: these premises are both about how things are in the actual world; in particular, they are about what the actual laws of nature are like. So to draw an inference from them to a counterfactual, we need to rely on some actual-to-counterfactual bridge principle. What bridge principle is the right one to appeal to here? Well—it seems that *NP itself*, or perhaps the special case of NP applicable to this very counterfactual, is the needed principle.

NP is a generalized conditional that licenses inferences from statements about the laws of nature to counterfactual conditionals, so it is what I have been calling an actual-to-counterfactual bridge principle. What's more, it seems to be the very bridge principle that we need to appeal to in order to empirically confirm the counterfactuals that must be true if NP is true. So if we want to use empirical evidence to confirm NP by means of confirming particular counterfactuals that are 'test-implications' of NP, then we are going to have to appeal to NP itself in arriving at these instances; as an empirical argument in favor of NP, this exercise will be blatantly circular.

To be sure, sometimes it is possible to get legitimate empirical evidence for a hypothesis by using that hypothesis itself as an auxiliary. For example, Newton's second law might be taken for granted in the measurement of the elasticity constant of a given spring, whose value will be taken for granted in a test of Newton's second law that employs masses attached to the end of that spring. But in cases like this, it is logically possible that the tests will yield empirical results that are incompatible with the hypothesis under test. This is not so in the case we have just been looking at: whatever the empirical evidence suggests about which propositions are laws of nature, that information, together with NP, will obviously imply exactly the counterfactuals that must be true if NP is true, given that information. So there is no possibility here of finding empirical evidence that will conflict with NP. When we use NP (or special cases of it) as auxiliary hypotheses in an empirical test of NP in the way just described, there will thus be no possibility of NP's failing the test; so it isn't a genuine test; so the results cannot yield any genuine empirical confirmation of NP.

Is there any other way in which we might find empirical evidence that confirms NP? I think the prospects are very slim. Since NP's content is exhausted by what it says about which counterfactuals are true, any empirical evidence for NP is going to have to be empirical evidence for one or more of the counterfactuals that follow from it. Any empirical evidence for one of these counterfactuals will have to consist in observations of actual-world facts that, together with some actual-to-counterfactual bridge principle, imply the counterfactual in question. If the bridge principle called upon is NP itself, or a special case or consequence of NP covering the particular counterexample in question, then this procedure is viciously circular and provides no real empirical support for NP. And it is hard to see how any of the counterfactuals implied by NP can be reached by inferences relying on any bridge principle that is not either NP or a special consequence of NP applying to it. For example, the counterfactual in the New-Planet case above is an example of a counterfactual that is implied by NP together with the actual nomological truths, and the actual-to-counterfactual bridge principle that it evidently relies on just is the special case of NP for the values of Q and P corresponding to the antecedent and consequent of the New-Planet-case counterfactual respectively. Without relying on NP—or some consequence of NP—it seems impossible to establish the truth of this counterfactual from the empirically ascertainable facts about the actual world.

7.3.3 NP a necessary presupposition of empirical science?

It seems to me that what all of these observations show is that NP is not at all the kind of proposition that can be empirically confirmed in the manner of a scientific hypothesis. It plays a very different role: that of a general principle lurking in the background of a great deal of scientific reasoning, that is not itself subject to direct test.

Many philosophers have held that the 'Principle of the Uniformity of Nature,' or the 'Same-Cause Same-Effect' principle, play a similar role in scientific reasoning: none of the ampliative inferences from empirical evidence employed in empirical science can be justified without taking such a principle for granted, and empirical evidence cannot be used to support the principle itself—or at any rate, so the old story goes.

What we have seen here is that if NP is something we can be justified in believing at all, then it must be an example of this kind of principle. Empirical evidence for NP could only come via empirical evidence for the particular counterfactuals that follow from NP, but evidence for those particular counterfactuals can actually manage to confirm those particular counterfactuals with the help of NP itself. This is a circle that we cannot break into from the outside, so NP cannot *come to be* justified on scientific grounds; it is either always justified within scientific contexts, or it never is. That is, the only way for the Science-Says-So Thesis to be true is for NP to be among the principles that must be presupposed in all justified scientific reasoning as such.

This, the only remaining possible way in which the Science-Says-So Thesis might be true, falls under the third of the three options considered above: NP is neither a logico-mathematical truth, nor empirically confirmable, but nevertheless justifiable on grounds that are not extra-scientific. For if NP is among the indispensable presuppositions of scientific inquiry as such, then whatever justifies us in believing it is surely not extra-scientific.

7.4 NP as a consequence of the presuppositions in any scientific context

How *could* NP be a consequence of assumptions that are indispensable to scientific reasoning? One objection to the very idea should be confronted immediately: in any possible situation, NP implies the truth of a set of counterfactuals, but it implies different sets of counterfactuals in different possible situations. This is just because which counterfactuals are implied by NP depends on which propositions are the laws of nature, and the laws of nature are contingent. Suppose that in the actual situation, the laws are a particular set of propositions, the @-LAWs. The lawhood of all and only the @-LAWs, together with NP, entail a certain set of counterfactuals, the @-Counterfactuals. So in the actual situation, NP is true just in case the @-Counterfactuals are. But it could hardly be an indispensable presupposition of scientific inquiry that all of the @-Counterfactuals are true. Unless we know which propositions are the laws of nature, we don't even know which counterfactuals are the @-Counterfactuals. And if we have false but justified beliefs about which propositions are laws of nature, then we may have false but justified beliefs about which counterfactuals are the ones implied by NP; we might even falsely but justifiably believe some counterfactuals that are in conflict with the @-Counterfactuals. Whatever indispensable presuppositions scientific reasoning might have, they cannot rule out scientists' having false but justified beliefs about which propositions are the laws of nature; for surely, scientists often have had (and presumably still have) false but justified beliefs about which propositions are laws. But if these presuppositions don't rule out false but justified beliefs about which propositions are the laws of nature, they cannot require us to believe all the @-Counterfactuals.

The reply to this worry is straightforward: if the Science-Says-So Thesis is to be vindicated, what must be shown is not that all of the @-Counterfactuals follow from the indispensable presuppositions of science; rather, what follows is just that the general claim NP is presupposed—which does not say which propositions are laws, and so does not by itself determine which counterfactuals it implies. It also follows that in any given scientific context, a certain bunch of counterfactuals are all true—but which bunch this is depends on what is presupposed about the laws of nature in that context. Let's define 'NP-modulo-k' as follows:

> For a given scientific context k, *NP-modulo-k* is the proposition that for every A and every C: if the presuppositions in k entail that A is consistent with all of the nomological truths, and that C is a consequence of the nomological truths, then A $\Box\!\!\rightarrow$ C.

In other words, NP-modulo-k asserts the truth of all of the counterfactuals that would be implied by NP if the nomological presuppositions in k were all true.

Here, I understand the *presuppositions in k* in the way Stalnaker understands them.[6] To a first approximation, a proposition is *presupposed in k* just in case all the speakers in k are taking it for granted for purposes of the conversation, and take it for granted that all of the other speakers take it for granted for purposes of the conversation, and so on. The reason why that is just a first approximation is that the presuppositions in a context are deductively closed: If $P_1, P_2, \ldots P_n$ are all presupposed in k, then so is every deductive consequence of the set $\{P_1, P_2, \ldots P_n\}$. If the indispensable presuppositions of science include NP, then NP (the general claim, which is independent of which particular propositions are the laws of nature) must be presupposed to be true in any scientific context. Since the presuppositions in k are deductively closed, NP is presupposed in k only if NP-modulo-k is. So, if NP is presupposed in every scientific context, then in any scientific context k, NP-modulo-k is presupposed.

The converse is true as well: if NP-modulo-k is presupposed in every possible scientific context k, then NP is an indispensable presupposition of

[6] Stalnaker (1975), p. 67.

scientific reasoning. To show this, let's divide and conquer. Break up all possible scientific contexts into three kinds:

- Contexts in which it is correctly presupposed that all and only the @-LAWs are laws of nature;
- Contexts in which it is falsely presupposed that all and only the members of some set *L* are laws of nature;
- Contexts in which the presuppositions leave it open whether some propositions are laws or not.

These categories are exhaustive.

Let k_1 be a context of the first kind, and suppose that NP-modulo-k_1 is presupposed in k_1. The counterfactuals implied by NP-modulo-k_1 are exactly the same as the counterfactuals implied by NP. But the content of NP is exhausted by the counterfactuals it implies. So, in k_1, the presuppositions include NP.

Now let k_2 be a context of the second kind, and suppose that NP-modulo-k_2 is presupposed in k_2. The presuppositions entail that the laws of nature are exactly the members of a certain set *L*. If that is so, it follows that NP-modulo-k_2 is true just in case NP is true. So, since the presuppositions are closed under deductive consequence, NP is presupposed in k_2.

Finally, let k_3 be a context of the third kind, and suppose that NP-modulo-k_3 is presupposed in k_3. Here, the presuppositions do not entail any complete specification of which propositions are laws of nature. Let N be the proposition that expresses everything presupposed about what is a law and what is not in k_3. N will not add up to a complete specification of what is a law and what isn't, since the presuppositions in k_3 leave it open whether some propositions are laws or not. In k_3 it is presupposed that all of the counterfactuals that follow from {NP, N} are true. But it does not follow immediately from this that the presuppositions in k_3 entail that NP is true. It could be that some of the counterfactuals that follow from NP are true and some are not, though the ones that are not all depend on nomological truths that are not presupposed in k_3. So, in k_3, the presuppositions seem to leave it open whether or not NP is true in full generality.

However, suppose that we are reasoning within the context k_3, and suppose we entertain, for the sake of argument, the hypothesis that NP is not true in full generality, since some of the counterfactuals it implies in conjunction with as-yet-unknown-to-us nomological truths are false. What would happen if new evidence became available to us, on the basis of which we came to learn all of those as-yet-unknown nomological truths, without giving up any of our present presuppositions except for ones that turn out to conflict with our new evidence? Well, since we are adopting for the sake of argument the hypothesis that NP is not true in full generality, we would then have to reject NP: its falsity would follow from what we would then presuppose. But then, we could no longer be in a scientific context—since, as we have just seen, any scientific context in which all of the actual nomological truths are correctly presupposed is one in which NP follows from its presuppositions. So, if we now adopted the hypothesis that NP is not true in full generality, we could infer on the basis of what we know now that if we come to discover all of the nomological truths, we would have to reject that hypothesis in order to continue reasoning scientifically. That implies that we can know now that if we want to continue reasoning in a scientific context even as we acquire more and more evidence about the nomological truths, we will eventually have to reject the hypothesis that NP is not true in full generality, and accept the hypothesis that it is true in full generality. But if we can know right now that continued scientific inquiry will, if sufficiently successful in uncovering nomological truths, force us to accept NP in full generality, then we are scientifically justified already in assuming NP in full generality. To suppose that in a scientific context we could coherently presuppose something that *we are in a position to know* we will have to reject if our further empirical researches are successful enough (even without knowing what the particular result of those further empirical researches are going to be), is absurd.

This completes the argument: NP is entailed by presuppositions of any possible scientific context if and only if NP-modulo-k is presupposed in every possible scientific context k.

It will be useful to give that condition a name:

> **NP-U**: In any scientific context k, the presuppositions in k include NP-modulo-k. In other words, the presuppositions in k include all the counterfactuals that would follow from NP, given what is presupposed in k about the nomological truths.

('U' here stands for 'universal scientific presupposition.' So, NP-U is the thesis that NP is universally presupposed in science.)

7.5 NP as true in all possible scientific contexts

If NP-modulo-k is presupposed in every possible scientific context k (that is, if NP-U is true), then not only is NP presupposed to be true in every possible scientific context; NP *is* true in every possible scientific context. Here is why:

First, unless there is something perverse about empirical-scientific reasoning as such (a possibility I will set aside), it cannot epistemically require us to affirm what is false in any case where the error cannot be blamed on misleading information or a lack of relevant information, and where the subject matter of inquiry is within the scope of empirical science. (That claim can serve as a pretty good definition of what it means for there to be nothing perverse about scientific reasoning: such reasoning would be perverse if, when we applied it to a question inside its proper subject matter, and did not suffer from misleading information or lack of relevant information, it nevertheless required us to affirm something false.)

Suppose for the sake of argument that NP-U is true. Suppose that we are in a scientific context—a context of discourse in which the subject of the conversation is within the subject matter of the empirical sciences, and in which no extra-scientific source of epistemic justification is appealed to in order to justify claims. It follows that NP is among our presuppositions, and that it will remain so as long as the context does not shift from a scientific one to a non-scientific one. So what would happen if by some miracle, we came to know all of the laws of nature as well as every other fact that was relevant to determining the truth values of the counterfactuals covered by NP?[7] Well, it would follow that we would then be committed to affirming all of the counterfactuals covered by NP. And we would not be suffering from any false information, or any lack of relevant information concerning those counterfactuals. But we saw above that scientific reasoning could not require us to affirm what was false in such a case. So in that case all of the counterfactuals covered by NP would be true. But that means that those same counterfactuals must all be true now, in our present context of discourse—since the only difference between the miraculous case and

[7] The counterfactuals *covered* by NP are the counterfactuals that must be true given NP and given all the facts about which propositions are laws and which are not. In the actual world, they are the ones I have been calling the @-Counterfactuals.

the actual one is that we know a lot more in the former. So all the counterfactuals covered by NP are true in our present context, and so NP itself is true in our present context (since all it takes for NP to be true is for all of the counterfactuals it covers to be true). But our context could have been any scientific context—hence, NP is true in any scientific context. Discharging our initial supposition: if NP-U is true, then NP is true in every scientific context.

If NP is true in all possible scientific contexts, then its truth in a given particular scientific context is not just a function of the standards of importance and salience that the speakers in the context happen to adopt; it is not just because they have decided to treat the laws of nature as the most important feature of the actual world, for purposes of counterfactual reasoning. Rather, it is a necessary consequence of the fact that they are engaging in empirical-scientific reasoning—discoursing about topics within the subject matter of empirical science, appealing to empirical-scientific reasoning to justify their claims, not respecting the claims of any other type of reasoning (e.g. theological reasoning) when these seem to conflict with what can be justified on empirical grounds, and so on. This goes a long way toward restoring the spirit of the scientific law-governed world-picture: NP is not true in all possible contexts, but neither is it only true in contexts where the speakers have contingently decided to treat the laws as special. It must be true in any context where empirical science is able to claim epistemic authority. This makes it fair to say that NP is a feature of the natural world that empirical science discloses to us; it is not simply something that we impose on the world via the contingent, psychological factors involved in our counterfactual reasoning.

Note that *the particular counterfactuals that we are justified in believing* in any scientific context need not be the same as *the particular counterfactuals that are true* in that context: we are justified in believing the general principle NP, and in believing all of the particular counterfactuals that follow from this general principle given what is presupposed in the context about which propositions are laws of nature; the particular counterfactuals that are true in the context are the ones that follow from the general principle NP given what the laws of nature really are.[8]

[8] What the laws of nature really are is perhaps relative to the context—and I must say that it is, since this is a consequence of the meta-theoretic conception of laws—but the laws relative to a context are

But so long as NP is true in every scientific context, we are in a position to put to rest some worries that first came up back in Section 5.4—namely, the worry that if the counterfactuals implied by NP are context-variable because their truth values can depend on what the speakers in a given context happen to regard as most important for purposes of the conversation, then the truth of NP in a given context may be nothing more than a reflection of the pragmatic goals and interests of the speakers, which would threaten NP's viability as an explication of the Governing Thesis. As we saw in Section 5.9, this worry can be put to rest if it turns out that NP is true in every possible scientific context.

Putting together what we have learned so far in this chapter:

- The Science-Says-So Thesis is true if and only if NP is an indispensable presupposition of all scientific reasoning.
- NP is an indispensable presupposition of all scientific reasoning if and only if NP-U is true.
- If NP-U is true, then NP is true in every possible scientific context.

And in Chapter 5 we learned:

- The Governing Thesis is true in a given context if and only if NP is true in that context.
- The Governing Thesis is true in a way that does not make it out just to be an expression of speakers' pragmatic goals and interests if NP is true in every possible scientific context.

From all of this, it follows deductively that:

> The Science-Says-So Thesis is true, and the Governing Thesis is true in a way that does not make it out just to be an expression of speakers' pragmatic goals and interests *if and only if* NP-U is true.

This completes a major part of the argument outlined back in Section 1.8: NP-U is the condition that must be fulfilled in order for the second half of the law-governed world-picture (the Governing Thesis and the Science-Says-So Thesis) to be correct.

not generally the same as the propositions that are presupposed to be laws in that context, so that does not take anything away from what I just said.

7.6 But how could it be so?

NP-U is a very strong claim, and it is not easy to see how it could possibly be true. If NP were a logically or conceptually necessary truth that must be true in all possible contexts of discourse (whether scientific or not), then there would be no problem. But since NP is context-variable, it can be true in all possible scientific contexts only if there is some kind of constraint on the evaluation of counterfactuals built into scientific methodology itself. How can we argue for the existence of such a constraint?

We could add some further stipulations about what we mean by a 'scientific context': we could say that in order for a context to count as 'scientific,' it must be one in which the speakers respect the counterfactual robustness of the laws of nature. Or we could proceed less directly, and say that in order for a context to count as 'scientific,' the speakers in it must recognize the laws of nature are the ultimate explanatory principles, and then argue that their explanatory ultimacy requires laws to be counterfactually robust in the way spelled out by NP-U. But to do either of those things would be to cheat. It would be essentially to build the law-governed world-picture right into our characterization of scientific reasoning, and so declare anyone who does not reason in a way that affirms that picture to be reasoning unscientifically.

What we must do, if we want to vindicate the law-governed world-picture, is to argue that in any context that counts as scientific, NP is presupposed. In order to give such an argument, we're going to have to assume something about what makes a context scientific. I've said before that a scientific context is one in which the conversationalists are seeking to exposit, apply, or extend the results of scientific inquiry. But this helps only if we can say what 'scientific inquiry' is.

Does this mean we need to give a solution to the demarcation problem? Maybe, but I think it turns out we don't need to give a very informative solution. Suppose we make only two very weak assumptions: first, that the sole source of ultimate evidence in empirical natural science comes from observations and empirical measurements; and second, that scientific reasoning involves inductive, abductive, and statistical inferences from that evidence. By 'ultimate evidence,' I mean evidence where the buck stops, inferentially and deferentially. Ultimate evidence contrasts with deferential evidence—such as evidence you get from someone's testimony, by appealing to someone's authority, from remembering the result of a measurement you made once, or from looking up something in a book. It also contrasts with inferential evidence—such as statements you arrive at by inferring them from the results of observations and measurements. To say that observations and measurements are the sole source of ultimate evidence is not to deny that observations and measurements are 'theory-laden'; even theory-laden measurements are new pieces of non-inferential evidence, and their results are not fully determined by the theories with which they are laden. 'Ultimate evidence' in the sense I mean is not evidence that you could possess even if you knew nothing else about the empirical world; it is just evidence that you got directly from the source (namely, our experience of nature), rather than by inferring it or being told about it by someone.[9]

The first of my two assumptions seems unassailable: science is distinguished from other modes of inquiry by the fact that its knowledge claims are supposed to be traceable back to observation and empirical measurement. This is not to say that the whole edifice of scientific knowledge can be built up brick-by-brick out of single pieces of pure empirical knowledge uncontaminated by theoretical presuppositions; it is just to say that the empirical evidence is supposed to be the sole ultimate court of appeal. My second assumption seems reasonably liberal: in science, we find many different kinds of arguments being employed, some that look like classical cases of abduction or 'inference to the best explanation,' some that fit the methods of textbook-statistics fairly well and seem to appeal to no explanatory considerations, some that look a lot like cases of enumerative induction, and some that look infinitely more sophisticated than that. If we want to be methodologists and prescribe behavior to scientists, then we should be much more picky than I am being here: we should say which inferences in the induction-abduction-statistics family are okay, which are not, and how the okay ones should be carried out. But our current project is to inquire how much is built into the very idea of empirical-scientific inquiry itself. I take it that some science has been done using just about any halfway-reasonable methodology you can dream up. Much of it may be bad science. But NP-U does not just quantify over all contexts in which

[9] See Sellars (1997). Sellars argues that non-inferential knowledge is not the same thing as knowledge you could have possessed though you possessed no other; what I mean by 'ultimate evidence' is roughly what Sellars means by 'non-inferential knowledge.'

impeccable science is getting done: it quantifies over all possible contexts in which the reasoning getting done is recognizable as science at all. So a reasonable defense of NP-U should proceed only from the strongest assumptions about what makes something science that allows every reasonable candidate for scientific status to qualify; any stronger constraint than that would run the risk of building too much into the concept of science, and thereby weaken the argument.

So let's suppose that scientific inquiry means inquiry in which only observation and empirical measurement are recognized as legitimate sources of ultimate evidence, and in which inferences of inductive, abductive, or statistical kinds are drawn from this evidence. Given that characterization of science, is it plausible that NP-U is true? That is, is it plausible that in any context where scientific inquiry is going on, the speakers are committed to evaluating counterfactuals in the way prescribed by NP, in the light of what they believe about which propositions are laws of nature?

In order for this to be so, scientific reasoning would have to impose a substantive constraint on the evaluation of logically contingent counterfactuals. In the following section, I'll present a thought-experiment that rules out a lot of possible sources for that constraint.

7.7 Attack of the Actual-Factualists

Imagine a group of scientists who are very skeptical about counterfactuals. In particular, they do not think that any counterfactual is true unless it is trivially true—that is, unless its antecedent logically entails its consequent. These scientists are not much like our own scientists. They are aliens, in a cultural sense if not a planetary sense. Perhaps they have good reasons for their peculiarly austere views of counterfactuals. Perhaps in their culture, matters of individual responsibility are thought of very differently: they think that one must have performed actions that logically necessitated a certain outcome in order to be responsible for that outcome. (So they are both stingy with praise and exceptionally forgiving, by our standards.) Since, like us, they tend to consider counterfactuals in deciding how to judge matters of personal responsibility ('Was Alph responsible for the accident?' 'Well, if he had taken better precautions, then would the accident still have occurred?'), their culture's way of thinking about responsibility all but forces them to take their peculiar view of counterfactuals. It seems reasonable to suppose that within the contexts of their own discourse, their austere view of counterfactuals is true. (By what right would we say that our own profligacy in affirming counterfactuals is correct, and their austerity is incorrect—even in the privacy of their own homes?) What this means in David Lewis's terms is that in their contexts of discourse, the similarity metric puts all non-actual possible worlds at the same distance from the actual world. All the worlds form the surface of a great sphere, which is completely hollow but for a point at the center occupied by the actual world. The logic of counterfactuals is considered much more boring by their philosophers than it is by ours.

It might seem to us that theirs is no way to run a culture. But the question I want to focus on is: could what their so-called scientists do really be science? If so, then in the scientific contexts inhabited by the aliens, all non-trivial counterfactuals are false, even ones that are supported by the laws of nature in the most straightforward way. For them, science is all about learning about what goes on in the actual world. They are interested in discovering regularities in the actual world, and in exploiting these regularities to make predictions and retrodictions and to aid their engineering projects. Their science is not at all concerned with how things would have gone, had things been different—except insofar as this is a matter of finding *logical* consequences of various hypotheses. For this reason, I will call the aliens the *Actual-Factualists*.

If there can be Actual-Factualist science that really counts as science, then NP-U is not true, and NP is not true in all scientific contexts, and so the Science-Says-So Thesis and the Governing Thesis are in trouble. What makes NP hold in *our* scientific contexts is a contingent feature of our culture, not shared by the Actual-Factualists, and so NP is not grounded in the nature of the laws themselves or in the nature of science itself. Its truth in *our* contexts of discourse is nothing more than a reflection that we consider the nomological truths to be more worthy of holding constant for purposes of evaluating counterfactuals than other contingent truths.

The Actual-Factualists are useful guinea pigs for a thought-experiment. In examining the question of whether they can do science, we might discover that there is no good reason to think they cannot, in which case we must reject the Science-Says-So Thesis, and with it the law-governed world-picture. Alternatively, we might find some good reason to think they cannot do genuine science, in which case we will have a clue as to what it is about the nature of science that makes NP true in all scientific contexts. Moreover, such a clue might shed light on the nature of lawhood. For whatever it is that makes the laws special must be connected to what it is that makes NP true in all scientific contexts (assuming that it is).

So, is there any reason to think that the Actual-Factualists could not practice genuine science? One might argue that they could not, since real science involves giving explanations, and one cannot give an explanation without committing oneself to at least some non-trivial counterfactuals. But if we ask the Actual-Factualists whether science is in the business of providing explanations, they might well reply that it is. Furthermore, they might point out that many philosophers of our own culture have articulated theories of explanation in which explanations do not automatically require the truth of any non-trivial counterfactuals: examples include epistemic accounts of explanation such as that of Hempel and Oppenheim (1965), unification accounts such as Friedman (1974) and Kitcher (1981), pragmatic accounts such as van Fraassen (1980), as well as the causal-mechanical account free of counterfactuals defended by Salmon (1994) and Dowe (2000). If any of these models of explanation provides a sufficient condition for explanation, then the Actual-Factualist scientists can offer scientific explanations.

Some of these accounts of explanation—including Hempel's and Dowe's—make use of the concept of a law of nature. But the Actual-Factualists are happy to talk about laws of nature: they afford them a special explanatory role, they regard them as the centerpieces of physical theories, they are very interested in what their symmetries are, they like statistical measures that are invariant under all evolutions consistent with the laws, and so on. They just don't think the laws support counterfactuals.

You might say that Actual-Factualism cannot make sense of the practice of experimental design. For experimentalists often contrive things in such a way that one of these counterfactuals might turn out to be true: 'If the hypothesis H were not true, then the data would not have fit H as well as it did'; 'If the hypothesis H were true, then the data would have fit H better than it did.' You might say that without being able to affirm such counterfactuals, the Actual-Factualists cannot engage in this kind of experimental reasoning. But you would be wrong. The problem with this argument is that the role played by such conditionals in experimental reasoning need not be played by counterfactuals. They can be played by indicative conditionals, or even by material conditionals. For if such a conditional comes into play, it is going to be used as the major premise of a modus tollens: 'If H were true, then the data would have fit H to at least a certain extent; they did not; therefore H is not true.' An indicative conditional (or even a material conditional) serves just as well as a counterfactual for purposes of such an argument.

On the other hand, you might try to argue that Actual-Factualists cannot make sense of inductive confirmation. The claim here is not that the Actual-Factualists cannot make sense of confirmation at all, but that they cannot makes sense of specifically inductive confirmation, which is distinguished from mere probability-raising. Probability-raising can be accomplished by mere *content cutting*, which is what happens when the probability that a run of ten tosses of a fair coin will all turn up heads is raised by observing that the first toss turns up heads. The result of heads on the first toss raises the probability that all ten coins will turn up heads by a factor of 2, but it does not at all affect the probability that any of the subsequent tosses will turn up heads. What is distinctive of inductive confirmation is that it involves a confirmation of one instance or consequence of a hypothesis which in turn confirms each of the other instances or consequences of that same hypothesis.[10]

Some philosophers have argued that there is a tight connection between counterfactuals and inductive confirmation. In broad strokes, the idea is that when we treat some regularity as capable of being confirmed inductively, we are treating it as *projectible*: other things being equal, the confirmation of one instance of the regularity confers confirmation upon other instances of the same regularity. These other instances include not only unobserved actual instances, but also counterfactual instances. For example, if I regard the regularity that all copper is conductive as projectible, then (other things being equal) I regard the confirmation of 'This block, which is made of copper, is conductive' as lending confirmation to 'If that block over there is made of copper, then it is conductive' as well as to 'If that block over there were made of copper, then it would be conductive' and 'If there were an additional block in the room, and it were made of copper, then it would be

[10] The importance of the distinction between inductive confirmation and mere content-cutting is discussed by Gemes (1998), p. 12.

conductive.' If all of this is right, then in order to inductively confirm any regularity at all, I must regard some non-trivial counterfactual conditionals as confirmed. In order to avoid commitment to non-trivial counterfactuals, it seems that an Actual-Factualist must forgo ever regarding a regularity as inductively confirmed.[11]

But this is far from conclusive. It is not at all obvious why an Actual-Factualist could not regard some regularities as projectible, in the sense that other things being equal, the confirmation of one instance lends confirmation to all the other instances, where the instances are construed as *indicative* conditionals. Thus, if the regularity that all copper is conductive is projectible, then the confirmation of 'This block, which is made of copper, is conductive' lends confirmation to 'If that block is copper, then it is conductive,' 'If the Eiffel Tower is made of copper, then it is conductive,' 'If there is a copper statue in the living room, then it is conductive,' and so forth. Why does the very practice of regarding some regularities as projectible require one to project it into the counterfactual domain? Why could there not be a rational practice of projecting certain regularities with respect to their indicative-conditional instances, without projecting them with respect to their counterfactual-conditional instances?

It seems that the Actual-Factualists could coherently engage in a great deal of reasoning that is inductive, abductive, or statistical in character. Bayesian confirmation requires only that we can assign probabilities to hypotheses, and update those probabilities via conditionalization as new evidence comes in; there is no reason to think that applying this procedure requires affirming any non-trivial counterfactuals. Hypothetico-deductive confirmation requires the use of *modus tollens*, as do many kinds of classical statistical testing; in a particularly simple case, we might reason like this: 'If the null hypothesis were true, then it would be enormously unlikely that we got results like these; we don't believe that what we saw was enormously unlikely; so we had better reject the null hypothesis.' Since *modus tollens* works with indicative or material conditionals as well as with counterfactuals, this sort of reasoning does not require us to positively evaluate any non-trivial counterfactuals. Even abduction, or inference to the best explanation, might be employed by the Actual-Factualists. For

[11] The *locus classicus* for this idea is Goodman (1954). A sophisticated extension of this idea is developed by Lange (2000), pp. 143 ff.

example, if they adopt some version of the Principle of the Common Cause, and they have some non-counterfactual conception of what causation is (perhaps a probabilistic conception), then they can infer from correlations to the existence of an undiscovered common cause without relying on any non-trivial counterfactuals.

The case for allowing that what the Actual-Factualists are doing can deserve the label 'science' is looking pretty good. Actual-Factualist discourse can contain an awful lot of what goes on in our own scientific discourse: predictions, retrodictions, inductive confirmation, and a broad range of explanatory claims. But it still holds that nothing said in a scientific context depends for its truth on the truth of any non-trivial counterfactual. The apparent possibility of Actual-Factualist science is a serious threat to NP-U—so it is a threat to the Science-Says-So Thesis too, and a threat to the idea that NP and the Governing Thesis are anything more than a reflection of our culture's own, possibly idiosyncratic, way of reasoning about counterfactuals.

Yet, I claim that this threat ultimately comes to nothing: despite initial appearances, the Actual-Factualists could not practice genuine empirical science. The reason is that empirical science relies on observations and empirical measurements as its source of ultimate evidence, and the Actual-Factualists are not in a position to recognize the existence of this sort of evidence. Explaining why is one task of the next chapter.

8

Measurement and counterfactuals

8.1 Where we are now

Here is a summary of the argument since Chapter 5:

What it means for the laws of nature to govern the universe is for the nomological truths—the truths about which propositions are laws of nature and which ones aren't—to be inevitable as a class. That means that these truths are maximally counterfactually stable: they would all still have been true no matter what else had been the case, so long as the what-else is logically consistent with the nomological truths themselves. This is what is codified in the principle NP.

But NP is not true in all possible contexts of discourse; there are possible contexts—including theological contexts and perhaps philosophical contexts as well—in which some of the counterfactuals implied by NP are false. This raises a worry about the Governing Thesis and the law-governed world-picture: if it turns out that NP is true in the contexts where it is true only because of pragmatic features of those contexts—such as what the speakers take the point of the conversation to be—then the Governing Thesis is deflated from an important thesis about the nature of the world supposedly taught us by the modern natural sciences into an expression of what we take the main points of some conversations to be. But this worry could be ameliorated if NP turned out to be true in every possible scientific context: in that case, the truth of NP in a given scientific context would not simply be a function of the pragmatic features of that context; rather, NP would be a non-negotiable aspect of any view of the world that was justified by scientific inquiry. That would be in the spirit of the law-governed world-picture.

It also turns out that the truth of NP in all possible scientific contexts is exactly what it would take for the Science-Says-So Thesis to be true:

since NP is not itself empirically confirmable, it can be part of what science justifies us in believing only if it is a consequence of presuppositions indispensable to scientific inquiry. It is a consequence of such presuppositions just in case the principle NP-U is true—which says that in any scientific context, the presuppositions entail all of the counterfactuals entailed by NP in the light of what is presupposed about which propositions are laws and which aren't. Furthermore, if NP is a consequence of such presuppositions, then it is true in all possible scientific contexts. So the truth of NP in all possible scientific contexts—or equivalently, the truth of NP-U—is exactly what it takes for the Governing Thesis and the Science-Says-So Thesis both to be true.

But it is not easy to see how NP-U could be true. For it to be so would require that scientific methodology itself involves non-negotiable constraints on how counterfactuals are evaluated in the light of what is known (or believed, or presupposed) about which propositions are laws of nature. The thought-experiment of the Actual-Factualists showed that we can conceive of creatures engaged in inquiry about the natural world that has a great deal in common with our science—in particular, employing the same kinds of reasoning from empirical evidence, reaching the same goals of prediction, retrodiction, and explanation—even though they refuse to affirm any logically contingent counterfactuals, and no such counterfactuals are true in the contexts of their discourse. If what the Actual-Factualists do really is science, then NP-U is false, and NP is not true in all possible scientific contexts, and the Science-Says-So Thesis is false, and the Governing Thesis is true in some contexts of discourse only qua reflection of the interests of the speakers in those contexts. In short: very bad news for the law-governed world-picture.

But there is a way out yet for the law-governed world-picture: we haven't yet seen any conclusive argument that what the Actual-Factualists engage in really is empirical science. In the last chapter, we focused on the ways in which Actual-Factualists reason from their evidence, and the kinds of applications they make of this reasoning. But there is another crucial feature of empirical science, having to do with where the evidence ultimately comes from. In any inquiry that deserves to be called *empirical science*, the evidence must ultimately come from empirical observations and measurements. I aim to show in this chapter that recognizing something as an empirical observation or measurement involves acknowledging the truth of some non-trivial counterfactuals. This is the sole place where scientific reasoning as such places constraints on how we evaluate counterfactuals. So, if NP is true in all possible scientific contexts, it must be so in virtue of this constraint. Recognizing that tells us a great deal about what lawhood is.

8.2 Measurements, reliability, counterfactuals

In any inquiry that counts as scientific, everything that counts as evidence consists ultimately of the results of empirical observations or measurements. For ease of exposition, I am going to use the word 'measurement' in a broad sense so that it covers all empirical observations: for example, an observation that a certain liquid is green can be construed as a measurement of a quantitative property of the liquid that has value 1 if the liquid is green and 0 otherwise. In this case and many others, construing an observation of a qualitative property as a measurement of a quantitative property can seem a little unnatural. But it will make life much easier if we can just speak of measurements of quantities (i.e. quantitative properties or magnitudes), and not constantly mention observations of qualitative properties as a separate case.

What is a measurement? First of all, a measurement is a token act (or set of acts, not necessarily all performed by the same agent) that involves the use of sense-perception and that culminates in a judgment about the value of some quantity Q. Moreover, what makes a given act count as a measurement is that it is a carrying-out of a legitimate measurement procedure—that is, it is a token following of a set of instructions, such that any token following of those instructions is a measurement. To say this is to deny 'singularism' about measurement: an act cannot count as a measurement 'all by itself'; a measurement has to be a proper carrying-out of a general measurement procedure or method (I'll use 'method' and 'procedure' interchangeably). If my act was a measurement, then any other act of the same kind carried out under sufficiently similar circumstances would also be a measurement, and it would be a measurement of the same thing that I measured. I take this to be obviously true.

A legitimate measurement procedure must be specifiable by a set of instructions which it is possible for an observer to carry out intentionally. It could be that the same procedure can be specified by different sets of instructions; so legitimate measurement procedures should not be individuated by their instruction-sets. Instead, I'll assume they are individuated by their sets of possible correct-carryings-out.

A legitimate measurement procedure can be characterized by three parameters (later on I will point out the need for a fourth). First, there is the quantity that is getting measured; I'll call this the *object variable* and will usually refer to it as 'Q'. Second, there is the *pointer variable* which I will usually refer to as 'P'; the pointer variable is the quantity whose value is determined at the last stage of the measurement, and from which the value of Q is 'read off.' In many typical cases, the pointer variable will be the position of a moving pointer that can move back and forth across a numbered scale that makes it easier to determine its position. (That's why P is called 'the pointer variable.') In others, it might be the color of a solution, the height of a column of mercury, the position on a ruler which the end of an object is adjacent to, or any number of other things. The one requirement is that the pointer variable must itself be measurable—otherwise, it would not be possible to determine its value and so complete the measurement. Third, there is a proposition which I will call the *set-up condition*, and will usually refer to as 'C.' The set-up condition specifies that all of the steps of the measurement procedure (not including the final reading of the pointer variable) have been carried out, that whatever enabling conditions must be in place for the measurement to be possible are true, and that any interferences or defeating conditions that would disrupt the measurement are absent.

So, for example, in the procedure that involves using an ordinary spring-scale to measure the weight of a middle-sized object, Q is the weight of the object placed on the scale, and P is the angular position of the pointer at the end of the measurement. C says that the scale has been constructed and calibrated according to certain specifications; that Q is within some range (not so small that we need a more sensitive scale, and not so great that the scale is going to get crushed); that nothing is resting on the scale other than the object getting weighed; that nothing save gravity, the object getting weighed, and the parts of the scale itself are pushing or pulling on the spring or the pointer; that the object getting weighed is not subject to any non-negligible non-gravitational forces; and that sufficient time has passed for the pointer to stop moving back and forth and come to rest. (I might have left something out, but you get the idea.)

So, we can designate a particular measurement procedure by an ordered triple $\langle Q, P, C\rangle$. But not every such triple designates a legitimate measurement method. For arbitrarily selected quantities Q and P and an arbitrarily selected proposition C, the procedure with Q as its object variable, P as its pointer variable, and C as its set-up condition will usually not be a legitimate measurement procedure. I'll call any such triple a 'procedure,' whether it is a legitimate measurement procedure or not.

The simplicity of the ordered triple $\langle Q, P, C\rangle$ might suggest that each individual measurement is a pretty simple thing, but this need not be so. The set-up condition C might, for example, require that one or more additional quantities (distinct from both P and Q) be measured along the way, in the course of carrying out the measurement; the pointer variable P might be some mathematical function of all of these intermediary quantities that were measured along the way. This is probably typical of the sophisticated measurement procedures found in contemporary science.

In the case of some methods of measurement, the pointer variable is simply the judgment that a competent observer feels inclined to make. For example, consider what happens when we measure the angular position of the pointer-needle on a spring scale by looking at it straight on. We don't find the value of this position by 'reading it off' from the value of some further quantity; we just look and see what the angular position of the pointer is. In cases like this, the only thing that could be playing the role of the pointer variable is the judgment that the angular position is thus-and-so, which the looker is strongly inclined to make. You might think it's a mistake to think that anything is playing the role of the pointer variable here at all. Whether this is a mistake depends on subtle questions about the epistemology of sensory knowledge that I don't think we need to try to settle here. Let it be understood as a local terminological convention that in cases like this, the judgment the competent observer is inclined to make shall count as the pointer variable. On some views of what is going on when we make an observation, this is just because this judgment simply is the pointer variable; on other views, we can still agree to count this judgment as the pointer variable by courtesy.

The pointer variable in such cases is itself measurable, of course: other observers can measure it by seeing what the first observer says, and the first observer can measure it by introspection. If we didn't allow for this, then the carrying-out of any measurement procedure would involve an infinite sequence of measurements: in order to determine the value of the pointer variable P, we would need to measure it by some method; so we would need to determine the value of the pointer variable P′ of some method for measuring P; in order to do that, we would have to measure P′ by some method; and so on *ad infinitum*. To block this debilitating regress, we need to assume (what is obviously true) that in some cases, a measurement can be made in one 'simple' act—simple, that is, as far as the agent is consciously aware—in which the value of the pointer variable P is determined by 'just looking,' and the value of Q is reported immediately without any consciously performed inference.[1]

In order for a procedure to count as a legitimate measurement procedure, it must be reliable: that is, when C is true, P is a reliable indicator of Q. For each legitimate measurement procedure ⟨*Q*, *P*, *C*⟩, there corresponds a condition that I will call the *reliability condition* of the method:

R: Whenever C, K(P, Q)

R should be understood to be universally quantified over time, and over any other positions in C occupied by singular terms.[2] 'K(P, Q)' stands for a condition that can take either of two forms: it can specify that the value of P is a certain mathematical function of the value of Q, or it can specify a statistical distribution for the value of Q in terms of P. (This allows for cases in which there are random measurement errors, as well as cases where there is no strict relation between P and Q but only a statistical one—for example, when we measure the amount of uranium in a sample by counting the number of clicks on a nearby Geiger counter in an interval of time, or when we measure the bias of a coin by flipping it 1,000 times and counting the number of heads.) I will call R the *reliability condition* for the procedure whose reliability it expresses.

At this point, we can see that we need to individuate measurement procedures in a more fine-grained way than we have so far. We have

[1] I do not mean to suggest that such 'simple' empirical judgments are really all that simple. The epistemology and psychology of such judgments is enormously complicated, and is the subject of much exciting recent research. But for my purposes here, I think it will be safe and convenient to 'black-box' such empirical judgments: I assume that we can make them somehow or other, and that in at least some circumstances we are pretty good at making them, and I will count them as examples of measurements of quantities that can be used as pointer variables in measurements of other quantities.

[2] For example, if C includes the condition that the scale being used has been calibrated, then in R, the antecedent will include the condition that x is a scale that has been calibrated, where x is a variable bound by a universal quantifier.

been assuming that once you specify the object variable Q, the pointer variable P, and the set-up condition C, you have effectively specified a particular measurement method. But a measurement method is a procedure for arriving at a justified belief about the value of a quantity. Two different possible methods, in two different possible worlds, might have the same Q, P, and C, but be such that the correlation between P and Q—the relation that gets plugged in for 'K(P, Q)' in the schema R—is different. For example, in one of the methods, this relation might be strict equality; in another, it might be a statistical relation involving a very narrow bell-curve, and in another a statistical relation involving a wider bell-curve. These methods yield different degrees of justification[3] for the judgment about the value of Q that they yield. This makes it not unreasonable to consider them different methods.[4] So, henceforth, I will assume that to specify a method, we must specify not only Q, P, and C, but also the correlation relation. In other words, a method can be identified by an ordered 4-tuple $\langle Q, P, C, K \rangle$. As before, not every method thus specified is a legitimate measurement method; in order for the method to be a legitimate measurement method, P must be measurable, C must be empirically confirmable, K must be some kind of significant positive correlation relation, and the reliability condition R must be true. These conditions are necessary for $\langle Q, P, C, K \rangle$ to be a legitimate measurement procedure. But they are not sufficient, for reasons that we need to confront now.

The truth of R guarantees that the method $\langle Q, P, C, K \rangle$ is a *de facto* reliable method of determining the value of Q. But not every *de facto* reliable method of determining the value of Q is a method of measuring Q. Suppose that Q is the apparent magnitude of the star Sirius. One way of determining the value of Q is to get an appropriately sensitive photometer and use it correctly. Another is to go the library and look up the apparent magnitude of Sirius in an astronomy text. Yet another is to

[3] Or maybe different kinds of justification; the important point is that the nature of the justification yielded by the methods will be different in some way.

[4] Moreover, within the same world, someone might use the method $\langle Q, P, C \rangle$ while falsely assuming that the correlation between P and Q is strict, while another uses the same method while correctly assuming the correlation to be only statistical. In a case like this, we could say that the first person is employing the method incorrectly, while the second is applying it correctly. But an equally legitimate and in some ways more perspicuous notation would be to say that we have here two distinct procedures, only one of which is a legitimate measurement procedure. If we want to talk that way, we have to distinguish procedures in a more fine-grained way than by ordered triples of the form $\langle Q, P, C \rangle$. What we have to add to the specification of a procedure is a correlation relation.

ask the friendly astronomer who lives down the street. The second and third methods may be quite reliable—in fact, for most of us, using either of these methods would give us a much more reliable answer than carrying out the measurement with the photometer ourselves. But only the first method is really a method of *measuring* the apparent magnitude of Sirius.

Why is this? Well, the obvious thing to say is that when we look up the answer in a text, or ask an expert, no new measurement is being performed—we are simply ascertaining the result of a measurement that has already been performed. A genuine measurement must be something that can yield *fresh empirical justification* for the claim made as its result. In other words, a measurement must involve a new empirical interaction with the world, and its result must depend on how that interaction goes—in such a way that the result is logically independent of the results of any previous measurements of the very same quantity. This is lacking when the method used involves taking someone's testimony (or a book's testimony, or even your own memory's testimony) about the result of a previous measurement.

There is another difference as well: if I make my own measurement of the apparent magnitude of Sirius, by constructing and correctly using a sensitive photometer and checking the reading on the photometer when I am done, then by calling my action a measurement, I am committing myself to the counterfactual reliability, and not merely the *de facto* reliability, of the procedure I used. But this is not so if I determine the apparent magnitude of Sirius by looking it up in a trusted book.

Here's what I mean by that: consider the case where I actually use the photometer to take a reading myself. I certainly believe that the reliability condition R of the method I use is true: if I didn't, then I should have no faith in the result I get. I must also believe that if Sirius had had a different apparent magnitude than it actually has, then the pointer variable would still have been a reliable indicator of the apparent magnitude (so long as the set-up condition C was still true)—so, the pointer variable would have had a different value. For otherwise, I am *just lucky* that Sirius happened to have the apparent magnitude it did; if it had had a different apparent magnitude, I might have gotten the wrong value even if I had done everything right.[5]

[5] Here I rely on one half of the 'might-would' duality affirmed by Lewis (1973): 'It is not the case that (if it had been the case that A, then it would have been the case that C)' logically entails 'If it had been

But if I made a proper measurement of the apparent magnitude of Sirius, then I am not just lucky in this way. Similarly, I must believe that if my pointer variable had had a different value than it does, then this pointer variable would still have been a reliable indicator of the value of Q. Otherwise, again, I am just lucky that I got the right result. Finally, if something apparently having nothing to do with the measurement had been otherwise than it actually is—say, if Dennis Kucinich had won the Democratic nomination in 2004—but the set-up conditions C were all still true (that is, I still used a photometer that was correctly constructed, calibrated, and shielded, and I still followed the instructions for using it correctly), then I had better believe that P would still have been a reliable indicator of Q. Otherwise, though I believe that P is a reliable indicator of Q, again my beliefs imply that I am just lucky—this time, I am lucky that Kucinich didn't win the nomination, for if he had, then I might have gotten the wrong result even if I had done everything just right. And again, this kind of luckiness is incompatible with my having made a genuine measurement.

But the same isn't true of the method of finding out the apparent magnitude of Sirius by looking it up in a book. It is, in a sense, lucky for me that the book I am using gives the correct value for this quantity. For in carrying out the look-it-up-in-a-book method—i.e., in seeing to it that the set-up condition of this method is satisfied—I didn't do anything to verify the measurement whose results it reports, or its report of the outcome of that measurement. If there had been a printer's error, or if the author had made a mistake, then the 'pointer variable' of this method would not have been an accurate indicator of the value of the object variable—even if I had done my part exactly right.[6] So, if there had been some such error,

the case that A, then it might not have been the case that C.' Or in symbols: $\neg(A \mathrel{\Box\!\!\rightarrow} C) \vdash A \mathrel{\Diamond\!\!\rightarrow} \neg C$. This half of the duality seems to me to be obviously true, though the other half (the converse implication) seems much less obvious. For a discussion of some shocking consequences of the other half of the might-would duality, see Hajek (unpublished).

[6] I assume here that the set-up condition C for the look-it-up-in-a-book method requires only that the book I am looking in is a non-altered copy of 'the right book'—volume S of the *Encyclopedia Americana*, as it might be. The truth of C does not place any constraints on how this book was produced. In other words, the procedure we're talking about starts only after the book is already written and printed; it begins when I go to the shelf to get that book. If instead we characterized the procedure as involving all the actions of those who produced the book, including those who gathered all the information reported in that book, then the set-up condition C might naturally be thought to include a condition that rules out any factual errors or misprints in the production of the book. In

then even if the antecedent of the reliability condition for this method had been true—even if I had carried out the procedure of going to the library, locating the right book, locating the right table on the right page, and correctly processing the numerals I find printed there—its consequent might have been false. In other words, the reliability condition itself might have been false, had things been different in some way or other. Thus, it is a striking difference between genuine measurement methods and other *de facto* reliable methods that the former must be counterfactually reliable, whereas the latter can be *merely de facto* reliable.

Why do we take some of our methods of ascertaining the values of quantities to be robustly counterfactually reliable, while we take other methods to be rather less robustly counterfactually reliable, or maybe even just plain *de facto* reliable? And why are the ones in the first group the ones we call 'measurements'? I think the answer to the first question is that we distinguish between our 'ultimate evidence' and our 'other-than-ultimate evidence,' where the former is drawn fresh from whatever the source of justification is (be it experience, a priori insight, divine revelation, or whatever) and the latter is drawn from such things as testimony, conclusions reached via inferences from ultimate evidence, and combinations of the two. And to recognize something as a source of ultimate evidence means acknowledging that when you use that source correctly and get a correct evidence-statement out of it, you aren't just getting lucky. And that absence of luckiness requires (at least) the counterfactual reliability of the sources of ultimate evidence. That is, recognizing something as a source of ultimate evidence is recognizing its robust counterfactual reliability.[7] I think the answer to the second question is that whenever we are doing science, the sole source of ultimate evidence that we recognize as legitimate is measurement. That is one of the defining features of empirical natural science, whether it is being practiced by us or by creatures very different from us—even when it is practiced by creatures as strange as the Actual-Factualists. That's why the Actual-Factualists can't really do empirical

this case, though, we would be talking about a different procedure, of which the procedure I have been talking about is a proper part. *That* procedure might well be counterfactually reliable. But it would be very misleading to call *that* procedure the look-it-up-in-a-book method, since it includes so much more human information-gathering than just my looking up something in a book. Thanks to Ram Neta here.

[7] At least. Maybe it is that plus something else.

natural science: they refuse to recognize the truth of the counterfactuals that they have to recognize as true in order to recognize something as a legitimate measurement procedure.

I need to head off a certain misunderstanding before going on. I say that legitimate measurement methods must be counterfactually reliable, because otherwise, when we use one and get the right result, our getting the right result is a matter of our being lucky, in a way that is not consistent with the kind of justification that reports of our ultimate evidence should be. When we correctly carry out a legitimate measurement method, and thereby form a true belief about the value of some quantity, our true belief is not an instance of sheer luck. But we must be careful not to overstate this point. Every real measurement procedure has a set-up condition C that is not entirely under our control, and we can mistakenly though reasonably believe that this C is true when it is not. For example, the spring-scale method of measuring the weight of a stone has a set-up condition that requires the absence of any non-negligible non-gravitational forces acting on the stone other than the contact force exerted by the scale's pan. Measurements that involve telescopic observations require the absence of any unknown lenses positioned between the telescope and the observed object. Cases are easily multiplied. Since it is not within my power to cause all the set-up conditions of my measurement to be satisfied, and I cannot achieve infallible certainty that these conditions are all in place on any given occasion, there is a sense in which I am lucky when things go well, when the set-up conditions are all in place and I get the right result from my measurement. Hence, if the justification yielded by measurement had to be independent of *all* varieties of good luck, then such justification would not be within our reach. And so, when I correctly carry out a legitimate measurement procedure and arrive at a true judgment about the value of Q, we must not suppose that my success in this enterprise is entirely due to my virtues and my efforts, and not in any way or to any degree attributable to my good luck. The only claim I am making here is a weaker one: when I reach a true judgment by correctly carrying out a legitimate measurement procedure, there is one particular place in the process where my own good luck must not have played a role. *Given that the measurement really was carried out correctly*—which requires that the set-up condition C be true, and which for that reason requires that some things be true that are not under my control, and which for that reason may be due in part to my good luck—there is no *further* luckiness on my part that was required in order for me to get a correct result.[8] Perhaps a better way to put this is that the procedure itself does not need to be lucky; even if we need some lucky-for-us cooperation on the part of the external world in order for the procedure to be implemented, the procedure once implemented needs no luck to yield a correct result. Once the procedure is correctly implemented, it *has* to yield a proper result; it isn't the case that it *might yet fail*. *This* is the kind of independence from luck that I am interested in here; I claim that it is more or less self-evident that sources of ultimate evidence must possess this kind of luck-independence. And for a legitimate measurement procedure to possess this kind of luck-independence is for its reliability condition to be counterfactually stable.

Before moving on, let me introduce an abbreviation: I'm going to be talking a lot about the reliability conditions of the legitimate measurement procedures. These are not the same as the reliability conditions, period—for every procedure has a reliability condition, even the procedures that do not deserve to be called 'legitimate measurement procedures' (though not all procedures have *true* reliability conditions). I'll call the reliability conditions of the legitimate measurement procedures the *measurement reliability conditions*, or the *MRCs* for short.

8.3 A general principle that captures the relation between measurement and counterfactuals

Here is what we have learned about legitimate measurement procedures so far: insofar as I take the method $\langle Q, P, C, K \rangle$ to be a legitimate measurement procedure, I am committed not only to the truth of its reliability condition R, but also to the claim that R would still have been true, even if Q or P had had a different value, and even if anything else had been different. R, in other words, is maximally counterfactually invariant.

[8] But note that 'a correct result' here means a result that does indeed bear the relation K to Q. If K is a statistical relation, then a 'correct' result need not be a true one—it is just one that is a statistically good indicator of Q.

It is tempting to understand that to mean this:

> For any proposition A, and any proposition R: if R is the reliability condition of a procedure I take to be a legitimate measurement procedure, then I am committed to the counterfactual A □→ R.

But that's not right—as we saw back in Chapter 5, maximal counterfactual reliability is subject to limitations imposed by logic. Suppose that B is logically inconsistent with R; then surely I am not committed to saying that R would still have been true even if B had been true. (That's a logical impossibility: a counterfactual with a logically possible antecedent but a consequent logically inconsistent with its antecedent.)

Suppose that D is logically consistent with R, but it is not consistent with the set of all of the MRCs I acknowledge.[9] For example, suppose that in addition to $\langle Q, P, C, K \rangle$ I also recognize another method $\langle Q', P', C', K' \rangle$ as a legitimate measurement procedure, and its reliability condition is R′. And suppose that D = (¬R ∨ ¬R′). So, D is logically consistent with R, but it is not consistent with the set of all of the MRCs I recognize. Am I committed to the counterfactual D □→ R? Well, if so, then I should also be committed to the counterfactual D □→ R′. By uncontroversial principles from the logic of counterfactuals, this means I am committed to D □→ (R · R′), and also to D □→ (D · R · R′). This last is a counterfactual with a logically possible antecedent and a logically impossible consequent; every such counterfactual is trivially false. So, we must not say that I am committed to D □→ R in this case.[10]

These *seem* to be the only restrictions on the original claim—that insofar as I am committed to calling a method a legitimate measurement procedure, I am committed to saying that it would still have been true no matter how things might have been different—that logic requires. That claim was motivated by the thought that when you get the right answer about the value of a quantity, and you did so by correctly carrying out a legitimate measurement procedure, it is not merely a matter of good luck that you got the right answer.[11] But, if the measurement

[9] That is: the reliability conditions of all the procedures I acknowledge as legitimate measurement procedures.

[10] I stole this argument from Lange, who uses it to make a similar point about laws rather than about MRCs; see his (2000), pp. 100–3.

[11] But see the qualifications at the end of Section 8.2.

might have given an incorrect answer had something else happened, even though you correctly carried out the measurement procedure, then your having got the right answer was a matter of good luck. So, when we recognize a procedure as a legitimate measurement procedure, we must take its reliability condition to be maximally counterfactually invariant. But now we see that 'maximal counterfactual invariance' must not mean invariance under any counterfactual suppositions whatsoever; it can only mean invariance under as broad a range of counterfactual suppositions as logical consistency allows. And this means, in the terminology of Section 5.5, that what we are committed to acknowledging is not the inevitability of all the MRCs one by one, but rather the inevitability of the MRCs *as a class*.

So, it seems that what we should say is this: insofar as we believe that $\langle Q, P, C, K\rangle$ is a legitimate measurement procedure, if R is its reliability condition, we are committed to this principle:

> For any proposition A that is logically consistent with the set of all of the MRCs we recognize, we are committed to the truth of: A $\Box\!\!\rightarrow$ R.

But that's not quite right either: there is one more kind of exception we need to build in. What if A is a counterfactual supposition that is logically consistent with the *de facto* truth of all of the MRCs we recognize, but it entails that the method $\langle Q, P, C, K\rangle$ is not really a legitimate measurement procedure? (For example, A could be the proposition *that if this method happens to give the right answer every time it is used then this is just a fluke, for the method is not a legitimate measurement procedure at all.*) In that case, surely we don't want to require that R would still have been true, even if A had been true. The motivation for thinking that R must be counterfactually reliable was that when we use the method and get the right answer, this isn't just good luck—but in the case we are considering, A *says that* it is just good luck if we always get the right answer when we use this method. So, we shouldn't require that R be counterfactually invariant even under that kind of counterfactual supposition. Here's what we get when we build in that exception:

> For any proposition A that is logically consistent with everything we suppose to be an MRC, and that is consistent with all of our presuppositions about which methods are legitimate measurement procedures, and

> any proposition R that we presuppose to be an MRC, we are committed to: A $\square\!\!\rightarrow$ R.

But, since the fact that a method is a legitimate measurement procedure entails that its reliability condition is true, we can simplify this:

> For any proposition A that is logically consistent with all of our presuppositions about which methods are legitimate measurement procedures, and any proposition R that we presuppose to be an MRC, we are committed to: A $\square\!\!\rightarrow$ R.

This can actually be strengthened a bit: under any such counterfactual supposition A, if A were true, then each of the legitimate measurement procedures would not just still be reliable—each of them would still be a legitimate measurement procedure as well. For surely that is why we think that each of these methods would still be reliable! (It would be very strange to say that if Kucinich had won the nomination, then my method of measuring the apparent magnitudes of stars would still always give the right answers, but that would just be a fluke since the method would not be a legitimate measurement procedure.) So, here is what we are committed to, insofar as we take there to be such things as legitimate measurement procedures:

> For any proposition A that is logically consistent with all of our presuppositions about which methods are legitimate measurement procedures, and any proposition C that is entailed by those presuppositions, we are committed to: A $\square\!\!\rightarrow$ C.

The 'we' in this condition means: we persons who are discoursing in a context k in which we are committed to recognizing legitimate measurement methods as the sole source of ultimate evidence. So we can reformulate it by saying that when we are reasoning within a scientific context k, we are at least implicitly committed to the following proposition, which I will call 'LMP-modulo-k':

> **LMP-modulo-k:** For every A and every C, if the presuppositions in k entail that A is consistent with all of the truths about which methods are legitimate measurement procedures, and they also entail that the truths about which methods are legitimate measurement procedures entail C, then A $\square\!\!\rightarrow$ C.

So the presuppositions of any scientific context k include LMP. Let's give this principle a name:

LMP-U: In any scientific context k, the presuppositions include LMP-modulo-k.

Why call the two preceding principles LMP-modulo-k and LMP-U? Well, consider the following principle:

LMP: For any proposition A that is logically consistent with all of the true propositions about which methods are legitimate measurement procedures, and any proposition C that is entailed by the truths about which methods are legitimate measurement procedures: A □→ C.

'LMP' stands for *legitimate-measurement preservation*; it says that the facts about which procedures are legitimate measurement procedures and which are not (which, again, entail that all of the reliability conditions of the legitimate measurement procedures are true) are maximally counterfactually stable; they are inevitably true as a class. LMP is analogous to NP: you can get LMP from NP just by substituting 'facts about which procedures are legitimate measurement procedures' for 'facts about which propositions are laws and which are not.' This substitution also turns NP-modulo-k into LMP-modulo-k, and NP-U into LMP-U.

Recall that the procedure $\langle Q, P, C, K \rangle$ is a legitimate measurement procedure just in case its associated reliability condition is not only true, but also one of the MRCs. (This is just a trivial consequence of the way we defined 'MRC.') So, the truths about which procedures are legitimate measurement procedures are equivalent to the truths about which propositions are MRCs. What LMP tells us, then, is that the MRCs are maximally counterfactually invariant.

Back in Section 7.5, we saw an argument that if NP-U is true, then NP is not only justified, but also true, in every possible scientific context. Due to the structural analogy between NP and NP-U, on the one hand, and LMP and LMP-U, on the other, an exactly parallel argument shows that if LMP-U is true, then LMP is true in every possible scientific context. This is how the nature of empirical-scientific inquiry as such places constraints on how counterfactuals are to be evaluated: the relation between measurement and counterfactual reliability that must be acknowledged in order for measurement to be recognized as the sole source of ultimate evidence requires that in every scientific context, the presuppositions about which procedures are legitimate measurement procedures entail further presuppositions about which counterfactuals are true, in the way expressed by LMP-U. And that, in turn, implies something about which counterfactuals are *true* in any given scientific context: for it implies that LMP is true in every possible scientific context.

8.4 What we can learn about lawhood from what we have learned about the counterfactual commitments of science

The example of the Actual-Factualists showed how implausible it is that the kinds of inference employed in science, and the goals of science (such as prediction, explanation, and technological application) imply that there are any constraints on the truth values and justificatory status of counterfactuals that hold across all possible scientific contexts. Now we have seen that the only way in which the nature of scientific inquiry itself exerts a constraint on counterfactuals is via the relation between measurements and counterfactual reliability. That is, if you want to engage in empirical science at all, you must be committed to acknowledging the counterfactual reliability of everything you acknowledge to be a legitimate measurement procedure, and so you must be committed to LMP-modulo-k. That's what stops you from being an Actual-Factualist. But apart from that, you can agree with the Actual-Factualists all you like, and keep on doing science. Acknowledge the counterfactuals that you must acknowledge in order coherently to acknowledge your measurement methods as sources of ultimate empirical evidence, and from then on you can be as stingy about acknowledging the truth of further non-trivial counterfactuals as you like; such stinginess won't stop you from drawing any of the scientific inferences or achieving any of the scientific goals that the Actual-Factualists are able to draw and achieve.

Now let's recall some of the lessons we learned earlier. First, the Governing Thesis and the Science-Says-So Thesis are both true if and only if NP is both true, and justifiably affirmed, in every possible scientific context. A necessary and sufficient condition for that is that NP-U is true.

NP-U says that the speakers in any possible scientific context are committed to affirming a whole bunch of non-trivial counterfactuals. But the only thing about scientific contexts as such that require the speakers in them to affirm any particular non-trivial counterfactuals at all is LMP-U. So, the law-governed world-picture can be correct only if LMP-U guarantees that NP-U is true. How could it do that?

Well, it could do that if the counterfactuals that LMP-U says the speakers in a scientific context are committed to are the same counterfactuals that NP-U says the speakers in that context are committed to. That would be so if the propositions that are presupposed to be laws of nature in a scientific context k have exactly the same logical closure as the propositions that are presupposed to be MRCs in k. For in that case, LMP-U and NP-U would both say that the same set of propositions is presupposed to be counterfactually stable in k. Thus:

> (1) If the logical closure of the set of propositions presupposed to be laws in a scientific context k is exactly the logical closure of the set of propositions presupposed to the MRCs in k, then the truth of LMP-U guarantees that of NP-U.

The converse is true as well. For, suppose otherwise: then there is some scientific context k in which the closure of the set of propositions presupposed to be laws of nature is not identical to that of the logically contingent propositions presupposed to be consequences of the MRCs. In that case, NP-U requires that the speakers in k are committed to some counterfactuals that LMP-U does not say they are committed to. For in that case, either there is a proposition presupposed to be a consequence of the laws in k that is not a consequence of the propositions presupposed to be MRCs in k, or vice versa. If there is a consequence L of the presupposed laws that is not a consequence of the presupposed MRCs, then NP-U implies some counterfactuals with L as the consequent, but LMP-U does not. If there is a consequence R of the presupposed MRCs that is not a consequence of the presupposed laws, then NP-U implies some counterfactuals with antecedents that are inconsistent with R, but LMP-U does not. So either way, the truth of NP-U is not guaranteed by the truth of LMP-U. Therefore: if it is not the case that the propositions presupposed to be laws in any given scientific context k have exactly the same logical closure as the propositions presupposed to be consequences of the MRCs in k, then the truth of

LMP-U does not guarantee that of NP-U. Taking the contrapositive: if the truth of LMP-U does guarantee the truth of NP-U, then in any given scientific context, the propositions presupposed to be laws have exactly the same logical closure as the set of propositions presupposed to be MRCs. Putting this together with (1), we get:

(2) The truth of LMP-U guarantees that of NP-U if and only if the propositions presupposed to be laws in any given possible scientific context have exactly the same logical closure as the set of propositions presupposed to be MRCs in that context.

But necessarily, every logically contingent consequence of the laws of nature is itself a law of nature.[12] So the set of laws of nature is necessarily identical to the set of logically contingent propositions that are in the logical closure of the set of laws of nature. It follows that the logical closure of the propositions presupposed to be laws is the same as the logical closure of the propositions presupposed to be MRCs just in case the propositions presupposed to be laws of nature are exactly the logically contingent consequences of the propositions presupposed to be MRCs. So:

(3) The truth of LMP-U guarantees that of NP-U if and only if the propositions presupposed to be laws in any given possible scientific context are exactly the logically contingent consequences of the propositions presupposed to be MRCs in that context.

As we have seen, the Governing Thesis and Science-Says-So Thesis are both true if and only if NP-U is true, and the only way for NP-U to be true is for its truth to be guaranteed by LMP-U. Hence:

(4) The law-governed world-picture is correct only if the propositions presupposed to be laws in any given scientific context are exactly the

[12] In the text, I am working on the assumption that it is a necessary truth that all logically contingent consequences of the laws of nature are themselves laws of nature. As I noted at the end of Section 2.4, there is an alternative view which I don't want to rule out of court: namely, that there is an objective, principled distinction between propositions that are sufficiently general to count as laws of nature and those that are not. For example, 'George is either a non-raven or he's black' is a logical consequence of the law that all ravens are black, but since it's just about George, and is not sufficiently general to count as a law of nature, perhaps we should consider it a nomologically necessary non-law. On this view, the logical closure of the laws is exactly the same as the logical closure of the nomological necessities, since every nomologically necessary non-law is a consequence of laws of nature. If we

logically contingent consequences of the propositions presupposed to be consequences of the MRCs in that context.

That is very big news.

8.5 A first-order account of laws or a meta-theoretic account of laws?

The principle (4) established in the preceding section tells us a great deal about lawhood. We can almost read an account of what lawhood is right off of it. Almost, but not quite. We face a choice between trying to accommodate (4) within a first-order account of laws, and trying to accommodate it within a meta-theoretic account of laws.

If we want to adopt a first-order account of laws, and accommodate (4), here's what we'll have to say:

> **FO:** It is an a priori truth that the laws of nature are exactly the logical consequences of the MRCs; moreover, the question of which propositions are MRCs—or equivalently, the question of which procedures are legitimate measurement procedures—is part of the first-order subject-matter of science; it is not a meta-theoretic matter.

(The second clause is needed because if it were false, then FO would not be a first-order account of laws at all, since it would analyze lawhood in terms of a meta-theoretic notion.) This is what we should say if we want a first-order account of laws that saves the law-governed world-picture in the light of (4), because what we want is a first-order account of laws that entails that what we presuppose to be the laws is identical with that we presuppose to be in the deductive closure of the MRCs; so what we want is a guarantee that whatever we presuppose to be a law, we also presuppose to be a consequence of the MRCs, and vice versa; this will be true just in case our set of presuppositions is closed under consequences of the principle that the laws are the consequences of the MRCs. Our set of presuppositions will automatically be closed under consequences of that principle just in case that principle is an a priori truth.

want to adopt this alternative view, then what I say in the text here should be reformulated, with 'nomological necessities' in place of 'laws.' Otherwise, the argument works in just the same way.

On the other hand, if we want to adopt a meta-theoretic account of laws, and accommodate (4), here's what we'll say:

> **MT:** The laws of a theory T are the logical consequences of the propositions that are MRCs according to T; or equivalently, the laws of T are the consequences of the propositions that are reliability conditions of procedures that are legitimate measurement procedures according to T.

The reason why this is what we should say if we want to save the law-governed world-picture, in the light of (4), with a meta-theoretic account of laws, is this: a meta-theoretic account of laws says that our presuppositions in a given context entail that the laws of nature are exactly the laws of the theory we presuppose in that context.[13] But (4) implies that the law-governed world-picture is true only if our presuppositions in a given context entail that something is a law just in case those presuppositions entail that it is a consequence of the MRCs. What our presuppositions entail to be the consequences of the MRCs is, of course, just the consequences of the MRCs of the theory we presuppose. Therefore, the laws of the theory we accept in any given context must be the propositions that are, according to that theory, consequences of the MRCs.

Which should we pick? I think there are compelling reasons to adopt MT rather than FO. But they won't emerge until we think through something else.

That something else is this: in a given scientific context, which propositions are presupposed to be MRCs? That's equivalent to this question: in a given scientific context, which procedures are presupposed to be legitimate measurement procedures?

8.6 What methods are presupposed to be legitimate measurement procedures?

8.6.1 Closure of the legitimate measurement procedures under a theory

In a given context k, which procedures are presupposed to be legitimate measurement procedures? The question isn't trivial: we can't answer it

[13] Because: according to any meta-theoretic account, it is true in context k that P is a law just in case P is a law of the salient true theory in k, and of course in k we presuppose that the theory we

just by saying, 'The procedures that the speakers in k explicitly believe to be legitimate measurement procedures.' For one thing, we can rely in practice on a measurement procedure (such as eyeballing a dial to see which number the pointer is pointing to) without ever giving it any explicit thought. Moreover, it is sometimes the case that what we explicitly believe commits us to the legitimacy of a method of measuring something that we have not yet thought of, due to lack of ingenuity or lack of trying. For example, it might be discovered that, given the body of theory we accept, there is a way of building a device with a pointer such that if we set things up in the right way, the position of the pointer will be reliably correlated with some quantity we would like to be able to measure. This is the kind of theoretical discovery that drives forward the technology of measurement.[14]

What happens in a discovery like this is that we discover that, given the body of knowledge already presupposed, it follows that:

Whenever C, then K(P, Q)

where C is some condition such that we can tell whether it is true via empirical means, P is some quantity we are already able to measure, and Q is a quantity we would like to measure (or, would like a new way of measuring).[15] Often, when we make a discovery of this kind, we immediately conclude that $\langle Q, P, C, K\rangle$ is a legitimate method of measurement. For example, when someone figures out a new way of building a device that, according to accepted theory, will reliably indicate the ambient temperature, we do not hesitate to say that they have invented a new thermometer—a new way of measuring the temperature. Since nothing here was discovered that did not follow from what was already presupposed, we were already committed to recognizing this method as a legitimate measurement procedure, and so to recognizing its reliability condition as an MRC—it's just that we were not explicitly aware of this commitment.

But it isn't always like that: sometimes, the reliability condition for some method follows from the body of theory we already accept, but

presuppose is true—hence it follows from our presuppositions that the laws just are the laws of the theory we presuppose.

[14] Which is not to say that the technology of measurement is driven forward only by theoretical discoveries.

[15] It should go without saying here that 'we' doesn't mean we philosophers; it means we humans, who have scientists among our number. But really, it just means the scientists.

it would not be appropriate to say that this shows that given that body of theory, this method is a legitimate measurement procedure. In the following subsections, I'll describe the kinds of exceptions that occur.

This point can be summed up by saying that the legitimate measurement procedures according to our theory are 'closed under our theory': if you can use what the theory says to show that under certain conditions, one quantity's value will be correlated with the value of some other quantity that we already know how to measure, then the latter correlation also forms the basis of a legitimate measurement procedure according to our theory. So the set of legitimate measurement procedures we are committed to acknowledging has a kind of closure property. But this closure is not unrestricted. Now we have to look at the restrictions.

8.6.2 The first exception: testimony

If we were already committed to the truth of all of the contents of an astronomical almanac which lists the masses of all of the planets, then we might 'discover' that we are committed to the reliability of a method of determining the mass of a planet: this method consists of turning to the right page of the almanac, looking at the right row and column, and seeing what numeral we find printed there. This, of course, is not a measurement method. To rule it out, we should say that no method, however *de facto* reliable it may be, can count as a legitimate measurement method if carrying it out involves taking testimony or consulting records of prior measurements, and the value of the pointer variable depends on what the outcomes of those prior measurement methods were.

8.6.3 The second exception: natural almanacs

Another kind of example involves cases where our accepted body of theory entails the existence of what we might call a *natural almanac.* A good example of what I mean by a natural almanac is a case where we have used surveyors' methods to measure the heights in meters of nine mountains, and used astronomical methods to measure the masses of the nine planets in kilograms, and found that the mass of the nth planet in kilograms was equal to the height of the nth mountain in meters (or, more likely, its height in some unit much smaller than the meter). If we added these results to our background theory, then that theory would imply the reliability of an unusual method of determining the mass of a planet: find the corresponding mountain, measure its height, and convert from meters (or whatever) to kilograms. In this case, we will have found that the mountains are a natural phenomenon that happen to be serviceable as a table of the masses of the planets; thus the phrase 'natural almanac.' Even if this happened, though, we would not be at all inclined to say that our background theory implies that this method of determining the mass of a planet is a genuine method of *measuring* the mass of that planet. What we are doing when we employ this method is just what we are doing when we look up the mass of the planet in a reference—it's just that the reference has been conveniently supplied to us by nature.

A real example of a natural almanac is supplied by the fact that, in our solar system, all of the planets go around the sun in the same direction. (Namely: counter-clockwise, if you are looking down on the solar system from above the Earth's north pole.) Knowing this, we can determine the orientation of one planet's orbit just by making an astronomical measurement to determine the orientation of some other planet's orbit, and then inferring that the orientation of the orbit of the planet we are interested in is whatever orientation we found for the planet we actually observed. Again, though we may be satisfied that this is a *de facto* reliable empirical method of finding out what we want to know, we would not call it a *measurement* of the quantity we are interested in.

Another way to see why empirical methods that exploit natural almanacs are not legitimate measurement procedures is to note that they lack the kind of counterfactual reliability that measurements have. For example, suppose that, contrary to fact, Saturn had a clockwise-oriented orbit. Suppose also that we correctly carried out the method described above—say, by observing Mars in order to determine its orbital orientation, and then inferring that Saturn has the same orientation we find Mars to have. All of this is logically consistent with the reliability of this natural almanac method.[16] If all of this were true, though, would the natural almanac method still have given us the right answer? That question is equivalent to this one: if Saturn had had a clockwise orbit, would Mars have had one too? Well, maybe it would have—in any context where the physical processes whereby all the planets were formed is important enough to be

[16] For everything I've just said is consistent with the proposition that all of the planets go round the sun in the clockwise direction—which is false, but not logically inconsistent.

held constant, then presumably all the planets would still have had the same orbital orientation, so Mars would have had a clockwise orientation. But what if, contrary to fact, Saturn had not been formed from the primordial spinning gas-disk from which the solar system was formed—rather, it was captured by the sun's gravity later on? That supposition is consistent with the truth of the proposition that all the planets (including Saturn) go around the sun in the same direction, but there is no good reason to believe the counterfactual that if that supposition were true, then Saturn *would* have had the same orbital orientation as the other planets. (Maybe it would have had the same orientation, and maybe it would have had the opposite orientation—nothing favors one possibility over the other.) So, the reliability of our natural almanac method is not sufficiently counterfactually stable for it to count as a measurement method: if we use it before we already know what the actual orientation of Saturn's orbit is, and we get the right answer, then we're just lucky that Saturn was not a captured planet—for if it had been, then we might just as easily have got the wrong answer.

When our background theory implies that some empirical method for determining the value of some quantity is reliable, it implies that this method is reliable as a natural almanac method rather than as a measurement method *when our background theory implies a specification of the value of that quantity, and of the 'pointer variable' used in the method, for every object we could measure using the method*. This is what happens in the mountains-planets case: here the pointer variable is the height of one of the nine mountains, and the object variable is the mass of a planet, and the background theory implies a specification of the value of the height of each of the nine mountains and a specification of the value of the mass of each of the planets. The same thing is true in the case of the orbital-orientation natural almanac: our background theory specifies the orbital orientation of each planet. More generally, what it is for our background theory to entail the reliability of a method qua natural almanac method is for it to specify the values of all the quantities we can measure using the method, and specify the values we will find for the pointer variable every time we use the method, in such a way that there is a neat correlation between the two. Whenever a theory entails that an empirical procedure is reliable in this way, that procedure is not a legitimate measurement procedure relative to the theory.

Of course, there will be times when our background theory does already include specifications of the values of a pointer variable P and an object variable Q, even when we can legitimately measure Q by a method that uses P as a pointer variable. (A case like this occurs whenever we make a repeatable measurement, record the result, and add the result to our total theory: our total theory still tells us that the method we used to make the repeatable measurement is a legitimate one, even though it also predicts what the values of P and Q will be if we ever repeat it.) Not every such case will automatically count as a natural almanac method. It will so count only if our total theory specifies the values of P and Q for *every case in which the method might be employed*. So, astronomical methods of measuring the masses of planets are not ruled out as natural almanac methods—even though our total theory now includes a specification of what result we will get whenever we employ such a method—because the same methods could be used to measure the masses of bodies we have not yet measured. Similarly, methods of measuring the mass-charge ratio of the electron are not ruled out because we can employ the same methods for measuring the mass-charge ratios of other bodies.[17]

8.6.4 The third exception: calibration-skipping

There is another tricky kind of case we need to consider. Suppose that we all presuppose Newtonian mechanics and gravitation theory, as well as Galileo's equation for free fall near the earth's surface; both of these belong to the total theory that we accept; let's call this total theory CT (for 'classical theory'). We design the following method of measuring the mass of an object in kilograms: weigh it (using newtons as the unit of weight) on earth at sea level using a spring scale, and divide the weight by 9.8 meters per second per second. This certainly seems at first to be a legitimate method of measuring mass. But though this method is *de*

[17] Here I am taking for granted that we know how to tell when two different token actions are carryings-out of *the same measurement procedure* or not. I said above that measurement procedure types should be individuated by their classes of possible correct carryings-out. But not just any cobbled-together set of possible correct carryings-out-of-some-method-or-other should count as a measurement-procedure type. (Otherwise, I couldn't say what I just said in the text: we could take any natural almanac method, throw its possible correct carryings-out into the same set with a bunch of correct carryings-out of a real measurement procedure, and claim that when we use the natural almanac method we are using a method that could also be used to measure other quantities whose values we don't know yet.) I'm going to take it for granted that we can distinguish genuine measurement-types from cobbled-together sets of carryings-out; I don't have a theory of this distinction to offer.

facto reliable, it is not counterfactually reliable. If the earth had had a greater mass than it does, or if the earth had had a different radius than it does, then this method would not have been reliable: the mathematical relation between weight-on-earth and mass would have been different. This seems to be a problem for much of what I said above. Either this method is not really a legitimate measurement method, or else legitimate measurement methods need not be as counterfactually reliable as I said they must be.

But the problem can be resolved. When we use this spring-scale method of measuring mass, we are really using a shortcut version of a more elaborate method of measuring mass. That method is this: drop a stone from a tower and time its descent in order to measure the acceleration due to gravity on earth; weigh the object you want to measure using a spring-scale; divide the weight by the acceleration you previously measured. The pointer variable here is the quotient of two quantities that have been measured along the way. This method is counterfactually reliable: it would still have been reliable even if the earth had a different mass, or a different radius. In performing our original method, we took a shortcut: we didn't measure the acceleration due to gravity ourselves, but depended on the known outcome of a previous measurement of it. Call the first method *the shorter scale method*, and the second one *the longer scale method*. Let's call any method like the shorter scale method—any method, that is, that is an abbreviated version of a longer method, skipping one step in the measurement by plugging in the result of some measurement that was previously carried out—a *calibration-skipping procedure*.

I claim that the longer scale method is a legitimate measurement method, and it is just as counterfactually reliable as I have argued that measurement methods must be. On the other hand, the shorter scale method is not a true legitimate measurement method, and neither is any calibration-skipping procedure. This seems a harsh judgment: when we use the shorter scale method to determine the mass of an object, we do seem to be measuring the mass of that object, and it doesn't feel like we are doing anything illegitimate! This intuition can be accommodated by noting that whenever a calibration-skipping procedure is carried out, a true measurement procedure is carried out, too. In the case of our employment of the shorter scale method, the longer scale method was carried out as well—it's just that we did not do it all ourselves. The measurement was a collaboration between us and whoever made the measurement(s) of the gravitational acceleration that we relied on: collectively, we and they carried out the longer method, which involves measuring the gravitational acceleration and measuring the weight of the object and then dividing one by the other. The different stages of the measurement procedure may have been performed centuries apart, but that doesn't take away from the fact that the entire method was correctly carried out. So there are two different ways of describing what we did: what we did was a complete correct carrying-out of the shortcut method, which is *de facto* reliable but is not a true legitimate measurement procedure for measuring mass; but it was also one part of a collaborative correct carrying-out of the longer method (which is a legitimate measurement method).

In ordinary talk, there is of course no harm in referring to calibration-skipping procedures as measurement procedures, calling them 'legitimate,' and so forth. But for our purposes, the important thing about legitimate measurement procedures is their counterfactual reliability. Since calibration-skipping procedures are not counterfactually reliable in the important way in which non-calibration-skipping procedures are, we need to exclude them. Doing this does not require us to discount any justified measurement activities—for again, whenever a calibration-skipping procedure is correctly performed, so is a legitimate measurement procedure.

It might seem as if calibration-skipping procedures are already disqualified from counting as legitimate measurement procedures by what we have already said. For whenever we perform a calibration-skipping procedure, we are in effect relying on testimony about the results of some measurement that was performed previously. But things aren't that simple. You *could* give the instructions for a calibration-skipping method by specifying that the results of some previous measurement should be consulted, and the results plugged into some calculation. But you need not do it that way—and we didn't do it that way when we defined the shorter scale method above: we just said to measure the weight of the object and divide the result by 9.8 meters per second per second. The reason why we trust this method, of course, is because we know that the gravitational acceleration near the earth's surface is about 9.8 meters per second per second, and we know this on the basis of past measurements. But the specification of the shorter scale method itself does not depend on this; its instructions do not require the measurer who correctly carries it out to consult any past measurements at all. So, we need to add something to our account of legitimate measurement procedures in order to rule out calibration-skipping.

8.6.5 Defining calibration-skipping

It's important to note that calibration-skipping is a *theory-relative* attribute of an empirical procedure: an empirical procedure that is a calibration-skipping method with respect to one theory might be a perfectly legitimate measurement procedure relative to a different theory. For example, the shorter scale method described in the preceding section is a calibration-skipping method relative to the classical theory CT described there, but it could be a legitimate measurement procedure relative to a pre-Newtonian theory that incorporates Galileian ideas about free fall but is innocent of Newtonian gravitation. For that sort of theory might imply that the shorter scale method is reliable, but not that the longer scale method is reliable—or that any other method of which the shorter scale method is a shortcut version is reliable.

There might also be a non-theory-relativized property of being a calibration-skipping method. But for our purposes, what is important is the theory-relative notion. The reason why is that we are in the process of defining the set of methods that are legitimate measurement methods relative to (or according to) a given theory; we want to know the conditions under which a given procedure should be included among the ones that anyone who accepts that theory is thereby committed to regarding as a legitimate measurement procedure. So, what is important here is not whether a procedure *really does* skip calibration in some way that excludes it from counting as a legitimate measurement procedure in its own right; rather, what is important is whether it does so according to the theory in question.

In the preceding section, I defined a calibration-skipping procedure as a reliable method for ascertaining the value of some quantity which is an abbreviated version of a longer method of ascertaining the value of the same quantity, in which a step is skipped by plugging in the known value of some quantity that is measured along the way whenever the longer method is carried out. Here is an obvious way to construe calibration-skipping, so characterized, as a theory-relative property:

> **First Stab at a Definition of Calibration-Skipping:** A procedure $\Pi_1 = \langle Q, P, C, K \rangle$ is a calibration-skipping procedure relative to theory T just in case:
>
> 1. T entails the reliability condition of Π_1: $C \rightarrow K(P, Q)$
>
> and:
>
> 2. There exists a second procedure $\Pi_2 = \langle Q, P', C', K' \rangle$ such that:
>   a) T entails the reliability condition of Π_2, and
>   b) Π_1 is a *shortcut* version of Π_2 in the sense that: For some function F, and some pair of measurable (according to T) quantities w and g, the identities $P = F(w_m, g_t)$ and $P' = F(w_m, g_m)$ hold, where w_m and g_m are measured values of w and g, and g_t is a value that T specifies for the measurable quantity q.

In the case of the shorter scale method, Π_2 is the longer scale method, w is the weight of the object being measured, g is the terrestrial gravitational acceleration, $g_t = 9.8$ meters per second per second, and the function F(x, y) is x divided by y.

Unfortunately, this definition won't work. It captures the formal relation that must hold between a calibration-skipping procedure and the longer method of which it is an abbreviation, but this formal relation to a longer method is not all there is to being a calibration-skipping method. So, satisfying the above definition is a necessary condition, but not a sufficient condition, for being a calibration-skipping method relative to a theory T.

To see why, suppose that Π_a is some measurement procedure that is legitimate according to T, and that Q is its object variable and P its pointer variable. Now consider a second procedure Π_w, which is carried out by: (i) finding the value of P in the same way one would if one were carrying out method Π_a; (ii) using a standard technique for measuring the boiling point of water in degrees Celsius; (iii) multiplying the first result by the second, and dividing the product by 100 degrees Celsius. If our theory T includes the information that the boiling point of water is 100 degrees Celsius, then it implies that the method Π_w is reliable if Π_a is. But Π_a

stands to Π_W in the same formal relation that Π_1 does to Π_2. So the formal test we just considered counts *every* reliable measurement method as a calibration-skipping procedure. This is surely an unacceptable result!

So what more is there to being a calibration-skipping method, over and above bearing the formal relation to some longer method in virtue of which it is a shortcut version of the latter? The obvious answer is that a calibration-skipping method (relative to a theory T) is one such that *the only reason why it is reliable* (so far as T is concerned) is that the longer method is reliable, the quantity g has the value it does, and the reliability of the shorter method follows from these two facts. This is what is going on in the case of the shorter scale method: by the lights of a Newtonian theory like CT, there is no particular reason why the shorter scale method (which, recall, just consists of weighing a body on the surface of the earth and dividing by the quantity g) should be reliable, except that the longer scale method is reliable by the Newtonian laws and the earth happens to have the dimensions and mass that it does. By contrast, in the case of Π_a and Π_W, Π_a is a method that is presumably reliable for reasons that have nothing in particular to do with the boiling point of water at all. Even though Π_a is, formally, a shortcut version of Π_W, the reason why it is reliable (by the lights of the background theory T) does not have anything to do with the fact that Π_W is reliable or the fact that water has the boiling point that it does.

But what does it mean to say that one procedure's reliability follows from a scientific theory T *only because* it follows from two other consequences of that theory? The logical relations among theories and propositions are what they are as a matter of logical necessity, after all; there are no causal relations among these logical relations, and if there are explanatory relations among logical facts, these explanatory relations are notoriously difficult to explicate. Fortunately, I think it's clear enough what we ought to say in the present case—even if it is not clear what it means in general for one logical relation to hold 'only because' another does.

What makes a procedure Π that is reliable according to theory T a calibration-skipping method relative to T is that T entails that Π is reliable in a way that depends crucially on the fact that T specifies the values of certain quantities that are measurable according to T. If you stripped T of this part of its content, what you were left with would not be sufficient to entail the reliability of Π.

That suggests that what we want to say is that Π is a calibration-skipping procedure relative to T if T entails its reliability condition *R*(Π) but no sub-theory T′ of T that fails to specify the value of any particular quantity that is measurable according to T entails this reliability condition. But this is not quite what we want to say—for no procedure satisfies this definition. This is because we can just take the sub-theory T′ to be *R*(Π) (together with all of its logical consequences); this T′ says only that the method Π is a reliable method; it doesn't specify the result you would get if you used Π to measure something. And obviously, this T′ does entail *R*(Π).

So what do we want to say instead? Here is what I propose: a procedure Π is *innocent of calibration-skipping* relative to theory T just in case its reliability condition *R*(Π) is entailed by a sub-theory T′ of T that satisfies the following two conditions:

1. T′ does not specify the value of any quantity that is measurable according to T;
2. Every quantity that is measurable according to T is also measurable according to T′.

Why is this a good test for calibration-skipping? First, let's see how the test works when applied to the case of the shorter scale method. Then, I'll explain why, in general, it is a good test.

If the reliability condition of a procedure is not entailed by any sub-theory T′ of our classical theory CT that satisfies the first of these conditions, then its reliability does indeed depend on the value of some measurable quantity; if that measurable quantity had had a different value, then the procedure would no longer be reliable, so the procedure is not counterfactually reliable in the way that it must be in order to be a legitimate measurement procedure. But if we stopped with this first requirement, our criterion for non-calibration-skipping would be too weak: many procedures that do commit calibration-skipping would pass. For example, the reliability of the shorter scale method is a consequence of a sub-theory T′ of our theory CT which includes only the proposition that the weight of a body near the surface of the earth is its mass times 9.8 meters per second per second, and nothing else. Plainly, this T′ does not entail anything about what the mass and radius of the earth are. However, this T′ does not entail the measurability of everything that CT entails the measurability of: using Newtonian mechanics, we can show the reliability of certain astronomical methods for measuring the mass-ratios among the bodies of the solar system,[18] but T′ does not imply the reliability of any method of measuring such mass-ratios. Moreover, in order to put enough of Newtonian theory back into our T′ in order to make these methods reliable, we would have to put back in the law of universal gravitation (or at least, the special case of it applying to one body that is attracted to another, much more massive body), and once this is added back into our sub-theory, it together with the reliability of the shorter scale method will entail the value of the ratio of the mass of Earth to the square of its radius—a measurable quantity according to our original theory CT. So, it seems that no sub-theory T′ that implies the reliability of the shorter scale method is going to be able to satisfy both of the conditions simultaneously. For this reason, the shorter scale method fails our test of innocence of calibration-skipping.

That shows that the test I have proposed works well for the case of the two scale methods. But why should we think that the test will give the right verdicts in general? Well, in order for Π to be innocent of calibration-skipping relative to T, it must be possible, assuming nothing more than T, to show that the reliability condition $R(\Pi)$ is true—and furthermore, it must be possible to do this drawing on some portion of T's content which is sufficient to entail the reliability of every procedure that is a legitimate measurement method relative to T, but does not entail a specification of the value of any particular measurable quantities.[19] But any portion of T's content that is sufficient to imply the reliability of all the legitimate measurement methods must be sufficient to imply that every quantity that is measurable according to T is indeed measurable. Hence, if $R(\Pi)$ is not a consequence of any sub-theory T′ of T that meets both condition 1 and condition 2, then Π cannot be innocent of calibration-skipping, relative to T.

That shows that passing the above test is a necessary condition of innocence of calibration-skipping; any procedure that fails it must be

[18] Newton employs such a method in Corollary 2 to Proposition 8 in Book III of the *Principia* (Newton 1999, p. 813).

[19] This is because the reliability of the genuine measurement methods should all be independent of the particular values that the measurable quantities happen to have; any method whose reliability depends crucially on the value of some other measurable quantity is a calibration-skipping method.

a calibration-skipper. But is passing this test a sufficient condition of innocence? In other words, can we be sure that it catches all the calibration-skipping methods?

This is a hard question to answer. My intuition is that it does, but I don't know how to give an argument for this claim that does not beg the question. As far as I am aware, every clear case of a procedure that should be considered a calibration-skipper, and so should not be regarded as counterfactually reliable in the way that a genuine measurement method should, is caught by this test. Still though, perhaps there are cases of calibration-skipping methods that satisfy my criterion for innocence. If there are, then my criterion of calibration-skipping will need to be revised. But I trust that it is clear enough what calibration-skipping is, and why being a calibration-skipping method relative to T is incompatible with being a legitimate measurement method relative to T.

So, for present purposes let me just say this: one of the ways in which an empirical procedure that is reliable according to a theory T can fail to be a legitimate measurement method according to T is for it to be a calibration-skipping procedure relative to T. Calibration-skipping is a matter of being a shortcut version of a longer method that crucially exploits the fact that T specifies the values that one or more quantities that are measurable according to T contingently happen to have. I have proposed a test for calibration-skipping that involves application of a non-trivial sufficient condition for calibration-skipping (equivalently: a necessary condition of innocence of calibration-skipping). In what follows, I will rely on this test. I believe that this test provides a necessary condition as well as a sufficient condition for calibration-skipping; I know of no good reason to think otherwise, though I have no compelling argument to offer.

8.6.6 Summing up

So, it is generally the case that when our body of presupposed theory implies that some method of empirically determining the value of some quantity is reliable, our theory also implies that that method is a legitimate measurement procedure—but there are three kinds of exceptions. One is when the method relies on consulting testimony or records of previous measurements; the second is when our theory implies the reliability of the method qua natural almanac method—which it does when it implies the reliability of the method by specifying the values of the object variable and pointer variable for each occasion when the method will be employed; the third is when the procedure is a calibration-skipping procedure—which it will be when its reliability is entailed by our theory, but is not entailed by any sub-theory of it that does not entail the values of any measurable quantities but does entail the measurability of every quantity that is measurable according to our theory.

Are there any other kinds of exceptions? It seems unlikely. Suppose that we have an accepted body of theory T, which tells us that a certain empirical procedure EP for determining the value of Q is reliable. Suppose that EP is not disqualified from counting as a legitimate measurement procedure on any of the three grounds described above. Then, whenever we carry out EP and reach a judgment about the value of Q, we have reached our judgment without consulting testimony, without inferring it from the values of measurable quantities that are already known, and without making essential use of known values of measurable quantities in the procedure. The judgment we reach is justified by empirical evidence; this empirical evidence is 'fresh' in the sense that we obtain it while carrying out EP and do not learn about it from some testimonial source, and the value for Q that we reach is not dependent on the values of any other quantities that we have measured previously. So our judgment has all the marks of a genuine empirical measurement. For this reason, there seems to be no reason to deny that T implies that the method is a legitimate measurement procedure.

Now we can give an answer to the question we started with: in a given context k, which procedures are presupposed to be legitimate measurement procedures? In other words, what are the measurement procedures of k?

In k, there will be a body of presupposed theory—call it T(k). If k is a context in which we are doing science, then T(k) will specify that some procedures are legitimate measurement procedures. Any other procedure whose reliability condition is entailed by T(k), whose pointer variable is measurable by some measurement procedure of k, which does not involve depending on testimony or records of the outcome of previous measurement, and whose reliability condition is not entailed by T(k) simply as a natural almanac method or a calibration-skipping procedure, will be a measurement procedure of k.[20] That tells us how to identify the methods that are presupposed to be legitimate measurement procedures in k; so it tells us how to find all the propositions that are presupposed to be MRCs in k.

8.6.7 What unifies the exceptional cases?

As we have seen, there are three different kinds of cases that pose exceptions to the general rule that when a theory T entails the reliability of a method M,[21] M belongs to the measurement methods of T. Each of these three kinds of cases is irreducible to the other two. There is something displeasing about this. Why should there be a list of exactly three separate exceptional cases? It would be so much nicer if we could combine the three into one elegant definition of the kind of case that gives rise to exceptions. Is there anything that unifies these three kinds of exception cases? Or are we stuck with a 'brute' list of three?

Piggy-back methods Well, there is something that all three cases have in common, in virtue of which they fail to be legitimate measurement methods. For they are all cases of empirical detection procedures that are in some way *derivative of* some other procedure (which happens to be a legitimate measurement procedure); they each involve one would-be measurement procedure trying to achieve measurement-status by piggy-backing on some other procedure that really deserves that status. In other words, though they confer empirical justification on the judgments they result in, this is not *fresh* empirical justification, since it 'recycles' the empirical justification of the measurement that it rides piggy-back on.

This characterization is suggestive but woefully imprecise. Unfortunately, I do not know a way to make it more precise while making sure that it applies equally well to each of the three kinds of exceptional case. The

[20] The definition looks circular, since it uses the phrase 'measurement procedure of k.' But it isn't circular; it is recursive: start with the procedures that are explicitly called legitimate measurement procedures by T(k); find all the measurement procedures of k that use those as pointer variables; then repeat the process.

[21] Where M's pointer variable is measurable by the measurement methods of T, and M's set-up condition is such that we can use the measurement methods of T to reach a justified judgment that it is true. This qualification is important, but it clutters up the page, so in the remainder of this chapter I'll skip it.

sense in which one procedure is 'derivative of' some other procedure is somewhat different in each of the three cases:

- In testimonial cases, the method in question is derivative of a second method because carrying out the first method crucially involves taking a report of the result of a carrying-out of the second method.
- In natural almanac cases, the method in question is derivative of one or more other methods because the former is known by the holders of the theory to be reliable *only because* they happen to know the results of particular carryings-out of the latter. For example, in the orbital-orientation example, the natural almanac method is known by us to be reliable only because we have measured the orbital orientations of all of the planets by other methods already.[22] In the case of the mountain range where heights line up nicely with the masses of the planets, we can be justified in believing that the method is reliable only if we have measured the heights of those particular mountains and the masses of all the planets.
- Finally, in calibration-skipping cases, our theory entails the reliability of the method in question only because our theory involves the result of some previous carrying-out of some other method.

Thus, we have three quite distinct senses of 'derivative' in which a disqualified method is derivative of some other method. Calibration-skipping methods are not derivative in the same way that natural almanac methods are, because we need not already know the result of every future carrying-out of a calibration-skipping method. Natural almanac methods are not derivative in the same way that calibration-skipping methods are, for one sub-theory of our theory just includes the regularity that the heights of these mountains are proportional to the masses of those planets without specifying the values of any of these heights or masses. Neither of these are derivative in the same way that testimonial methods are since in principle a calibration-skipping method or a natural almanac method could be carried

[22] Of course, everything we know on empirical grounds, we know because of evidence that ultimately consists in measurements. But what we know on the basis of inductive or abductive reasoning does not in general depend crucially on our having made *some one particular measurement*, or some *particular set of measurements*. For example, we need not have measured the color of any particular raven in order to have reached the conclusion that all ravens are black. But the orientation of Mars, that of Venus, etc. must all have been measured in order for us to be justified in believing that all the planets have the same orbital orientation.

out without taking any testimony from anyone. In other words: all three cases are cases of procedures that deliver 'non-fresh' empirical justification, but non-freshness comes in at least three different mutually irreducible varieties.

So this first characterization of what the three exception cases have in common does not permit us to eliminate our list of three in favor of a single, unified criterion for exception cases. However, this characterization does bring out an intuitive gloss that applies to all three exception cases. So it helps somewhat to alleviate the unattractiveness of a brute list of three cases.

Detecting one value by measuring another There is also a somewhat different (though related) way of characterizing what the three exception cases have in common. Note that in each exception case, we have a *de facto* reliable empirical method for reaching a judgment about the value of a quantity Q, where:

- The value q that we judge Q to have co-varies counterfactually with the value q* of some other quantity Q*; and
- we know that Q* is a reliable indicator of Q because, and only because, this is implied by some past measurement, either because:
  - the fact that the past measurement was correctly carried out itself implies that Q* is a good indicator of Q, or
  - some mathematical relation between Q and Q* (such as their ratio) has been measured by a carrying-out of some other method.

In other words, what poses as a measurement of Q is nothing but a measurement of Q*, which is able to pass itself off as a measurement of Q because of some crummy fact about the relation between Q and Q* that we know because we did some *other* measurement. So the alleged measurement of Q is, so to speak, trying to acquire for itself the status of a *measurement of* Q, but it tries to do so by illegitimately piggy-backing on *other* measurements.

There are three different ways in which this illegitimate piggy-backing can take place, which are exhibited by the three different exception cases:

- In testimonial cases, Q* is the judgment that was reached about the value of Q in the past token measurement that the testimony reports.

We know that Q^* is a good indicator of Q because Q^* just is the value Q was judged to have as the result of carrying out a legitimate method of measuring Q.

- In natural almanac cases, Q^* is the pointer variable P of the method itself, and we know that P is a good indicator of Q because we have already measured both and found them to be equal. For example: when we use the orbital-orientation natural almanac method described above, where P is the orientation of Mars and Q is that of Saturn, the result of our measurement is a counterfactually reliable indicator only of the orbital orientation of Mars; we happen to know that this is identical to the orientation of Saturn because our background theory incorporates the results of previous measurements of both planets' orientations.
- In calibration-skipping cases, the result counterfactually co-varies not with the object variable Q, but rather with some function of Q and another quantity, whose known value we plugged in when we took our shortcut. We can infer the value of Q from the value of this function because we also happen to know the value of that other quantity. For example: in the shorter scale method, Q^* is the product of the mass of the stone and the local gravitational acceleration. We know that Q^* is a good indicator of Q—in particular, that you can find Q simply by dividing Q^* by 9.8 meters per second per second—because the ratio between Q^* and Q—i.e., the gravitational acceleration—has itself already been measured.

Thus, in each of the three kinds of exception case, a *de facto* reliable method for ascertaining the value of Q consists of a counterfactually reliable way of ascertaining the value of a different quantity, namely Q^*, which we know to be a *de facto* reliable indicator of Q because of some other token measurement that has been carried out. So it is natural to say that in such cases, what we *really* measure is Q^*, and we exploit some contingent and counterfactually fragile fact—one we know because of a particular measurement that has been performed—in order to infer a value of Q from the measured value of Q^*.

Unlike the characterization I considered above, this does give us a unified and precise characterization that seems to pick out exactly what it is about the three exception cases that makes them exceptional. This makes it tempting to throw out the answer I reached above to the question of which methods are the legitimate measurement methods of our background theory, and replace it with this:

> Method $M = \langle Q, P, C, K \rangle$ is a legitimate measurement procedure relative to our background theory so long as that theory entails M's reliability condition, *and* there is no quantity Q* such that our theory entails that the value of P counterfactually co-varies with Q*, and we know that the value of Q is a certain function of the value of Q* because (and only because) of a particular token measurement that has been previously carried out.

This is much simpler than the account I reached at the end of Section 8.6.6. Its availability helps to make it clear that the three exception cases are not an arbitrary or ad hoc list of three troublesome cases that are excluded by fiat; it shows that they are simply different ways in which a single condition can be satisfied, where this single condition is intuitively sufficient to disqualify a *de facto* reliable procedure from counting as a *bona fide* measurement method.

The only trouble with this new account is that it freely appeals to the implications our background theory has for which quantities counterfactually co-vary with which others. There's nothing wrong with that as such, but it is a move that I am not entitled to in the present context. I assume that our background theory itself does not imply anything about which counterfactuals are true; for me, which counterfactuals are true depends on features of the context other than our background theory. Our background theory does, however, bring with it a commitment to affirming certain counterfactuals *given that we are reasoning in a scientific context.* The reason why this is so, according to me, is that in any scientific context, everything we take to be a legitimate measurement procedure is something we are committed to treating as counterfactually reliable. This, on my view, is a *special* feature of *scientific* contexts; it need not be true in, say, a theological or a meta-ethical context.[23] So on my view, the background theory itself cannot be what implies that some things counterfactually co-vary with others (for the same background theory might be presupposed in some non-scientific context). But the background theory *brings something to* any

[23] See Chapter 6.

scientific context in which it is presupposed, which in that context does imply that certain counterfactuals are true. That *something* is just *what the theory implies about which procedures are legitimate measurement methods*. So, on the view I am developing here, it is a context-independent feature of a body of theory that it implies that certain procedures are legitimate measurement procedures, whereas it is a context-dependent feature of that same body of theory that anyone who presupposes it is committed to affirming certain counterfactuals. So, these two features of the body of theory cannot be identified, and the former cannot be reduced to the latter. It follows that in giving my account of the conditions under which a theory implies that a given procedure is a legitimate measurement method, I cannot appeal to the relations between measurement procedures and counterfactual co-variation—for the former is context-independent and the latter is not. For this reason, the above indented characterization of the procedures that are legitimate measurement methods according to our background theory is not one I can make use of at this stage of my argument; I have to stick with the more clunky one reached in Section 8.6.6.

Nevertheless, the indented characterization above is helpful. For the fact that it is so plausibly true—in scientific contexts, at least—shows that, when viewed from a scientific context, the three kinds of exception-cases are not just three random items thrown together in an ad hoc way in order to make a definition yield the right verdicts. To see how it shows this, assume for the sake of argument that in scientific contexts, legitimate measurement procedures are those in which the pointer variables counterfactually co-vary in a certain way with the quantities getting measured. Now, procedures that fall under the three exception cases will all share a common salient feature—robust counterfactual covariation with something *other than* the object variable, together with *counterfactually fragile de facto* co-variation between this third thing and the object variable. This common feature marks all three kinds of procedure as failing to exhibit the kind of counterfactual co-variation *between pointer variable and object variable* that we have assumed to be typical of genuine measurement methods. When we attend directly to the definitions of these three kinds of exception cases, we might not see any common 'natural kind' under which they all fall. Nevertheless, from a point of view in which it is assumed that being a good measurement procedure is a matter of the right sort of counterfactual co-variation between pointer variable and object variable, these three kinds of cases appear simply to be the three different ways in which a common feature can be exemplified—a feature that is obviously inconsistent with being a good measurement method, given our initial assumption. In short: if we are willing, at the beginning, to accept a definition of the class of procedures we are committed to regarding as legitimate measurement methods that seems clunky and ad hoc, then by the end of the day, we will be able to see a respect in which that was exactly the right definition to give. What appeared to be an arbitrary list of three unrelated types of exception cases turns out at the end of the day to be a catalogue of the different ways in which a common salient feature can be exhibited.

8.7 Why we must adopt a meta-theoretic account of laws

8.7.1 Problems for the first-order account

Suppose that we adopt the first-order conception of laws FO. Now, consider a context in which the presupposed body of the theory is the set of all true propositions about what goes on in the natural world—call this 'GOT' (for 'God's Own Theory'). Since GOT specifies the values of all measurable quantities, it only implies the reliability of *any* empirical method of ascertaining the value of *any* quantity qua natural almanac method. Thus, in this context, there are no legitimate measurement procedures, and so no laws. But whatever is true in a context where the background theory is GOT must be true *simpliciter*—GOT contains all and only the truths, after all. Therefore, there are no laws of nature. This is an unhappy result.

It doesn't help to point out that we are never going to get our hands on GOT. Instead of GOT, consider some theoretical context in which correct values of the masses of all elementary particles are presupposed—and it is presupposed that these are indeed all the elementary particles that there are. In any theoretical context like that, none of the reliability conditions of methods for measuring the masses of elementary particles are going to count as laws of nature. In any context where our background theory included that one, LMP-U and NP-U would not require us to acknowledge the counterfactual stability of any of the laws that imply that those methods are reliable—since all those methods would be natural almanac methods. The general point is just that whenever our background theory is rich enough in specific information, it will undermine something's claim to being a law of nature. Moreover, if a sufficiently rich theory is true (whether we will ever discover it or not), then that theory already undermines the claim of every proposition to lawhood.

It won't help either to say, 'So, we must have made a mistake back in Section 8.6 when we defined natural almanac methods, and declared them all not to be legitimate measurement methods.' We introduced that clause in our account because of an important problem, that has to be addressed somehow. The problem starts with the observation that measurement procedures have a kind of closure property: if there is a method for measuring P, and there are empirically determinable circumstances in which P is correlated with Q, then that yields a procedure for measuring Q. It won't do to ignore this closure property of the set of measurement methods; if we do that, we miss out something important about the way measurement methods and background theory can be used together to design new measurement methods. But the existence of egregious natural almanac methods (like the mountain-planet method, or the orbital-orientation method) shows that we have to formulate the closure principle with care: it cannot just be that *whenever* some true portion of background theory entails that the measurable P is correlated with Q, this yields a procedure for measuring Q. There must be some boundaries here—under some circumstances, the truth of the reliability condition for the procedure $\langle Q, P, C, K \rangle$ does not guarantee that that procedure is a legitimate measurement procedure. On the first-order account FO, where those boundaries lie is a first-order question for science: science must have some theory-neutral way of distinguishing between the ones that are good measurement procedures and the ones that are not. This difference, we have seen, lies in the counterfactuals: the reliability conditions of the legitimate measurement procedures are counterfactually reliable, whereas the reliability conditions of the *de facto* reliable procedures (like natural almanac methods) need only be actually true.

But we cannot find out empirically which propositions are laws of nature by means of finding out empirically which counterfactuals are true, for reasons we saw back in Section 7.3.2. Since we can observe only what actually takes place, and not what would have taken place under different conditions, empirical evidence can be brought to bear on such counterfactuals only with the assistance of what I called 'actual-to-counterfactual bridge principles' back in Section 7.3.2. For reasons we saw in the same section, the bridge principles we will need to use in order to bring empirical evidence to bear on competing hypotheses about which propositions have the counterfactual resilience typical of laws will need to include NP, or at least special cases of NP. But NP doesn't tell us anything at all about which counterfactuals are true unless we already know something about which propositions are the laws of nature. Thus, empirical investigation of which propositions are counterfactually resilient depends on our having prior empirical information about which propositions are laws of nature. So it seems that if empirical investigation of which propositions are laws of nature depends on empirical investigation of which propositions are counterfactually resilient, then we can never get started on either task. So if FO is right, then the boundaries between the theory-neutrally legitimate measurement procedures and the theory-neutrally merely *de facto* reliable procedures are boundaries that we cannot locate empirically. This means that we will not be able to determine empirically where the boundary between the laws and the true non-laws lies; the Discoverability Thesis will be threatened.

We avoid all these problems, though, if we adopt the meta-theoretic account MT. MT lets the question of which methods are legitimate measurement procedures be meta-theoretic: a procedure can be a legitimate measurement procedure relative to a theory, and in a given context it is true that procedure $\langle Q, P, C, K \rangle$ is a legitimate measurement procedure just in case it is a legitimate measurement procedure relative to the true theory that is salient in the context.

But what is it for a procedure to be a legitimate measurement procedure *relative to a theory*?

8.7.2 Legitimate measurement procedures relative to a theory

In practice, we never find a scientific theory in use without a set of assumptions (either implicit or explicit—but almost never entirely explicit) about what are the right ways to measure the quantities mentioned by the theory. Two different practitioners, if asked, might provide two different lists of the 'right measurement procedures.' It might be that either of these two lists, together with the theory itself, implies the legitimacy of all the procedures on the other list, via the limited closure principle

I have been talking about since Section 8.6. In that case, there is no disagreement between the two practitioners; they share a common theory, with a common empirical interpretation, though they may formulate both differently. On the other hand, if the two lists do not agree, then the two practitioners make use of theories that, by their respective lights, have different implications about the results of possible measurements—for they disagree about which kinds of acts are measurements in the first place. In this circumstance, it seems fair to say that the two practitioners do not really hold the same theory, after all. Even if their formal statements of their theories look identical, they give different empirical interpretations to the common formalism, yielding different accounts of what the empirical world is like.

So for present purposes let's identify scientific theories with *interpreted theories*, where an interpreted theory is to be understood as having two parts: a theoretical part, and an empirical interpretation. The theoretical part might be a set of propositions, or a set of sentences in some natural or formal language; on the other hand, it might be a class of models. Here I want to remain neutral between these two influential ways of thinking about what theories are.[24] The empirical interpretation may include many elements, but I assume that it at least includes a specification of a set of legitimate procedures for measuring the quantities mentioned by the theoretical part of the theory (or figuring in its models). The set of specified measurement procedures cannot include any methods that involve taking testimony, or any method $\langle Q, P, C, K\rangle$ such that the values of Q and P are already specified by the theoretical part of the theory for every case in which this method can be used to measure Q—for such methods do not yield fresh empirical justification for the judgments about the value of Q they yield. I also assume the set of specified legitimate measurement procedures to be *closed under the theory*, in the following sense:

For any scientific theory T, if:

- P is measurable by one of the legitimate measurement methods specified by the empirical interpretation of T,

[24] In the case of a theory that is best construed as a set of models, what it means for that theory to entail that P is that P is true in all of its models.

- C is a condition such that the legitimate measurement procedures of T make it possible to tell whether C obtains,
- the theoretical part of T entails the reliability condition for the method $\langle Q, P, C, K\rangle$—that is, it entails that whenever C, then K(P, Q),
- C does not specify that testimony has been taken or records consulted about the results of any past measurements,
- the theoretical part of T does not specify the values of Q and P for every case in which $\langle Q, P, C, K\rangle$ may be used to determine the value of Q, and
- the reliability condition for $\langle Q, P, C, K\rangle$ is entailed by some sub-theory of T that does not specify the value of any quantity that is measurable according to T, but that does entail the measurability of every quantity that is measurable according to T,

then: $\langle Q, P, C, K\rangle$ is one of the legitimate measurement methods specified by the empirical interpretation of T.

Given this closure requirement, there are liable to be infinitely many legitimate measurement procedures specified by any interesting scientific theory. But by the same token, we don't have to list them all in order to specify the whole set: some subset of primitive measurement methods could be specified, from which the rest of the methods are generated recursively by the closure clause. There need not be a *unique* set of primitives that would suffice to generate the whole set of legitimate measurement methods, given the theoretical part of the theory and the closure requirement. So, just as there can be alternative axiomatizations of the theoretical part of a theory, so there can be alternative sets of primitive measurement procedures that generate the same empirical interpretation of a theory. Adding this closure property is a way of acknowledging that even after a theory has been formulated, we can still discover new methods that turn out to be legitimate measurement procedures, according to that theory.

The closure requirement is what allows the theoretical part of the theory to generate new legitimate measurement procedures, by entailing that those procedures exploit real correlations between pointer variables and object variables. But of course, the closure requirement won't allow the theoretical part of the theory to generate any legitimate measurement methods at all unless there are already some supplied by the empirical interpretation of the theory. Unless we have some already-measurable quantity we can use as a pointer variable, then all the positive correlations among quantities in the world won't help us design a measurement procedure. So, there must be some quantities that figure in a theory that can be measured by procedures that are legitimate and reliable otherwise than because the theoretical part of the theory entails that they are. Let's call these procedures the *basic* measurement procedures of our theory, and let's call the quantities they can be used to measure the *basic measurables* of our theory.

Anyone who accepts and uses a given theory will of course have to believe (at least implicitly) that these basic methods are reliable. But they need not agree on the form of their reliability conditions—they might have different views about what the K relation is. For example, suppose our theory is some theory of celestial mechanics, and suppose one of the basic measurables is the elevation of a planet above the horizon, and that one of the basic procedures for measuring apparent position involves using a sextant and a working human eyeball. The object variable here is the elevation of a planet at a time, and the pointer variable is the judgment reached by the owner of the eyeball. Suppose you and I disagree about the way in which this method is reliable, because we have different views concerning the reliability of eyeballs. I think that the K relation occurring in the reliability condition of the sextant-eyeball method is a statistical correlation represented by a bell-curve with a very narrow spread, whereas you think that the spread is somewhat wider. We have a disagreement—but our disagreement is not about celestial mechanics; it's about human visual perception. Under these circumstances, we ought to say that we share the same theory of celestial mechanics: our common theory of celestial mechanics has an empirical interpretation in which the sextant-eyeball method is a basic method for measuring elevation; we agree that this method is reliable, but we disagree about the form of its reliability condition. Therefore, the reliability condition of this method is not part of the content of our common theory of celestial mechanics—though the fact that this method is reliable, and also a legitimate measurement procedure, is part of our common theory. Cases like this show that if we want to talk about a single theory (rather than a total body of theory), its legitimate measurement procedures, and its laws, then we must allow that the theory leaves open the form of some of the reliability conditions of some of its legitimate measurement procedures; there will be no determinate law of the theory about these measurement procedures. That seems right: in the present example, we don't want to say that our shared theory of celestial mechanics has any determinate laws about the reliability of human visual perception.

Note that the disagreement between you and me on the precise form of the reliability condition for the sextant-and-eyeball method does not imply disagreement between us on any other measurement procedures that use elevation as a pointer variable: if our theory tells us we can design and use a measurement procedure that measures the distance from a planet to the sun using the elevation of that planet as the pointer variable,[25] then the reliability condition of *this* procedure does not depend on what form the reliability condition of the sextant-eyeball method takes. We may disagree on how much we can confidently say about how far a given planet is from the sun, but that is not because we disagree about the nature of the correlation between elevation and distance from the sun; it's because we disagree about how precisely we know the elevation in the first place. In general, disagreement about the degree and kind of reliability of a method of measuring a pointer variable does not imply disagreement about the kind of correlation that exists between that pointer variable and the quantity it is used to measure.

So, the empirical interpretation of a scientific theory will include a specification of some basic measurement procedures of basic observables, whose reliability conditions are not entailed by the theoretical part of the theory itself; the precise form of the correlation conditions of these measurements need not be specified by the theory. Let's identify *the legitimate measurement procedures relative to the theory* as the ones whose reliability conditions *are* specified by the theory; so, they won't include the basic measurement procedures. In practice, it may be quite arbitrary just where we draw the line between the basic measurement procedures of a theory and the other procedures whose reliability and legitimacy are

[25] We would have to have a pretty strange theory of celestial mechanics to believe this, but it makes for a simple example.

implied by the theory. That means it will be arbitrary where we draw the boundary around the legitimate measurement procedures relative to the theory, and so, given the meta-theoretic account of laws I'm in the middle of developing, it will be arbitrary just where we draw the boundary around that theory's laws.

But this should be no surprise, and it is no worry: in practice, we use a number of different theories, and the boundaries between them can be arbitrary. If the precise boundaries of a given theory are vague, then the boundaries around that theory's set of laws can be vague, too. Once we precisely fix which theory we are talking about, though—that is, once we precisely fix what is entailed by that theory, what is not, and how that theory is empirically interpreted—we have precisely fixed which measurement procedures are the basic methods of its empirical interpretation, and which are among the legitimate measurement procedures relative to the theory. So if, as I am going to propose, we define the laws of a theory in terms of its legitimate measurement procedures, we will have then fixed what the laws of that theory are.

The empirical interpretation of a theory, then, will specify a set of basic measurables and a set of basic measurement methods for those measurables. Given those, the theoretical part of the theory and the closure property on legitimate measurement procedures generates a larger set of legitimate measurement procedures. But the procedures we will call *the legitimate measurement procedures relative to the theory* will just be the ones whose reliability conditions are part of the content of the theoretical part of the theory.[26]

I will assume that a scientific theory—the kind of thing that a law-of-a-theory is relativized to—is a pair consisting of a theoretical part and an empirical interpretation, where the empirical interpretation specifies a set of legitimate measurement procedures that is closed under the theory in the above sense. The meta-theoretic account of laws we have been working toward can now be stated as follows: the laws of any theory T are the propositions that are logical consequences of the reliability conditions of the legitimate measurement methods relative to T.

[26] So in the example I have just been discussing, you and I agree in accepting a certain theory of celestial mechanics, which has a certain definite set of laws. But you and I accept *total* bodies of theory that have at least some differences in their laws. In particular, they have different laws about human vision.

8.7.3 God's Own Theory revisited

Now, if we adopt MT, what can we say about the problem of GOT, mentioned at the beginning of this section? Relative to GOT, there are no legitimate measurement procedures: every reliable procedure for determining the value of any empirical quantity is a natural almanac method, since the value of every quantity is already specified by the theory. This means that there are no laws of GOT, according to MT. It does not follow from this that there are no laws of nature—for in any context where we are liable to find ourselves, the true salient theory (which will be comprised of all the true theoretical commitments held by us and the other members of our epistemic community—see Chapter 3, Section 3.3.7) will be considerably weaker than GOT; it will not specify the values of all empirical quantities, so it will be able to have some legitimate measurement procedures that are not ruled out on natural almanac grounds. Relative to any theory we are ever likely to accept, there are laws of nature, which means that in any scientific context we are liable to find ourselves in, there are laws of nature.

This result might seem weird at first, but it is actually consonant with the spirit of the view we have been developing. According to this view, lawhood is an important scientific concept because of its relation to measurement, a concept that is absolutely crucial to science. We need to make measurements because, insofar as we are engaged in scientific inquiry, they are our only ultimate means of learning more about the layout of the natural world; we need to adopt theories which have laws because we need to suppose that some methods are legitimate measurement procedures, and every legitimate measurement procedure is reliable by virtue of some law. Now, if things were different—if we had a God's-eye view of the cosmos—then we would not need to rely on measurements in order to find out what was going on in the world. The concept of a law of nature would then have no role to play. So it is only natural that relative to God's Own Theory, there are no laws. Laws are characteristics of theories that are employed by beings like us—whose only epistemic access to the world is empirical.

By contrast, if we try to accommodate conclusion (4) (from Section 8.4, above) within a first-order account of laws, this result will be disastrous. Since GOT is *ex hypothesi* a true theory, its laws must be exactly the laws of nature. Hence, there are no laws of nature, since there are no laws of GOT.

For this reason, we must accommodate (4) within a meta-theoretic account of laws. The essence of that account is now on the table. It will be the subject of the next chapter.

9

What lawhood is

9.1 Where we are now

We saw in Chapter 8 that the Governing Thesis and the Science-Says-So Thesis are both true just in case the laws of nature are the consequences of the reliability conditions of the legitimate measurement methods. But the latter condition might be integrated into either a first-order account of laws or a meta-theoretic account of laws. We saw that trying to integrate it into a first-order account is going to lead to disaster. So, if we want to save the Governing Thesis and the Science-Says-So Thesis—and thereby save the law-governed world-picture—the only way to do that is by adopting a meta-theoretic account of laws, according to which the laws of any theory are the consequences of the reliability conditions of the legitimate measurement methods of that theory.

The meta-theoretic account we need is one I will call *the measurability account of laws*, or the MAL for short. It has already been developed in the previous chapter; given that what we are looking for is a meta-theoretic account rather than a first-order account, it can be more or less read off of the conclusion (4) drawn in Section 8.4. In this chapter, I will give it its final formulation, discuss an objection to it, and argue for its plausibility.

9.2 The Measurability Account of Laws

The Measurability Account of Laws can be summed up as follows:

Scientific theories: A scientific theory T consists of a theoretical part—which may be a set of propositions or a set of models—and an empirical interpretation—which specifies a set of procedures for empirically determining the values of the quantities that figure in T, called *the legitimate measurement methods relative to T.*[1]

Closure of legitimate measurement methods: The legitimate measurement methods relative to a theory T must be *closed under T* in the following sense: for any scientific theory T, any quantities Q and P, any condition C, and any positive-correlation relation K, the measurement method with object variable Q, pointer variable P, set-up condition C, and correlation relation K—for short: the method $\langle Q, P, C, K\rangle$—must be one of the legitimate measurement methods relative to T if all the following conditions are satisfied:

- P is measurable by one of the legitimate measurement methods relative to T;
- C is a condition such that the legitimate measurement procedures of T make it possible to tell whether C obtains;
- the theoretical part of T entails the reliability condition for the method $\langle Q, P, C, K\rangle$—that is, it entails that whenever C, then K(P, Q);
- C does not specify that testimony has been taken or records consulted about the results of any past measurements;
- the theoretical part of T does not specify the values of Q and P for every case in which $\langle Q, P, C, K\rangle$ may be used to determine the value of Q; and
- the theoretical part of T has some sub-theory T′ that entails the reliability condition for $\langle Q, P, C, K\rangle$, that does not specify the value of any quantity that is measurable according to T, but that does entail the measurability of every quantity that is measurable according to T.

The law role: P is a law of theory T just in case P is a logically contingent logical consequence of the set of reliability conditions, entailed by the theoretical part of T, of all of the legitimate measurement methods relative to T.[2] (Note that since the variable 'K' can take as its value a

[1] Some but not all of these methods have reliability conditions that are entailed by the theoretical part of T. The ones that don't may be called the *basic* methods of T. See Chapter 8, Section 8.7.2.

[2] But see the qualification at the very end of Section 2.4: you might want to add the requirement that P be sufficiently general to count as a law of nature. This will exclude as laws-of-T only non-general

statistical relation, the laws of a theory can include statistical propositions. This makes room for probabilistic laws.)

Salient theories: The default salient theory in a context k is that theory which comprises all the true theoretical commitments of the members of the extended epistemic community of the speakers. But this default is canceled, and another theory becomes the salient one, whenever this is necessary in order for (i) someone's statement about the laws of some non-actual world to be true, or (ii) someone's modal statement about laws of nature to be true, or (iii) the antecedent of someone's counterfactual-conditional statement to be true at any possible world. When that happens, if a particular scientific theory has been singled out for attention, it becomes the salient theory; otherwise, if there is a unique theory T such that the modal or counterfactual statement that has been asserted would be true if T were salient, then T becomes the salient theory; otherwise, it becomes indeterminate what the salient theory is, but determinate that the salient theory is one that renders the asserted modal statements or counterfactual antecedents true.

Laws of nature: 'P is a law of nature' is true at world w in context k just in case P is a law of the salient theory in k, and the salient theory in k is true at w.

9.3 Brief review of the case for the MAL

The MAL must be the correct account of lawhood, if the law-governed world-picture is correct. Two necessary conditions for the correctness of that picture are the Governing Thesis—which says that the laws of nature govern the universe—and the Science-Says-So Thesis—which says that the Governing Thesis is part of what we can be justified in believing by engaging in scientific inquiry; it is not projected onto the world by our adoption of a convention, it is not an unjustified leap of faith, and its justification does not depend on extra-scientific metaphysical or theological reasoning.

I argued in Chapter 5 that the Governing Thesis is true just in case the principle NP is true—which says that the truths about which propositions

propositions that are logical consequences of laws-of-T. I'll ignore this in the text since nothing else seems to turn on it.

are laws and which are not are maximally counterfactually stable. I argued in Chapter 6 that NP is not true in all possible contexts of discourse; in particular, in some possible theological and philosophical contexts it is false. However, I also argued that we seem to have no clear counterexamples to the truth of NP in scientific contexts. I also argued that if NP is true in all possible scientific contexts, then there is no reason to worry that its truth is merely a reflection of our own pragmatic interests, rather than the important truth about the nature of the universe that it is supposed to be.[3]

In Chapter 7, I argued that the Science-Says-So Thesis is true just in case NP is a consequence of indispensable presuppositions of scientific inquiry as such. This, in turn, is true just in case NP is among the presuppositions of every possible scientific context. And that, in turn, is true just in case NP-U is true; NP-U says that in any possible scientific context, the presuppositions entail the truth of all counterfactuals that are entailed by the general thesis of NP together with the specific presuppositions about which propositions are laws in nature that are in play in that context. Moreover, NP-U entails that NP is true in every possible scientific context—which is just what we need to establish in order to establish that the Governing Thesis is true in every possible scientific context, and is not just a reflection of our own pragmatic interests in the contexts we happen to inhabit.

At this point, the fate of the law-governed world-picture hinges on NP-U, a principle that imposes strong constraints on which counterfactuals can be true in any possible scientific context. At the end of Chapter 7, I introduced the thought-experiment of the Actual-Factualists, which seems to show that none of the basic kinds of inferences that must be employed in science, and none of the basic goals that science serves, require that scientists affirm any non-trivial counterfactuals.[4] This left only one possible way in which science might have indispensable presuppositions that imply NP: namely, via the commitment of science to regard empirical measurement (construed broadly so as to include qualitative empirical observations) as the sole source of ultimate evidence.

[3] This worry arose once we realized that NP cannot be true in all possible contexts, suggesting that its truth value might vary from context to context in the same ways and for the same reasons that counterfactual conditionals generally do.

[4] By 'non-trivial counterfactual,' I mean a logically contingent counterfactual—that is, one whose antecedent does not logically entail its consequent.

I argued in Chapter 8 that this commitment of science implies that in any possible scientific context, it must be presupposed that the reliability conditions of the legitimate measurement procedures are, as a class, maximally counterfactually stable. Since this is the sole source of constraint on the evaluation of counterfactuals imposed by the nature of science as such, this constraint must imply NP-U if NP-U is true at all. Then I argued that this constraint does imply NP-U if and only if the propositions that are presupposed to be laws of nature in any given scientific context k are exactly the logical consequences of the reliability conditions of the procedures that are presupposed to be legitimate measurement procedures in k.

That last conclusion is almost an account of lawhood by itself. But there are two ways to interpret it: on the first, the laws are part of the first-order subject matter of science; it is an a priori truth that the laws are exactly the consequences of the reliability conditions of the legitimate measurement methods; for this reason, in every scientific context, it is presupposed that the things presupposed to be laws are exactly the things presupposed to be consequences of the reliability conditions of measurement procedures.

This proposal leads to trouble. First, it threatens to yield the consequences that there are no laws of nature. The only way to avoid this consequence is to suppose that in order to discover which propositions are laws, science must discover which reliable empirical procedures are true measurement procedures and which are merely *de facto* reliable procedures. And settling this question empirically would require empirical testing and confirmation of hypotheses that differ from one another only with respect to which counterfactuals they imply, and not at all on what they said about the occurrent history of the actual world. As we saw in Section 8.7.1, this leads to an epistemological disaster that threatens the Discoverability Thesis.

The alternative is to adopt a meta-theoretic account of both laws and legitimate measurement procedures: the laws of a theory are just the consequences of the reliability conditions of the legitimate measurement procedures relative to that theory. For this reason, the propositions that the presuppositions of a context imply to be laws are just the propositions that the presuppositions of that context imply to be consequences of the reliability conditions of measurement methods: for the laws in this context *are* the laws of the salient true theory, and the measurement procedures of this context *are* the measurement procedures relative to that same theory; given what theory is presupposed in the context, its laws must be the consequences of the reliability conditions of its measurement procedures. Hence, what the presupposed body of theory entails to be the laws is exactly what that same body of theory entails to be the consequences of the reliability conditions of the measurement methods.

This meta-theoretic account is exactly the MAL, spelled out more carefully above.

It is worth noting that the case for the MAL just outlined doesn't really depend crucially on the assumptions about what it would take for the Governing Thesis to be true that I made in Chapter 5. Instead, we could skip that part of the argument and begin with NP: to many philosophers, what is most conspicuously distinctive of laws of nature is their relation to counterfactuals, and for many philosophers that relation is summed up in NP or some closely related principle. The arguments of Chapter 6 show that NP could not be true in every possible context of utterance. But if laws of nature are distinguished from other truths by their counterfactual robustness, then it is natural to expect that they will exhibit this robustness in any context of discourse in which laws should be expected to play their most characteristic roles—that is, in scientific contexts. So, governing or no governing, it is natural to expect that NP should be true in all possible scientific contexts. And from there on out, the argument is the same as the one sketched above.

9.4 A note about hedged laws

Many philosophers hold that some (or all) laws of nature are *hedged laws*, or '*ceteris paribus* laws.' These are laws that do not take the form of strict or statistical regularities, but rather the form of regularities (whether strict or statistical) that are qualified by hedge clause, such as 'so long as nothing interferes.' This hedge clause cannot be replaced *salva veritate* with a more explicit or precise statement that effectively defines what counts as an 'interference.'[5]

I have argued elsewhere that there are no such things as hedged laws. (However, statements that appear to state hedged laws can have an important role to play in science—it's just that it's a mistake to think

[5] For example Cartwright (1983), Essay 3; Lange (1983a); Pietroski and Rey (1995); Lange (2002).

of these statements as statements of a special sort of fact that is usefully described as a 'hedged law of nature.')[6] I still believe that there are no such things, but I don't think their existence is incompatible with the MAL. Those who disagree with me about whether there are hedged laws need not reject the MAL for that reason.

The way that the MAL can admit hedged laws is by admitting irreducible and non-eliminable hedge clauses to occur in the antecedents of reliability conditions. Recall that a reliability condition takes the form: 'Whenever conditions C are satisfied, P and Q are correlated (either strictly or statistically).' The only restriction on the condition C is that it is possible in principle to be empirically justified in believing that it holds. Proponents of hedged laws typically argue that even though the hedge clause cannot be stated explicitly without the use of hedging language (such as 'interference,' 'disturbance,' 'other things being equal,' 'the cases to which this law is meant to apply,' and so on), we can still be justified in particular cases in believing either that this clause was or was not satisfied. (See, for example Lange 1993a.) If they are right about this, then there is no objection to allowing C itself to include a hedge clause as a conjunct.

9.5 How plausible is the MAL?

9.5.1 Are laws too scarce according to the MAL?

According to the MAL, the laws of a theory T are all reliability conditions of measurement methods, or else logical consequences of such propositions. It might seem that these propositions could not contain all of the laws of a typical scientific theory T. The reliability conditions of measurements all have to do with very specific sorts of physical interactions; laws of nature, on the other hand, are typically completely general, applying even in situations where nothing that looks much like a measurement is going on. So it can seem as if the MAL is bound to leave out a lot of laws of nature.

In addressing this worry, the first thing to do is to recall from Chapter 8 that the set of measurement methods-associated with a theory has a closure property: whenever T together with the reliable measurability of one

[6] Earman and Roberts (1999); Earman, Roberts, and Smith (2002).

quantity entails that another measurement method is legitimate the reliability condition associated with the latter belongs to the laws of T. This is so whether or not the scientists who formulate and use T are actually technologically able to employ the measurement method in question; in fact, it is so whether or not the scientists are even explicitly aware of this method. For this reason, a sufficiently strong scientific theory can be expected to entail reliability conditions corresponding to many more measurement methods than one might expect. So the laws of a theory, according to the MAL, might turn out to be far richer than one might expect.

For example, consider a theory that includes Newton's second law of motion, $\mathbf{f} = m\mathbf{a}$. This is a very strong generalization, with a great variety of special cases. Every one of its special cases that states a correlation that could be exploited in order to design a reliable measurement procedure using some measurable quantity (such as an acceleration) as its pointer variable will count as playing the law role relative to the theory in question. If (as does not seem implausible) *every* special case of this generalization is like that, then every special case of the proposition plays the law role; since the laws of the theory are closed under deduction, and the generalization is simply the conjunction of all of its special cases, this means that $\mathbf{f} = m\mathbf{a}$ itself will be a law of this theory. So there is no obvious, a priori reason to think that the characterization of the law role we have arrived at will admit too few laws of a typical theory to be plausible.

9.5.2 Testability of the MAL

But in the end, whether the MAL arrives at a plausible verdict about which propositions are laws of which theories can only be decided by looking at particular cases. For this reason, the MAL, or any other meta-theoretic account of laws worked out in sufficient detail, is testable in a way that most first-order accounts of laws are not. A meta-theoretic account of laws should (and the MAL does) specify the law role in enough detail to enable us to look at examples of scientific theories and see which propositions play that role in those theories. The results ought to classify propositions of these theories as laws or nomologically contingent truths in the same way as our ordinary judgments do. To the extent that they don't, the particular meta-theoretic account of laws in question is 'disconfirmed,' and to the extent that they do, this should count in that account's favor.

This kind of test can be performed on any particular meta-theoretic account. But it cannot be performed on, for instance, the universals account of Armstrong, Dretske, and Tooley. Whatever the laws of a particular theory happen to be, the proponent of the universals account can simply say that if that theory is true, then the universals are related by the necessitation relation in corresponding way. Similarly, an advocate of Lewis's best-system analysis invokes a notion of 'our standards of strength, simplicity, fit, and the balance among these,' on which there seem to be few if any independent constraints. Whatever a scientific community says it thinks the laws of nature are, an advocate of the best-system analysis can adopt the hypothesis that that community's standards are whatever they need to be to reach the verdict that those putative laws are in the best system. Similar remarks apply to the necessitarian/essentialist accounts of laws defended by Swoyer (1982), Ellis (2001), and others, as well as for the non-reductive realist view of Carroll (1994).

Thus, the MAL (as well as any other meta-theoretic account) is testable in a way that first-order accounts of laws typically are not; its tires make contact with the road of scientific practice in a way that they do not. I am not sure whether this in itself counts as a virtue of the MAL (and meta-theoretic accounts in general). On the one hand, it seems that testability is always a virtue, other things being equal; but on the other hand, that maxim applies primarily to empirical scientific theories, and it is not entirely clear whether a philosophical account of laws should be subject to the same norms. One thing is certain, though: if an account is testable, then it had better pass its tests if we are going to consider accepting it.

I think the MAL performs well when it is tested in this way. For example, consider Newton's theory of mechanics and gravitation. We just saw (in Section 9.5.1) a reason to think that the MAL will count Newton's second law of motion as a law of this theory. One of this theory's non-laws is the regularity that all planets go around the sun in the same direction. Can this regularity be exploited as the reliability condition of a measurement method? For example, could we rely on it to design a method of measuring the orbital orientation of a given planet by first using astronomical techniques to determine the orbital orientation of Venus, and then inferring that the planet in question has the same orientation? According to Newton's theory, this method is *de facto* reliable. However, it does not qualify as a legitimate measurement method relative to Newton's theory; it is excluded on natural almanac grounds.[7] So it seems that the regularity about the orientation of the planets' orbits will not qualify as a law of Newton's theory, according to the MAL. (I will take up this example in more detail in the Appendix.)

I will not attempt the Herculean task of applying the MAL to every theory in the history of modern science in order to see whether it gives the right verdicts concerning what their laws are. But in the Appendix, I will consider how the MAL fares in the face of a few theories that seem to be representative.

9.5.3 The MAL and conceptual analysis

One objection to the MAL that many people have raised in conversation is that the MAL just doesn't seem to capture what's involved in our concept of lawhood. When we reflect on our concept of lawhood, it does not seem to amount to the concept of a principle that underwrites the reliability of a method of measurement; when we reflect on our concept of a law of a theory, it does not seem to amount to the concept of a principle that underwrites the reliability of a method that is a good method of measurement according to that theory. And it seems easy to conceive of counterexamples—easy, that is, to conceive of a situation in which there is some law that fails to imply the reliability of any measurement method at all.

My first reply to this objection is that it misunderstands what the MAL is trying to do. The MAL isn't supposed to be an analysis of our concept of a law of nature, or an explication of our folk theory of lawhood, or anything like that. But this reply faces an immediate counter-reply: the MAL is a theory about the truth conditions of lawhood-ascriptions; if it is true, then it is necessarily true; most of the reasons in its favor are largely a priori (or at least, they're about as a priori as anything other than pure mathematics and logic can be). All of that makes it look as if the MAL must be an attempt at conceptual analysis—for what other than conceptual analysis can give us a priori knowledge of necessary truths? And so, in order for the MAL to be successful on its own terms, it must be plausible that the MAL just makes explicit what was implicitly built into our concept of a law of nature all along. But that isn't plausible: the idea that lawhood is connected to

[7] See Chapter 8, Section 8.6.3, and the fifth subclause of the definition of the closure of measurement methods in Section 9.2.

measurement in the way the MAL says is not something we can discern just from reflecting on our concept of a law, paying attention to the way in which we decide how to classify things as laws or non-laws, and so on. So how can I deny that its implausibility as a conceptual analysis is a major liability of the MAL? If the MAL's account of the truth conditions of lawhood-ascriptions is not made true by something built into the concept of a law nature, then what could make it true, and how could we know it?

This objection is based on a particular traditional view of what the enterprise of theoretical philosophy is all about: there exists a realm of concepts, and the philosopher's job is to make a faithful map of this realm, which she does by investigating a priori the criteria we use for applying or withholding our concepts. The case I have made for the MAL cannot be reconciled with this picture of the enterprise of philosophy. It is based on a very different picture, according to which our conceptual framework, like our view of the world, is a perpetual work-in-progress, and philosophical progress can consist of reforms in the conceptual landscape as well as faithful representations of what is already there. Such reforms are never forced upon us, but they are sometimes useful. What is 'built into' our concepts is what we have put there—the criteria we have adopted for deciding how and when to apply them. But we don't just build such criteria into our concepts; we also expect them to do certain jobs for us, and it can turn out that a concept does not have enough built into it to do the job it has been assigned. In the case at hand, our ordinary concept of a law of nature does not have built into it the relation to the concept of a method of measurement that the MAL imposes; yet, I have argued that the concept of a law can do a job that has been assigned it—that of representing features of reality that *govern the universe* in accordance with the law-governed world-picture—only if it does have this relation built into it. So we have a choice: we can keep our old concept of a law of nature in its original unencumbered state, refusing to recognize any necessary connections between it and other concepts (such as the connection between lawhood and measurement that the MAL imposes) that we cannot already recognize to be there through a priori reflection—and leave the concept unable to play its part in the law-governed world-picture. Or, we can reform the concept, impose the necessary relations between it and the concept of measurement imposed by the MAL, and thereby enable it to play its role in the law-governed world-picture. The latter reform will not make much (if any) difference in practice, I claim—for the examples considered in the Appendix show that, to a large extent, if we adopt the MAL, we'll end up calling the same propositions 'laws of nature' that we always did. The reform comes with a low cost and offers a big payoff. So it's a good reform to make.

To philosophers who insist on the meta-philosophy that I oppose, this will not be persuasive. They will insist that a non-logical necessary constraint on the truth conditions of law-statements—such as the MAL proposes—can be true only if it unpacks what is, as a matter of fact, already built into the concept of lawhood as we have been using it all along. I don't have an argument against their meta-philosophy to offer here, but I think I have shown in effect that if they are right, then there is little that is philosophically interesting in the concept of a law of nature. For if they are right, and the concept of lawhood does not have the relation to measurement proposed by the MAL built into it, then (if the argument of Chapters 5 through 8 succeeds) the law-governed world-picture is untenable.

9.5.4 Can the MAL explain our ability to recognize the laws of a theory?

The upshot of the last section was that the MAL is not intended as an analysis of our pre-existing concept of a law of nature, and so it should not be judged by the standards appropriate to such an analysis; in particular, it should not be faulted on the grounds that when we decide whether to classify some truth as a law or a non-law, it does not seem as if we do so on the basis of whether it underwrites the reliability of some measurement method or not. But it might seem that an argument I used earlier in this book commits me to saying that the MAL does, after all, capture the criteria we rely on in deciding whether to call something a law—which the MAL plainly does not. This would spell trouble for me.

Back in the first section of Chapter 3, I offered a plausibility argument for the meta-theoretic approach to laws that ran as follows. It is frequently possible to tell what the laws of a scientific theory are from a presentation of that theory that gives only its non-nomological content; let's call this fact *the recognizability of laws*. On the first-order conception, the recognizability of laws is mysterious: the non-nomological content of a theory radically underdetermines its laws, so it is hard to see how knowledge of only the former could enable us to discern the latter. But on the meta-theoretic conception, there is a natural explanation. For, when we learn a paradigm case of a law-positing theory, such as Newtonian mechanics, and learn which propositions are its laws, and what jobs those laws do in the use of the theory, we come to acquire an implicit understanding of the distinctive role that the laws of a theory play within that theory. So, when we later learn another theory—say, classical electrodynamics—we can recognize that certain propositions are playing the same role within it. This is not the only possible explanation, but it is a particularly natural and simple one; it is a virtue of the meta-theoretic conception that it makes this explanation possible. Thus, in spite of its strangeness and initial counterintuitiveness, the meta-theoretic conception has at least one important apparent advantage; in this way, I argued that the meta-theoretic conception deserves a hearing.

The phenomenon of the recognizability of laws thus seemed to point to an advantage of the general meta-theoretic approach to laws. But can the MAL enjoy this advantage? It seems that in order for the MAL (or any other meta-theoretic account of laws) to successfully explain the recognizability of laws, the truth conditions it attributes to statements of the form 'P is a law of T' must faithfully correspond to the criteria we actually use when deciding whether to classify P as a law of T or not. For otherwise, what makes P a law of T is not what inclines us to say that P is a law of T. So our ability to recognize the laws of a theory without being told what they are explicitly remains a mystery.

It seems that the MAL fails this test: when the hypothetical physics student from the first section of Chapter 3 learns classical electrodynamics and recognizes that Maxwell's equations must be among its laws, it is just not very plausible that she does this by recognizing that those equations all guarantee the reliability of one or more good methods of measurement. Similarly, when she learned classical mechanics and what its laws were, it might not ever have occurred to her that the law of universal gravitation can be used to guarantee the reliability of certain methods of measuring the mass-ratios among the planets—or, indeed, that this law can be used to guarantee the reliability of any method of measuring anything at all. So it is not very plausible that when she learned to recognize the law role being played when she sees it, what she learned to recognize was the measurement-underwriting role that the MAL identifies with the law role.

The upshot is that if the recognizability of laws is a genuine phenomenon, then it is just as mysterious if the MAL is true as it is if the first-order conception of laws is true; so, an advocate of the MAL cannot in good faith appeal to that phenomenon in order to support the general meta-theoretic approach, and thereby seek to advance the cause of the MAL.[8]

This is an impressive objection, but I think it is mistaken. What the recognizability of lawhood appears to show is that the laws of a theory are determined by the non-nomological content of that theory—since many people are pretty good at reading the former off of the latter. Its appearing to show this depends on its also appearing to show that people with some training in science are able to do this reading-off: that when presented with the non-nomological content of a scientific theory, they can tell what the laws of that theory are. Nothing follows about *how* such people are able to perform this trick. It might be because they have some implicit awareness of a set of necessary and sufficient conditions for lawhood-relative-to-a-theory, which they bring to bear in the recognition task, and which a good philosophical account of the law role should make explicit. But a priori, there is no reason to assume that this is how things must be. We have reliable abilities to recognize all sorts of things whereof we could not formulate the necessary and sufficient conditions of identity of the things recognized—for example, faces, scents, species of animal, and genres of music. These things might have necessary and sufficient conditions of identity, even if our way of recognizing them does not depend on any awareness, explicit or implicit, of those conditions, but rather on abilities to notice resemblances (grounded perhaps in something like connectionist networks in our brains). In cases like that, the way to find out what those principles are would not be to reflect on the cues and criteria we rely on in making our recognitional judgments. The fact that we are reliable recognizers of a kind of thing can give us a good reason to believe that there really is a kind of thing there, whereof it might be fruitful to investigate the conditions under which something belongs to this kind—without giving us any reason to think that those conditions must correspond to criteria that we somehow employ in making our recognitional judgments. Why couldn't it be like that with the laws of a given scientific theory?

9.5.5 Laws, counterfactuals, and the MAL

The fundamental idea behind the MAL is that lawhood is essentially linked to measurability: to be a law is to make something measurable. Back in

[8] I am grateful to Marc Lange for raising this objection.

Section 1.10.1, I motivated this idea by appealing to the counterfactual robustness of both laws and measurement methods: when we regard something as a legitimate measurement method, we regard the proposition that it is reliable as resilient under a broad range of counterfactual suppositions; when we regard something as a law, we do likewise; so if we assume that the laws of a theory are the propositions of that theory that express the reliability of measurement methods, then we can explain why laws are counterfactually robust by appealing to the counterfactual reliability of measurements. The counterfactual reliability of measurements, in turn, is to be explained in terms of the distinctive epistemological and methodological role of measurements in science: a method can play this role within our scientific practice only insofar as we regard it as counterfactually reliable.

This argument was pretty rough: in particular, it was not very precise about exactly what the 'counterfactual robustness' of laws, or the 'counterfactual reliability' of measurements consists in. So as it stood, it was at best a plausibility argument, an argument that the basic idea behind the MAL was worth taking seriously. But in the meantime, a lot more detail has been provided. The way in which laws must be related to counterfactuals in order for them to govern the universe has been examined, and so has the way in which our commitments concerning the legitimacy of measurement methods are related to our counterfactual commitments. The two match up just right in the form of the MAL.

But I should reply to an objection to this way of defending the MAL that will no doubt occur to many readers almost immediately:

> Okay, so the laws are counterfactually stable, and the propositions expressing the reliability of measurement methods are counterfactually stable, and perhaps this gives us some reason to suspect that the laws are the propositions that express the reliability of measurement methods. But nothing is *explained* by this hypothetical identity. It is mysterious, and in need of philosophical explication, why *any* logically contingent truth should be counterfactually stable. If laws of nature are a special sort of fact, the nature of which explains why its instances should be counterfactually robust, then the identification of laws and propositions expressing the reliability of measurement methods could be used to explain why the

latter are counterfactually stable. But the order of explanation here goes like this:

Metaphysical nature of laws → Counterfactual stability of laws → (via identification of laws with propositions expressing reliability of measurement methods) → Counterfactual reliability of measurements.

What the MAL proposes is a very different order of explanation, namely:

Counterfactual reliability of measurements → (via identification of laws with propositions expressing reliability of measurements) → Counterfactual stability of laws.

The first order of explanation—which is plainly the right one!—leaves no mysterious counterfactual robustness unexplained. The second order of explanation—the one proposed by the MAL—does; it leaves unexplained and mysterious the counterfactual reliability of measurements.

Things are not as simple as this objection portrays them, though. For one thing, it is not at all clear how the metaphysical nature of the laws of nature can *explain why* they are counterfactually stable.[9] Counterfactuals seem mysterious at least in part because they seem to be logically cut off from the realm of actual fact; the gulf between what is and what would have been had certain things been otherwise seems as logically unbridgeable as the gap between what is and what ought to be. If it seems impossible to infer an 'ought' from an 'is,' then it seems just as impossible to infer a 'would have been' from an 'is.' The Stalnaker-Lewis approach to counterfactuals makes the truth conditions of counterfactuals depend on the standards of similarity among possible worlds that are salient in the conversational context. Which standards of similarity are the salient ones in a given context depends on the interests and attitudes of the speakers—the aspects of the actual world that are most important to hold fixed and take into account when evaluating counterfactuals. We might gloss this by saying that on the Stalnaker-Lewis approach, the truthmakers for counterfactuals are found (at least partly) in our *counterfactual attitudes*. Now, for any metaphysical nature that some feature of the actual world might have (such as its laws of nature), there is

[9] See Swoyer (1982) for a powerful criticism of the candidate explanation offered by Armstrong (1983), Dretske (1977), and Tooley (1977); see Chapter 2, Section 2.5 for a criticism of the candidate explanation Swoyer offers in place of the former.

no apparent impossibility in our taking counterfactual attitudes that do not privilege the features of the actual world that have that metaphysical nature; the metaphysical nature of something is a matter of what that thing is really like independently of us, whereas our counterfactual attitudes are a matter of how we reason. So if, as the Stalnaker-Lewis approach has it, counterfactuals are made true (at least in part) by our counterfactual attitudes, it is not at all obvious what kind of 'metaphysical nature' the laws of nature might have that explains why they have to be counterfactually robust.

Pursuing the analogy with the 'naturalistic fallacy' in ethics a little further: the projectivist approach to ethics locates the ethical properties of the world ultimately in our moral attitudes. On this kind of view, the metaphysical nature of some state of affairs, all by itself, cannot explain why that state of affairs ought to obtain. A metaphysical nature, which is a particularly heavyweight 'is,' cannot entail an 'ought' all by itself, without the cooperation of our moral attitudes. Similarly, on the Stalnaker-Lewis approach to counterfactuals, no metaphysical nature such as the laws of nature might possess could entail their counterfactual stability, without the cooperation of our counterfactual attitudes. So on this approach to counterfactuals, the order of explanation favored by the objection above is lacking: the first term in the chain of explanations is impotent to support the first explanatory arrow all by itself.

Of course, not all ethicists are projectivists, and not all theorists of counterfactuals accept the Stalnaker-Lewis approach. Ethical naturalists who are not projectivists face the challenge of explaining how an 'is' can entail an 'ought,' in spite of the apparent logical gap pointed out by Moore.[10] And in a parallel fashion, anyone who wants to ground the truth conditions of counterfactuals in facts about the actual properties and natures of actual things, *other than* our own counterfactual attitudes, must meet a similar challenge. They must explain how something's *being the case in the actual world* can entail that things *would have been different* had the world been different in various ways. Facts that are necessary evidently would *have* to have been the same, even if the world had been different in other respects. But at least some laws of nature are metaphysically contingent.[11] The mere fact that some metaphysically contingent fact holds in the actual world does

[10] I do *not* mean to imply here that this challenge cannot be met! Only that it must be met in some way or other.

[11] Again, see Section 2.5.

not seem to have what it takes, all by itself, to entail that that contingent fact would still have held had things been different in some way.

So the order of explanation favored by the objection is not as straightforward as at first appears. It is not at all clear how 'the metaphysical nature of the laws' *could* explain why laws are counterfactually stable. On the other hand, the order of explanation favored by the MAL is not as lacking as the objection portrays it as being. This order of explanation need not start where the objection says it starts—with the counterfactual reliability of measurements. Prior to this node is another one: *the epistemological and methodological role of measurements in the practice of empirical natural science.* If the role played by measurements within the practice of science is such that no one can treat something as a method of measurement without also treating it as counterfactually reliable, then we have an explanation for the counterfactual reliability of measurements.

Anyone sympathetic to the objection rehearsed above is not likely to be impressed by this. They are likely to reply that even if scientists must treat the methods they regard as measurement methods as counterfactually reliable, this must be because they regard the reliability of these methods as *objectively* counterfactually stable. Our beliefs about what is a good measurement are answerable to our beliefs about the objective counterfactual facts, not the other way around. But this line of thought is plausible only if there are such things as 'objective counterfactual facts,' which are what they are independently of our counterfactual attitudes. These objective counterfactual facts will either have to supervene on the way things are in the actual world—in which case, we face the same difficulties discussed above—or else they 'float free of the actual facts,' in which case it is mysterious how scientists can ever discover them, limited as they are to empirical evidence, which reveals only what actually happens, never what would have happened otherwise.

And there is an alternative: perhaps scientists cannot pursue science at all without accepting that certain methods are good ones for measuring things, and thereby committing themselves to the counterfactual reliability of these methods. There is no one set of methods that scientists must recognize as good measurement methods, no one set of counterfactuals they must adopt, no one set of propositions they must recognize as laws; but there is no question of a choice about whether to recognize any measurement methods, counterfactuals, or laws at all: if you want to do science, you have to recognize as legitimate some measurement methods or other, so you must accept some counterfactually stable reliability conditions, and your total theory must have some laws. It is not a question of whether to accept counterfactuals and laws, but only a question of which counterfactuals and laws to accept. That decision can be made by empirical testing and confirmation of scientific hypotheses and theories. But only if the laws and counterfactuals implied by a theory are already implied by the non-nomological content of that theory (as they are on any meta-theoretic account of laws); otherwise, different sets of nomological hypotheses can be coherently combined with the same set of non-nomological hypotheses, and the empirical evidence will be unable to help us decide which ones to accept.

If this is how it is, then the truth values of counterfactuals, and the lawhood of certain propositions, are features of any scientific theory of the world, which are there not because the world being represented by the theory contains objective facts which they reflect, but rather because the methodology and practice of science as such requires that any product of scientific theorizing have such features. On this view, the metaphysics of counterfactuals and laws is 'post-Kantian' rather than 'pre-Kantian':[12] We cannot (scientifically) understand the world except as governed by laws and containing true counterfactuals—simply because we cannot (scientifically) understand the world without recognizing some methods as good measurement methods; but it does not follow that laws of nature and counterfactual facts are features of the world that are radically independent of our ways of theorizing, and which our theories faithfully mirror. Whether this 'post-Kantian' line is in step with the law-governed world-picture is a question I will turn to in Chapter 10.

9.6 What if we don't care about the law-governed world-picture?

The main argument of the last few chapters has sought to establish that the MAL is the account of lawhood we have to accept if we want to

[12] I use the terms 'pre-Kantian' and 'post-Kantian' in a loose and popular sense, not one informed by serious Kant scholarship.

vindicate the law-governed world-picture; on no other possible account of laws are all four of the theses making up that picture true. Assuming the argument has been successful, there can be no better argument for an account of lawhood—for someone committed to the law-governed world-picture. But what about people who come to the table with no particular commitment to that picture—or those who bear outright hostility toward it? Do they have any good reason to accept the MAL?

As I hinted back in Section 1.8, I think they do. The main source of hostility to the law-governed world-picture is the idea that that picture involves some extravagant metaphysics that is in no way relevant to what goes on in science. But note that the MAL is very parsimonious in its metaphysical commitments: the only undefined non-logical primitive concept that it uses is that of a legitimate measurement procedure. This is a concept that science cannot do without; if we can't classify procedures according to whether they are legitimate measurement procedures or not, we cannot even engage in science at the most basic level. If the idea of a legitimate measurement procedure is metaphysically problematic, it is a problem that science is stuck with.[13]

The form the MAL takes allows us, if we like, to think of it as a stipulative definition of a predicate, 'is a law of nature.' This predicate looks a lot like an old one that has been in play for a while, but the new predicate, unlike the old one, is precisely defined. It turns out that if we adopt this definition, then we can truly say a lot of things with it that mirror pretty closely the things that have been said using the old, lexically similar predicate: in particular, that the things it applies to support counterfactuals in a powerful way, and that there is a genuine sense in which they govern the universe. Moreover, as I'll try to show in the Appendix, if we adopt this definition and apply it in contexts where various historically important physical theories are presupposed, we will find ourselves applying the new predicate to exactly those propositions that the proponents of those theories tend to apply the old, similar predicate to. If we banished all talk of 'laws of nature' (the old predicate), it would be relatively cheap and easy

[13] Another, similar ground of hostility toward the law-governed world-picture is the thought that it is incompatible with the thesis of Humean Supervenience, which is an article of faith for many philosophers. In Chapter 10, I will argue that the MAL is consistent with Humean Supervenience—in fact, it entails it—even though it is also consistent with the law-governed world-picture. So fans of Humean Supervenience need not reject the law-governed world-picture.

to introduce a new, precisely defined, and metaphysically unproblematic predicate that does pretty much all the same work that the old predicate did—including the business about 'governing the universe.' In the light of this, resistance to the law-governed world-picture seems futile—if you kill it, it can pop right back up. It also seems pointless—for the law-governed world-picture can live and thrive without giving birth to metaphysical monstrosities after all.

9.7 Newton's god and Laplace's demon

The MAL has a curious consequence. Recall 'God's Own Theory,' or GOT: this is the theory that consists of all the non-nomological truths about our world.[14] What would the laws of this theory be? According to the MAL, GOT has no laws at all.

There are two very different reasons why this is so. The first is that in order for a theory T to have any laws (other than the logical necessities), T must not contain all truths, for otherwise any regularity found in T will be eliminated from law-status on natural almanac grounds (see Chapter 8, Section 8.6.3). The second is that in order for a theory T to have any laws, T must be associated with empirical procedures designated as legitimate methods of measurement; their reliability conditions will be the generating axioms of the set of T's laws of nature. It is doubtful whether a theory meant to represent a transcendent omniscient being's cognition of the universe will designate any procedures as legitimate measurement methods, since such a being will not be dependent on empirical measurements as a source of information.

This might seem to be an unwanted consequence. In fact, I think this consequence is consilient with the spirit of the MAL. God's Own Theory has no laws, for laws are a feature of theories used by subjects who know only a tiny fraction of the contents of space-time, and need to rely on measurements whenever they want to find out more. It is the essence of lawhood that the laws of a theory are whatever underwrite the legitimacy of the measurements that the users of that theory employ; it is the essence of measurement that when we measure we make a fresh judgment about

[14] I discussed GOT in Chapter 3, Section 3.3.3, and in Chapter 8, Section 8.7.3.

whatever we have measured, mediated both by the body of theory we accept and a non-redundant contribution from our empirical interaction with the world; any theory that already gave everything away, leaving nothing needing to be measured, is not a theory that could ever be used by a subject who needs to use measurements to learn about the world. Scientists as such are people who use measurements to investigate the world in developing, testing, and applying their theories—so God's Own Theory is not a theory that can ever be accepted by scientists (without their ceasing to be scientists). *It is not a scientific theory, and it has no laws.*

This consequence of the measurability approach to laws does violence to a common interpretation of the modern-scientific conception of the world, one suggested by Laplace's famous demonic thought-experiment. We often tend to think of the world as the product of a divine intelligence who went about His work in a particular way: He laid down laws of nature to govern creation, then set up the initial conditions, and then stepped back to allow things to unfold. What God knows in this picture is sufficient to determine everything about the world (if the laws He laid down are deterministic). For He knows the laws, He knows the initial conditions, and everything else follows from there. God, in this picture, is in the position of Laplace's demon: a super-intelligent being who knows all the laws of nature and knows the complete state of the universe at a given moment.[15]

From the point of view of the MAL, this picture is wrong. God (or Laplace's demon) might well know the truth of all the propositions that are laws of some true theory, as well as the complete initial state of the universe. But He does not know these laws *as laws*; for He does not hold any true theory within which they play the law role.

For those who accept the MAL, the story of Laplace's demon is still a helpful parable for illustrating the concept of a law of nature, but it needs a different interpretation. Laplace's demon is a *demon*, not a god: it does not create the universe, but rather finds itself within the universe, needs to find its way around in the universe, and hits on a certain method for doing so: that of using the laws of nature to predict and retrodict its way to a complete map of space-time. This demon is thus an extremely idealized version of a modern (that is, post-Newtonian) physicist. The idealization here has (at least) two components. First, the demon has unlimited computational

[15] Laplace (1952), p. 4.

power;[16] second, and more importantly here, the demon is aware of the values of all measurable quantities pertaining to a single time. (And third, the laws are perfectly deterministic; though Laplace himself probably did not think of this as an idealization.) Given these idealizations, the demon has no need to ever measure anything again. The values of all measurable quantities are computable via perfectly reliable inferences from what it already knows. Something that Laplace conspicuously leaves out of his story is how the demon ever came to know the complete state of the universe at a single instant. If the demon's epistemic access to the contingent facts about the universe is, like ours, entirely empirical, then it must have performed some measurements at some point. (Or else it relied on the testimony of someone who did.) What goes on in most cases of measurement is not entirely different from what the demon does in making its predictions and retrodictions: measurement is the activity of inducing the value of one quantity to reveal itself in the value of another; the result of the measurement is an inference from the pointer variable to the measured variable, an inference underwritten by laws, just as the demon's predictions and retrodictions are. In fact, the demon's prediction and retrodiction of the entire history of the universe is a limiting case of a measurement: it uses the present total state of the universe as a pointer variable for detecting the total trajectory of the universe. The demon, then, is a scientist who has already measured everything that is there to be measured. Once this universal measuring task has been completed, there is no longer any need to measure anything, and nothing will ever be called upon to play the law role again. (Hence, relative to the demon's total theory, there are no laws. Laws are a ladder that the demon has already climbed all the way up, and can now throw away.)

Of course, we will never be in the demon's position. We will always have many things left to measure. And so, so long as we always remain capable of measuring things, our total theory will always have something in it that plays the law role (though what this something is will no doubt change from time to time). The demon is thus a projection from our current state, in which we have already accomplished all the empirical tasks we could ever hope to accomplish. It is natural to think of the demon as

[16] In fact, the demon would have to be mathematically omniscient, so it wouldn't even have to rely on computations; the mathematical problems it would have to solve in order to predict and retrodict the whole history of the universe would be uncomputable.

knowing, among other things, all the laws, but this is a mistake, since laws as such are things that play a special role within the total theory of someone who is not yet at that stage; that is, of someone who has not finished needing to be a scientist. The demon has finished needing to be a scientist; scientific practice as such will have come to an end for the demon, and so everything that is what it is in virtue of the role it plays in scientific practice (e.g., the laws of one's total theory of the world) will likewise fall away for the demon.

This is why the consequence that GOT has no laws is not a *reductio* of the MAL, but rather something anyone who embraces the MAL should expect. If the laws of a theory are the elements of that theory that make measurement possible, then no theory according to which there is nothing left to measure should have any laws.

10

Beyond Humean and non-Humean

10.1 Two views of laws

Much of the contemporary philosophical conversation about laws of nature concerns a conflict between two broad views, or families of views, about what laws are and how they relate to the rest of the world. On one side, we have *Humean* views of laws, which are also called *regularity accounts* or *reductionist accounts*; the basic conception of laws they embrace is sometimes called the *non-governing* or *summarizing* conception of laws. On the other side, we have the *non-Humean* views of laws, which are sometimes called *strong-laws views*, *non-reductionist* or *realist* views; they embrace what is called the *governing* conception of laws.[1]

The two camps defy easy definition, but they are readily described in intuitive, imaginative terms. The Humean view takes off from David Hume's denial of non-logical 'necessary connexions' in nature. It conceives of the world as a big mosaic of 'loose-and-separate' matters of fact. There are regular patterns in the mosaic, but we seek in vain for some kind of hidden *arche* standing behind these patterns, producing and enforcing them. The regularities we call laws are simply descriptions of the most prominent patterns; the ones that play the most fundamental roles in the theories we construct to cope with the world; the ones that convey to us simply and elegantly a great deal of valuable information about the layout of the cosmic mosaic.

The non-Humean view, on the other hand, thinks Hume made a serious error when he denied 'necessary connexions.' Non-Humeans think our world is really governed by laws—in some genuine sense that is difficult

[1] See Beebee (2001) for an illuminating discussion of this divide.

to define precisely—and that these laws offer genuine explanations of why we find the regularities in the world that we do. These laws may not be logically or metaphysically necessary (though some non-Humeans think they are), but they certainly have some grade of necessity. The notion of the physical or natural or nomological impossibility of violating a law is a serious and legitimate one; there is a real sense of 'can't' at work in 'you can't break the laws of nature.'

These are broad-stroke metaphysical pictures. Let's try to get down to details and see exactly what the two camps disagree about. There are in fact at least four distinct (though related) controversies on which the two sides take opposing positions. These concern the relation between laws and counterfactuals, the notion of nomological necessity, the choice between the governing conception of laws and the summarizing conception of laws, and the thesis of Humean Supervenience.

10.1.1 The first divide: Laws and counterfactuals

First, there is *the question of the relation between laws and counterfactuals*. All sides agree that in our everyday practices of counterfactual reasoning, we tend to respect the principle that the laws support counterfactuals. If things had been different, then the laws would still have been the same. Non-Humeans hold that we evaluate counterfactuals in a way that respects this principle because the principle is true: it is an objective feature of the world.

Humeans cannot accept this; the great mosaic of loose and separate matters of fact is a wholly actual and occurrent thing; it does not include any would-have-beens among its stones. They hold that all non-trivial counterfactuals[2] are true, when they are true, because of which features of the actual world are most salient to the speakers and evaluators. When we ask how things would have been if A had been true, what we are really asking is how things would have been if A had been true *and everything else had remained the same, as much as possible.* Changing one aspect of the actual situation logically requires changing lots of others, and these changes are not generally related in any single hierarchy running from 'most like the actual situation' to 'least like the actual situation.' In deciding whether to affirm a counterfactual, then, we must (at least implicitly) make a decision

[2] A *non-trivial* counterfactual is one whose antecedent does not logically entail its consequent, for example: 'Had I remembered my umbrella this morning, I would not be soaking wet right now.'

about which features of the actual situation are most important or salient: which ones we are least willing to allow to vary in our counterfactual reasoning. When I wonder what would happen if I were to drop a crystal glass onto a stone floor, I consider what things are like in a possible situation where I do so, and the most important features of the actual situation hold, to as great an extent as possible. In the actual world, this particular glass does not shatter—but dropped objects fall, and glasses that fall onto stone floors shatter. I cannot conceive of a possible world where I drop this glass and yet all three of these actual truths are still true. One of them has to go. Since the general facts about dropped objects and the fragility of glasses are so much more salient to me than the fate of this one particular glass, the actual truth that I let go of is the truth that this glass does not shatter. Thus, I reach the conclusion that had I dropped this glass, it would have shattered. In general, the important regular patterns in the world are more important to me than the local truths about particular objects, so they tend to be the ones that I hold onto. And the laws of nature are the most important regular patterns in the great actual mosaic of matters of fact. Hence, we tend to count possible worlds where the laws of nature are true as more similar to the actual world than worlds where they are violated. This is the explanation for why we tend to respect the principle that laws hold up under counterfactual suppositions. The explanation appeals to our standards of importance and salience for features of the actual world. Unlike the Non-Humean, the Humean holds that the counterfactual-supporting power of laws is entirely dependent on these standards of ours.

10.1.2 The second divide: nomological necessity

Our talk of laws of nature frequently gets mixed up with modal locutions. What is consistent with the laws of nature is physically possible, or naturally possible, or nomologically possible. What is not consistent with them is physically or naturally or nomologically impossible. What follows from them is physically or naturally or nomologically necessary. How are we to make sense of this modal talk?

The Humean has a simple answer: most of the modal operators that occur in ordinary language are restricted modalities of one sort or another.[3]

[3] See Lycan (1994) for an illuminating discussion of this phenomenon.

So it is with nomological modality. To say that something is nomologically possible is to say that it is compossible with the laws of nature;[4] to say that it is nomologically necessary is to say that its negation is not nomologically possible.

Thus, we can define a pair of modal operators (a necessity operator and a possibility operator) in terms of the laws of nature, with the result that the necessity operator applies to the laws and their consequences and to nothing else. This, for the Humean, is all it takes to capture the notion that there is such a brand of necessity.

But the fact that it is possible to do this is not anything special about the laws of nature; the same trick could be pulled for any set of true propositions you like. Thus, we could define a pair of modal operators 'It is GVE-necessary that' and 'it is GVE-possible that' as follows:

> It is GVE-possible that P iff P is compossible with all the truths about the contents of Nelson Goodman's pockets on VE Day.
>
> It is GVE-necessary that P iff ¬P is not GVE-possible.

What we can do for the laws of nature, or the GVE truths, we could do for any set of truths we like. So the fact that the laws are necessary in the sense of necessity supplied by the definition of nomological necessity given above does not distinguish the laws from any other set of truths; every set of truths is necessary after its own fashion. We might put this point by saying that the possibility of defining nomological modal operators in the way described above shows only that the laws have a kind of *trivial* necessity.

It might be objected that since almost all the modal operators we use in ordinary language are restricted modalities definable in the same way, this line of thought proves too much: it shows that all the necessities we speak of on a daily basis are merely trivial necessities. But it can be replied that these restricted modalities, while in themselves trivial (they have no particular metaphysical import), are important for the purposes of ordinary conversation because of the interests and attitudes of the speakers. Thus, when I say it is not possible for me to help you secretly move the dead body in your garage, what I mean is that my doing so is not compossible with my

[4] Here, 'compossible' means jointly possible, in the broadest legitimate sense of 'possible' there is. That broadest legitimate sense might be metaphysical possibility, or it might be logical possibility; different Humeans might disagree about this.

carrying out the plans I have already committed myself to (which include not risking a lengthy prison sentence). Compossibility with my carrying out the plans I have settled on is an important matter in the context of our conversation, but from a metaphysical point of view it is trivial indeed: there is nothing especially important or interesting that is shared by all and only the possible worlds in which I carry out my actual plans.

The upshot is that if there is nothing more to nomological modality than a pair of modal operators defined in terms of compossibility with a certain set of truths, even if this modal operator is particularly salient in the context of human conversations, then the necessity of the laws does not mark anything particularly special about them. It makes them no more special than the set of truths to the effect that I am going to carry out the plans I have settled on. Both are necessary in the sense of necessity provided by some artificial modal operator that is helpful to appeal to in conversation. Neither are necessary in any stronger sense.

For this reason, non-Humeans object to the Humean treatment of nomological necessity. They argue that it is in the nature of the laws themselves that they have a 'modal character.'[5] There is a sense in which laws are necessary, and to attribute this necessity to them is to say something important about what they are really like, rather than to invoke a made-up restricted modality that happens to suit the needs of a particular conversation. Some non-Humeans go so far as to say that the laws of nature are *metaphysically* necessary; even those who do not go this far nonetheless strive to find some lesser grade of necessity, reflecting something important about the nature of the world rather than our own interests, to attribute to them. Thus, for D. M. Armstrong, the laws involve a *necessitation* relation, which is also exhibited in singular causation; for John Carroll, laws have an irreducible *modal character*.[6]

We can sum up this dispute by saying that for non-Humeans, but not for Humeans, laws and their consequences are distinguished by some kind of *non-trivial necessity*.

10.1.3 The third divide: governing versus summarizing

For Humeans, what is special about the laws of nature is that they provide an elegant summary of the non-nomic history of the world. The simplest

[5] See Carroll (1994), pp. 1, 7.

[6] Armstrong (1993); Carroll (1994).

Humean view of laws is what is usually called (disparagingly) the *naive regularity account of laws*. According to this account, the laws are simply the true statements that take the form of universally quantified conditionals: all Fs are Gs. It should be added that the predicates F and G appearing in a law must be 'purely qualitative'; gruesome predicates are forbidden. On this account, the laws consist of a big set of descriptions of general patterns in the great mosaic of the world. They convey much less information than a complete specification of every element in the mosaic would. But the complete set of laws is also a great deal more compact than such a complete specification would be.

The difficulties of the naive regularity account are well known, and they are legion.[7] Most modern-day Humeans reject it in favor of some more sophisticated regularity account. The most prominent example is the best-system analysis (or BSA) of David Lewis.[8] For Lewis, being a true universally quantified regularity statement is a necessary condition for being a law, but it is not a sufficient condition. The BSA can be seen as an attempt to improve on the virtues of the naive regularity account by making the laws turn out to be an even more compact summary of the world's history. For any given possible world, there is a set of eligible deductive systems at that world: these are deductively closed, axiomatized sets of propositions that are true and whose truth supervenes on the occurrent, non-nomic history. One will include all such truths; it will be fantastically informative, but ridiculously complicated. Another will include only the logical truths: it will be admirably simple, but woefully uninformative. Between these two extremes are systems with more simplicity than the first and more information content than the second. These two virtues tend to trade off: the more information you want, the more axioms you need, and adding axioms to a system tends to make it less simple. If nature is kind, then one system will strike the best balance between the two virtues. If nature is kind in this way, then the universally quantified propositions belonging to the best system are the laws of nature; if nature is unkind, then there are no laws of nature.

Thus, if there are any laws of nature, then collectively they provide a maximally good summary of the history of the world: they provide the

[7] Armstrong (1983), Part I contains a classic, relentless, devastating assault on this account.

[8] See Lewis (1973), the Introduction to Lewis (1986), Lewis (1994), Chapter 5 of Earman (1986), and Loewer (1997).

most information about what happens as simply as possible, so to speak. This, on Lewis's view, is what it is for some set of propositions to be the laws of nature: the laws are a set of truths that collectively convey in a very economical form a great deal of useful information about the layout of the great mosaic we live in. If our mosaic has no unique best system, then we live in an unsummarizable world, and there are no laws of nature.

By contrast, the non-Humeans think that what it is for a set of propositions to be the laws is not for it to provide a unique best summary of the world (though the laws might do that). The laws are a set of propositions that govern or constrain the evolution of the world. They provide an explanation for why our world is laid out in the way that it is; they could not be a mere summary of the world, for a summary is impotent to offer an explanation of why what it summarizes is the way it is.

It is natural to view the Humeans and non-Humeans as focusing on two distinct elements in the familiar concept of a law of nature. On the one hand, there is the idea that for there to be laws of nature is for there to be a cosmic order to the universe—for there to be harmonious regular patterns into which all particular events fit. The laws are the principles that provide a key for discerning this grand pattern. On the other hand, there is the idea that for there to be laws of nature is for there to be an inevitable compulsion at work in the evolution of the universe; the laws are that which you couldn't get around no matter how hard you tried. It is conceivable for either of these two elements to be present without the other: perhaps we live in a mosaic world in which the loose and separate elements happen to cohere in a grand cosmic pattern; perhaps we live in a monstrous chaos in which each episode unfolds under the constraint of an irresistible compulsion resulting in no large-scale cosmic order at all. We might also live in a world where both elements are found. The Humean view takes the harmonious-order element to be most central to our concept of a law of nature; the non-Humean view takes the irresistible-compulsion element to be most central.

10.1.4 The fourth divide: Humean Supervenience

The Humean view that the world is nothing but a great mosaic of loose and separate matters of fact can be captured in a supervenience thesis. The relevant supervenience base here is what is usually called *the Humean base*; it is supposed to consist of all the loose and separate matters of fact that make up the mosaic. Less picturesquely but more informatively, the Humean base can be defined as the set of particular, occurrent, non-nomic facts. These will presumably include the facts about the spatiotemporal structure of the universe, as well as the assignments of natural contents to spacetime locations and of non-nomic natural properties to locations and their contents. Different authors have given different detailed accounts of what belongs to the Humean base, but this rough-and-ready characterization should suffice for present purposes.[9] Humean Supervenience is the thesis that the laws are completely determined by the Humean base; there can be no difference in the laws without a difference in the Humean base. That is:

> **HS:** No two possible worlds agree completely on their Humean bases while differing in their laws of nature.

This thesis is universally endorsed by philosophers on the Humean side of the controversy about laws, and is almost universally rejected by philosophers on the non-Humean side.[10]

On the BSA, that paradigm of a Humean account of laws, it is clear that HS must be true. Once the Humean base of a possible world is fully specified, all the propositions that can be members of the eligible systems at that world are fixed. The standard of informativeness, simplicity, and the balance between them used to determine the 'best' system are rigidly fixed: they are supposed to be the standards employed by actual human scientists for purposes of theory selection. Hence, there is no room left for the laws of nature to wiggle in.

By contrast, consider one paradigm case of a non-Humean account of laws: the universals account defended by Armstrong. According to this view, it is a law that all Fs are Gs just in case the universals F and G are

[9] The term 'Humean Supervenience' was introduced by Lewis (1986), who characterized the supervenience base as 'the spatiotemporal distribution of local qualities.' For a survey of other formulations, see Earman and Roberts (2005a).

[10] Lewis adds a qualification I have dropped: the quantifier in his version of HS ranges over only worlds that contain instances of no 'alien properties' not instantiated in the actual world; thus he makes HS a contingent thesis, and leaves room for bizarre possible worlds out there containing 'non-Humean rubbish.' Advocates of HS include Earman (1986), Loewer (1997), Beebee (2001), and Earman and Roberts (2005b). Deniers of HS include Armstrong (1983) (see especially p. 71), Tooley (1987), and Lange (2000) (see pp. 88–90), among others. Not all of the authors just mentioned use the term 'Humean Supervenience.'

related by a certain second-order relation N, which has the property that N(F, G) entails that $\forall x(Fx \supset Gx)$ but not conversely. Consider a particular possible complete Humean base, and now consider the set of universal regularities that are true given this Humean base. On Armstrong's view, it is possible for *any* subset of this set of regularities to be the laws of nature, consistently with that specification of the Humean base.[11] Thus, HS is false; there are possible worlds with the same Humean base but different laws.

10.2 Humean Supervenience and the meta-theoretic conception

Evidently, many of the important characteristics of a particular philosophical approach to laws depend on whether that approach belongs to the Humean or the non-Humean camp. So it seems worthwhile to consider the question of which side the MAL lies on. I'll begin by considering the fourth divide between Humeans and non-Humeans: the question of Humean Supervenience. What is the relation between the MAL and HS? Does the MAL entail that HS is true, or entail that it is false, or remain neutral on the question?

This question is complicated by the fact that the MAL is a meta-theoretic account of laws. For if one accepts the meta-theoretic conception of laws, then there is no such thing as the laws at a given possible world, full stop. Lawhood is relativized not only to a possible world, but also to a context of utterance: a proposition P is a law at world w relative to context k just in case P plays the law role relative to the theory that is salient in k and that theory is true at w. So the statement of HS seems incomplete, at least if we are going to talk about it in the same breath as the meta-theoretic conception. It quantifies over possible worlds, and uses the notion of a law at a possible world, but it says nothing of the contexts relative to which attributions of lawhood are relativized.

But this difficulty is easily got around. Suppose that the statement of HS itself is uttered and evaluated within a given context. Within the present

[11] Armstrong himself affirms this consequence of his account on p. 71 of his (1983), though he does not use this terminology.

context of utterance, some theory T is the salient theory. In this context, 'P is a law of nature' is true at world w just in case P plays the law-role relative to T and T is true at w. But theories themselves, and the facts about which propositions play the law-roles within them, do not vary from world to world. So, in the present context, the statement of HS is true just in case for any two worlds w and v, w and v do not differ on whether T is true unless they also differ in their Humean bases. But on the meta-theoretic conception, T must (like all scientific theories) be completely non-nomological in its content. Hence, the truth or falsity of T supervenes on the Humean base. So, HS is true in the present context. This argument depends on no assumptions about what the present context is, or which theory is the salient theory in it. Hence it generalizes: in any context of utterance whatsoever, HS is true. So, whether we take HS to be a context-bound statement made and evaluated in a particular context of utterance, or alternatively take it to be a trans-contextual statement intended to quantify over all possible contexts of utterance, we get the same result: HS is true.

This might seem to be a problem for the meta-theoretic conception of laws. For many impressive arguments against HS have been advanced in the literature. These arguments were not designed as attacks on the meta-theoretic conception; their intended targets are Humean first-order accounts of lawhood, such as Lewis's BSA. But whatever the motives of their authors, these arguments purport to show that the thesis of HS itself must be false. It will turn out, however, that the meta-theoretic conception of laws has ways of responding to these objections not available to first-order Humeans such as Lewis.

We can divide these arguments against HS into two categories: the first attack HS by attacking the Humean picture of the universe. They purport to show that any account of lawhood that satisfies HS must miss something important about laws, namely the sense in which they *govern* the world, or the sense in which they are *necessary*; it follows that they are unable to account for the counterfactual robustness and explanatory power of laws. I'll set aside this kind of argument for the time being, and return to it later. The second kind of anti-HS argument goes after HS directly, by posing a counterexample. Let's look more closely at these arguments, and how a friend of the MAL might respond to them.

10.3 Alleged counterexamples to Humean Supervenience

10.3.1 How the counterexamples work

Many arguments of this kind have been given, some of them very sophisticated.[12] But for my purposes it will suffice to consider an extremely simple version. It is possible for the laws of nature to be exactly what Newton thought they were, and these laws are consistent with there being nothing in the universe save a single particle traveling eternally through the void with unwavering velocity. It is also possible for the laws of nature to be like Newton's laws except that the second law, force = mass times acceleration, is replaced by the law that force = mass times the square of acceleration. It is consistent with these modified Newtonian laws, too, for there to be nothing in the universe save one particle, traveling on its own forever with a constant velocity. Thus, we have two *lonesome-particle worlds*: one where the laws are Newtonian, and one where the laws are the modified Newtonian ones. These worlds have different laws of nature. Yet everything that actually goes on in them is exactly the same, so they have the same Humean base. So these worlds pose a direct counterexample to HS.[13]

As John Carroll has shown, this conclusion can be reinforced by considerations having to do with the way laws support counterfactuals.[14] Adapting Carroll's discussion to the lonesome-particle example, we get the following argument: suppose for the sake of argument that we are living in a Newtonian universe. Now, what would it be like if there were nothing but a solitary particle making an eternal, uniform trek across the void? This supposition is logically consistent with the laws of nature, so it seems that the laws should still have been exactly what they actually are even if it were true. So, we have this true counterfactual:

> If the lonesome-particle scenario were realized, then the laws would be the Newtonian laws.

[12] One example is Tooley's example concerning a universe containing particles of ten fundamental kinds; see Tooley (1977). Another is Carroll's Mirror Argument, presented in his (1994), chapter 3.

[13] Examples like these are presented in chapter 5 of Earman (1986) and in Lange (2000), pp. 85–90.

[14] See Carroll (1994), section 3.1.

It is obvious that if a counterfactual A $\Box\!\!\rightarrow$ C is true, and A is possible, then C must be possible as well, and so must be the conjunction of A and C. Since the antecedent of our counterfactual is obviously possible, so must be the conjunction of it with the consequent. Hence, it is possible that there is nothing but a lonesome particle and the laws are Newtonian. In other words, there is a lonesome-particle world where the laws are the Newtonian laws.

Now, consider beings living in a world where the laws of nature are the modified Newtonian laws considered above. They could go through exactly the same reasoning we just did, and their reasoning would be equally cogent. They would reach the conclusion that there is a lonesome-particle world where the laws are the modified-Newtonian ones. Hence, there is such a possible world.

In my (1998), I described a way in which a first-order Humean might reply to this argument. Carroll isn't convinced that this reply works, and I think it achieves at best a stalemate between the pro-HS and anti-HS positions. But I think an advocate of the meta-theoretic conception of laws is able to offer a much better reply.

10.3.2 How a meta-theoreticist can respond to the counterexamples

Suppose that the meta-theoretic conception of laws is correct. Then HS is true, so there is only one lonesome-particle world. Why does it seem to us as if there must be more than one?

On the meta-theoretic conception, the truth value of a law-statement is relative not only to the possible world at which it is to be evaluated, but also to the context from which it is to be evaluated. Suppose that we are in a context where the salient theory is that of Newtonian mechanics. Then, our statement 'Newton's second law of motion is a law of nature' will be true at the lonesome-particle world just in case both (a) Newton's second law plays the law role within the theory of Newtonian mechanics (it does!), and (b) the theory of Newtonian mechanics is true at the lonesome particle world (it is!). Now, consider a different context, in which the salient theory is the modified-Newtonian theory considered above. In this context, a statement of 'It is a law that $\mathbf{f} = \mathrm{m}\mathbf{a}^2$' is true just in case both (a) the equation in question plays the law role within the theory of modified Newtonian mechanics (which, presumably, it does), and (b) the modified Newtonian theory is true at the lonesome particle world (which it is).

When someone asks you to consider a possible world that is modified Newtonian in its laws, the salient theory in the context becomes the modified Newtonian theory.[15] So, in such a context, it is true that there exists a possible world at which the modified Newtonian laws are indeed laws of nature. For in such a context, it is true that at the lonesome-particle world, each law of the modified Newtonian theory is a law of nature, and no other proposition is. On the other hand, when someone asks you to assume for the sake of argument that we are living in a Newtonian universe, the salient theory becomes that of Newtonian mechanics. So in this context, it is true that the laws of nature in the lonesome-particle world are the laws of the Newtonian theory. Our 'two lonesome-particle worlds' which seemed to pose a counterexample to HS are not two distinct possible worlds; they are one possible world, considered from two different points of view—one possible world referred to in two different contexts of utterance. Since it's just one possible world, it does not have any incompatible properties; nonetheless, different things can be correct to say of it in different contexts of utterance. In this way, our modal and counterfactual reasoning can 'have access' to a lonesome-particle world with Newtonian laws in some contexts, and to a lonesome-particle world with modified Newtonian laws in other contexts, without there being anything at any genuinely possible world that threatens the truth of HS.

Now consider the reinforcement of the argument against HS by appeal to the counterfactual-supporting power of laws. Suppose for the sake of argument that we are living in a Newtonian universe. (I just made our context one in which the salient theory is Newton's.) Since the lonesome-particle scenario is consistent with everything that can be truly called a law—in fact, it is consistent with the lawhood of exactly the Newtonian laws—it is true that if that scenario had been realized, the laws would (still) have been the Newtonian ones. (This is a consequence of NP, which the MAL entails to be true in all scientific contexts.[16]) This is a true counterfactual with a possible antecedent, so the conjunction of its antecedent with its consequent is possible. Thus, there is a possible world at which there is nothing but a lonesome particle and the laws are Newtonian.

[15] See Section 3.3.8.

[16] NP was introduced in Chapter 5; in Chapters 8 to 9, the MAL was tailored to entail that NP is true in all possible scientific contexts.

Now, consider beings living in a modified Newtonian universe. They can go through a structurally identical argument, and arrive at the conclusion that there is a possible world at which there is nothing but a lonesome particle and the laws are modified Newtonian. Both our conclusion and theirs are correct, yet we have not discovered two distinct possible worlds. There is just one possible world here: the unique lonesome-particle world. But in our context, it is correct to say that the laws at this world are Newtonian; in their context, it is correct to say that the laws at this world are modified Newtonian. So both of our conclusions are true, even though there is no violation of HS. Moreover, after we have gone through the reasoning I described us going through, we can consider the fact that there are possible worlds where the laws are the modified Newtonian ones, and go through the same reason I just described the inhabitants of the modified Newtonian world as going through. At the end, we will reach the same conclusion they did. We, as well as they, can acknowledge a possible lonesome-particle world in which the laws are the modified Newtonian laws. It's just that in order to do that, we've got to take the extra step of getting ourselves into a context where the salient theory is the modified Newtonian theory—which we do when we follow an argument that begins with the words, 'Consider a possible world where the Newtonian laws are false, and the laws of nature are the modified Newtonian laws...'

This meta-theoreticist's reply to the alleged counterexamples to HS is much friendlier to our intuitions than any reply open to the first-order Humean. A first-order Humean who wants to defend HS against counterexamples like the lonesome-particle example must deny the reality of at least one possible world that seems, intuitively, to be possible. But the meta-theoreticist need not deny any such thing. She can give a reply to the counterexamples that does not involve saying that any claim about laws and possible worlds that is supported by our intuitions and mobilized in the anti-HS argument is false. According to her reply, after we have taken the steps in the thought-experiment that we are asked to take, we are exactly right to say that there are the kinds of possible worlds that we find it intuitive to say there are. We do not have to reject any claim we find pre-theoretically intuitive. All we have to do is adopt a new view of the truth conditions of law-statements. And none of the pre-theoretic intuitions marshaled by the anti-HS arguments have anything to say about the formal semantics of law-statements; they are just about which modal-nomological statements *are true*, not about what the truth conditions of those statements are. It might be countered that this meta-theoreticist reply to the counterexamples involves just as much violation of our pre-theoretic intuitions as does the first-order Humean reply; the only difference is that now we are violating semantic intuitions whereas before we were violating modal-nomological ones. But it is not very plausible that we have any 'pre-theoretic' intuitions about the context-dependence (or lack thereof) of our law-statements; this is a matter of formal semantics, a theoretical enterprise *par excellence*. And at any rate, the meta-theoretic account of the semantics of law-statements has an awful lot to say for it, as I have argued in Chapters 3 and 4, even if it seems surprising at first.

10.4 Governing and non-trivial necessity

There is still another worry about the meta-theoretic conception to consider. Since it implies HS, it seems natural to classify it as a Humean conception of laws. And the Humean way of thinking about laws is subject to an important objection that does not depend on generating counterexamples to HS. Namely, *the Humean picture of laws makes the laws out to be nothing more than grand patterns in a big mosaic of loose-and-separate states of affairs; thus it cannot do justice to the idea that the laws of nature govern the world, or to the idea that the laws enjoy a non-trivial kind of necessity*.

Of course, Humeans can reply: 'So much the worse for the outdated notion of a universe governed by necessary laws; laws of nature *govern* only in a metaphorical sense that cannot be rigorously cashed out; they are *necessary* only insofar as we find it useful to employ a modal operator defined in terms of them.'

I think we should resist giving this reply. As I argued back in Section 1.5, the notion of nomological possibility does some real work in scientific practice, and it is hard to see how it could do this work if the distinction between the nomologically possible and the nomologically impossible were just an artifact of the modal operators we happen to employ in our discourse. Furthermore, the notion of a universe governed by laws, vague as it may be, appears to have explanatory power, and much of the sense of understanding we get from modern natural science seems to depend on this power. Neither of these points is anything like a conclusive argument in favor of the idea that laws govern and are non-trivially necessary. But they do suggest that this idea is not to be dismissed lightly.

What reasons do Humeans offer for dismissing it? For one thing, the big-mosaic picture of the world seems to be more ontologically parsimonious than the alternative; for another, the Humean view of laws seems to be better than the alternative at making it intelligible how laws might be empirically discoverable; finally, Hume himself gave us reasons to think that the very concept of non-logical natural necessity involved in the non-Humean view of laws is unintelligible. These are all impressive considerations, even if there is room for philosophers to disagree about how they should be weighed against the advantages of the non-Humean view. The Humean case in a nutshell is that no matter how disadvantageous it is to throw out the concept of non-trivial nomological necessity and the idea of the law-governed universe, our hands are tied here: ontological considerations (Occam's Razor), epistemological considerations (whatever laws are, they had better be epistemically accessible to empirical science), and conceptual/semantic considerations (the concept of a law had better be intelligible) all militate against the non-Humean view of laws. It would be philosophically irresponsible not to embrace the big-mosaic view of the world.

But what if it turns out that we can have it all? That is, what if there is an account of laws available that satisfies all of the Humean's strictures, and yet provides a legitimate sense in which laws govern the world, and an acceptable account of non-trivial nomological necessity? Then the case for rejecting the idea of the law-governed universe would be seriously undercut. One could still retain doubts about whether there really are such things as non-Humean laws of nature, but the advantages of that view would still be there, and the argument that we cannot responsibly enjoy those advantages would have fallen away.

I say that we *can* have it all: the MAL is the account I have just been describing.

10.5 How the MAL lets us have it all

The MAL satisfies the Humean ontological stricture by positing a basic ontology no richer than that of the big-mosaic picture: that is to say, it is fully consistent with (and even entails) HS. It satisfies the Humean conceptual/semantic stricture: the truth conditions, in any context, of any law-statement, can be specified in terms that should be acceptable to a Humean. For the truth conditions it supplies are articulated solely in terms of the truth value of a theory formulated in non-nomological terms, and the relation between a theory and a proposition. As argued in Chapter 4, it satisfies the Humean epistemological stricture as well—or at the very least, the epistemological difficulties that beset first-order non-Humean accounts of laws do not threaten it.[17]

All those things are equally true of any meta-theoretic account of laws. What is special about the MAL is that it satisfies those Humean strictures while giving us what non-Humeans want. As we saw in Chapters 5 through 8, the MAL implies that there is a very strong sense in which laws support counterfactuals—in fact, the laws and the nomological truths support counterfactuals in the strongest way possible: in any scientific context, for any A that is consistent with the nomological truths, it is true that had A been the case, then the nomological truths would all still have been true.[18] This assigns to the nomological truths, in any possible scientific context, the maximal degree of counterfactual resilience: they are a set of true propositions that would still have been true, no matter how things had been different otherwise—so long as they weren't different by virtue of those very propositions being false. As Lange has argued, this is just the ordinary sense of 'necessity': that which is necessary is that which would still have been so no matter what else had happened (see e.g. Lange 2000, p. 105). For any old set of truths you like, you can define a modal operator □ such that □P is true just in case P is compossible with all the truths

[17] The qualification is needed because I have not, of course, provided a complete epistemology of science that shows that belief in laws can be empirically justifiable. That is a great task beyond the scope of this book. What I think I have established there is that a meta-theoretic account of laws is better placed than any first-order account—whether Humean or non-Humean—to allow for the possibility of empirical knowledge of laws. If laws are empirically discoverable at all, then some meta-theoretic account must be true.

[18] Recall that a 'nomological truth' is a truth of the form *it is a law that P* or *it is not a law that P*.

in that set. But not just any old set of truths is such that in any scientific context[19] every member of that set would still have been true under any counterfactual circumstances logically consistent with the set itself. Thus, the laws enjoy a status that deserves the name 'necessity,' and it is far from trivial that they do so.[20]

What about the idea that the laws govern? It is not entirely clear whether this idea differs from the idea that laws possess a brand of non-trivial necessity. Perhaps giving a clear sense to the notion that laws are necessary is sufficient for giving a clear sense to the notion that they govern the world: that which governs is that which constrains, and any non-trivial kind of necessity can be thought of as a kind of constraint. But this might be too quick. Clearly there is a non-trivial sense in which the truths of logic are necessary; are we 'governed' by the laws of logic? Maybe. But there is something uncomfortable about the idea. For it is natural to think of governing as a matter of drawing distinctions among possibilities, declaring some possibilities (or at least one) permitted and all others forbidden. The truths of logic don't seem to do this; they do not draw a distinction between two sets of ways the universe could behave, and tell the universe that the first set is allowed and the other set is not allowed. There simply are no possibilities in the forbidden set. A 'government' that forbids nothing except that which is not there to be done anyway is not a real government. Hence, for a set of truths to be necessary in some non-trivial sense does not seem to suffice for that set of truths to 'govern' in any robust sense.

But the kind of non-trivial necessity that the MAL attributes to the laws seems especially well suited to capture the intuitive notion of governing. Suppose the laws govern the universe, including us; what does this amount to? Well, for one thing, the laws deny us certain prospects—for example, the prospect of making something go faster than the speed of light, or that of building a perpetual-motion machine. That prospect is out there in logical space for us to grasp: we have a perfectly coherent and consistent conception of what it would be to achieve one of these prospects. Yet the laws tell us there is nothing we could do that would result in the

[19] Recall that I am construing 'scientific context' very broadly, so that it covers any context in which the aim of the discourse is to exposit, apply, or extend empirical knowledge of the natural world.

[20] Back in Chapter 5, I described the status of laws in terms of 'eternal inevitability,' which is plausibly construed as a kind of necessity—just the kind of necessity that non-Humeans take the laws of nature to enjoy.

achievement of such prospects: the truth of the laws implies that we will not achieve them, and their being the laws implies that no matter what else we did, we would not achieve them. And there's nothing special about us: in the same way that the lawhood of the laws implies that there is nothing we could do that would result in the falsity of a law, they also imply that there is nothing any finite natural agent could do that would have such a result. This seems to capture exactly one of the key elements of the intuitive notion that the universe, including us, is governed by the laws of nature: there are certain logical possibilities that are denied us by the lawhood of the laws; we natural creatures cannot do certain things, because no matter what we might do, those things would remain undone.

Thus, the MAL effectively attributes a kind of non-trivial necessity to the laws and provides a satisfying sense in which the universe is governed by the laws, and it does both in virtue of the relation between laws and counterfactuals that it implies. Does it not thereby supply everything that the non-Humeans want from an account of laws?

Some non-Humeans might object that it does not. For all of the non-Humean goodies that the MAL purports to give us rest on the relation between laws and counterfactuals. But the relation between laws and counterfactuals that the MAL provides is context-dependent, in two different ways. First, according to the MAL, the counterfactual stability of the laws is guaranteed to hold only in scientific contexts. Second, according to the MAL, which propositions are truly called laws (and so, which propositions are counterfactually stable, and thus necessary, and so govern the universe) can vary from scientific context to scientific context.[21] It could be objected that these two kinds of context-dependence do not fit well with the non-Humean picture of laws. The necessity and governance of the laws are, for the non-Humean, 'out there in the world,' and are not subject to the contingencies of evolving discursive contexts. Non-Humean laws have an 'oomph' to them, which is not a creature of us, our practices, or the changing characteristics of our discursive contexts. The 'oomph' of the laws is due to Nature itself; we do not have the power to create it. Any view of nomological necessity and the governing relation between laws and the world that makes the truth about them context-dependent fails to capture this. Or, so the objection goes.

[21] See Section 3.3.4.

First, let me respond to the worry about the first kind of context-dependence. The dependence of the necessity and counterfactual robustness of the laws on our being in a scientific context is not something we can avoid. As the God Cases show,[22] in many theological or metaphysical contexts, there are counterfactuals that violate the kind of necessity that laws enjoy—that is, counterfactuals in which the antecedent is compossible with the lawhood of exactly the actual laws, but the consequent is not. This is an inescapable consequence of the fact that the necessity of laws of nature is an aspect of the *natural* order: in any context where what is under discussion are supernatural or non-natural matters which are subject only to necessities other than the nomological, we are going to be able to exploit these other necessities to find violations of the counterfactual resilience of laws. More plainly: once we start talking about God, all bets are off. If it is a necessary truth that what God says goes, then surely this necessity outweighs whatever necessity the laws of nature enjoy, and this fact should be reflected in the counterfactuals.[23] So, this contextual limitation of the necessity-making counterfactual resilience of the laws is inescapable. Fortunately, it is not too painful to accept: the range of contexts in which the laws are counterfactually resilient in the way that makes for non-trivial necessity is extremely broad; it stops only at the border of the natural-scientific. In any scientific context—which means, any context in which the aim of the conversation is to exposit, apply, or extend our empirical knowledge of the natural world—laws exhibit their distinctive kind of counterfactual stability and hence their distinctive kind of necessity.

The second worry about context-dependence is that according to the MAL, within a single possible world different truths are laws of nature in different scientific contexts—even though in each scientific context, the truths that are laws are the ones that are necessary in the way distinctive

[22] See Section 6.2.

[23] This discussion does not presuppose theism, or that there are metaphysical or theological necessities that go beyond the nomological necessities. The important point is only that, so long as it is possible that there are supernatural or non-natural sources of the natural order, then there are possible contexts in which God Cases arise, and in any such possible contexts, there are true counterfactuals that violate the counterfactual stability of the laws. And it seems to me that we should prefer an account of laws and their necessity that is autonomous of theology, compatible both with theism and with its denial. Hence, our account of the necessity of laws ought to allow for the possibility of God Cases. That means that the counterfactual robustness of laws, which makes for their non-trivial necessity, should not be assumed to extend even to theological contexts.

of laws. So, in different scientific contexts, different truths are necessary in that way. But what kind of *necessity* is it that can shift from truth to truth as one moves from context to context?

The first thing to point out is that it is not as if the MAL allows us to make any proposition we like a law just by moving into the right conversational context. A proposition is correctly called a law in a context only if it plays the law role within some theory that is *true* in that context. These theories themselves are formulated in non-nomological terms, and are true or false at a given possible world independently of the context. And what propositions play the law role within a given theory is fixed by the necessary conditions formulated by the MAL. So the variability of the laws from context to context is not really that great or that flexible.

Still, the MAL does allow for the possibility that different propositions are laws in different contexts. Recall the example from Section 3.3.4 of the alien scientists who accept the theory T*, which differs from our own theory only with respect to some uninstantiated instances of a single functional law. In our context, one proposition is a law, and another is a true non-law; in the aliens' context, the verdict is reversed. Neither is 'really' a law, from a context-neutral perspective. So, which one belongs to a counterfactually stable set? Which one is non-trivially necessary, and plays a role in the government of the universe? The MAL, like any meta-theoretic account of laws, cannot give a context-neutral answer here. Does this undermine the pretensions of the MAL to satisfy the non-Humean demand for an account of non-trivially necessary laws governing the universe?

In order to address this worry, I need to say a little more about the picture of laws, counterfactuals, and necessity that the MAL puts forward. The context-dependence the MAL finds in statements about which propositions are nomologically necessary is a form of the context-dependence of counterfactuals. But it is not your garden-variety context-dependence of counterfactuals. In typical cases where a shift of context makes for a shift in the truth values of counterfactuals, what the shift of context does is change which features of the actual situation are most salient for the conversationalists. Thus, I can make it true that if I had pushed the button then there would have been an explosion by directing your attention to the way the wires are hooked up to the dynamite; then, I can make it true that if I had pushed the button then I would have made sure to disconnect the wires from the dynamite first, by directing your attention to my own obsessive concern for safety. I can make it the case that if Philip K. Dick had been a compatriot of Stanislaw Lem then Dick would have been Polish, and then make it the case that if Lem had been a compatriot of Dick then Lem would have been American, simply by changing the word-order of the conditionals that I assert. What I do in each case is cause one feature of the actual situation to stand out vividly before your mind, so that you will keep your eye on it and not let it shift around when you imaginatively visit other nearby possible worlds.

The way in which, according to the MAL, changes in context make for changes in what is correctly called a law (and so, in which counterfactuals are true) is not like this. The context we are in makes the propositions that are laws in this context counterfactually robust not because this context makes those propositions especially vivid before our mind. Rather, it is because in this context we are carrying out, or applying, or expositing, an empirical inquiry, and like all empirical inquiries this one requires that there are empirical procedures (crude or sophisticated) that we assume can be counted on as legitimate measurements. And to treat an empirical procedure as a legitimate measurement procedure *is* to treat it as counterfactually reliable. The principles that underwrite the reliability of these measurements are thus counterfactually stable, by virtue of a role they play in the present context. But we cannot change which principles play this role in the context simply by changing our minds about which features of the actual situation we are most interested in at the moment. To change our context in such a way as to change which propositions are counterfactually stable in the way that laws are, we would have to adopt a new set of commitments concerning what is a legitimate measurement procedure and what is not. That can be done, of course; as the history of science progresses, one of the things that changes is what gets counted as a legitimate measurement and what does not. But such changes cannot be effected simply by changing our interests, or by having someone draw a particular fact about the actual situation to our attention and thereby induce us to 'hold it constant' in our imagined trips to other possible worlds. Such a change has radical implications for which claims are empirically justified, and how it is possible to empirically justify a claim, for such a change modifies the very foundation (such as it is) of our practice of empirical justification.

For the MAL, there is context-to-context variation in the truth of law-statements, so there is such variation in the truth of statements about which propositions are nomologically necessary and govern the universe. But some things are true in any scientific context: there can be no context of scientific discourse—save ones in which the epistemic community of the participants accepts no true theories at all[24]—in which there is not a set of truths that are maximally counterfactually invariant. Which set of truths this is can vary from context to context, but this can happen only when there are changes in the factual, non-nomic presuppositions of the communities of the speakers, or radical revisions in the empirical epistemic practices of these communities (in particular, changes in which natural quantities are regarded as measurable), or both. In short, insofar as you are pursuing empirical knowledge of the natural world, it is not open to you not to be committed to the counterfactual stability of some set of truths, and it is open to you to change the identity of this set only when you acquire new factual knowledge of the world or revise your basic modes of empirical access to the world. Thus, the context-dependence of the laws and the counterfactuals (and so which propositions are non-trivially necessary and govern the universe) does not put them at the mercy of our whims. It is not something that we have 'a free choice' about in any significant sense. The truth of statements about what is a law, what is counterfactually stable, and what is non-trivially necessary are determined by what the non-nomic truths of our world are, what we know of these truths, and what our basic modes of empirical access to the world are. The laws are thus something we are *subject to*; they are not of our making.

Nonetheless, there *is* variability of the laws across possible scientific contexts. That might be enough to make the MAL unattractive to a philosopher of strong non-Humean proclivities. But the MAL does not fit the Humean mold, either. For it rejects the first three of the four elements of the Humean picture distinguished above: the counterfactual-supporting character of the laws is *not* a matter of which features of the world are most salient or important to us, but is rather determined by which true theories we accept and what quantities we can measure; there is a natural sense of necessity that the laws possess that goes beyond the trivial fact that it is always possible to define a modal operator in terms of some set of truths; this natural sense of non-trivial necessity captures the notion that the laws

[24] In which case there will be no true law-statements in the context. This is not a damaging qualification; a context in which no one knows anything about the natural world will be one in which we should not expect the counterfactuals to be very well behaved.

govern the universe. Moreover, the MAL does not purport to achieve an account of nomological necessity and governing simply by redefining those notions to fit its own picture of the world—as an advocate of Lewis's BSA might simply fashion Humean definitions of 'necessity' and 'governing' and then declare 'spoils to the victor.'[25] As I argued above, the notions of non-trivial necessity and governing offered by the MAL are well motivated on the basis of intuitive considerations of what those concepts amount to: necessity is a matter of being such that you would still have been true no matter what else had happened (so far as logical possibility allows this); natural governing is a matter of implying that certain acts that are logically possible not only will not be done, but could not have been done no matter what else had been done (again, so far as logical possibility allows). The fundamental special feature of the laws here is their counterfactual stability, and since the MAL respects the context-dependence of all non-trivial counterfactuals, this means that it introduces a certain context-dependence to all of these special features. That context-dependence might leave many non-Humeans unsatisfied. But it does not amount to an adoption of the standard Humean view, with its big mosaic of 'loose and separate' facts; it does not endorse the Humean claim that there is nothing special about the laws other than the fact that they provide a simple and informative summary of the world and we are consequently prone to treat them as especially important or salient.

10.6 Humeanism? Non-Humeanism?

The MAL does not fit the first three elements of the standard Humean view of laws and their relation to the universe. Yet, the MAL does include the fourth element of the Humean picture: Humean Supervenience. Because it does so, it is immune to the standard Humean complaints about the non-Humean picture: its ontology is no greater than that of the Humean; it does not render laws empirically undiscoverable; and it has no truck with an unexplicated and unintelligible notion of 'necessary connexions.'

So is the MAL a Humean account or not? The question is pointless. One could simply define a 'Humean' view of laws as one committed to HS,

[25] As Lewis seems to be willing to do in his (1994), pp. 478–9.

but this would deflate much of the meaning of the label. The concepts of 'Humean views' and 'non-Humean views' that have been at work in the literature on laws are cluster-concepts, and it turns out that the elements of the clusters do not necessarily cohere together. The MAL offers a way of combining the best elements of both clusters.

10.7 What is the significance of the idea of the law-governed universe?

Back in Chapter 1, I said that the philosophical problem of laws is important mainly because we want to answer the basic metaphysical question of what kind of universe we live in. Accepting the law-governed world-picture, I said, must have a profound effect on our world-view, but it is not clear what this effect should be. A good philosophical account of what laws of nature are and how they govern the universe should help us clear that up.

So, what effect should it have on our overall world-view if we accept the version of the law-governed world-picture I have been defending? I am afraid that what I have to say about this is disappointingly brief and sketchy. But since I advertised the importance of my topic by highlighting its connections to some perennial deep problems of philosophy, I should not end the book without addressing those connections at all.

10.7.1 Theism, atheism, laws, and explanation

To some people it seems that the law-governed universe points beyond itself to a supernatural creator; hence, the fact that science presents us with a picture of the universe as law-governed provides an argument for the existence of God. On the other hand, to some people it seems that the law-governed universe actually eliminates any need to call on God to do any explanatory work at all; hence, the fact that science presents us with a picture of the universe as law-governed provides an argument against the existence of God. It would be nice to find a good account of lawhood that settles this issue for us. The account of lawhood I have defended in this book does not settle the substantive question, but I think it does resolve this particular debate. For it implies that neither argument works: the argument from the law-governed world-picture to theism is a failure, and so is the argument from the law-governed world-picture to atheism. But there is something constructive to be learned from this. For both arguments fail because they both depend on a particular picture of how the creator would be related to the universe, if there were a creator. What the MAL teaches us about this issue is that if the law-governed world-picture is right, and the universe has a supernatural creator, then the relation between the creator and the universe is not as simple as it is often assumed to be.

Suppose that our universe is indeed governed by laws of nature. Now suppose, for the sake of argument, that our universe is the product of a supernatural creator. These two suppositions each say something about the explanatory structure of the universe. The law-governed picture tells us that things go as they do in our universe because they are constrained to go that way by laws that govern the course of events; the theistic picture tells us that the true ultimate explanation of the existence of the universe and of all its parts and aspects traces back to the creative acts of the deity. How can these two ideas fit together?

Let's start by focusing on the theistic picture. If that picture is right, then how exactly is the creator related to the universe? In other words, if there is a creator, then in what way do the creator's actions bring about the existence of this law-governed universe? This is a strange question, and it is natural to wonder what kind of answer I am looking for. I am not looking for any kind of deeper explanation of the creator's creative power, or for any kind of mechanism that might account for how a universe like ours comes into being out of nothingness. What I am looking for is an account of the plan and order of the creator's creative acts. So one possible answer is that the universe as a whole—presumably a great four-dimensional continuum filled with various sorts of contents—is conceived in the divine mind as a single unit, all at once, in a flash, and it is all created in one act. Each part of the universe and each aspect is there as part of the whole that was envisioned and actualized in a single act. So there is no part or aspect of it whose creation took any kind of precedence or priority over the creation of any other part or aspect. A very different sort of answer is that the creator creates the universe one instant of history at a time, making it up as he or she goes along. At each instant, the creator selects a possible state to put the universe in out of an infinite range of options; when the work of creation is complete, it will be a great serial, each part of which was written in a way unconstrained by what came before.

Both of those possible answers seem incompatible with the law-governed world-picture. If the universe is really governed by laws, then it seems that the true explanation of it must have a certain structure. That structure is the familiar one found in covering-law explanations: in the simplest cases, particular phenomena are explained by derivations from the laws of nature together with earlier conditions. Those earlier conditions may be explained by further derivations from the laws together with still-earlier conditions, and the laws might be themselves explained by derivations of them from more general laws. This means that there is a richly articulated structure of explanatory dependencies in the natural universe—something that would seem to be impossible if the whole four-dimensional world were envisioned and created in a flash, or if it were built up piece by piece out of loose-and-separate bricks.

This suggests that if the law-governed and theistic pictures are both true, then the creator must have a different sort of relation to the universe. The explanations that trace everything back to the creative acts of the deity must not be incompatible with the ones that attribute the character of our universe to an evolution governed by laws. And that suggests that the theistic explanations must graft smoothly onto the covering-law explanations without undermining them, yielding one comprehensive explanatory scheme. This leads us straight to a familiar account of how God made the universe: first, he selected the laws of nature and invested them with the authority to govern the universe; then, he selected an initial state for the universe, and placed it in that state; then, he sat back to let the universe unfold, evolving from that initial state in accord with those laws. This familiar account is flexible in many ways: it is consistent with the idea that the laws of nature are deterministic, but also that those laws institute stochastic processes whose outcomes are undetermined. It is consistent with the thought, common to Leibniz and the deists, that once the universe has been set up and allowed to start running, God will never interfere with it again, but also with the thought that God reserves the right to tinker directly with the course of events from time to time, authorizing exceptions to the laws (miracles) on a case-by-case basis. It is consistent with any number of different ideas about what might have been the motive for the creation in the first place. What is essential to the account is the thought that the act of creation involved two distinct acts: the setting-up of the laws of nature, and the setting-up of the initial state of the universe. These two things have to be kept separate, because they play such different roles in covering-law explanations: in order for the theistic explanation to graft smoothly onto the nomological explanatory structure without upsetting it, the theistic part of the story must explain (or at the very least, respect) the distinction between these two very different explanatory elements.

I am going to call that account of how this law-governed universe came into existence *the nomo-theological account*. It seems to be taken for granted both by a popular argument for theism, and a popular argument for atheism. The argument for theism goes roughly like this: in science, we seek hypotheses that explain the known phenomena; scientists have standards for evaluating the quality of putative explanations, and other things being equal, they prefer hypotheses that offer explanations that are better according to these standards. Now consider two grand explanatory hypotheses: one is the complete set of covering-law explanations offered by an ideal, completed science; the second is the first together with the hypothesis that the fundamental laws of nature and the initial conditions of the universe were selected and set up by an intelligent creator—in other words, the second is a complete articulation of the nomo-theological account. We are at present unable to spell out either of these grand explanatory hypotheses in much detail. But we are in a position to evaluate their relative explanatory virtues, as measured by the standards employed in science. The first traces all explanatory chains back to the fundamental laws of nature and the initial conditions of the universe, but it can offer no explanation for the fundamental laws and the initial conditions themselves; these must simply be taken as brute facts. By contrast, the second grand explanatory hypothesis explains both the fundamental laws and the initial conditions by appeal to the creative activity of God. It also explains by means of a simpler fundamental postulate; the existence of a supremely good being is less arbitrary and conceptually simpler than any plausible candidate for the basic laws of nature. What is more, the particular laws of nature we find in our universe are very special: unlike most possible sets of laws of nature, the ones we have lead to the kind of universe in which intelligent life can evolve and thrive. So the first grand explanatory hypothesis not only explains less than the second; it also suffers from the theoretical vice of positing very surprising and improbable brute facts in order to carry a heavy explanatory burden. In science, we prefer explanations that are simpler, explain more, and refrain from positing improbable brute facts in order to explain important phenomena. So, by the standards of science itself, the second hypothesis is preferable to the first. But the second hypothesis is just the explanation that theism believes in; the first hypothesis is the best that we can do if we adopt the view that the natural universe is all that is. Therefore, we have a good reason to believe in God, and this reason is of a piece with the reasons we have to accept successful scientific theories. (So concludes the theistic argument.)[26]

The argument for atheism proceeds in the same way as the argument for theism, except that it gives the opposite verdict on the competing virtues of the two grand explanatory hypotheses. What the second, theistic hypothesis adds to the first one does not augment its empirical content at all. It leads to no new predictions, and is not subject to any tests that are not simply tests of the first grand hypothesis. So what it adds is scientifically otiose; it is an idle wheel tacked on to a successful theory. What is more, the theistic hypothesis is not as simple as it claims to be: any being with the capability to design the physical universe and the means to bring it into existence must be enormously complex indeed. In sum, the first of our two grand explanatory hypotheses is preferable to the second, according to the standards employed in science. So we have good reasons, of the same kind as the reasons we have to accept good scientific theories, to believe that the explanatory buck stops with the fundamental laws of nature.[27]

The difference between these two arguments is very localized: they agree on everything except which of the two explanatory hypotheses gets a higher score when graded by the criteria that scientists use in deciding which theories to accept. The heart of the difference might be even more localized than that. For the most basic clash of intuitions here seems to be between this principle:[28]

> An absolutely perfect being would be very simple—in the same sense of 'simplicity' in which simpler hypotheses are rightly preferred to more complex ones in science.

[26] Arguments that follow this basic strategy have been given many times by many people; one recent example is Swinburne (1996).

[27] This argument, too, has appeared in many places. One example is Dawkins (1986), especially chapter 6.

[28] See Swinbrune (1996), pp. 43–7, for a case for this view.

and this one:[29]

> Any being capable of creating our universe would have to be very complex—in the same sense of 'complexity' in which simpler hypotheses are rightly preferred to more complex ones in science.

So if we could only find a manifestly correct analysis of the notion of simplicity that figures in scientific theory choice, and which validates one of these principles and invalidates the other, we might be able to sort out which argument wins.

I am afraid that I am pessimistic about our prospects for sorting out this particular tussle in a way that does not beg the question one way or the other. But if I am right, we do not need to do that, for both sides are mistaken. Both arguments take it for granted that if the law-governed world-picture is basically right, then if the theistic picture is basically right too, then covering-law explanations will need to meld smoothly with theistic explanations in the way they do according to the nomo-theological account. Hence (both sides assume), the question of whether we should believe in God comes down to how well the nomo-theological account measures up against the alternative. If the MAL is the right account of lawhood, though, the nomo-theological account cannot be right.

The easiest way to see this is to recall a conclusion from Chapter 8, Section 8.7.3 and Chapter 9, Section 9.7: according to the MAL, God's Own Theory of the universe has no laws. More precisely: the theory that contains all the truths about what goes on in the universe—the limiting case of a true scientific theory that sums up what would be known about the universe by an omniscient being—is such that no logically contingent proposition is a law relative to it. As spoken by God to himself or to another omniscient being, then, 'It is a law of nature that P' is always false, for any contingent proposition P. Neither an omniscient God creating the universe, nor a hypothetical omniscient being watching on as a Godless natural universe develops in its self-sufficient way, would conceive of the universe in question as a law-governed one. The law-governedness of the universe is something that shows up only from the perspective of a finite cognizer with only limited empirical access to information about the natural universe. To put that point more precisely:

[29] See Dawkins (1986), p. 200.

there are truths of the form 'P is a law of nature' (where P is not a strictly necessary truth) only in conversational contexts where the body of presupposed information about the universe is incomplete. To put the point more colorfully: if we could take the 'view from nowhere' upon the universe, we would not see any laws of nature—although we do see a law-governed universe no matter which 'view from somewhere' we take.

What does this mean for the question about the relation between God and the laws of nature? Well, if it is legitimate to think of all that goes on in the natural universe as somehow explanatorily traceable back to God, then this tracing-back must not follow the path outlined in the nomo-theological account: it must not be that God made the universe *by means of* selecting a set of laws of nature and selecting an initial state, putting the world in that initial state, imposing those laws of nature on it to govern its evolution, and letting it run. For the very distinction between laws of nature and other features of the world is one that cannot show up from the point of view of God, or any other omniscient being.

It does not follow that there is no supernatural creator whose plan for the universe in some way explains what happens. There may be some coherent way to achieve a fusion of traditional monotheistic theology and modern natural science. But the nomo-theological account is not it. Explanations of the universe in terms of divine creative acts, and explanations of it in terms of law-governed evolution, cannot be grafted smoothly together into a single coherent explanatory structure. So if both kinds of explanation exist, then they must have some other mode of co-existence; perhaps they are fundamentally different kinds of explanation, neither of which interferes with the other.

So philosophical debate between theists and atheists would be more fruitful if it left behind the nomo-theological account and the question of its merits as a scientific hypothesis. A better strategy for the theist would be to try to articulate the non-scientific kind of explanation that theism supplies, show that this kind of explanation need not interfere with scientific covering-laws explanations, and argue that we have good reason to believe that the world has this kind of explanation in addition to a scientific explanation. A better strategy for the atheist would be to try to argue that the idea of such a non-scientific kind of explanation is an illusion.

10.7.2 Freedom and responsibility

The idea that the universe is governed by laws of nature seems to threaten our sense of ourselves as free and responsible agents. If all natural events are under the jurisdiction of the laws, and our actions themselves are among these natural events, and the laws are inevitably true, then it seems that our actions themselves are inevitable in a way that is not compatible with our responsibility for them. Even if the laws themselves are statistical, so that the inevitability of the laws themselves does not make each one of our actions inevitable, this seems to provide little help.

Of course, I cannot take on the difficult topic of freedom and responsibility in any serious way here. But I want to note one apparent implication of the MAL that seems important for that topic: if the MAL is correct, then the inevitability that characterizes the laws of nature is something that must exist in the world in order for us to be free and responsible agents at all. Therefore, if the MAL is correct, then either the very idea that we are free and responsible agents is compatible with the law-governedness of the universe, or else that idea is incompatible with something that it necessarily implies and is therefore self-undermining. So the law-governed world-picture itself poses no threat to our freedom and responsibility: either the idea that we are free and responsible is self-undermining to begin with, or else it can be true right alongside the law-governed world-picture. One might have thought there was a third possibility here, namely that we are free and responsible beings living in a universe that is not governed by laws of nature; this third possibility is closed off if the MAL is the right account of lawhood.

Why do I say this appears to be an implication of the MAL? One important part of what it is for us to be free and responsible agents is our epistemic responsibility. If it cannot ever be to our credit when we form true beliefs about our surroundings, or to our blame when we form false ones, then much of our structure of practices for assigning credit and blame for our actions fails to make sense; so does our conception of ourselves as responsible for much of what we do. Back in Chapter 8, I argued that the laws of nature are inevitably true because our basic procedures of empirical measurement and observation are counterfactually reliable. If these procedures were not counterfactually reliable, then it would just be a matter of epistemic good luck when our most basic empirical beliefs are true. I argued that if the truth of our most basic empirical beliefs is a matter of epistemic luck, then they cannot be the primary source of evidence supporting our scientific knowledge. Or to put the point the other way around: necessarily, if scientific knowledge deserves the name 'knowledge,' and observations and measurements are the ultimate source of evidence supporting that knowledge, then it cannot just be a matter of epistemic good luck that those observations and measurements are generally reliable. They must be counterfactually reliable too, and their counterfactual reliability is what turns out to make the laws of nature inevitable. What is more, if the truth of most of our most basic empirical beliefs were just a matter of epistemic good luck, then we would not really be epistemically responsible. So, it is not only the status of natural science as legitimate knowledge, and the status of observation and measurement as the ultimate evidential basis of that knowledge, that requires the inevitable truth of the propositions we call laws of nature; our status as free and responsible agents requires this inevitable truth as well.

10.8 Where in the world are the laws of nature?

Back in Section 10.7.1, I introduced a slogan: you can see no laws of nature when you take the 'view from nowhere,' but no matter which 'view from somewhere' you take, you will see a law-governed universe. Let me close this book by spelling out what that slogan means.

I assume that we have epistemic access to the character of the natural world only via the methods of empirical science. The products of these methods—scientific theories—are such that they *have laws*. Their laws are the parts of their contents that secure the measurability of the properties and quantities they refer to. No complete body of scientific theory can be without laws, for anyone engaged in the activity of doing science or applying science must be committed to the legitimacy of some methods of measuring some quantities. Being committed to a theory that has laws is part of the price of accepting any body of scientific theory.

Once you are committed to a theory that has certain laws, you are committed to the proposition that those laws govern the universe, in the sense that they are counterfactually stable: while doing or applying science, you must evaluate counterfactuals in a way that respects the principle that the laws of your theory would still have been true, and would still have been the laws, however things might have been different otherwise. The source of this commitment lies in three facts: first, scientific activity as such involves recognizing legitimate measurement methods as the sole source of ultimate evidence; second, recognizing something as a source of ultimate evidence involves regarding it as not merely *de facto* reliable, but rather as counterfactually reliable; and third, the laws of a scientific theory are exactly the propositions that express the reliability of the measurement methods that theory calls legitimate.[30]

We cannot theorize about the natural universe otherwise than as governed by some set of laws. The force of this 'cannot' is epistemic: the only epistemically justified means of theorizing about the workings of the natural universe available to us is the empirical-scientific way, and the norms of scientific practice require deferring to measurements as the ultimate source of evidence, and treating measurement methods as counterfactually reliable, and the counterfactual reliability of measurement methods is what the law-governedness of the universe consists in. Thus, the reason why we must represent the universe as law-governed, and what this law-governedness amounts to, are both grounded in the nature of the manner of justified theorizing that is available to us. You might put this by saying that the law-governedness of the universe is grounded in *our way of representing the universe*, rather than in *the universe that we represent*. Some philosophers will call this a disappointing non-realism about laws of nature; it portrays the laws as 'projected onto the universe by us.' But the view I have defended implies that the law-statements we make are either true or false, independently of what we happen to believe, so it is a realist view in an important sense. And it is not friendly to projectivism, since it leaves no room for us to be able to describe on the one hand a lawless universe 'as it is in itself,' and on the other hand, human activity that makes laws and projects them onto the lawless universe. A law-governed universe is the only kind of universe that we can have any justification for believing in.

[30] Or more precisely: those together with their logically contingent logical consequences.

APPENDIX

The MAL in action: A few examples of scientific theories and their laws

In this Appendix, I will apply the MAL to a handful of typical theories that seem to posit laws of nature. In each case, the MAL implies a definite answer to the question, 'Which of the propositions implied by this theory are among its laws, and which are its nomological contingent implications?' It turns out that in each case, the answer implied by the MAL agrees with our common judgments.

All the examples that I address in detail here come from physics. But there is no obvious reason to think that the MAL implies that only physics has laws, and I suspect that the MAL implies that many theories from the special sciences have laws too. For example, perhaps the principle of natural selection is a law of the Neo-Darwinian theory of evolution, on the grounds that it underwrites the reliability of methods of measuring fitnesses; perhaps Dalton's law of partial pressures counts as a law of modern chemical theory, on the grounds that it underwrites the reliability of methods of measuring the number of moles of a given gas in a mixture; perhaps some of the generalizations of econometrics provide methods of measuring the values of some economic variables by performing computations on the measured values of other variables, and thereby count as laws of econometrics.

But the main purpose of this Appendix is to test the MAL by comparing its implications with our common judgments about what the laws of various theories are; physical theories work better for this purpose, because these judgments seem to be more clear and unanimous in the case of physics than in the cases of other sciences. For example, no one doubts that Maxwell's equations are laws of electrodynamics (even though their name does not contain the word 'law'), but it is not obvious whether it is really a law of ornithological theory, or simply a nomologically contingent local consequence of evolution, that ravens are black.

A.1 NEWTON'S THEORY AS A PARADIGM EXAMPLE

Consider the contents of Books I and III of Newton's *Principia* (Newton 1999) as a single theory; let's call the theory N.

Part of this theory's content consists of laws—laws of N, if not laws of nature. But not all of it does: it also contains many claims that are, from the point of view of N, nomologically contingent. These include, for example, that the solar system contains six planets, all of which move around the sun in the same direction (namely, counterclockwise, if the solar system is viewed from above earth's north pole). Any plausible meta-theoretic account of laws ought to get this right: it ought to turn out that the propositions of N that have the word 'law' in their familiar names—the three laws of motion, and the law of universal gravitation—play the law role in N, and none of the propositions about the contents and arrangement of the solar system do. Let us see how things turn out if the law role is what the MAL says it is.

The MAL takes a theory to consist of a theoretical part and an empirical interpretation. The theoretical part of N includes all of the following propositions: the existence of absolute space and time, the three laws of motion, the law of universal gravitation,[1] and that the solar system fits the description given in Book III: there are a sun and six planets, with each planet in an approximately elliptical orbit with the sun at one focus, all these orbits lying approximately in a common plane, with the planets going around the sun in the same direction, and so on. So it also entails every proposition in the deductive closure of these. The theoretical quantities of N include masses, forces (that is, individual component forces, such as the gravitational force impressed on the moon by the earth), time intervals, (absolute and relative) positions, velocities, accelerations, and so on, as well as all quantities defined as functions of these. The empirical interpretation of N will include a designation of procedures for measuring many of these quantities (many of these are not explicitly described in the *Principia*, but would have been taken for granted by its intended readers). These procedures include ones for measuring time intervals, relative positions, relative velocities, absolute accelerations, and weights of terrestrial objects. They also include procedures for measuring other quantities that are functions of these, as well as any additional quantities that can be measured via methods that N's propositions entail to be reliable and that use pointer variables that are themselves measurable. Recall from Section 8.7.2. that the legitimate measurement methods relative to a theory are 'closed under the theory,' so that not all these methods need have been mentioned (or even thought of) by Newton or his intended audience.

The MAL says that the laws of N are the propositions that are in the deductive closure of the reliability conditions of the legitimate measurement methods of N. These are propositions of the form:

R: Whenever C, then K(P, Q)

[1] Here I am simply calling these propositions by their familiar names, which contain the word 'law.' I am not presupposing that they are laws of N according to the MAL. But it is clear that they had better turn out to be laws of N according to the MAL, if the MAL is to be at all plausible.

where C is a set-up condition, P is the pointer variable, Q is the object variable (the quantity getting measured), and K is a positive correlation relation that may be either strict or statistical. Since Newton's theory does not ascribe any objective probabilities, the correlation relations that are entailed by the theoretical part of N[2] will all be strict correlations (that is, P will be correlated with Q in the sense of being *equal* to some function of Q). It does not follow from this that given N, all measurement methods are perfectly reliable. For a strict correlation means that Q can be measured in a perfectly reliable way only if P can be measured in a perfectly reliable way. The basic measurement methods will have limitations of both precision and reliability, and these will carry over to all measurements made via the methods whose reliability is guaranteed by the reliability conditions entailed by N.[3]

What we must show in order to vindicate the MAL for the case of the theory N is that every instance of the propositions we think of as the laws of N is a consequence of the reliability conditions of the legitimate measurement methods relative to N, and that no proposition of N that we do not think of as a law of N is.

A.1.1. The laws of N

The first two laws of motion Consider first the second law of motion: for every body at every time, the total impressed force on that body is equal to its mass multiplied by its acceleration. This proposition serves as the reliability condition for a certain class of measurement procedures: those in which the pointer variable is one of the three quantities it relates, and the object variable is the appropriate function of the other two; those in which the object variable is one of the three quantities it relates, and the pointer variable is the appropriate function of the other two; and those in which the object variable is one of the three related quantities, the pointer variable is one of the others, and the set-up conditions require that the third have been empirically determined to have a particular value. In each case, the correlation relation K is equality. Since acceleration is a basic measurable of

[2] This excludes the correlation relations in the reliability conditions of basic methods of measurement such as determining the position of a needle by eyeballing it. The reliability of those sorts of measurement procedure belongs to the empirical interpretation of N, and is not within the scope of its theoretical part.

[3] Recall from Section 8.7.2. that a *basic measurable* is a theoretical quantity that is measurable according to the theory, but not because the theory itself entails that a particular method of measuring it is reliable. (They are *not* necessarily quantities referred to in a 'pure observation language,' or whose values are among 'the Given,' or anything like that.) The basic measurables of N will presumably include displacements and spatiotemporal coincidences. Since we are only able to estimate these to within a certain degree of precision and subject to measurement errors, this will also be true of all measurement methods whose reliability is assured by reliability conditions entailed by N. A full analysis of the reliability of actual measurements that can be carried out in practice would no doubt include a statistical theory of measurement errors. But the probabilities or frequencies employed in this analysis will not be derived from N itself; they will be derived from theories or empirical studies of actual human measurements.

N, it follows that at least one of the three related quantities is eligible for use as a pointer variable. The set-up conditions of none of these methods requires anyone to take any testimony, and the values of all the pointer and object quantities in particular cases of the uses of these methods are not already part of the content of N. None of these methods is a 'calibration-skipping method,' since the reliability of each is entailed by Newton's second law of motion, which does not specify the value of any measurable quantity. Hence, at least some of the methods for which the second law of motion serves as reliability condition are legitimate measurement methods relative to N. So, the second law is among the laws of N, according to the MAL.

The first law of motion is a direct consequence of the second law; hence, it counts as a law of N. There is a case to be made for denying that the first law is 'merely a special case' of the second law. For example, the first law can be seen as providing a criterion for inertial frames of reference, without which the second law cannot even be properly stated. But this point can be granted without denying that the first law is a deductive consequence of the second law (which it manifestly is). The latter point is all that I need here.

The third law of motion The third law of motion states that for every force exerted by one body on another, there is a force of equal magnitude and opposite direction exerted by the second on the first. This law is a consequence of the set of all of its special cases, and each of its special cases can serve as a reliability condition expressing the reliability of some method of measurement. One simple paradigm case is that of a measurement of the tension in a rope. Suppose that a rope is attached to a hook, hanging down vertically from the point of its attachment, and at the other end it is attached to a stone. The third law of motion tells us that the force exerted by the stone on the rope is equal and opposite to that exerted by the rope on the stone. If we can measure the weight of the stone, as well as its acceleration (which is of course zero in the case as described), then if conditions are such that we are justified in believing that no non-negligible forces act on the stone other than its weight and that exerted on it by the rope, then we have a way of measuring the force exerted on the stone by the rope: it will be equal in magnitude and opposite in direction to the gravitational force on the stone (by Newton's second law). Then we can use the third law of motion to determine the force exerted by the stone on the rope: it is equal in magnitude and opposite in direction to that exerted on the stone by the rope; hence it is equal in both magnitude and direction to the gravitational force on the stone. (A similar procedure allows us to determine the forces exerted by the rope on the hook and vice versa: if the rope is motionless (has zero acceleration), then by the second law of motion and the results just found, the hook exerts on the rope a force equal in magnitude and opposite in direction to the gravitational force on the stone; by this and the third law of motion the force exerted on the hook by the rope has the same magnitude and direction as the gravitational force on the stone.)

The reliability of the method employed to measure the force exerted by the stone on the rope is expressed by the following:

> The force exerted by the stone on the rope = −(the force exerted by the rope on the stone)

which has the form of a reliability condition: the object variable here is the force exerted by the stone on the rope; the pointer variable is the force exerted by the rope on the stone (which is measurable by a method employing the second law of motion); and the enabling condition C is the trivial condition that is automatically satisfied. This reliability condition is obviously just one instance of the third law of motion. Every instance of the third law in which the force on one side of the equation is measurable will similarly be a reliability condition expressing the reliability of a possible measurement. Again, the method does not involve taking testimony concerning the results of distinct measurements, and its reliability is not beholden to any specifications N makes of the values of particular measurable quantities. It follows that the MAL implies that every instance of the third law of motion is a law of Newton's theory, from which it follows that the third law itself is a law of Newton's theory.

The law of universal gravitation Things are more tricky with the case of the law of universal gravitation. It states that for every pair of bodies $<B_1, B_2>$ B_1 exerts an attractive force on B_2 the magnitude of which is given by the following equation:

$$|\mathbf{F}_{12}| = \frac{GM_1M_2}{D_{12}^2}$$

where $\mathbf{F}_{12}$ is the force exerted by body B_1 on body B_2, G is the gravitational constant, M_1 and M_2 are the masses of B_1 and B_2 respectively, and D_{12} is the distance separating the two bodies. Equivalently:

$$M_1 = \frac{|\mathbf{F}_{12}|\, D_{12}^2}{GM_2}$$

which is a reliability condition for a method of measuring the mass M_1 of body B_1. For the expression on the right-hand side of this equation is a function of quantities each of which are measurable according to N: masses, distances, impressed forces, and the gravitational constant (which is measurable via an experiment like that of Cavendish[4]). This equation thus expresses the relation between the pointer variable and the object variable in a method of measuring the mass of body B_1. Depending on what kind of body B_1 is, it might be carried out in a laboratory using a Cavendish-type torsion-balance experiment, or by means of astronomical observations. In either case, actually employing the method will require that it is possible to measure the gravitational force impressed by B_1 on B_2; such

[4] Cavendish (1798).

measurements can be performed, though their execution conditions require that all of the other component forces acting on B_2 are either negligible or else measurable in some other way. So measurements of this kind are far from trivial to carry out; nonetheless, we have here a method of empirically determining the mass of B_1, this method is in principle possible to carry out if N is true, and this method qualifies as a measurement method relative to N. Of course, a carrying-out of this method must include measurements of all the various measurable quantities on the right-hand side of the last equation. In practice, scientists might simply rely on past measurements of, say, G or M_2. But this shows only that there are calibration-skipping methods (of the kind discussed in Section 8.6.4.) whose reliability is guaranteed (in part) by instances of the law of universal gravitation; every such method is, however, a shortcut version of a genuine measurement method.

In short, each instance of the law of universal gravitation is equivalent to a reliability condition for a method of measurement, and so each instance is a law of N. Therefore, the law of universal gravitation is a consequence of the whole set of such reliability conditions; so by the MAL, it is a law of N.

A.1.2. The non-laws of N

Consider first the proposition that there are six planets in the solar system. What measurement method is guaranteed reliable by this proposition? It seems that none are. This proposition does guarantee the reliability of many methods of reaching judgment about the number of planets in the solar system. One such method is to multiply the first two prime numbers together, and form the judgment that the number of planets in the solar system is equal to the product. But this fails to be a legitimate measurement method relative to N, since it is ruled out on natural-almanac grounds: N itself entails what the values of the pointer variable and the object variable will be every time the method is employed.

Consider next the proposition that all of the planets go around the sun in the same direction. This does not seem to guarantee the reliability of any measurement methods, either. It does enable us to determine the orientation of one planet's orbit by means of determining the orientation of some other planet's orbit. But the orientation of the second planet's orbit is already specified by the theory N itself, so this method too fails to count as a measurement method on natural-almanac grounds (see Chapter 8, Section 8.6.).

There are other methods that are guaranteed reliable by parts of N that include apparently nomologically contingent propositions. But these are similarly ruled out as legitimate measurements relative to N. Here is one example: if we construe the theory N as including a proposition about the mass and radius of the earth, and as specifying the value of the gravitational constant,[5] then one of its consequences

[5] This is anachronistic, of course.

is that the acceleration due to the gravitational force near the surface of the earth is approximately 9.8 meters per second per second, and another is that the non-gravitational force required to hold an object at rest near the surface of the earth is equal to its mass times this acceleration. Thus, this theory entails the reliability of the following method of measuring the mass of a stone on earth: use a spring scale or some other method of measuring the weight of the stone in newtons, and then divide the result by 9.8 meters per second per second. But it is not guaranteed by what we ordinarily think of as the laws of Newton's theory that such a method is reliable, for it is not a consequence of the laws of Newton's theory that the earth has the mass and radius that it does. So it will be a big problem for the MAL if it implies that the principle that guarantees the reliability of this method is a law of N.

Fortunately, the MAL does not imply this. The method of determining the mass of the stone in question is exactly the shortcut scale method discussed in Section 8.6.4., my paradigm example of a calibration-skipping method that does not count as a legitimate measurement method in its own right.

A.2 CLASSICAL SPECIAL-FORCE LAWS

One way of modifying Newton's theory is to add additional special-force laws to it: for example, Hooke's law of the spring force, or Coulomb's law of electrostatic attraction. It is pretty clear that Hooke's law is a law of the theory that results from adding it to Newton's theory, and that Coulomb's law is a law of the theory that results from adding it to that theory. The MAL saves this phenomenon.

Consider first Hooke's law: it says that for any object that we call a *spring*, compressing or stretching the spring from its equilibrium point and thus decreasing or increasing its length will result in a force that tends to restore it. The force is given by this equation:

$$F = -kx$$

where F is the strength of the force on an end of the spring, x is the difference between the spring's present length and its length when at equilibrium, and k is a positive constant that is characteristic of the spring, which I'll call the *elasticity constant*.

The theory that consists of N plus Hooke's law contains an additional theoretical quantity that N alone lacks: the elasticity constant of a given spring. The instances of Hooke's law are trivially equivalent to equations of the form:

$$k = \frac{-F}{x}$$

which is the reliability condition for a method of measuring the elasticity constant k for a given spring. Hence, all instances of Hooke's law are laws of the theory in question; therefore so is Hooke's law itself.

Coulomb's law states that any two electrically charged bodies exert a mutual force given by an equation of the same form as the universal law of gravitation, but with the charges of the bodies in place of their masses. So just as the instances of the law of gravitation are all reliability conditions for methods of measuring the mass of a body, so are the instances of Coulomb's law reliability conditions for measuring the charge of a body. The argument here goes exactly the same as it did there, with 'charge' substituted for 'mass.' Hence, Coulomb's law does indeed play the law role within the theory that consists of N plus Coulomb's law.[6]

There is a general pattern here that we can reasonably expect to repeat itself in any other cases of additions of special-force laws to Newtonian mechanics: the special force in question is given by an equation in which some new theoretical quantity characterizing the object exerting the force and/or the object on which the force is exerted, and the instances of this equation provide correlation conditions for methods of measuring this new theoretical quantity. So the equation is a law of the theory that includes it.

A.3 GEOMETRICAL OPTICS AND ONE OF ITS LAWS

Consider a simple theory of geometrical optics—call it GO—which includes the law of refraction: for any light ray that crosses the boundary between two transparent dieletric media, the following equation holds:

$$n_1 \sin\theta_1 = n_2 \sin\theta_2 \qquad \text{(A.1)}$$

where n_1 and n_2 are the refractive indices of the two media, and θ_1 and θ_2 are the angles with which the light ray approaches the boundary and leaves the boundary, respectively—i.e., the angle of incidence and the angle of refraction. Intuitively, whatever else GO includes, the law of refraction should count as one of its laws. And according to the MAL, it does: for we can use the above equation as the reliability condition of a measurement procedure in which the ratio between two refractive indices are measured using the ratio between the sines of the two angles (which are presumably basic measurables of GO) as the pointer variable.

Suppose GO also includes the proposition that a particular object—say, the transparent block I use as a paperweight—has a refractive index of 0.5. Intuitively, this should not count as a law of GO; it is a nomologically contingent fact about the properties my paperweight happens to have. Does it count as a law of GO according to the MAL?

Here is an argument that it does: one method of measuring the refractive index of a given chunk of some medium is hold a flat face of it right up against my paperweight, shine a light beam through the chunk and into my paperweight,

[6] Note that this theory is not that of classical electrodynamics; it is (a fragment of) that of classical electrostatics.

measure the angles of incidence and refraction, take the sines of the two angles, find the ratio of the sine of the angle of refraction to the angle of incidence, and multiply by 0.5 (the known index of refraction of my paperweight) to get the index of refraction of the given chunk. The reliability of this procedure is guaranteed by GO; it's reliability condition can be written (suppressing the set-up condition C) as follows:

$$X = 0.5 \frac{\sin \theta_1}{\sin \theta_2} \tag{A.2}$$

Equations A.1 and A.2 are both consequences of GO. Applying both of them to a single situation in which the method just described yields:

$$\frac{\sin \theta_1}{\sin \theta_2} = \frac{X}{0.5}$$

and:

$$\frac{\sin \theta_1}{\sin \theta_2} = \frac{X}{\text{(the index of refraction of my paperweight)}}$$

Therefore: the index of refraction of my paperweight is 0.5. So, this fact about my paperweight is a consequence of two laws of GO; so it is itself a law of GO. This is an unwelcome result.

Fortunately for the MAL, this argument doesn't work. For equation A.2 is not a law of GO, according to the MAL. It is indeed the reliability condition of an empirical method for determining indices of refraction which is reliable if GO is true. But this method is not a legitimate method of measurement relative to GO. It is a calibration-skipping method, since its reliability is not entailed by any sub-theory of GO that does not entail that my paperweight's index of refraction is 0.5 but does entail that indices of refraction are measurable. For, in order to entail the latter, it would have to entail the law of refraction (equation A.1), and if it entailed both that and the reliability of the method in question, it would entail equation A.2—and we have seen already that any theory that entails both of those also entails that my paperweight's index of refraction is 0.5. This example illustrates why the exclusion of calibration-skipping methods (introduced back in Section 8.6.4.) is so important to the way the MAL works.

A.4 LOCAL DETERMINISTIC FIELD THEORIES

Suppose that FT is a local, deterministic theory of fields. That is, suppose that it is a physical theory with the following properties:

(1): FT posits the existence of one or more fields, represented mathematically as differentiable functions that assign values (which may be scalars, vectors, or tensors) to each point of space-time.

(2): FT includes field equations that are local and deterministic.

The *locality* of these equations consists in the fact that they impose only mathematical relations among the values of the fields and their derivatives at each point; they do not directly impose any relations among the values of fields or their derivatives at different points. Each bounded space-time region R has a *domain of dependence* D(R), which is a region such that if the values of all fields and their derivatives throughout R are specified, then the field equations determine their values at all points in D(R).[7] So, for example, in a special-relativistic field theory, a point p is in D(R) just in case R includes a complete space-like cross-section of one of the two lobes of p's light-cone. The *determinism* of the field equations consists in the fact that each finite, bounded region of space-time is within the domain of dependence of some disjoint region; that is, there is no region within space-time where the values of the fields and their derivatives are unconstrained by what is going on everywhere and everywhen else.

(3): FT might also include some information in addition to the above equations—for example, that there are nine planets, or that all the coins in Goodman's pocket on VE day were made of silver. (All of these facts will of course have to be translated into field-theoretic terms.)

The set of propositions entailed by the theoretical part of T is just the deductive closure of all the information mentioned in 2 and 3.

(4): Certain functions of the values of the fields and their derivatives, and all quantities definable in terms of these functions, are among the basic observables of FT, so that they can serve as pointer variables in measurements.

(5): Any field value at a given space-time point is in principle measurable given T.

Many real physical theories share these features—classical and special relativistic electrodynamics (construed as a field theory rather than a theory of fields and particles), for example. It might be objected that these theories consist of their field equations, and they do not contain any of the additional information mentioned in 3. But with a little license, we can take FT to be the background knowledge presumed by a community of scientists who take for granted a theory like the ones just described as well as some other salient facts—e.g., where their lab is located, what they have in their pockets, what time they usually break for lunch, etc. My motivation for including the information in 3 in the content of FT is that I want to argue that even if the information in 3 belongs to FT, it will not belong to the laws of FT, according to the MAL. Thus, nothing in 3 will get to count as a law of FT, which is what our intuitions would lead us to expect.

Given FT, how could you design a measurement method? Suppose that the pointer variable P is a function of the field values (or, the values of the fields and

[7] Earman (1986), p. 58.

their derivatives) in some region R_P; the set-up condition C requires that the fields satisfy certain conditions within some region R_C; and the object variable Q is some function of the field values (or, the values of the fields and their derivatives) in a region R_Q. Since C must entail that there is a correlation between P and Q, it follows that R_Q had better be inside the domain of dependence of $R_P \cup R_C$. The correlation condition, then, will take the form:

Whenever C, then Q = f(P)

for some function f. We can reformulate this as a condition that says that given that the field values (and their derivatives) satisfy certain constraints throughout $R_P \cup R_C$, they must also satisfy certain constraints in a certain region within that region's domain of dependence:

E: if $H_i(R_P \cup R_C)$ then $K_i(R_Q)$

where '$H_i(R_P \cup R_C)$' means that the fields in region $R_P \cup R_C$ satisfy the constraint that C is true and the value of P is P_i (where P_i is any possible value of P), and '$K_i(R_Q)$' means that the fields in region R_Q satisfy the constraint that the value of Q equals f(P_i).

E expresses a constraint that the fields in one region exert, in the light of the field equations, on the fields in that region's domain of dependence. Any such constraint could be written in the form of E. But the field equations themselves are exhausted by their consequences of the form E: all of the constraints that the field equations impose on the field are captured by constraints of the form, 'If it is like so in region R, then it must be like thus in the domain of dependence of region R.'

Hence, the correlation conditions corresponding to legitimate measurement methods relative to FT have the same deductive closure as the field equations of FT. The laws of FT are exactly its field equations.

And intuitively, the deductive closure of these equations is the set of laws of a theory of this kind. That's a significant victory for the MAL. Relative to this kind of physical theory, the MAL says that the laws are exactly what we intuitively take the laws of the theory to be.

One might object to this argument as follows. The information in clause (3) of T might include e.g. that all electrons have charge q, that all electrons have spin ½, that all electrons have mass m. Of course, T was defined as a theory of fields, rather than a theory of particles; but perhaps this problem can be finessed: perhaps we can identify particles with regions of space-time in which the field values (which might include mass density, charge density, etc.) satisfy certain constraints, and identify the mass of a particle, spin of a particle, etc. with certain properties of the field values in the region identified with an electron. The proposition that all electrons have a certain charge, a certain mass, and a certain spin could, it seems, be laws of the theory T. But since they do not appear to be consequences of the field equations—rather, they are included in the information in clause (3)—it seems that the MAL will imply that they are not among the laws of T. This looks like a problem.

My reply to this objection addresses two possible cases in turn. In the first case, clause (3) of T entails that having the right values for charge, mass, spin, and so forth is both necessary and sufficient for being an electron. In that case, the proposition that all electrons have certain values for those quantities is a law relative to T. For it entails the reliability condition for a method of measuring electronhood: take the particle (region of space-time) you're interested in, measure it's charge, mass, spin, etc., and perform the obvious calculation. A certain function of this result (which will be identified with the pointer variable of the measurement method) will be 1 if the particle (space-time region) is an electron, and 0 otherwise. So in this case, the alleged law is indeed a law of T according to the MAL.

In the second case, clause (3) of T implies that all electrons have the right values of charge, mass, spin, etc., but this is not a sufficient condition for electronhood, for there are other particles that share all the measurable characteristics of electrons but are not in fact electrons. In this case, I would argue that the concept of an electron has been given no empirical meaning, and we should not expect T to entail any laws concerning electrons. In neither case is there a threat to the MAL.

Someone sympathetic to the objection might offer the following rejoinder. Perhaps T entails that every particle with charge q and spin ½ also has mass m, and by the lights of a theory like T this might well be a law of nature, even if it is not a consequence of T's field equations. Forget about the property of electronhood; the important point here is that there could be laws of nature relating one basic property of an elementary particle (which, recall, we are supposing to be identified with a region of space-time) to its other basic properties.

My reply is that such a correlation among the basic measurable properties of elementary particles would not be a law of the theory T, even if T entailed that it was true. It would be a striking correlation that might lead us to suspect that there is some more fundamental theory to be found, which would explain why these particle properties always have to go together. But just saying, 'It's a law that these properties always go together' would not provide a deeper explanation. A genuine deeper explanation might appeal to a theory that posits more fundamental particles (by positing more fundamental fields to characterize the dynamical state within the regions identified with particles) with different basic properties (quark color, for example), which can only combine in certain ways, giving rise to larger particles that only come in certain varieties. In that case, the correlation among mass and charge in T might well be a consequence of the laws of the more fundamental theory. But that does not make them laws of T.

Summing up: in the case of a local, deterministic theory such as T, it is very plausible that the propositions the MAL calls laws of T will match what we would intuitively call the laws of T. So the MAL is extensionally correct for local, deterministic field theories, a broad and interesting class of physical theories. Moreover, it seems to be extensionally correct for the right reason (or at least, it's no accident that it is extensionally correct): in a deterministic theory, the laws are plausibly just what ensures the determinism, and on the MAL they are just what ensures reliability of the measurement methods, and both of these hold for the same reason—determinism and the reliability of measurement methods are both a matter of the field values in one region of space-time being determined by those values in another region.

References

Albert, David Z. (2000). *Time and Chance*. Cambridge, MA: Harvard University Press.

Armstrong, D. M. (1983). *What is a Law of Nature?* Cambridge: Cambridge University Press.

—— (1993). 'The Identification Problem and the Inference Problem.' *Philosophy and Phenomenological Research*, 53(2): 421–2.

Balashov, Yuri (1992). 'On the Evolution of Natural Laws.' *British Journal for the Philosophy of Science*, 43(3): 343–70.

Barbour, Ian (1997). *Religion and Science: Historical and Contemporary Issues*. New York: HarperCollins.

Beebee, Helen (2001). 'The Non-Governing Conception of Laws of Nature.' *Philosophy and Phenomenological Research*, 61(3): 571–94.

Bigelow, John; Ellis, Brian; and Lierse, Caroline (1992). 'The World as One of a Kind: Natural Necessity and Laws of Nature.' *British Journal for the Philosophy of Science*, 43(3): 371–88.

Bird, Alexander (2004). 'Strong Necessitarianism: The Nomological Identity of Possible Worlds.' *Ratio* (new series), 17(3): 256–76.

Burge, Tyler (1979). 'Individualism and the Mental.' *Midwest Studies in Philosophy*, 4: 73–121.

Callender, Craig (2004). 'Measures, Explanations, and the Past: Should "Special" Initial Conditions Be Explained?' *British Journal for the Philosophy of Science*, 55(2): 195–217.

Carroll, John (1994). *Laws of Nature*. Cambridge: Cambridge University Press.

—— (2007). 'Nailed to Hume's Cross?', in J. Hawthorne, T. Sider, and D. Zimmerman (eds.), *Contemporary Debates in Metaphysics*. Oxford: Basil Blackwell.

Cartwright, Nancy (1983). *How the Laws of Physics Lie*. Oxford: Oxford University Press.

—— (1999). *The Dappled World: A Study of the Boundaries of Science*. Cambridge: Cambridge University Press.

Cavendish, Henry (1798). 'Experiments to Determine the Density of the Earth.' *Philosophical Transactions of the Royal Society of London*, 88: 469–526.

Chisholm, Roderick (1946). 'The Contrary to Fact Conditional.' *Mind*, 55: 189–307.

Churchland, Paul and Hooker, Clifford (eds.) (1995). *Images of Science: Essays on Realism and Empiricism, with a Reply from Bas C. van Fraassen*. Chicago: University of Chicago Press.

Dawkins, Richard (1986). *The Blind Watchmaker: Why the Evidence of Evolution Reveals a Universe without Design*. New York: Norton.

DeRose, Keith (1995). 'Solving the Skeptical Problem.' *Philosophical Review*, 104(1): 1–52.

Dowe, Phil (2000). *Physical Causation*. Cambridge: Cambridge University Press.

Dretske, Fred I. (1977). 'Laws of Nature.' *Philosophy of Science*, 44: 248–68.

Earman, John (1978). 'The Universality of Laws.' *Philosophy of Science*, 45(2): 173–81.

____(1986). *A Primer on Determinism*. Dordrecht: Reidel.

____and Mosterin, Jesus (1999). 'A Critical Look at Inflationary Cosmology.' *Philosophy of Science*, 66(1): 1–49.

____and Roberts, John T. (1999). '*Ceteris Paribus*, There Is No Problem of Provisos.' *Synthese*, 118: 439–78.

________(2005a). 'Contact with the Nomic: A Challenge for Deniers of Humean Supervenience, Part One.' *Philosophy and Phenomenological Research*, 71(1): 1–22.

________(2005b). 'Contact with the Nomic: A Challenge for Deniers of Humean Supervenience, Part Two.' *Philosophy and Phenomenological Research*, 71(2): 253–86.

________, and Smith, Sheldon Russell (2002). 'Ceteris Paribus Lost.' *Erkenntnis*, 57(3): 281–301.

Ellis, Brian (2001). *Scientific Essentialism*. Cambridge: Cambridge University Press.

____(2005). 'Marc Lange on Essentialism.' *Australasian Journal of Philosophy*, 83: 75–9.

____and Lierse, Caroline (1994). 'Dispositional Essentialism.' *Australasian Journal of Philosophy*, 72: 27–45.

Fine, Kit (2002). 'The Varieties of Necessity,' in Tamar Szabo Gendler and John Hawthorne (eds.), *Conceivability and Possibility*. Oxford: Oxford University Press, pp. 253–81.

Fodor, Jerry A. (1991). 'You Can Fool Some of the People All of the Time, Everything Else Being Equal; Hedged Laws and Psychological Explanation.' *Mind*, 100(397): 19–34.

Foster, John (2004). *The Divine Lawmaker*. Oxford: Oxford University Press.

Friedman, Michael (1974). 'Explanation and Scientific Understanding.' *Journal of Philosophy*, 71(1): 5–19.

Gemes, Ken (1998). 'Hypothetico-Deductivism: The Current State of Play; The Criterion of Empirical Significance; Endgame.' *Erkenntnis*, 49(1): 1–20.

Giere, Ronald (1999). *Science without Laws*. Chicago: University of Chicago Press.

Goodman, Nelson (1945). *Fact, Fiction and Forecast.* Cambridge, MA: Harvard University Press.

Graner, F. and Bubrulle, B. (1994). 'Titius-Bode Laws in the Solar System. 1: Scale Invariance Explains Everything.' *Astronomy and Astrophysics*, 282(1): 262–8.

Guth, Alan (1997). *The Inflationary Universe: The Quest for a New Theory of Cosmic Origins.* Reading, MA: Addison-Wesley.

Hajek, Alan (unpublished). 'Most Counterfactuals are False.'

Halpin, John (1999). 'Empiricism and Nomic Necessity.' *Noûs*, 33: 630–43.

Harre, Rom and Madden, E. H. (1975). *Causal Powers: A Theory of Natural Necessity.* Oxford: Blackwell.

Hempel, Carl G. and Oppenheim, Paul (1965). 'Studies in the Logic of Explanation,' in Hempel Carl G. (ed.), *Aspects of Scientific Explanation and Other Essays in the Philosophy of Science.* New York: Free Press, pp. 245–90. (Originally published in *Philosophy of Science*, 15: 133–75 in 1948.)

Jackson, J. D. (1975). *Classical Electrodynamics*, 2nd edition. New York: Wiley.

Kaplan, David (1989). 'Demonstratives,' in Joseph Almog, John Perry, and Howard Wettstein (eds.), *Themes from Kaplan.* New York: Oxford University Press.

Khinchin, A. I. (1949). *Mathematical Foundations of Statistical Mechanics*, tr. G. Gamow. New York: Dover.

Kitcher, Philip (1981). 'Explanatory Unification.' *Philosophy of Science*, 48: 507–31.

Kripke, Saul (1980). *Naming and Necessity.* Cambridge, MA: Harvard University Press.

Lange, Marc (1993a). 'Natural Laws and the Problem of Provisos.' *Erkenntnis*, 38(2): 233–48.

—— (1993b). 'When Would Natural Laws Have Been Broken?' *Analysis*, 53(4): 262–9.

—— (2000). *Natural Laws in Scientific Practice.* Oxford: Oxford University Press.

—— (2002). 'Who's Afraid of *Ceteris Paribus* Laws? Or: How I Learned to Stop Worrying and Love Them.' *Erkenntnis*, 57(3): 407–23.

—— (2004). 'A Note on Scientific Essentialism, Laws of Nature, and Counterfactual Conditionals.' *Australasian Journal of Philosophy*, 82: 227–41.

—— (2005). 'Laws and Their Stability.' *Synthese*, 144: 415–32.

Laplace, Pierre Simon (1952). *A Philosophical Essay on Probabilities*, tr. Frederick William Truscott and Frederick Lincoln Emory. New York: Dover.

Laudan, Larry and Leplin, Jarrett (1991). 'Empirical Equivalence and Underdetermination.' *Journal of Philosophy*, 88: 449–72.

Lewis, David (1973a). *Counterfactuals.* Cambridge, MA: Harvard University Press.

—— (1973b). 'Causation.' *Journal of Philosophy*, 70: 556–67.

—— (1979a). 'Counterfactual Dependence and Time's Arrow.' *Noûs*, 79: 455–76.

—— (1979b). 'Scorekeeping in a Language Game.' *Journal of Philosophical Logic*, 8: 339–59.

—— (1986). *Philosophical Papers*, Volume 2. Oxford: Oxford University Press.

—— (1994). 'Humean Supervenience Debugged.' *Mind*, 103: 473–90.

—— (1996). 'Elusive Knowledge.' *Australasian Journal of Philosophy*, 74(4): 549–67.

Lierse, Caroline (1996). 'The Jerrybuilt House of Humeanism,' in Peter J. Riggs (ed.), *Natural Kinds, Laws of Nature, and Scientific Methodology*. Dordrecht: Kluwer, pp. 29–48.

Lipton, Peter (1991). *Inference to the Best Explanation*. London: Routledge.

Loewer, Barry (1997). 'Humean Supervenience.' *Philosophical Topics*, 24: 101–26.

Lycan, William G. (1994). *Modality and Meaning*. Dordrecht: Kluwer.

Manson, Neil A. (ed.) (2003). *God and Design: The Teleological Argument and Modern Science*. New York: Routledge.

Maudlin, Tim (2007). *The Metaphysics in Physics*. Oxford: Oxford University Press.

Maxwell, Grover (1962). 'On the Ontological Status of Theoretical Entities,' in Herbert Feigl and Grover Maxwell (eds.), *Minnesota Studies in the Philosophy of Science, Volume III*. Minneapolis: University of Minnesota Press, pp. 3–27.

Mill, John Stuart (1904). *A System of Logic*. New York: Harper and Row.

Milton, J. R. (1998). 'Laws of Nature,' in Daniel Garber and Michael Ayers (eds.), *The Cambridge History of Seventeenth-Century Philosophy*, Volume 1. Cambridge: Cambridge University Press, pp. 680–701.

Mumford, Stephen (2004). *Laws in Nature*. London: Routledge.

Needham, Joseph (1951). 'Human Laws and Laws of Nature in China and the West, Parts I and II.' *Journal of the History of Ideas*, 12(1): 3–30 and 12(2): 194–230.

Neta, Ram (2003). 'Contextualism and the Problem of the External World.' *Philosophy and Phenomenological Research*, 66: 1–31.

Newton, Isaac (1999). *The Principia: Mathematical Principles of Natural Philosophy*, tr. I. Bernard Cohen and Anne Whitman. Berkeley: University of California Press.

Pietroski, Paul and Rey, Georges (1995). 'When Other Things Aren't Equal: Saving Ceteris Paribus Laws from Vacuity.' *British Journal for the Philosophy of Science*, 46: 81–110.

Price, Huw (1996). *Time's Arrow and Archimedes's Point: New Directions for the Physics of Time*. Oxford: Oxford University Press.

Putnam, Hilary (1974). 'On the "Corroboration" of Theories,' in Paul A. Schillp (ed.), *The Philosophy of Karl Popper*, Volume I. La Salle, IN: Open Court, pp. 221–40.

—— (1975). 'The Meaning of "Meaning",' in Keith Gunderson (ed.), *Minnesota Studies in the Philosophy of Science*, Volume VII. Minneapolis: University of Minnesota Press, pp. 131–93.

Ramsey, F. P. (1978). *Foundations of Mathematics*. Atlantic Highlands, NJ: Humanities Press.

Rescher, Nicholas (1970). *Scientific Explanation*. New York: The Free Press.

Roberts, John T. (1998). 'Lewis, Carroll, and Seeing through the Looking Glass.' *Australasian Journal of Philosophy*, 76: 426–38.

——(1999). '"Laws of Nature" as an Indexical Term: A Reinterpretation of the Best-System Analysis.' *Philosophy of Science*, 66(3) (supplement): S502–S511.

——(2004). 'Measurability and Physical Laws.' *Synthese*, 144(3): 433–47.

——(unpublished). 'Some Laws of Nature Are Metaphysically Contingent.'

Ruby, Jane E. (1986). 'The Origins of Scientific "Law".' *Journal of the History of Ideas*, 47(3): 341–59.

Salmon, Wesley C. (1994). 'Causality without Counterfactuals.' *Philosophy of Science*, 61(2): 297–312.

Schiffer, Stephen (1991). 'Ceteris Paribus Laws.' *Mind*, 100(397): 1–17.

Sellars, Wilfrid (1948). 'Concepts as Involving Laws and as Inconceivable without Them.' *Philosophy of Science*, 15: 287–315.

——(1997). *Empiricism and the Philosophy of Mind*. Cambridge, MA: Harvard University Press. (Originally published in H. Feigl (ed.), *Minnesota Studies in the Philosophy of Science*, Volume I. Minneapolis: University of Minnesota Press, 1956.)

Shoemaker, Sydney (1980). 'Causality and Properties,' in Peter van Inwagen (ed.), *Time and Cause*. Dordrecht: Reidel, pp. 109–36.

Sidelle, Alan (2002). 'On the Metaphysical Contingency of Laws of Nature,' in Tamar Szabo Gendler and John Hawthorne (eds.), *Conceivability and Possibility*. Oxford: Oxford University Press, pp. 309–36.

Sober, Elliott and Hitchcock, Christopher (2004). 'Prediction versus Accommodation and the Risk of Overfitting.' *British Journal for the Philosophy of Science*, 55(1): 1–34.

Stalnaker, Robert (1975). 'Indicative Conditionals.' Reprinted in *Context and Content*. Oxford: Oxford University Press, 1999, pp. 63–77. (Originally published in *Philosophia*, 5: 269–86.)

Swinburne, Richard (1996). *Is There a God?* Oxford: Oxford University Press.

Swoyer, Chris (1982). 'The Nature of Natural Laws.' *Australasian Journal of Philosophy*, 60: 203–23.

Teller, Paul (2004). 'The Law Idealization.' *Philosophy of Science*, 71(5): 730–41.

Tooley, Michael (1977). 'The Nature of Laws.' *Canadian Journal of Philosophy*, 7: 667–98.

——(1987). *Causation: A Realist Approach*. New York: Oxford University Press.

van Fraassen, Bas C. (1980). *The Scientific Image*. Oxford: Oxford University Press.

——(1989). *Laws and Symmetry*. Oxford: Oxford University Press.

Ward, Barry (2002). 'Humeanism without Humean Supervenience: A Projectivist Account of Laws and Possibilities.' *Philosophical Studies*, 107(3): 191–218.

Weinert, Friedel (1995). *Laws of Nature: Essays on the Philosophical, Scientific, and Historical Dimensions*. Berlin: Walter de Gruyter.

Wilson, Mark (1982). 'Predicate Meets Property.' *Philosophical Review*, 91(4): 549–89.

Woodward, James and Hitchcock, Christopher (2003). 'Explanatory Generalizations, Part I: A Counterfactual Account.' *Noûs*, 37(1): 1–24.

Zilsel, Edgar (1942). 'The Genesis of the Concept of Physical Law.' *Philosophical Review*, 51(3): 245–79.

Index